THE RADICAL FACE OF THE
ANCIENT CONSTITUTION

St. Edward's "Laws" in Early Modern Political Thought

Building upon the seminal work of J. C. Holt and J. G. A. Pocock, this book deals with the ways in which medieval and early modern historians, lawyers, and politicians deployed their own national history to justify opposition to the English kingship. In particular, it is a study of the origins and development of the historical construct known as the "radical ancient constitution," a version of the past that originated in the eleventh, twelfth, and thirteenth centuries from three sources of conspicuous importance: the *Modus tenendi Parliamentum*, the *Mirror of Justices*, and, most important of all, the so-called "laws" of Edward the Confessor.

The book tells how a cult of kingship, centered around Edward's "laws," was transformed from a cult that sacralized the upstart Norman dynasty into one which desecrated the Stuart monarchy. In telling the whole story of the "ancient constitution" from the middle ages down to the eighteenth century, the book also corrects two widely held assumptions about Stuart England: first, that the so-called whig version of history was concocted by seventeenth-century dissidents who deliberately distorted medieval history in the service of their own agendas; and, second, that argument from history was inherently conservative, while argument from natural law and natural rights was inherently radical. Finally, the author's arguments serve as a corrective to revisionist histories that erase "revolution" from the "century of revolution" and reduce the role played by political principle in seventeenth-century England.

JANELLE GREENBERG is Professor of History at the University of Pittsburgh. Her previous publications include *Subjects and Sovereigns: the Grand Controversy over Legal Sovereignty in Stuart England* (1981, with Corinne C. Weston).

THE RADICAL FACE OF THE ANCIENT CONSTITUTION

St. Edward's "Laws" in Early Modern Political Thought

JANELLE GREENBERG

CAMBRIDGE
UNIVERSITY PRESS

PUBLISHED BY THE PRESS SYNDICATE OF THE UNIVERSITY OF CAMBRIDGE
The Pitt Building, Trumpington Street, Cambridge, United Kingdom

CAMBRIDGE UNIVERSITY PRESS
The Edinburgh Building, Cambridge CB2 2RU, UK
40 West 20th Street, New York, NY 10011–4211, USA
10 Stamford Road, Oakleigh, VIC 3166, Australia
Ruiz de Alarcón 13, 28014 Madrid, Spain

© Cambridge University Press 2001

First published 2001

Printed in the United Kingdom at the University Press, Cambridge

Typeface Baskerville 11/12.5 pt   *System* 3B2   [CE]

A catalogue record for this book is available from the British Library

ISBN 0 521 79131 6 hardback

For Corinne Comstock Weston

The historical sense involves a perception, not only of the pastness of the past, but of its presence.

T. S. Eliot, "Tradition and the Individual Talent," in *The Sacred Wood*.
Quoted by permission of Faber and Faber Ltd.

Contents

Acknowledgments

I have had the good fortune of growing up in a department filled with first-rate scholars and gentle colleagues, who over the years have supported and sustained me in any number of ways. Successive chairmen – the late Richard Hunt, Peter Karsten, Seymour Drescher, Richard Smethurst, Edward Muller, and Reid Andrews – have encouraged and prodded in equal measure, and I am genuinely grateful to them. My friends and colleagues have also been ever ready to serve as sounding boards and to read whatever I handed them, responding with incisive and on-the-mark criticisms. I am particularly grateful to Hugh Kearney, who always thought that this project was worthwhile. He has played a major role in the development of my career, and I am very fortunate indeed to have him as a colleague and friend. I have also been lucky to have Pete Karsten looking over my shoulder and nudging me forward. He has never let me forget that I have something to contribute to our discipline.

In addition, I owe much to Amy Remensnyder, Fritz Ringer, Bruce Venarde, Alison Stones, Paula Baker, and Evelyn Rawski. All read chapters and some read numerous drafts, thereby saving me from many an error. Marcus Rediker helped by providing information and citations about St. Edward's cult in North America. I am grateful to Peter Koehler, former Dean of the Faculty of Arts and Sciences, who did whatever he could to facilitate my scholarly efforts. In a special category is my good buddy Laura Marin, who sat beside me in the British Library and the Bodleian Library at Oxford, taking notes and then later poring over much of this manuscript. Her keen editorial eye has improved every single page she read. She also provided needed support and comfort along the way, as did my good friends Mary and Fritz Ringer, Robert Marin, Bill Chase, Maurine Greenwald, Akiko Hashimoto, Ann Jannetta, and Amy, Bruce, Hugh, and Reid. Finally, those of us who work in the History

Department at the University of Pittsburgh have the honor of associating over the years with an excellent staff, in particular, Judy Macy, Faye Schneider, and Grace Tomko. These smart, efficient, and infinitely patient women make coming into work downright pleasurable.

I owe a very special debt of gratitude to a special friend, Patricia Goetz. Although not an historian, at least of the usual sort, she more than anyone has helped me to understand (and accept) the insistence with which the past impinges on the present. That I was able to complete this work owes much to her own skill, fortitude, and dedication.

Scholars and friends at other universities vastly improved the quality of this book. James Burns and Annabel Patterson read the entire manuscript twice, offering many valuable suggestions and comments. Bruce O'Brien shared his knowledge of medieval legal texts and thereby saved me from certain embarrassment in chapters 1 and 2. Emily O'Brien, who is writing her doctoral dissertation on Edward the Confessor at Oxford University, also commented on chapters 1 and 2. Brian Simpson went to some length to tutor me on the doctrine of prescription, and Paul Brand helped out in a similar fashion. Melinda Zook brought her expertise on late Stuart England to bear on the last chapters. I am also obliged to Johann Sommerville and Daniel Woolf for helpful criticisms, as well as to the two anonymous reviewers for Cambridge University Press. Finally, along with everyone who works in this area, I stand on the shoulders of James Burns, Michael Clanchy, James Holt, Hugh Kearney, Annabel Patterson, John Pocock, Lois Schwoerer, Quentin Skinner, and Corinne Weston. The remaining errors are, of course, my own.

The kind efficiency of the staff at the University of Pittsburgh Hillman Library eased my labors over the years, in particular, Charles Aston and Ann Macleod. I am also grateful to the staff at the British Library, especially the North Library and the Manuscript Room, as well as to the librarians in the Cambridge University Manuscripts Collection and Bodleian Library, Oxford University. I must also thank the staff at Cambridge University Press, in particular William Davies and Kay McKechnie, for their careful and close attention to my manuscript. Mark Harvey, Assistant Serjeant at Arms of the House of Commons, provided special assistance, graciously escorting me through inaccessible areas of the Houses of

Parliament so that I could view paintings, drawings, and sculpture related to my interests.

I received welcome financial aid from the National Endowment of the Humanities, the American Philosophical Society, the Faculty of Arts and Sciences at the University of Pittsburgh, the Nationality Rooms fund, and the University's Center for West European Studies. Without this support I could not have completed my research. I am also grateful to my students Chris Kovac, Linda Loewer, Mary Redd Magnotta, and Ben Reilly for favors along the way.

My husband Martin helped out in ways far too numerous to mention, serving over the years as my most enthusiastic cheerleader and my best friend. He is always an inspiration, both scholarly and otherwise. My children, Joshua, Rebecca, and Steven, also did their part, reminding me, whether I liked it or not, that the living are sometimes more interesting than the dead. On occasion my family, to its everlasting credit, even indicated some slight interest in my work, though I would not want to push this too far.

Finally, I want to acknowledge my debt to my good friend, colleague, and mentor Corinne Comstock Weston. It was she who first piqued my interest in English history and taught me to be an historian. In a way, she is the co-author of everything that I write. I dedicate this book to her with deep respect, abiding affection, and lasting gratitude.

CHAPTER I

Hagiography and historiography: the long shadow of Edward the Confessor

INTRODUCTION

When present-day visitors to the Houses of Parliament pass through St. Stephen's Hall, which connects medieval Westminster Hall with the Central Lobby and the House of Commons, they see on its walls a series of large murals centered around the theme "The Building of Britain." Created in 1927, these paintings portray scenes associated with the history of parliament in general and the House of Commons in particular. Visitors who know their English history will appreciate the inclusion of depictions such as Sir Thomas More's refusal to grant Henry VIII a subsidy without proper debate in the Commons. And the very knowledgable will associate St. Stephen's Hall itself with the history of parliament, since St. Stephen's Chapel served as the meeting place of the Commons from 1547 until the great fire of 1834.[1]

However, the meaning of the huge mural above the entrance to St. Stephen's Hall will require clarification even to the most erudite of visitors. A reproduction of a portion of the Painted Chamber associated with Henry III (1216–1272), it depicts three figures: St. Stephen in the center, his namesake King Stephen (1135–1154) to the right, and St. Edward the Confessor (1042–1066), the penultimate Saxon ruler before the Norman conquest and the only English king ever to be canonized, to his left. The presence of the two Stephens makes sense in a room devoted to the history of parliament. And Holy Edward's representation is understandable given Henry III's utter devotion to his patron saint. Indeed, Henry sponsored the

---

[1] Nikolaus Pevsner, *The Buildings of England. I. The Cities of London and Westminster*, revised by Bridget Cherry, 3rd. edn. (Harmondsworth, 1973), pp. 527–8. C. C. Pond, *The Palace of Westminster* (Westminster, 1994), pp. 5–6. Robert Wilson, *The Houses of Parliament* (Norwich, 1994), p. 28.

creation of a cult of kingship that revered the Confessor as a national king and a great law-giver, the veritable symbol of a just and virtuous ruler who brought peace to the realm. And he rebuilt Westminster Abbey as the supreme tribute to St. Edward, after whom he named his son and heir.

But what is less well appreciated is that St. Edward deserves a place of highest honor in a room memorializing significant moments in the history of parliament and its sometimes stormy relationship to the crown. In fact, throughout the seventeenth century his was a name frequently associated with opposition to the kingship and forcefully evoked to support the idea of a monarchy limited by parliament and the law. More than this. From the civil wars of the 1640s to the Glorious Revolution of 1689, St. Edward served as the patron saint of dissidents who vigorously promoted the quintessential radical causes of the century, including rebellion, deposition, even regicide. Indeed, when all is said and done, St. Edward figures much more prominently in the broad sweep of English history than the better-known St. George.

In this book I will examine the transformation of the Confessor from a medieval symbol that sacralized the kingship into an early modern weapon that utterly defaced it. My study thus concerns the making of a political ideology that loomed large in the seventeenth century. But this book also deals with early modern historiography, for St. Edward successfully lent himself to such radical usage because he stood at the center of a credible and compelling historical narrative that commanded the deepest respect in the seventeenth century. This was the ancient constitution, within which lurked a version of medieval history redolent with polemical possibilities of the most radical sort.[2]

---

[2] The modern authority on the ancient constitution is J. G. A. Pocock, *The Ancient Constitution and the Feudal Law. A Study of English Historical Thought in the Seventeenth Century. A Reissue with a Retrospect* (Cambridge, 1987). Recently his work has been expanded by such scholars as Glenn Burgess, *The Politics of the Ancient Constitution. An Introduction to English Political Thought* (University Park, Pa., 1992); Paul Christianson, "Young John Selden and the Ancient Constitution, ca. 1610–1618," *Proceedings of the American Philosophical Society* 128 (1984), 271–315; Paul Christianson, *Discourse on History, Law, and Governance in the Public Career of John Selden, 1610–1630* (Toronto, 1996); Corinne C. Weston, "England: Ancient Constitution and Common Law," in *Cambridge History of Political Thought*, vol. II *Medieval Political Thought, 1450–1700*, ed. J. H. Burns and Mark Goldie (Cambridge, 1991), pp. 375–411; Johann P. Sommerville, *Politics and Ideology in England, 1603–1640* (London, 1986); William Klein, "The Ancient Constitution Revisited," in *Political Discourse in Early Modern Britain*, ed. Nicholas Phillipson and Quentin Skinner (Cambridge, 1993), pp. 23–44; Colin Kidd, *British Identities*

While radical ancient constitutionalists – as I call those Stuart dissidents who, beginning in the 1640s, pressed their medieval history into the service of rebellion, deposition, and regicide – exploited this version of the past, they did not themselves create it.[3] They merely hijacked a rendition of their national past that descended to them through the writings of medieval chroniclers and Renaissance historians and antiquaries. Although first fully articulated in Reformation England, an ancient constitution was in place in the middle ages. Indeed, according to three eminent modern scholars – J. C. Holt, R. W. Southern, and Patrick Wormald – it could be found as early as the tenth, eleventh, and twelfth centuries, its foundations laid by monks, monarchs, and magnates who created it to enhance their own powers. Moreover, in the middle ages it sometimes served much the same political purpose as did the early modern version of the ancient constitution during the century of revolution, that is, it was used to justify resistance against the king.[4] Importantly, this traditional ancient

---

Before Nationalism. Ethnicity and Nationhood in the Atlantic World, 1600–1800 (Cambridge, 1999), chapters 4 and 5.

[3] As used to describe seventeenth-century politics, the term "radical" is, of course, anachronistic. In this book I employ the label to classify certain political ideas and actions, in particular, those that aimed at destroying or using force against an established form of government. In this understanding, making war against, deposing, and/or killing a ruler, as well as justifications for the same, merit such a description. I also include under the label "radical" arguments to the effect that a ruler who governed as a tyrant instead of a king deposed himself, since in seventeenth-century England these almost always served as a cover for rebellion, deposition, and regicide. On this understanding, supporters of monarchical rule, for example, advocates of both the papal and imperial sides in the late eleventh- and twelfth-century Investiture Controversy, as well as some sixteenth-century Jesuits might well be called "radical." For further discussion of this issue see Melinda Zook, *Radical Whigs and Conspiratorial Politics in Late Stuart England* (University Park, Pa., 1999), p. xx; Gary De Krey, "Rethinking the Restoration: Dissenting Cases for Conscience, 1667–1672," *Historical Journal* 38 (1995), 53–83; J. C. Davis, "Radicalism in Traditional Society: the Evaluation of Radical Thought in the English Commonwealth, 1649–1660," *History of Political Thought* 3 (1982), 193–213; and Conal Condren, *The Language of Politics in Seventeenth-Century England* (New York, 1995), pp. 140–67. I am grateful to James Burns for advice about this matter.

[4] Holt, "The Origins of the Constitutional Tradition in England," in *Magna Carta and Medieval Government. Studies Presented to the International Commission for the Study of Parliamentary Estates* (London, 1985), pp. 1–22. Holt, "The St. Albans Chroniclers," in *ibid.*, pp. 265–87, especially 276. Holt, *Magna Carta*, 2nd. edn. (Cambridge, 1992), pp. 18–22 and *passim*. Southern, "Aspects of the European Tradition of Historical Writing: 4. The Sense of the Past," *Transactions of the Royal Historical Society*, 5th series, 23 (1973), 243–63, especially pp. 246–56. Wormald, *The Making of English Law: King Alfred to the Twelfth Century*, vol. 1 *Legislation and its Limits* (Oxford, 1999), chapter 3 and *passim*. Unfortunately, Wormald's magisterial work, which will set a new agenda for research, appeared too late for me to take full advantage of its rich contents.

constitutionalist narrative – as I term the historical construct before its radicalization during the civil wars of the 1640s – enjoyed the imprimatur of the greatest scholars of the Tudor and Stuart eras, including William Lambarde, William Camden, John Selden, Sir Henry Spelman, and Sir Roger Twysden. Their seal of approval sanctioned a reading of the past that provided a firm foundation for the most basic tenet of radical ancient constitutionalist theorizing, namely, the immemorial nature and continuity of English political and legal institutions. In particular, the traditional narrative taught that the governmental arrangements of the Stuart era dated back at least as far as the Saxon period and perhaps even earlier. Moreover, medieval and early modern writers identified the traditional ancient constitution with St. Edward himself, whom they considered the father of common law. Importantly, they suggested that the Confessor declared this body of law in conjunction with a parliament that included at least the House of Lords and perhaps the House of Commons as well. In this traditional reading, an essentially Saxon constitution enjoyed an unbroken continuity that extended from the early middle ages down to the Stuart period. In other words, no deep and abiding fissure such as a Norman conquest interrupted the flow of medieval and early modern English history.

From this conventional narrative, radical ancient constitutionalists created a theory of government based on elective kingship, a contractual relationship between ruler and ruled, and finally, a right to resist, depose, and even kill a king who broke the terms of his agreement with the people. In their version of the ancient constitution, parliament stood at the center of government and political society, its job to ride herd on over-mighty sovereigns. This "whiggish" narrative of the past, both in its traditional and radicalized versions, has been much attacked by many modern scholars who see the Norman conquest as a cataclysmic event in English history. In this view, William I abolished Saxon laws and institutions and introduced others with a decidedly Norman flavor. Moreover, neither common law nor parliament dated from the Saxon period: common law came into existence in the late twelfth and thirteenth centuries, while parliament originated in the late thirteenth and fourteenth centuries and did not regularly include the lower house until the late middle ages. Further, we now understand that both the common law and parliament owed their existence to kings who not only created them but generally used them for their own purposes.[5]

As for St. Edward and his high reputation as a great law-giver, modern scholarship makes clear that he, unlike his predecessors Edgar, Cnut, and Ethelred, neither legislated nor codified; no dooms survive him. Indeed, little from his reign suggests that he was destined for such a fabulous and exalted future. But we must never assume that the people of early modern England knew what we know. They did not. From their point of view, all that mattered was that the traditional ancient constitution, with St. Edward as its cynosure, carried the blessings of generations of chroniclers, scholars, and antiquaries. When radical ancient constitutionalists put their own spin on this familiar narrative, they imbued their political theorizing with an aura of sanctity and a persuasive power that it could have attained in no other way. In so doing, they made the most revolutionary of innovations appear as the innocent restoration of pristine practices.

The two main contentions of this book – that medieval English history lent itself to the most radical of early modern political causes, and that seventeenth-century dissidents merely expanded on and embellished the traditional ancient constitution whose roots stretched back to the middle ages – fly in the face of much recent scholarship. Thus, Quentin Skinner posits that late sixteenth- and early seventeenth-century English historical writing ran in an entirely different direction from what I suggest here. In his opinion these histories emphasized discontinuity rather than continuity. Especially in their characterizations of the Norman conquest, "the old fashioned chroniclers brought down with unconscious violence the twin pillars of whig historiography. They made no denial of the conquest; they allowed no continuity from Saxon institutions." Unable to draw on these sources, Stuart rebels concocted a "bogus" and "propagandist" historical account that suited their ideological agendas.[6] Other scholars look to the early seventeenth century for the origins of the ancient constitution. Christopher Brooks and Kevin Sharpe discover its roots in the reign of James I, when, in their view, common lawyers created it as a counterweight to a

---

[5] However, Wormald argues convincingly that the development of common law owed much to tenth- and eleventh-century Anglo-Saxon kings. *The Making of English Law*, vol. 1.

[6] Skinner, "History and Ideology in the English Revolution," *Historical Journal* 8 (1965), 151–78, especially p. 160.

potential incursion of civil law that they feared with the ascension of a Scottish ruler. The ancient constitution was, then, the result of tactical moves initiated in a particular set of political circumstances. Brooks further notes that the Tudor period shows few signs of belief in an ancient constitution because Renaissance humanism, with its emphasis on Roman law and Aristotelianism, characterized the legal mind.[7] Paul Christianson also sees the early seventeenth century as critical in the formation of the ancient constitution, adding that several different versions of an ancient constitution then competed for ascendancy.[8]

Then again some scholars find its origins in the sixteenth century. Firmly linking the ancient constitution with the common law that stood at its core, J. G. A. Pocock, for one, looks to the reign of Queen Elizabeth, when common lawyers attempted to defend themselves and their law from aggressive conciliar courts. Or, conversely, perhaps common law thought solidified as a result of Tudor policies that enhanced its already great authority.[9] Glenn Burgess and John Guy also focus on the sixteenth century, noting that Henrician and Protestant reformers reached back to the Saxon past to prove the antiquity of English religious institutions against the claims of Rome.[10] I agree with these scholars that the sixteenth century proved vital to the precise articulation of ancient constitutionalist thought. However, in what follows I intend to focus on and illuminate the earliest origins of this particular approach to history and political theory, for it was the medieval sources to which Stuart rebels themselves turned.

Just as many modern scholars tend to slight the early origins of the ancient constitution and its wide acceptance among learned English people of the sixteenth and seventeenth centuries, so do they generally doubt that medieval history easily lent itself to radical

---

[7] Brooks and Sharpe, "History, English Law and the Renaissance," *Past and Present* 72 (1976), 133–42. Brooks, "The Place of Magna Carta and the Ancient Constitution in Sixteenth-Century English Legal Thought," in *The Roots of Liberty. Magna Carta, Ancient Constitution, and the Anglo-American Tradition of Rule of Law*, ed. Ellis Sandoz (Columbia, Mo. and London, 1993), pp. 57–88.

[8] Christianson, "Ancient Constitutions in the Age of Sir Edward Coke and John Selden," in *The Roots of Liberty*, ed. Sandoz, pp. 89–146.

[9] Pocock, *The Ancient Constitution and the Feudal Law*, pp. 31–2.

[10] Burgess, *The Politics of the Ancient Constitution*, pp. 17–18. Guy, *Tudor England* (Oxford, 1990), chapters 5–8 *passim*. Guy, "Thomas Cromwell and the Intellectual Origins of the Henrician Revolution," in *Reassessing the Henrician Age. Humanism, Politics and Reform 1500–1550*, ed. Alistair Fox and John Guy (Oxford, 1986), pp. 151–78.

causes in Stuart England. According to recent literature, a tension exists between two poles of anti-court theorizing. On the one side is argumentation from history and law, and on the other, argumentation from natural law and natural reason. The first many modern scholars characterize as essentially conservative, and the latter as inherently radical. Thus, according to this view, from the Levellers of the 1640s to John Locke and the Green Ribbon Club of the 1680s, extremists turned to natural law as the idiom of choice. Less extremist opponents of the Stuarts, as exemplified by the noted common lawyer William Petyt, are portrayed as relying almost entirely on the historical mode of argumentation – so the usual comment runs. Mark Goldie, for one, speaks the conventional wisdom when he writes that, whereas the argument from English law and history "made it difficult to deny the historical fact of the king's supremacy over parliament," natural law "liberated the community to refashion itself as it thought fit." Further, "a right of resistance was ultimately an appeal beyond history to natural or divine right, exercised by the community beyond the framework of the constitution."[11] Burgess takes a similar approach, suggesting that, while "appeals to the past as a legitimating force did not disappear from the thought of the 1640s," from the civil wars onward they had to compete with other modes of discourse. The eclipse of ancient constitutionalism, he suggests, resulted from its inability to justify extremist claims such as the Long Parliament's right to control the militia.[12]

---

[11] Goldie, "The Roots of True Whiggism," *History of Political Thought* 1 (1980), 209–10. See also Goldie, "The Revolution of 1689 and the Structure of Political Argument," *Bulletin of Research into the Humanities* 83 (1980), 486–7, 489–90; H. T. Dickinson, *Liberty and Property* (New York, 1977), chapter 2; J. P. Kenyon, "The Revolution of 1688: Resistance and Contract," in *Historical Perspectives. Studies in English Thought and Society in Honour of J. H. Plumb*, ed. Neil McKendrick (London, 1974), pp. 43–70; Kenyon, *Revolution Principles* (Cambridge, 1977), chapter 1; Martyn P. Thompson, "Significant Silences in Locke's *Two Treatises of Government*," *Historical Journal* 31 (1988), 275–94. For a similar argument about Charles II's reign see B. Behrens, "The Whig Theory of the Constitution in the Reign of Charles II," *Cambridge Historical Journal* 8 (1941–43), 42–71, *passim*. Martyn Thompson and Richard Ashcraft, noting the ease with which late seventeenth-century polemicists moved from history to reason in their argumentation, seem to view the argument from reason and natural law as necessarily more radical. Thompson, "A Note on 'Reason' and 'History' in Late Seventeenth Century Political Thought," *Political Theory* 4 (1976), 491–503. Thompson, "The History of Fundamental Law," *American Historical Review* 91 (1986), 1103–28. Ashcraft, *Revolutionary Politics and Locke's Two Treatises of Government* (Princeton, 1986), pp. 208–9, 210–11, 572. See also Johann P. Sommerville, "History and Theory: the Norman Conquest in Early Stuart Political Thought," *Political Studies* 24 (1986), 249–61.

[12] Burgess, *The Politics of the Ancient Constitution*, pp. 79, 116–19, 221–31.

However, not all modern scholars find historical arguments inimical to radical theorizing. Indeed, Pocock notes with typical acuity "that there can be no greater error than to suppose that the argument from natural rights by its nature tended toward radicalism, the appeal to history towards conservatism."[13] In this work I have taken his brief admonition to heart. To it I would add that the marked tendency of modern scholars to underestimate the radicalism in polemical appeals to history has led to a distorted view of late Stuart England in general and the Glorious Revolution in particular. According to many historians, mainstream whigs justified the Revolution in predominantly historical and therefore "conservative" terms, as befitted the political nature of the Revolution settlement itself.[14] Although revised in the last decade by scholars such as Robert Beddard, Tim Harris, Lois G. Schwoerer, W. A. Speck, Corinne C. Weston, and Melinda S. Zook, this view of the Revolution has never gone out of style.[15] And with some reason. After all, Englishmen who argued from law and history did not go so far as to insist that James II's policies had resulted in the dissolution of government, as Locke's ideological followers, the "true whigs," believed. Nevertheless, as I contend here, radical ancient constitutionalists argued that the political nation, through its representatives, might resist and depose a despotic ruler and settle the crown on a successor. This is hardly a conservative or even a moderate position.

That Stuart dissidents appreciated the polemical potential of the ancient constitution appears from their persistent use of the three medieval sources on which this version of history solidly rested.

---

[13] Pocock, *Virtue, Commerce, and History* (Cambridge, 1985), p. 226. See also Pocock, *The Ancient Constitution and the Feudal Law*, pp. 57–8, 360–1.

[14] See, for example, Ashcraft, *Revolutionary Politics*, pp. 560–62; Tony Claydon, *William III and the Godly Revolution* (Cambridge, 1995); Goldie, "The Roots of True Whiggism," pp. 209–10; Dickinson, *Liberty and Property*, chapter 2; Kenyon, *Revolutionary Principles*, chapter 1; Howard Nenner, "Constitutional Uncertainties and the Declaration of Rights," in *After the Reformation: Essays in Honor of J. H. Hexter*, ed. Barbara Malament (Philadelphia, 1980), pp. 291–308; Lawrence Stone, "The Results of the English Revolution of the Seventeenth Century," in *Three Revolutions*, ed. J. G. A. Pocock (Princeton, 1980), p. 64; John Morrill, "The Sensible Revolution of 1688," in *The Nature of the English Revolution*, ed. Morrill (London, 1993).

[15] Beddard, "The Unexpected Whig Revolution of 1688," in *The Revolution of 1688*, ed. Beddard (Oxford, 1991), pp. 11–101. Harris, "The People, the Law, and the Constitution in Scotland and England: a Comparative Approach to the Glorious Revolution," *Journal of British Studies* 38 (1999), 28–58. Schwoerer, *The Declaration of Rights, 1689* (Baltimore, 1981). Speck, *Reluctant Revolutionaries: Englishmen and the Revolution of 1688* (Oxford, 1988). Zook, *Radical Whigs and Conspiratorial Politics*. Corinne Weston and Janelle Greenberg, *Subjects and Sovereigns: the Grand Controversy over Legal Sovereignty in Stuart England* (Cambridge, 1981).

These were the *Modus tenendi Parliamentum*, the *Mirror of Justices*, and, most critical of all, the so-called laws of St. Edward. These treatises, which were thought to date from the Saxon period, described the workings of English law and government before the Norman conquest. Two of the sources, St. Edward's laws and the *Modus*, told how the Normans so admired the Saxon laws and legal institutions that William I decided to make them a permanent part of his new regime. Despite the centrality of these sources in Stuart political ideology, their role has been little studied hitherto. Christopher Hill, Pocock, and Weston have noted the parliamentarian and whig dependence on St. Edward's laws, Weston underlining their import-ance when she wrote that "it is difficult to see how the claim to English rights and liberties could have made substantial headway without them." And Weston has also discussed the role of the *Modus* in legitimizing opposition to the Stuart monarchy.[16]

Still, no detailed and systematic study of their ideological impact exists, despite the fact that St. Edward's laws, the *Modus*, and the *Mirror* were every bit as influential as the Bible and Magna Carta in shaping political thought in the century of revolution.[17] Perhaps even more so. This relative neglect can probably be accounted for by the fact that modern scholars now know that these sources are apocryphal and their stories false. As a matter of fact, the Confessor's laws, the *Modus*, and the *Mirror* dated not from the Saxon period at all but from the early twelfth and fourteenth centuries, when they were manufactured by clergymen and politicians who backdated them in order to produce the illusion of antiquity. Still, early modern lawyers, scholars, and antiquaries generally took them as authentic accounts of the way things used to be. They had little reason not to. Although the *Modus* and the *Mirror* fell under attack in the seven-teenth century, Locke recommended both as worthy guides to the English past, and throughout the seventeenth century references to them are thick on the ground.[18] The Confessor's laws boasted a

---

[16] Weston, " 'Holy Edward's Laws': The Cult of the Confessor and the Ancient Constitution," in *Restoration, Ideology, and Revolution*, ed. Gordon J. Schochet, *Proceedings of the Folger Institute Center for the History of British Political Thought*, 4 (1990), 307. Pocock, *The Ancient Constitution and the Feudal Law, passim*. Christopher Hill, "The Norman Yoke," in *Puritanism and Revolution* (London, 1958), pp. 58, 62, 73. See also M. I. Finley, "The Ancestral Constitution," in *Uses and Abuses of History* (Harmondsworth, 1971), pp. 34–59.

[17] See Janelle Greenberg, "The Confessor's Laws and the Radical Face of the Ancient Constitution," *English Historical Review* 104 (1989), 611–37.

[18] *The Educational Writings of John Locke*, ed. James L. Axtell (Cambridge, 1968), pp. 400–1.

particularly impressive pedigree. Thus, medieval writers made several attempts to compile and record them. As Bruce O'Brien notes, the *Laga Edwardi* can be found in collections of Old English laws such as the *Textus Roffensis*, in translations such as *Quadripartitus*, and in original treatises, namely, the *Leges Edwardi Confessoris*, *Leis Willelme*, the *Deceta* (or *Articuli*), and the *Leges Henrici Primi*.[19] The most important of these was the *Leges Edwardi Confessoris*, first published in 1568 by the eminent common lawyer and antiquary William Lambarde under the title *Archaionomia*. Two later editions followed in 1644, one by the equally esteemed Sir Roger Twysden and the other by the noted Cambridge Saxonist Abraham Whelocke.[20] In 1623 Selden, universally respected for his legal learning then and now, used the *Textus Roffensis* as the basis of his own edition of the Confessor's laws.[21]

Equally important, avid supporters of the Stuarts accepted the Confessor's laws as genuine. John Cowell, Regius Professor of Civil Law at Cambridge and reputedly the most learned civilian of his age, used them repeatedly in his law dictionary *The Interpreter*, published in 1607.[22] Sir Edward Hyde, later earl of Clarendon, referred to them in his answer to Hobbes, and his fellow royalists Fabian Philipps, John Northleigh, Robert Sheringham, and Roger Coke accepted them at face value. Even Dr. Robert Brady, the *doyen* of high tory historians, accepted their authenticity in some, though not all, of his writings. So did his fellow royalist Sir William Dugdale, perhaps the greatest medievalist of the seventeenth century.[23] Thus,

---

[19] See O'Brien, *God's Peace and King's Peace* (Philadelphia, 1999), chapters 1 and 2.

[20] William Lambarde, *Archaionomia, sive de priscis anglorum legibus libri* (London, 1568). Roger Twysden, *Archaionomia, sive De Priscis Anglorum* (Cambridge, 1644). Abraham Whelocke, *Archaionomia, Sive De Priscis Anglorum Legibus libri* (Cambridge, 1644). These editions are hereafter referred to as *Archaionomia*.

[21] John Selden, *Eadmeri . . . historiae novorum sive sui saeculi libri vi . . .* (London, 1623).

[22] Cowell, *The Interpreter* (Cambridge, 1607), under "Danelage," "Peter's Pence," "Tearn," "Thridborow," "Leet," "Non Terme."

[23] Edward Hyde, earl of Clarendon, *A Brief Survey of the Dangerous and pernicious Errors to Church and State, In Mr Hobbes's book, Entitled Leviathan* (Printed at the Theatre, 1676), pp. 109–10. John Northleigh, *Remarks Upon the most eminent of our Antimonarchical Authors and Their Writings* (Westminster, 1699), pp. 551–2. This is a reprint of a tract first published in 1685. Fabian Phillips, *The Established Government of England, Vindicated from All Popular and Republican Principles and Mistakes . . .* (London, 1687), pp. 2–4, 7, 177, 179. Robert Sheringham, *The Kings Supremacy Asserted* (London, 1682), pp. 42–5. Roger Coke, *Justice Vindicated* (London, 1660), pp. 43, 104–5. Robert Brady, *A Full and Clear Answer to a Book, written by Mr. Petyt* (London, 1681), pp. 46, 55, 57. Sir William Dugdale, *Origines Juridicales* (London, 1666), pp. 2–5. See also David C. Douglas, *English Scholars* (London, 1939), pp. 31–59; Pocock, *The Ancient Constitution and the Feudal Law*, pp. 182–5. For Brady's turn-about-face see *A Complete*

when seventeenth-century Englishmen cited St. Edward's laws, the *Modus*, and the *Mirror* in their quarrels with their kings, they appealed to an established historical tradition with long and eminently respectable roots.

THE ANCIENT CONSTITUTION IN TUDOR–STUART ENGLAND

In the rest of this introductory chapter I will further discuss the major principles associated with the ancient constitution, explain their origins, especially in legal terms, and point forward to their later application in the service of radical political agendas. As mentioned earlier, seventeenth-century radical ancient constitutionalists enlisted St. Edward's laws, the *Modus*, and the *Mirror* to establish the principle nearest and dearest to them. This was the essential continuity of Saxon laws and political institutions, which, despite centuries of change and upheaval, descended basically intact to Stuart Englishmen. More particularly, Stuart radicals cited the three sources as proof that the king held his office upon trust and condition and by compact and consent; the people, however defined, elected rulers and owed them obedience only so long as they governed lawfully. Monarchy, therefore, originated in a governmental contract which bound kings and subjects alike. Consequently, the ruler who failed to live up to his part of the bargain freed his people from allegiance.

Thus Nathaniel Bacon, in an immensely influential tract written in 1647, found St. Edward's laws apt in justifying the war against Charles I. In particular, they proved that "a Saxon king was no other than a *primum mobile* set in regular motion, by laws established by the whole body of the kingdom." The king who broke those laws unkinged himself, leaving his subjects free to elect another in his place. And what was true for Saxon kings held equally for their seventeenth-century successors.[24] John Milton, for his part, viewed St. Edward's laws as the "most important" evidence that the king was subject to the law. Moreover, he defended the regicide by claiming that St. Edward's laws, which he identified with an original governmental contract, sanctioned king-killing if the ruler degener-

History of England . . . (Wherein it is Shewed the Original of Our English Laws) (London, 1685), pp. xxx–xxxi, lxvii, 144, 155.

[24] Nathaniel Bacon, *An Historical Discourse of the Uniformity of the Government of England* (London, 1647–51), pp. 49–50, 53, 112ff.

ated into a tyrant. Milton also found the *Modus* and the *Mirror* suitable for radical theorizing. On numerous occasions he cited all three "Saxon" sources to prove the ultimate right of the people to destroy the monarch, the monarchy, and establish a republic.[25] Although Milton hardly merits inclusion in the ancient constitutionalist lists, his appeals to history, even if a rhetorical device, suggest that he deployed these sources in the expectation that his audience would find such arguments persuasive and compelling.

Next radical ancient constitutionalists utilized St. Edward's laws, the *Modus*, and the *Mirror* to sustain another fundamental assumption of their political ideology. This was the belief in an "immemorial" common law and parliament, whose preeminence over kings stemmed from their greater antiquity. As proof they often quoted the *Mirror of Justices*, which told how the Saxons initially called the kingship into existence. And they also referred to the Confessor's laws, declared, their sources told them, in a full parliament and synonymous with the common law itself. Importantly, both the *Modus* and the *Mirror* described the existence of a contemporary parliament, complete with a lower house, in pre-conquest England. This "historical" evidence proved useful when the regicides had to vindicate the right of the lone House of Commons to try and execute Charles I. As the commonwealthman John Sadler wrote in 1649, the medieval sources guaranteed the Commons a place of preeminence over both the king and the House of Lords. Indeed, the Confessor's laws bound the king "to confirm the just laws which the Commons (not the Lords but the Commons) shall elect or choose."[26]

Inextricably interwoven with the issue of antiquity was the nature of the Norman conquest, a subject that provoked one of the fiercest historical and ideological battles of the early modern period. By the mid-seventeenth century, many politically articulate Englishmen acknowledged that if Duke William had conquered England, he ruled as a conqueror and thus as an absolute king. In this case, his will, not a governmental contract, served as the basis of his legitimacy. From this it also followed that he constituted the earthly source of political authority, with the power of parliament and the common law flowing from the royal reservoir. To many seventeenth-century Englishmen, this meant, in turn, that the Stuart kings, as the

---

[25] John Milton, *A Defence of the English People* (n.p., 1692), pp. 206, 208, 210, 225, 233–4, 491–2. The work was originally published in 1651. *Eikonoklastes* (London, 1649), pp. 41, 44, 45, 234.
[26] Sadler, *Rights of the Kingdom and People* (London, 1649), pp. 87–91 and *passim*.

Conqueror's heirs and successors, likewise reigned as absolute monarchs. Put differently, to admit that the Normans conquered England was to deny the continuity of Saxon laws and institutions through the ages. This led in turn to the conclusion that, because the ancient constitution was not ancient after all, it possessed no life independent of the monarchy.[27]

Such reasoning gravely threatened radical ancient constitution-alist causes, and from the 1640s onward anti-court elements labored mightily to prove the contrary. At first sight, theirs was a daunting task, since medieval chroniclers roundly acknowledged that William and his forces had defeated the English army, slain Harold God-winson, and then laid waste to large areas of the country, especially in the north and the west. *The Anglo-Saxon Chronicle*, for example, described 1066 and its aftermath as a time when men suffered "grievous oppression and manifold injuries."[28] The catastrophic nature of the Norman invasion was also noted by Gervase of Canterbury, John of Worcester, William of Malmesbury, Matthew Paris, and Henry of Huntingdon.[29] If such widespread violence and wholesale destruction did not merit the label "conquest," what did?

This was by no means a merely rhetorical question in the Stuart century because, as Pocock notes, a conquest worthy of the name necessarily involved the obliteration of the laws of the vanquished and the imposition of those of the victor. If in 1066 the Normans defeated Saxon laws and legal institutions, then William reigned as a conqueror. If not, not.[30] Put differently, not all conquests threatened the belief system of ancient constitutionalists. In fact, they easily tolerated a conquest in which the Normans wiped out Harold

---

[27] Pocock, "Robert Brady, 1627–1700. A Cambridge Historian of the Restoration," *Cambridge Historical Journal* 10 (1951), 189–90; Pocock, *Ancient Constitution and the Feudal Law*, pp. 53, 280–9, 300–2, and *passim*; Burgess, *The Politics of the Ancient Constitution*, pp. 82–6. Cf. Sommerville, "History and Theory: the Norman Conquest in Early Stuart Political Thought," pp. 249–61.

[28] *The Anglo-Saxon Chronicle*, trans. G. N. Garmonsway (London, 1954), pp. 220–1. See also pp. 200, 203–4, 218.

[29] William of Malmesbury, *Gesta Regum Anglorum, atque Historia Novella*, ed. Thomas Duffus Hardy (London, 1840), pp. 421–3, 428. Henry of Huntingdon, *Historia Anglorum. The History of the English People*, ed. Diana Greenway (Oxford, 1996), pp. 403ff. Matthew Paris, *Historia Anglorum*, ed. Sir Frederic Madden (London, 1866), vol. I, pp. 8, 22. *The Chronicle of John of Worcester*, ed. R. R. Darlington and P. McGurk, trans. Jennifer Bray and P. McGurk (Oxford, 1995), p. 607. Gervase of Canterbury, *The Historical Works of Gervase of Canterbury. The Minor Works Comprising the Gesta Regum with its Continuation, the Actus Pontificum, and the Mappa Mundi*, ed. William Stubbs (London, 1880), vol. II, p. 62.

[30] Pocock, *The Ancient Constitution and the Feudal Law*, p. 283 and *passim*.

Godwinson and his army, and even one in which the military victors introduced Norman institutions such as trial by jury and new tenures. What mattered was the survival of ancient laws and customs as a whole, not in every particular. That is, only the complete and total abolition of Saxon legal institutions would be theoretically incompatible with the ancient constitution.[31]

The supreme value of the Confessor's laws, the *Modus*, and the *Mirror* lay precisely in the fact that all seemed to point to the continuity of a core of ancient custom across the great divide of 1066. The Confessor's laws proved particularly helpful in this regard. Associated with a sainted king who stood at the center of a cult of kingship that venerated his person and his law-making, these laws, along with the *Modus*, described how William I himself promised to abide by them. Moreover, his successors throughout the ages issued similar confirmations, sometimes in coronation charters, as in the case of Henry I, King Stephen, and Henry II, later through the new coronation oath of 1308. The most momentous confirmation came in the Magna Carta of 1215, which contemporaries saw as another in the steady drumbeat of royal promises to abide by St. Edward's laws. In other words, the continued existence of Saxon laws told against the sort of conquest that threatened the ancient constitution. John Pym expressed this sentiment when in the Commons' debates on the Petition of Right (1628) he stated that, while William conquered the kingdom, "he conquered not the law."[32] Equally to the point were the words of the whig barrister Edward Cooke, who in 1682 championed excluding the duke of York from the throne by reference to St. Edward's laws, which William I promised "inviolably to keep." This proved that "the mighty conqueror is himself conquered, and solemnly renouncing all arbitrary will and power, submits his will to be regulated and governed by justice, and the ancient rights of English men."[33]

Also relevant to the early modern debate over 1066 was the title by which William claimed to rule England. Did he take by conquest or as the legitimate and rightful successor to Edward the Confessor?

---

[31] *Ibid.*, pp. 289, 298. For a discussion of the varieties of conquest see R. R. Davies, *Domination and Conquest. The Experience of Ireland, Scotland, and Wales 1100–1300* (Cambridge, 1990).

[32] *Commons Debates 1628*, ed. Robert C. Johnson and Maija Jansson Cole, assisted by Mary Frear Keeler and William B. Bidwell (New Haven, 1977), vol. II, p. 106.

[33] Cooke, *Argumentum Antinormanicum: Or An Argument Proving From Ancient Histories and Records, That William, duke of Normandy, Made no Absolute Conquest of England by the Sword; in the sense of our Modern Writers* (London, 1682), pp. xxx.

Here, once again, medieval sources came to the aid of radical ancient constitutionalists. Chronicler after chronicler acknowledged that, although William wreaked havoc upon England, he took the crown by right and as the lawful heir to Edward the Confessor, as well as by the promise of Harold Godwinson. This was the story told by the Bayeux Tapestry, Orderic Vitalis, Henry of Huntingdon, Matthew Paris, Ralph de Diceto, the Dunstable chronicler, Thomas Walsingham, and the anonymous author of *Le Livere de Reis de Brittanie*.[34] The lesson was not lost on rebels such as the Leveller Edward Hare. In his tract *St. Edward's Ghost* (1647), he wrote that William "was admitted as legatee of St. Edward, and upon his oath to preserve our laws and liberties."[35] Following the regicide, the Rumper Bulstrode Whitelocke justified the supremacy of parliament over kings by noting that "King William I, unduly styled the Conqueror," "both claimed and governed the kingdom as an heir, and successor; not as a Conqueror, but according to the laws of the nation, which he found here and confirmed."[36]

In sum, well respected medieval sources enabled radical ancient constitutionalists to argue the unarguable and defend the indefensible, namely, that, whatever else happened in 1066, no conquest worthy of the name occurred. In Nathaniel Bacon's words, William never shook "off the clog of Saxon law" or "raise[d] the title of conquest"[37] – a conclusion which, in turn, encouraged a belief in the continuity of Saxon laws and institutions throughout the centuries. However, we must keep one particularly critical point in mind: until the civil war period, the traditional ancient constitutionalist narrative had little intrinsic political valence of a distinctly

---

[34] *Le Livere de Reis de Brittanie e le Livere de Reis de Engleterre*, ed. John Glover (London, 1865), pp. 125, 127, 133, 141. Thomas Walsingham, *Chronica Monasterii St. Albani*, ed. Henry T. Riley (London, 1876), pp. 64, 69–70. Ralph de Diceto, *The Historical Works of Master Ralph de Diceto, Dean of London*, ed. William Stubbs (London, 1876), vol. I, pp. 193, 198, 199. Henry of Huntingdon, *Historia Anglorum. The History of the English People*, ed. Greenway, pp. 384–5, 392–3. Paris, *Historia Anglorum*, ed. Madden, vol. I, pp. 5–6. *Annales Prioratus de Dunstaplia*, ed. Henry R. Luard (London, 1866), vol. III, p. 12. For the Bayeux Tapestry see Antonia Gransden, *English Historical Writing* (Ithaca, 1974), pp. 103–4; *The Bayeux Tapestry*, ed. David Wilson (New York, 1985).

[35] Hare, *St. Edward's Ghost* (London, 1647), pp. 15, 18–19. A notation in the Thomason tracts indicates that this work was written in 1642.

[36] Whitlocke, *Notes Uppon the King's Writt For Choosing Members of Parlement XIII Car. II. Being Disquisitions on the Government of England By King, Lords, and Commons* (London, 1766), vol. II, pp. 134, 140, 185, 187. This tract was written around 1660.

[37] Bacon, *An Historical Discourse of the Uniformity of the Government of England*, pp. 16off. See also pp. 115–16, 118, 155ff.

partisan sort. With hardly any strain whatsoever it could be used for ends as divergent as shoring up the medieval kingship, supporting the barons in their opposition to King John, justifying the Henrician reformation, and bracing both the critics and supporters of extra-parliamentary taxation in the early seventeenth century. In other words, pre-civil war writers who used this story-line were by no means "proto-radical" oppositionists with ideological axes to grind. Rather they followed their sources and drew conclusions that, in the light of modern scholarship, were sometimes right, sometimes wrong.

Another general point about the ancient constitution bears mention. As Johann Sommerville demonstrates, deploying the national past for political purposes was by no means an exclusively English practice. On the contrary, the same national pride that motivated the English to reach back into their past also motivated continental writers to do the same. In Sommerville's words, "In a number of European countries people argued that their own state had existed, and at least in some respects remained unchanged, since the remotest antiquity."[38] Moreover, the ancient constitutionalist narrative did not provide the only theory of government popular in early modern England. As Sommerville, Weston, James Burns, and Derek Hirst note, concepts of royal absolutism also found favor. Indeed, some of the ancient constitution's most avid fans, for example, Sir Edward Coke and Sir John Davies, were able to harmonize a belief in divine right monarchy with a reverence for an immemorial parliament and common law.[39]

At the heart of the ancient constitution that Stuart radicals commandeered lay a series of beliefs about the relationship between past and present, preeminent among which was the assumption that a study of the way things were provided a reliable guide to the way

---

[38] Sommerville, "The Ancient Constitution Reassessed: the Common Law, the Court, and the Language of Politics in Early Modern England," in *The Stuart Court and Europe. Essays in Politics and Political Culture*, ed. Malcolm Smuts (Cambridge, 1996), pp. 46–52, especially p. 48.

[39] Hirst, *Authority and Conflict. England, 1603–1658* (Cambridge, Mass., 1986), p. 87. Burns, *The True Law of Kingship. Concepts of Monarchy in Early-Modern Scotland* (Oxford, 1996), chapters 7 and 8. Sommerville, "English and European Political Ideas in the Early Seventeenth Century: Revisionism and the Case of Absolutism," *Journal of British Studies* 35 (1996), 168–94. Sommerville, "Introduction," *King James VI and I. Political Writings*, ed. Sommerville (Cambridge, 1994). Sommerville, "Absolutism and Royalism," in *The Cambridge History of Political Thought, 1450–1700*, ed. Burns and Goldie, pp. 347–73. Weston and Greenberg, *Subjects and Sovereigns*, chapters 1 and 2.

things are and ought to be. Indeed, as Keith Thomas explains, "the *only* respectable justification for the study of the past was that it could be of service to the present."[40] Put differently, for early modern ancient constitutionalists the essence of history was not the pastness of the past but rather its presence. Indeed, the very term "ancient constitution" referred to a set of laws and political institutions which, while originating at some distant point in time, existed very much in the present.[41] The presence of the past meant that early modern English people might profitably look to history for guidance in politics, law, and government.

Their belief in the essential continuity of the English experience went hand in hand with their reverence for custom and tradition. It also explained why they searched medieval records with such diligence and enthusiasm, harvesting precedents, glossing texts, studying actors and events – all in an effort to find solutions to present-day problems. It was this mind-set that Sir Dudley Digges expressed when he reminded the House of Commons during the 1628 debate on the Petition of Right that "out of the mouth of antiquity itself the cause ought to be shown."[42] As late as 1703 John Locke recommended the study of history, especially the history "of a man's own country," as the best means of learning the art of politics and government.[43]

Nowhere was this mentality more evident than in the workings of the common law, the legal system associated with the ancient constitution and often considered virtually synonymous with it. Importantly, a knowledge of common law was not limited to professional practitioners; many Englishmen other than working lawyers possessed a general familiarity. The Inns of Court, where the common law was taught, constituted a third university in the early modern period. There young gentlemen down from Oxford and Cambridge often studied before beginning their careers in other fields. Moreover, land owners and business people needed a sound knowledge of the law in order to prosper, a fact which probably accounts for the rather vigorous market in law books. As for political

---

[40] Thomas, "The Perception of the Past in Early Modern England" (University of London, The Creighton Trust Lecture, 1983), p. 1.

[41] Burgess, *The Politics of the Ancient Constitution*, pp. 7–11. See also D. R. Woolf, *The Idea of History in Early Stuart England. Erudition, Ideology, and "The Light of Truth" from the Accession of James I to the Civil War* (Toronto, 1990), pp. 3–44.

[42] B.L. Stowe MSS 366. fo. 32.

[43] *The Educational Writings of John Locke*, ed. Axtell, pp. 400–1.

life, common lawyers easily eclipsed other professions, not only at
the center of government but in the localities as well. Thus, justices
of the peace spent time in London learning about the laws which
they had to enforce in the counties. Further, there were almost 2,000
practicing attorneys serving the royal courts at Westminster, in
addition to the nearly 500 barristers. As for parliament, the influence
of the common lawyers far exceeded their numbers, the lower house
in particular boasting strong contingents.[44] Finally, to an unusual
extent, English political thought was legal thought, shaped and
articulated by men, both professional and lay, whose own thinking
was heavily influenced by the common law mind. In Pocock's words,
"the attempt to understand English politics through the history of
English law was an all but universal pursuit of educated men in the
seventeenth century," while Glenn Burgess states that the language
of the common law attained "hegemonic status" in the early Stuart
period.[45] Indeed, as Alan Cromartie puts it, by the 1620s "common
law was touching more lives, in more places, than ever before."[46]
Therefore, to speak of common law understandings of history and
government is to cast an exceedingly wide net.

The essence of the common law lay in its reliance on past usage.
In contrast to statute law which was made in parliament, common
law consisted primarily of customs, in particular, those that had
earned the blessings of the king's courts. As Sir John Davies, James
I's attorney general and solicitor general for Ireland and a well-
respected antiquary, wrote, the common law "is nothing else but the
common custom of the realm" which "hath been tried and approved
time out of mind, during all which time there did thereby arise no
inconvenience."[47] In addition, common law must be consonant with
natural law, divine law, and reason. The "reason" in question was

---

[44] Wilfred Prest, "Lawyers," in *The Professions in Early Modern England*, ed. Prest (London, 1987),
pp. 72–5. Prest, *The Inns of Court under Elizabeth and the Early Stuarts, 1590–1640* (London,
1972). Prest, *The Rise of the Barristers* (Oxford, 1986), especially Introduction and chapters 3
and 4.

[45] Pocock, *The Ancient Constitution and the Feudal Law*, pp. 237, 240, 276. Burgess, *The Politics of the
Ancient Constitution*, pp. 117–19, 212. At least Burgess suggests that this was true of the
language of common law in the sixteenth and early seventeenth centuries. But cf.
Sommerville, "The Ancient Constitution Reassessed," pp. 39–64.

[46] Cromartie, "The Constitutional Revolution: The Transformation of Political Culture in
Early Stuart England," *Past and Present* 163, (1999), 85.

[47] Davies, *Le Primer Report des Cases & Matters en Ley* (Dublin, 1615), preface. Note that Davies,
like all common lawyers, distinguished between the customs of the king's courts which were
applied universally and the customs of localities, such as gavelkind and burgage tenure.

not only the "legal" or "artificial" reasoning that came with the study of common law but also natural reason, or, as some would have it, "nature's laws for England."[48]

Seventeenth-century English people associated the idea of custom and customary usage very closely with the common law doctrine of prescription. All were spoken of in the same breath with such terms as "immemorial," "time out of mind," and "time whereof the memory of man runneth not to the contrary."[49] Prescription, however, differed from custom, in particular, local custom such as gavelkind tenure. Custom served as a source of law and, in the words of the eminent Elizabethan lawyer Edmund Plowden, "is a thing disagreeing from the common law but not contrary."[50] Prescription, on the other hand, constituted a means of acquiring rights by "long user," especially rights to incorporeal hereditaments such as easements, profits, and the right to use the local commons.[51] At first sight, then, prescription concerned only "private law" matters and therefore appeared irrelevant to polemical disputes about the nature of kingship and law. However, demonstrating once again how easily history and law could be deployed in the service of political causes, radical ancient constitutionalists converted the doctrine into a mainstay of their theorizing. Because critical points of seventeenth-

[48] Sommerville, "The Ancient Constitution Reassessed," pp. 51–5. Sommerville, *Politics and Ideology*, pp. 93–4. Cromartie, "The Constitutional Revolution," pp. 83–4. Cromartie, *Sir Matthew Hale, 1609–76: Law, Religion, and Natural Philosophy* (Cambridge, 1995), chapter 1 *passim*.

[49] In Coke's words, "Prescription and custom are brothers and ought to have the same age, and reason ought to be the father and congruence the mother, and use the nurse, and time out of memory to fortify them both." *Rowles v. Mason* (1612). Quoted in G. C. Cheshire, *The Modern Law of Real Property*, 6th. edn. (London, 1949), p. 277. J. W. Salmond wrote that custom and prescription "are two species of the same thing" and "are originally governed by essentially similar rules." *Salmond on Jurisprudence*, ed. P. J. Fitzgerald, 12th. edn. (London, 1966), p. 36.

[50] *Hale's Case*, 1596. Quoted in J. H. Baker and S. F. C. Milsom, *Sources of English Legal History: Private Law to 1750* (London, 1986), p. 594. In general common law applied throughout the land. But a local practice, so long as it was reasonable and not contrary to fundamental principles of common law, could derrogate from the common law and become a sort of local law. However, those who pleaded local custom had to prove that it was immemorial. I am grateful to A. W. B. Simpson for advice about this matter.

[51] Incorporeal things were entities of an intangible nature in which a person could claim a heritable right and to which the laws of real property applied. In addition to easements, profits, and commons, such things included advowsons, tithes, rents, offices, and franchises. Another difference between prescription and local custom is that custom applied to a geographic area and prescription to a person or community. See Frederick Pollock and Frederic William Maitland, *History of English Law* (Cambridge, 1898, repr. 1968), vol. II, pp. 124–49; A. W. B. Simpson, *A History of the Land Law*, 2nd. edn. (Oxford, 1986), pp. 105–9.

century argumentation depended on prescription, we must examine it as well as its relationship to the ancient constitution and radical ideology in some detail.

The doctrine of prescription, which medieval lawyers such as William Raleigh and Henry Bracton borrowed from Roman law, rested on the principle "that long acquiescence in the continued existence of a given state of things entitles others to assume that state of affairs will continue to exist." Importantly, long user must be "without force, without secrecy, without permission."[52] For example, if X and his heirs have regularly and openly exercised a right of easement in Y's lands, albeit without his permission, and Y has failed to object, they are entitled to assume that Y will not enforce his right of ownership now or in the future. Conversely, if in this situation Y constantly builds barriers to impede X's coming and going, Y thereby defeats X's easement. Thus, acquiescence breeds prescription. A right constantly exercised grows ever stronger, while a right exercised intermittently or not at all grows ever weaker.[53]

Time, in other words, was of the essence. But how old was "ancient"? How much time needed to pass before a usage could be called "long"? What, exactly, did early modern Englishmen mean when they described a particular right as "immemorial," or as having existed "time out of mind," or "since the mind of man runneth not to the contrary"? These questions are of the greatest import, for they relate directly to the defining characteristics of the ancient constitution. Equally to the point, these questions cast light on the current tendency to underestimate the radical potential of appeals to the past. According to many modern historians, terms such as immemorial referred to an ancient constitution that literally

---

[52] *Stephen's Commentaries on the Laws of England*, ed. A. D. Hargreaves, 21st. edn. (London, 1950), p. 341. W. S. Holdsworth, *An Historical Introduction to Land Law* (London, 1927), p. 272. Simpson, *A History of the Land Law*, pp. 109–10. R. E. Megarry and H. W. R. Wade, *The Law of Real Property*, 2nd. edn. (London, 1959), p. 803. For a discussion of prescription and its Roman law and canon law origins, as well as its history in medieval England, see Ernst Kantorowicz, *The King's Two Bodies. A Study in Mediaeval Political Theology* (Princeton, 1957), pp. 164–73. Paul Brand has established Raleigh as the author of *De Legibus Consuetudinibus*, though Bracton served as later editor. Brand, "The Age of Bracton," in *The History of English Law: Centenary Essays on "Pollock and Maitland"*, ed. John Hudson, *Proceedings of the British Academy* 89 (1996), 78–9.

[53] *Stephen's Commentaries on the Laws of England*, ed. Hargreaves, pp. 341–3. See also Simpson, *A History of the Land Law*, pp. 109–12; J. H. Baker, *An Introduction to English Legal History*, 2nd. edn. (London, 1979), pp. 355–6; William Holdsworth, *A History of English Law* (London, 1966), vol. III, pp. 166–71; *ibid.*, VII, pp. 341–3; Digby, *An Introduction to the History of Real Property*, pp. 128–9; *Salmond on Jurisprudence*, ed. Fitzgerald, p. 36.

had no beginning in time or whose beginnings were unknown. From this it followed that an ancient constitutionalist view of law and government was not only ahistorical, it was inimical to theories of law and government based on contract. In other words, the ancient constitution could not be both immemorial and have originated at a particular time in a contractual agreement between king and people. Indeed, if we want to find contract theory in political argumentation, we are told to peruse obviously radical writers such as Locke. Thus, the putative incompatability of appeals to the past and contract theory becomes further evidence of the conservative nature of ancient constitutionalist thought.

Burgess, for one, takes this tack. In his words, "the language of original contracts and natural rights is totally alien to ancient constitutionalism; an original contract contradicted the doctrine of immemoriality," which he defines as meaning of unknown origins. There is truth in this statement: seventeenth-century English people did speak of common law and the ancient constitution as being of unknown origin, and they also sometimes described it as having existed forever. But it is possible to read such terms differently. Sometimes, for example, people used the words as synonymous with "old." For lawyers, however, the language typically referred to 1189 – the date of legal memory – or to the memory of any person then living. If contemporaries had either of these meanings in mind, then an ancient constitutionalist interpretation of law and history would prove perfectly compatible with contract theory. But Burgess states that there "is almost no evidence from the *pre*-civil war period" to indicate such an association. Not until the late seventeenth century, he posits, did the English link terms such as immemorial with 1189, and by then ancient constitutionalism had run its course.[54]

However, an examination of the medieval and early modern context within which people thought about these matters suggests otherwise. Indeed, those with any legal learning at all associated phrases such as immemorial either with 1189 or with the memory of any person then living.[55] This interpretation removes any theoretical

---

[54] Burgess, *The Politics of the Ancient Constitution*, pp. 74, 90–1, 96, 256 n. 60. Burgess, *Absolute Monarchy and the Stuart Constitution*, p. 168.

[55] Weston, Sommerville, and I have argued this point more briefly elsewhere. Sommerville, *Politics and Ideology in England, 1603–1640*, pp. 90–1. Weston and Greenberg, *Subjects and Sovereigns*, pp. 132–6, 342, n. 16. Weston, "England: Ancient Constitution and Common Law," pp. 376–9. See also Cromartie, *Sir Matthew Hale*, pp. 12–13, 37, 104–5, 121.

differences that might exist between ancient constitutionalism and contract theory.[56] In order to illuminate the point, we must go back to the eleventh and twelfth centuries. Before this time, litigants who attempted to prove prescription or custom depended on the memory of the oldest living persons. According to Frederic W. Maitland, early prescriptive claims usually used words such as "I and those whom I represent have commoned here – always – from before the Norman conquest – from time immemorial."[57] Michael Clanchy agrees. Whatever preceded the earliest memory was considered to be time out of mind and constituted a point beyond which a litigant did not have to go. By the twelfth century, the beginning of each reign was seen as a convenient dividing point for legal memory. Thus, in the reign of Henry II the date of legal memory was set at the beginning of Henry I's reign; and at the beginning of Richard I's reign, it became the beginning of Henry II's reign. These moveable dates served as statutes of limitation.

The situation, Clanchy continues, changed dramatically with the reforms of Hubert Walter, who served as justiciar to Richard I and chancellor to King John. Walter laid the foundations for reliable record keeping by mandating that the royal government preserve its records. In so doing he made it possible to rely on written documents rather than human memory, which in turn made such up-dating unnecessary. By the late thirteenth century the development of an official archive enabled the government to be more precise in designating a period of limitation. In 1275 the statute Westminster I fixed the date of legal memory at September 3, 1189 in cases begun by a writ of right. This designation was confirmed by the *Quo Warranto* statute of 1290. As Clanchy notes, in these two statutes Edward I conceded that, henceforth, royal courts would not require documentary proof of any earlier date than 1189. The coronation date of Richard I thus marked "the formal beginning of the era of artificial memory." Paul Brand makes a similar point, though he suggests that in the first century after the Norman conquest the meaning of "time out of mind" was uncertain and variable.[58] A Year

---

[56] Simpson, *A History of the Land Law*, especially pp. 109–10. Cheshire, *The Modern Law of Real Property*, pp. 242–4. David J. Hayton, ed., *Megarry's Manual of the Law of Real Property*, 6th. edn. (London, 1982), pp. 417–18. See also Paul Brand, "'Time Out of Mind': the Knowledge and Use of the Eleventh- and Twelfth-Century Past in Thirteenth-Century Litigation," *Anglo-Norman Studies*, 16 (1994), 37–54.

[57] Pollock and Maitland, *History of English Law*, vol. II, p. 142.

[58] Clanchy, *From Memory to Written Record. England 1066–1307*, 2nd. edn. (Oxford, 1993), pp. 3,

Book case from 1313 made the connection firmly. In *King v. Wickham Breux* a *quo warranto* proceeding was begun against one Breux, who claimed a prescriptive right to fine his demesne tenants for breaches of the assizes of bread and ale. His claim referred to his father as purchaser of the manor. It failed because, according to the court, his father made the purchase after the reign of Richard I, which was within time of legal memory.[59] Note that the origin of the right was indeed known; what mattered to the court was that the franchise began after 1189.

Sir Thomas Littleton's late fifteenth-century treatise on tenures also associated time out of mind with 1189. The earliest printed work on English law and the most important law book between the thirteenth and seventeenth centuries, the treatise was known in the early modern period primarily through Sir Edward Coke. His influential *First Part of the Institutes of the Laws of England* (1628), which Richard Helgerson describes as the work "that would introduce Englishmen to the legal order" under which they lived, used Littleton as a foundation. Indeed, Coke described Littleton's treatise as " 'the most perfect and absolute work that was ever written in any humane science' " and placed Littleton on the same plane as Gaius, Ulpian, and Justinian.[60] A jurist of great practical experience as well as legal learning, Littleton served as king's serjeant, a justice of assize, and by 1466 as a justice in the court of Common Pleas.[61] His words, then, reflected both book law and its application in common law courts. As Littleton expressed it, "time out of mind should be said from time of limitation in a writ of right, that is to say, from the time of King Richard the first after the conquest, as is given by the Statute of Westminster 1."[62]

Tudor lawyers also defined immemorial in relationship to 1189. In

---

68–73, 152–3, 328–9. Cheshire, *The Modern Law of Real Property*, pp. 242–3, 246–7. Brand, *The Making of the Common Law* (London, 1992), pp. 403 and n. 47, 405 and n. 60. Brand, " 'Time Out of Mind.' "

[59] *Year Books of Edward II. The Eyre of Kent 6 and 7. A.D. 1313–1314*, ed. William C. Bolland, Selden Society XXIX (London, 1913), pp. 179–80. Simpson, *A History of the Land Law*, p. 103.

[60] Helgerson, *Forms of Nationhood. The Elizabethan Writing of England* (Chicago, 1992), pp. 91–2. Coke is quoted in Charles M. Gray, "Parliament, Liberty, and the Law," in *Parliament and Liberty from the Reign of Elizabeth to the English Civil War*, ed. J. H. Hexter (Stanford, 1992), p. 157.

[61] David M. Walker, *The Oxford Companion to Law* (Oxford, 1980), p. 772.

[62] Littleton, *Tenures*, ed. E. Wambaugh (Washington, DC, 1903), section 170. Coke, *The First Part of the Institutes of the Laws of England, or, A Commentary on Littleton*, ed. Charles Butler, 19th. edn. (London, 1832), pp. 113a–15b.

1520, for example, Chief Justice Fyneux struck at the practice of ecclesiastical sanctuary partly on the ground that its usage was not time out of mind, that is, before 1189.[63] Sir Robert Brooke noted in *La Graunde Abridgement* (1568) that time before the memory of man referred to the beginning of Richard I's reign.[64] That Brooke should use this language is telling. No ordinary common lawyer, he sat in parliament in 1554, where he served as speaker of the House of Commons. In the same year he was made chief justice of Common Pleas. As a man of great legal stature, he well knew the meaning of time beyond memory; and his sentiments undoubtedly reflected the opinions of the wider legal community. Moreover, *La Graunde Abridgement* was a treatise of some renown and was frequently referred to in early modern legal literature.[65]

Despite the close association of 1189 with prescription, from the late thirteenth until the sixteenth century litigants often satisfied legal requirements if they could show a long user according to the memory of any man then living. If this was possible, then the court accepted the fiction that the practice had begun before 1189. That is, prescriptive claims based on long user could still be proved by reference to living memory. Littleton commented pointedly on this matter. After noting the association of time out of mind with 1189, he wrote that terms such as immemorial could also refer to a "time whereof the mind of man runneth not to the contrary . . . that is as when such a matter is pleaded that no man then alive has heard any proof to the contrary, nor hath no knowledge to the contrary."[66] Christopher St. German's *Doctor and Student*, written in the early sixteenth century, also defined immemorial as not within the memory of any man now living. So did the noted common lawyer and antiquary Sir John Dodderidge, who cited Littleton as one of his authorities.[67] In his *Institutes*, first published in 1605, the civilian John

---

63 *Reports of Sir John Spelman*, ed. John Baker, Selden Society XCIV (London, 1978), vol. II, p. 65. See also Guy, "Thomas Cromwell and the Henrician Revolution," pp. 167–68.

64 Brooke, *La Graunde Abridgement* (London, 1573), fo. 149b.

65 Walker, *Oxford Companion to English Law*, p. 155. For seventeenth-century references to Brooke see Sir John Dodderidge, *The English Lawyer* (London, 1631, repr. 1980), pp. 116, 219; William Lambarde, *Eirenarcha or the Office of Justices of the Peace* [1581] (London, 1972), p. 79. See also Cromartie, *Sir Matthew Hale, 1609–1672*, p. 14.

66 Littleton, *Tenures*, ed. Wambaugh, section 170. Coke, *The First Part of the Institutes on the Laws of England*, pp. 113a–15b. Holdsworth, *A History of English Law*, vol. III, pp. 344–5, and n. 4. Simpson, *A History of the Land Law*, p. 103.

67 St. German, *Doctor and Student*, ed. T. F. T. Plucknett and J. L. Barton, Selden Society, XCI (London, 1974), pp. 61, 318. Dodderidge, *The English Lawyer*, p. 102.

Cowell defined time out of mind in this way, citing St. German and Littleton. Remarking on the variety of meanings which the term carried in England, Cowell further pointed to statutory limits on the time period within which an action could be brought. Although he did not mention 1189, he was surely aware that Westminster 1 had associated that particular date with legal memory.[68]

Confining time beyond memory to the memory of any person now living relieved litigants from having to prove an impossibly long user that grew ever more distant with the passage of time. However, according to A. W. B. Simpson, "unhappily" the view which came to prevail in the seventeenth century was the view found in the early Year Books: user had to be shown since 1189. If this were not possible, or if the right could be shown not to have existed at any time since 1189, then the claim failed. This interpretation placed an intolerable burden on many who deserved the protection of prescription, and in the course of the seventeenth century courts began to rule that, with regard to some incorporeal hereditaments, a continuous user of twenty years raised a presumption of a grant made before 1189. The courts neglected, however, "to restrict *legal memory* to the same period."[69]

In the early seventeenth century such terms as time out of mind remained closely connected both with 1189 or with a limited period of years. Coke's commentary on Littleton linked him with these definitions, and Dodderidge has been quoted to the same effect. Other common lawyers agreed. In his abridgment of cases at common law, the eminent seventeenth-century jurist Sir Henry Rolle wrote: "the said time of memory was the beginning of the reign of King Richard." Twysden expressed a similar opinion.[70] Admittedly, Rolle and Twysden published their works later in the

---

[68] Cowell, *Institutes of the Lawes of England* (London, 1651), pp. 102–4.

[69] Simpson, *A History of the Land Law*, pp. 109–10. Cheshire, *The Modern Law of Real Property*, p. 243. The limitation of twenty years was probably drawn by analogy from the 1623 Limitation Act, which limited the amount of time within which an action for ejectment could be brought to that time period. *Ibid*. Megarry and Wade, *The Law of Real Property*, p. 808. In the eighteenth century, judges began to instruct juries to assume the existence of a fictitious grant that spelled out the prescriptive right but had been lost sometime after 1189.

[70] Rolle, *Un Abridgment des plusiers Cases et Resolutions del Commun Ley*, ed. Matthew Hale (London, 1668), pp. 264–72. The Long Parliament appointed Rolle as justice of King's Bench in 1645. In 1648 he became chief justice of King's Bench, and in 1649 was elevated to the position of Lord Chief Justice of Upper Bench. Sir Roger Twysden, *Certaine Considerations upon the Government of England*, ed. John Mitchell Kimbell, Camden Society XLV (London, 1849), p. 126.

seventeenth century, a fact which might seem to support Burgess's contention that few pre-civil war writers thought of immemorial in the ways I suggest. However, as far as Rolle (c. 1590–1656) is concerned, the exact dates at which he composed his treatise are unknown. But surely his educational and professional experiences in the early seventeenth century shaped his views about law and legal history. Entering Inner Temple in 1609 and called to the bar in 1617, he served in the last three parliaments of James I and the first three of his son.[71] When Rolle referred to immemorial and 1189 in the same breath, he likely reflected knowledge that he picked up in the early years of the seventeenth century. As for Twysden, he wrote *Certaine Considerations upon the Government of England* in 1642 and 1643, and his treatise probably also revealed early seventeenth-century legal thought.[72]

The association of immemorial with 1189 and living memory continued throughout the Stuart period. Writing sometime after the Restoration of 1660, the noted common lawyer and justice Sir Matthew Hale noted that any right which originated before 1189 was considered as "without a beginning, or at least such a beginning as the law takes notice of." With these words Hale implied not that the origins of a right were necessarily unknown – though they might be – , or that it had always existed. Rather he meant that the origins were irrelevant for legal purposes.[73]

Thus, from the thirteenth to the seventeenth century, noted common lawyers and learned justices often viewed time before memory as referring either to 1189, to the memory of any man then living, or to a definite period of years.[74] When they used such phrases they implied neither a belief in the timelessness of their legal institutions nor an understanding that the origins were necessarily unknown. Their education, training, and professional experience primed them to think of immemorial in a very different way. Moreover, by linking terms such as immemorial to specific dates and periods of time, they inadvertently set the stage for an argument that combined both the strength and familiarity of the ancient consti-

---

[71] *DNB*. Prest, *The Rise of the Barristers*, pp. 388–9.

[72] Frank W. Jessup, *Sir Roger Twysden 1597–1672* (New York, 1965), pp. 188–9. Cromartie, *Sir Matthew Hale*, p. 51.

[73] Sir Matthew Hale, *The History of the Common Law*, ed. Charles M. Gray (Chicago, 1971), p. 4. See also Cromartie, *Sir Matthew Hale*, pp. 104–5.

[74] Cf. D. R. Woolf, "Memory and Historical Culture in Early Modern England," *Journal of the Canadian Historical Association* 2 (1991), 293–308, especially pp. 303–4.

tution with a theory of government founded upon a contract between king and people. Not that lawyers and politicians considered themselves obliged to prove the origins of precious institutions such as parliament and the common law. Nor did they believe it necessary to lay their hands on any specific agreements describing the precise moment at which king and people entered into a contract. Indeed, learned Englishmen of various political stripes recognized that the loss of early records to fire, unscrupulous borrowers, and raids by tyrants such as Richard II left some origins shrouded in uncertainty. Here prescription came in particularly handy, because it provided the means by which a claim of right could be made in the absence of written records. Here, too, medieval chroniclers proved valuable, since their writings sometimes filled the gaps in the official records.[75]

Because belief in an ancient constitution proved perfectly compatible with contractual theories of government, radicals such as Milton could, as mentioned earlier, identify St. Edward's laws with an original contract. This sort of theorizing also suited the leading parliamentarian pamphleteer William Prynne, who used it on a number of occasions. So did William Atwood, who defended the Glorious Revolution by noting that the Confessor's laws constituted a "noble transcript of the original contract."[76] Moreover, throughout the seventeenth century, ancient constitutionalists, both traditional and radical, interpreted the coronation ceremony, where the king took an oath to abide by these laws before the people gave their allegiance, as a most public proof of the existence of such a contract.[77] Admittedly, natural law theorists such as Locke made much more of contract, placing it at the center of their models of political society. But this is not to say that ancient constitutionalists

---

[75] On the problem of lost records see William Hakewill's speech on impositions in the parliament of 1610, published by command of the House of Commons as *The Libertie of the Subject* (London, 1641), pp. 127–8; Sir Robert Holbourne, in *A Complete Collection of State Trials*, ed. T. B. Howell (London, 1816), vol. III, pp. 983–4, 987; Sir Francis Weston, in *ibid.*, p. 1073; Sir George Croke, in *ibid.*, p. 1153.

[76] Prynne, *The Third Part of The Soveraigne Power of Parliaments and Kingdomes*, 2nd. edn. (London, 1643), pp. 3–6, 13, 118–32 *passim*. William Atwood, *Fundamental Constitution of the English Government* (London, 1690), p. iv.

[77] See, for example, *Several Speeches Delivered At a Conference concerning the Power of Parliaments, to proceed against their Kings for Misgovernment* (London, 1648), pp. 27–8, 42ff., 58–9; *Some Special Arguments For the Scottish Subjects lawfull defence of their Religion and Liberty* (London, 1642), p. 6; William Ball, "The Power of Kings discussed" (1649), in *Somers Tracts*, ed. Walter Scott (London, 1811), vol. V, p. 135; Sadler, *Rights of the Kingdom*, pp. 20–2, 32–3, and *passim*.

ignored it. On the contrary, they consistently combined both appeals to history with theories of contract in their justifications for rebellion, deposition, and regicide.

In making my case for linking immemorial to the date 1189, I confront a potentially devasting fact: if what I have said is correct, then Stuart radicals could have settled for proving that the ancient constitution existed before 1189. But they did not. Most strongly committed themselves to the view that an ancient constitution existed in the pre-Norman period. And in this they followed in the footsteps of their more traditional ancient constitutionalist brethren. How, then, can we account for the fact that 1066 loomed as large as, indeed larger than, 1189 in ancient constitutionalist thinking? Why, in other words, did radical ancient constitutionalists not opt for the more easily proven date of legal memory when pleading their case against Stuart kings? If they had, then the events of 1066 would cease to be relevant to their political thought.

The answer lies in the fact that they worked within an intellectual and historical tradition which taught them that the origins of the ancient constitution lay in the period before 1066. That is, the ancient constitution was ancient not simply because it was very old in the sense of deriving generally from the middle ages. Rather, its ancientness stemmed from the "fact" that it dated from the Saxon period if not earlier.[78] Indeed, the situation could not have been otherwise when so many literate people had cut their eye teeth on canonical sources that told of the existence of common law and parliament long before 1066. St. Edward's laws, the *Modus tenendi Parliamentum*, and the *Mirror of Justices* stood witness to this simple fact. Ancient constitutionalists of all persuasions assumed it as a matter of course; they took it as a given. Then there were the writings of the greatest scholars and antiquaries of the early modern period – for example, Lambarde, Camden, Selden, and Twysden – who, for all of their talk about the Norman conquest, nevertheless confirmed the essential continuity of the common law from Saxon down to Stuart times. In other words, the ancientness of the ancient constitution was beyond dispute because its origins lay before 1066 which was outside legal memory.

Thus, by the beginning of the seventeenth century the ancient constitutionalist version of the past already occupied the high

---

[78] See Burgess, *The Politics of the Ancient Constitution*, pp. 69–72.

ground. It was not, as some scholars suggest, constructed in response to James I's policies or to civil war royalists. Because Stuart radical ancient constitutionalists took the pre-1066 existence of the ancient constitution as axiomatic, they understandably bristled when their opponents claimed that William I had conquered both the Saxons and their laws. Moreover, unless they convincingly rebutted this wrong-headed view of English history – for so their evidence indicated it to be – the entire structure of their political argument collapsed. In a way, then, their implicit acceptance of this premise and these sources made them captives of a particular view of early English history. This mind-set, in turn, encouraged them to develop theories which not only suited their political agendas but corresponded perfectly with their readings of history. Schooled in this version of the past and bolstered by St. Edward's laws, the *Modus*, and the *Mirror*, Stuart radicals found themselves well equipped to preach the ancientness, and hence autonomy, of the ancient constitution. And they perfectly positioned themselves to associate the ancient constitution with an original contract between king and people.

Radical ancient constitutionalists also made political hay out of another feature of common law reasoning, namely, the requirement that a particular custom, in addition to being immemorial, must also have been exercised regularly, continually, and peacefully without interruption.[79] Here they once again extrapolated from "private law" matters such as incorporeal hereditaments to issues of a broader and more constitutional import. In particular, they used this reasoning to strengthen their claim that both William I and his Stuart successors reigned not absolutely but in accordance with St. Edward's laws, which monarchs confirmed throughout the centuries. The common law doctrine of prescription came to their aid in the following way. If the Normans had abolished Saxon law and imposed a new legal system upon the conquered English, and if the Saxons had acquiesced in this extinction of their legal heritage, kings then as well as now could claim a prescriptive right to disregard the ancient laws of the kingdom and to govern as absolute sovereigns. Put differently, in this reading of early English history, seventeenth-century Englishmen enjoyed no prescriptive right to be governed by St. Edward's laws because their ancestors had not fought to maintain

---

[79] Weston, "England: Ancient Constitution and Common Law," pp. 376–7.

them. They were in the position of the land owner who acquiesced in his tenant's easement and thereby lost his full and unencumbered proprietary interest.

But, on the other hand, an entirely different scenario unfolded if the Saxons and their successors, rather than submitting peacefully, continually pestered the Norman kings and their successors to confirm the ancient laws of the kingdom. In this case, prescription told for St. Edward's laws and the ancient constitution, kept alive through the centuries by the steady beat of royal promises. Nor did it matter that subjects sometimes used force to get their way, despite royalist assertions to the contrary.[80] As the common lawyer Thomas Hedley told the Commons in the 1610 debate over impositions, "if a man get possession of lands by disseisin by force, yet if he get but one release or confirmation from the disseised in lawful and peaceable manner, this wrongful possession is made rightful and lawful forever." Translated to a broader context, this meant that even when subjects "obtain a grant of their ancient laws and liberties at the conqueror's hands, though it be first gotten by force, yet if after at several times and in several ages in time of peace it be confirmed by continual consent and oath of king and people and hath so continued and been continually approved for many hundred years, then they will be as firm and strong as any human laws whatsoever."[81] This reading of the doctrine of prescription would later enable radical ancient constitutionalists to take the sting out of the royalist claim that coerced concessions did not bind the king.

But the common law doctrine of prescription did not protect radical ancient constitutionalists from all royalist sallies. They had to contend with the sound legal argument that the positions of king and subject were not entirely analogous: the passage of time did not affect them in the same way. Indeed, in the words of Sir Robert Brooke, "no one can prescribe against the king." As royalists throughout the seventeenth century delighted in pointing out, the king enjoyed a decided advantage, namely, the maxim *nullum tempus occurrit Regi* – time does not run against the king. Because the king, as the keeper of the kingdom, could not be expected to keep track of all of his rights and properties, he enjoyed freedom from the ticking of the clock. That is, the passage of time and non-user did not diminish

---

[80] See, for example, James I's remarks concerning Magna Carta. Sommerville, "The Ancient Constitution Reassessed," p. 60.
[81] *Parliamentary Debates in 1610*, ed. Elizabeth Read Foster (New Haven, 1966), vol. II, p. 190.

his rights as they did those of his subjects. Hence, while he might prescribe against them, they could not prescribe against him.[82] If this were true, then ancient constitutionalist explanations for interruptions in the enforcement of St. Edward's laws failed.

Once again, however, medieval law came to the rescue. Writing in the mid-thirteenth century, William Raleigh and his later editor Henry Bracton drew a distinction which endured into the early modern era, namely, that between those essentials "which make the Crown what it is" and "accidentals." The *nullum tempus* prerogative protected the king in the former case but not in the latter.[83] This meant that kings, unlike subjects, did not always have to be eternally vigilant for fear of losing "public law" rights through non-user. Importantly, however, limiting the maxim to "essentials" left the door open for radical ancient constitutionalists to dispute the issue.

The predisposition to think in terms of prescription explains why the opponents of James I and Charles I went to such great lengths to enter protests to certain royal policies. Clearly the common lawyer William Noy had prescription in mind when, in the 1621 fight over parliamentary privileges, he warned the House of Commons that its members "must use whatsoever liberties we have hitherto used . . . To use our liberties is the best maintenance of our liberties."[84] Serjeant Francis Ashley, chairman of the committee that produced the *Protestation*, echoed this thinking, reminding the Commons that "A legal use breedeth a right; and [is] as good as a legal grant."[85] Oliver St. John, counsel to John Hampden in the *Ship Money Case*, put the matter even more bluntly. Arguing that Charles I could tax only in parliament, he noted that previous kings had regularly done so without objection. Their acquiescence amounted to "non-claims" which should be taken "as so many *le voets* and declarations of their general consents." Importantly, St. John added, the *nullum tempus* clause did not apply in this situation, where the proprietary rights of subjects were concerned.[86] As Weston notes, seventeenth-century

---

[82] Brooke, *La Graunde Abridgement*, fo. 151. See also William Noy, *The Principal Grounds and Maximes, with an Analysis; and A Dialogue and Treatise of the Laws of England* (Abingdon, 1821, repr. 1985), pp. 339–40. This work was written in the 1620s.

[83] For the medieval history of this maxim see Kantorowicz, *The King's Two Bodies*, pp. 164–73.

[84] *Commons Debates, 1621*, ed. Wallace Notestein, Hartley Simpson, and Frances Relf (New Haven, 1935), vol. VI, p. 240.

[85] *Journal of the House of Commons* (London, 1803), vol. I, pp. 664, 666.

[86] *A Complete Collection of State Trials*, ed. Howell, vol. III, p. 923.

English people of many political hues well understood that "the law aids the vigilant, not those who slumber on their rights."[87]

· One final issue remains in this introductory discussion of the ancient constitutionalist view of law and history, namely, the supposed origins of the ancient constitution and the institutions associated with it. Opinions varied among sixteenth- and seventeenth-century writers. Many early modern antiquaries and politicians, including Lambarde, Owen, Digges, and Pym, identified the Saxons as its authors. The common lawyer Nicholas Fuller, on the other hand, found the common law originating in "the first preaching of the Gospel in this island." Others, for example, Coke and Dodderidge traced it to the Britons. For Hakewill and Selden, the ancient constitution consisted of a melange of Saxon, Danish, and Norman customs, though with the Saxon influence predominating. Despite these variations, the majority of Tudor and early Stuart writers adhered to what Burgess terms the "standard model" of ancient constitutionalism: virtually all found the origins of their laws and government before 1066 and understood that these institutions descended to them essentially intact.[88]

The theme of continuity between Saxon and Stuart England echoed throughout both traditional and radical ancient constitutionalist thought, a direct outgrowth of the assumption that the past existed in the present. However, to say that ancient constitutionalists believed in the essential continuity of English history is not to imply that they necessarily considered their history as literally unchanging. Nor did they believe that the laws that governed their polity were no different from those of their ancestors. To be sure, the vast majority of writers maintained that the basic character of a government was established at its first building, and some seemed comfortable asserting the unchanging nature of the English constitution. Sir John Fortescue, for example, wrote in the late fifteenth century that from the age of the Britons "the realm has been continuously regulated by the same customs as it is now"; and Coke made similar remarks in the seventeenth century.[89] But Coke also viewed the common law as

[87] Weston, "England: Ancient Constitution and Common Law," p. 378.
[88] Burgess, *The Politics of the Ancient Constitution*, pp. 69–71, 82–4.
[89] Sir John Fortescue, *On the Laws and Governance of England*, ed. Shelley Lockwood (Cambridge, 1997), p. 26. According to Lockwood, Fortescue meant that "English customs have always been the same because they have always been the customs of the English people, that is, they have always been the usages of the English people." *Ibid.*, n. 95.

having been refined "by the wisdom of the most excellent men, in many succession of ages."[90] He recognized, in other words, that the laws of England had undergone change. Moreover, like virtually every common lawyer he acknowledged that statutes, for example, *De Donis Conditionalibus* of 1285, sometimes accounted for that change. But parliaments, Coke warned, ought to have a care when they drafted measures that altered the common law because such statutes could wreak havoc. Witness, once again, the statute *De Donis*, which, by creating the entailed estate, sanctioned perpetuities and thereby corrupted English land law.[91]

Other writers described the ancient constitution not as static but as in perpetual flux. Thus, for Thomas Hedley the common law grew with England as the skin with the hand.[92] His contemporaries Selden and Owen turned to another metaphor to illustrate both the changing and changeless nature of the ancient constitution. Following in the footsteps of medieval Romanists such as Accursius and Baldus, they likened it to a ship which retained its essential form even though its planks and sails had been continuously replaced over the years.[93] It was in this sense that the ancient constitution, and the English state of which it was a constituent part, remained essentially the same since its founding. It was in this sense, too, that Saxon laws and legal institutions could be seen as descending intact to Stuart England.

Ancient constitutionalist thought, then, allowed for continuity as well as change. With regard to the latter, Tudor and Stuart lawyers, antiquaries, and scholars were especially alert to changes in ele-

---

[90] Coke, *The Seventh Part* of the *Reports*, fo. 3b. See also Sommerville, *Politics and Ideology in England, 1603–1640*, p. 92.

[91] Coke, *The First Part of the Institutes of the Laws of England*, lib. 2. c. 10. sect. 170. *The Second Part of the Institutes of the Laws of England* (London, 1797), proem. *The Fourth Part of the Institutes of the Laws of England* (London, 1797), p. 36. See also Sir Robert Holbourne's remarks in the *Ship Money Case*, Howell, *A Complete Collection of State Trials*, vol. III, pp. 97, 978, 979, 982, 1000–1.

[92] *Proceedings in Parliament in 1610*, ed. Foster, vol. II, p. 50. See also Nicholas Fuller, *The Argument of Master Nicholas Fuller, in the Case of Thomas Lad, and Richard Maunsell, his Clients* (London, 1607), pp. 13–14.

[93] Selden, "Notes on Fortescue," in Sir John Fortescue, *De Laudibus Legum Angliae*, trans. Robert Mulcaster (London, 1616, repr. 1672), pp. 17–18. For Owen's views see Klein, "The Ancient Constitution Revisited," pp. 40–1. Kantorowicz notes that the metaphor of the ship to express the principle of "'identity despite changes'" or "'within changes'" can be found in Roman law. Thus, Accursius wrote in the *Glossa Ordinaria* (c. 1250) that "'even if the ship has been partly rebuilt, and even if every single plank may have been replaced, it is nonetheless always the same ship.'" To this his successor Baldus added: "'Notice, that where the form of a thing does not change, the thing itself is said not to change.'" Quoted in Kantorowicz, *The King's Two Bodies*, pp. 294–5.

venth-century Saxon life. They recognized, for example, that the English language and culture underwent alterations and that Saxon laws took on a French tinge. However, these transformations they often ascribed to Edward the Confessor and his mother, not to William I. This line of reasoning – which was partly correct – made perfect sense to Elizabeth I's historian, William Camden, as well as to Sir Henry Spelman.[94] Such historical constructions would later provide a respectable pedigree to dissidents like James Tyrrell, whose defense of the Glorious Revolution included the argument that "the laws and customs of Normandy came from the English laws and nation, either not long before or after Edward the Confessor's time."[95]

Thus, radical ancient constitutionalists draped themselves and their political arguments in a mantle of legitimacy woven of medieval threads. Admittedly, sometimes they had to work hard at putting a radical spin on St. Edward's laws, the *Modus*, and the *Mirror*. Admittedly, too, they sometimes drew conclusions far from the minds of those who fabricated them. But we must keep in mind that they labored within a highly esteemed historical tradition that rested upon a trinity of sources saluted as sound by protagonists of various political persuasions. Moreover, this tradition encouraged using the past for present purposes. And it saw no particular virtue in the modern practice of interpreting a given document within its proper historical context and with an eye toward the original intent of the author. As Holt notes, this earlier approach to history invited a partial selectivity and "encouraged error." But, he suggests, it was not the "simple anachronism of superimposing the present on the past with which Petit-Dutaillis charged Stubbs" and for which Herbert Butterfield took to task generations of historians. Rather, this historical method grew out of a reverence for custom and tradition, which reflected and reinforced "the common memory of how society was organized and social relations conducted. It was the expression of stability." The enormous appeal and staying power of this tradition leads Holt to recall the words of Lewis Namier:

---

[94] Camden, *Remains Concerning Britain*, ed. R. D. Dunn (Toronto, 1984), pp. 294–5. Spelman, "Of the Antiquity and Etymology of Terms and Times for Administration of Justice in England," in *A Collection of Curious Discourses*, ed. Thomas Hearne (London, 1775), vol. II, pp. 344ff, 369ff. Susan Reynolds notes that there were few differences between Norman and English customs. *Kingdoms and Communities* (Oxford, 1984), p. 266.

[95] Tyrrell, *Bibliotheca Politica* (London, 1694), p. 753.

" 'What matters most about political ideas is the underlying emotions, the music to which the ideas are mere libretto, often of inferior quality.' "[96]

The sense of history that assumed the presence of the past as well as its pastness spawned both the ancient constitution and its radicalized form, the "whiggish" version of history. And the community of respected medieval texts imbued the historical constructions with plausibility and legitimacy. To this tradition the seventeenth century was heir, and to it the people of Stuart England happily paid tribute.

[96] Holt, "The Ancient Constitution in Medieval England," pp. 51, 55. Holt, *Magna Carta*, chapters 2–4 *passim*. Holt, "The St. Albans Chroniclers and Magna Carta," in *Magna Carta and Medieval Government*, pp. 265–87, especially 266.

CHAPTER 2

"Those most noble and equitable laws of St. Edward": from the cult of the Confessor to the cult of the Confessor's laws

Every tradition grows ever more venerable – the more remote is its origin, the more confused that origin is. The reverence due it increases from generation to generation. The tradition finally becomes holy and inspires awe.

Friedrich Nietzsche

ST. EDWARD AND THE SACRALIZATION OF ENGLISH KINGSHIP

As the preceding chapter noted, St. Edward's laws deserve pride of place among the trinity of texts that formed the foundation of the ancient constitution. And St. Edward himself constituted the actual, non-legendary ancestor upon whom the ancestral constitution was based.[1] This is a fact of some importance, since an historical construction founded on a mythical figure such as Brut might well have been extinct by the mid-seventeenth century, a casualty of the increasingly sophisticated scholarship associated with Sir Henry Spelman, John Selden, and Sir William Dugdale. As it was, the ancient constitution, with the exalted Confessor at its center, boasted a long and respectable medieval pedigree, nourished and sustained by generations of esteemed sources and writers. This chapter explores the early origins and literature of the ancient constitution and examines the beginnings of the process by which a cult of kingship was transformed into a cult of law.

The story commences in the early middle ages, when both Saxons and Normans discovered that linking themselves to the English past carried distinct political and legal advantages. Thus, English Benedictines, eager to defend their lands and way of life from the Norman invaders, constructed histories in which they described

---

[1] M. I. Finley, "The Ancestral Constitution," in *The Use and Abuse of History* (Harmondsworth, 1971), pp. 34–59.

36

their liberties as existing in Saxon times and surviving the conquest intact. This was the picture painted by monastic writers such as Eadmer, John of Worcester, Symeon of Durham, Wulfstan, and William of Malmesbury, who collected and transcribed Saxon charters, laws, and legal texts in an effort to depict the conquest as a relatively inconsequential event in their history. Indeed, R. W. Southern credits the Benedictines with initiating the first historical revival in England as well as with "bringing Anglo-Saxon history into existence."[2]

Early Norman kings also played a part in the story, attempting to legitimize their rule by tapping the immense prestige associated with the Saxon past in general and the Saxon kingship in particular. Thus, William the Conqueror, in addition to imposing foreign laws upon the conquered kingdom and disseising Saxon landholders, constantly appealed to English customs, ordering in early charters that the practices of Saxon kings be followed under the new regime.[3] There were, for example, his charters to the city of London and to churches such as Westminster, Canterbury, Wells, and Bury St. Edmunds, granting that they could continue to enjoy those privileges which they had known in Saxon times.[4] Moreover, Anglo-Norman

[2] R. W. Southern, "Aspects of the European Tradition of Historical Writing: The Sense of the Past," *Transactions of the Royal Historical Society*, 5th series, 23 (1973), 243–63, especially pp. 246–56. See also J. C. Holt, "The Origins of the Constitutional Tradition in England," in *Magna Carta and Medieval Government. Studies Presented to the International Commission for the Study of Parliamentary Estates* (London, 1985), pp. 1–22; Holt, "The Ancient Constitution in Medieval England," in *The Roots of Liberty. Magna Carta, Ancient Constitution, and the Anglo-American Tradition of Rule of Law*, ed. Ellis Sandoz (Columbia, Mo., 1993), pp. 22–56; Nancy Partner, *Serious Entertainments. The Writing of History in Twelfth-Century England* (Chicago, 1977), p. 5. Patrick Wormald, *The Making of English Law: King Alfred to the Twelfth Century*, vol. 1 *Legislation and its Limits* (Oxford, 1999).

[3] David C. Douglas, "William the Conqueror: Duke and King," in *Time and the Hour. Collected Studies in Legal and Constitutional History* (London, 1977), p. 204. The extent to which William imposed French ways on the English or merely adapted Saxon institutions to his own use has been a topic of debate for nearly two centuries. Douglas suggests that despite the introduction of wide-scale change, the conquest "proved almost as important for what it preserved as for what it created." *Ibid.* See also H. G. Richardson and G. O. Sayles, *The Governance of Medieval England from the Conquest to Magna Carta* (Edinburgh, 1963), pp. 27, 33, 118; Ann Williams, *The English and the Norman Conquest* (Woodbridge, 1996); Bruce R. O'Brien, *God's Peace and King's Peace. The Laws of Edward the Confessor* (Philadelphia, 1999), chapter 1; Wormald, *The Making of English Law*, pp. 398–401. But cf. Hugh F. Kearney, *The British Isles. A History of Four Nations* (Cambridge, 1989), chapters 4 and 5; R. C. van Caenegem, *The Birth of the English Common Law*, 2nd. edn. (Cambridge, 1988), pp. 6–9; Elizabeth van Houts, "The Trauma of 1066," *History Today* 46 (1996), 9–15. For an especially measured view see Holt, *Colonial England, 1066–1215* (London and Rio Grande, Oh., 1997), Introduction, chapters 1 and 9.

[4] F. Liebermann, *Die Gesetze der Angelsachsen* (Halle, 1903), vol. 1, p. 286. *Liber Albus: the White*

writers told how William even asked the English to select those laws by which they would be governed. According to the twelfth-century chronicler Wace, they chose the laws of St. Edward: "these they wanted, these they demanded, these pleased them, these they took. This was their wish, and the king granted it to them." The story of William I's confirmation of the Saxon laws was repeated by Roger of Hoveden, Henry of Huntingdon, and Henry Knighton.[5] Then came William's coronation at Westminster Abbey on Christmas Day, 1066, where, according to *The Anglo-Saxon Chronicle*, he promised to "govern this nation according to the best practice of his predecessors" in return for the loyalty of his new subjects.[6] Nor is this all that can be said about William's propensity for things Saxon. The early twelfth-century chronicler Orderic Vitalis could write that he even struggled to learn the English language so that he might better understand Saxon ways.[7]

Most decisive of all in the formation of an ancient constitution were the efforts of early Norman monarchs to associate themselves with Edward the Confessor. Their attempts, as we shall see, created a cult of kingship that promoted Edward as the kingdom's prime symbol of kingly piety, justice, and virtue. Like other cults of kingship in the high middle ages, the cult of the Confessor enabled, indeed invited, contemporary kings to identify with a holy and revered

---

Book of the City of London. Compiled A.D. 1419 by John Carpenter, Common Clerk, and Richard Whitington, Mayor, ed. Henry Thomas Riley (London, 1861), pp. 427–8. David C. Douglas, *William the Conqueror* (Berkeley, 1964), p. 258. O'Brien, *God's Peace and King's Peace*, pp. 7, 25–6 *passim*, 112–15.

5 *Le Roman de Rou de Wace*, ed. A. J. Holden (Paris, 1971), vol. II, lines 8997–9014. I am indebted to Dr. Dolores Buttry for this citation and translation. See also Henry of Huntingdon, *Historia Anglorum*, ed. Diana Greenway (Oxford, 1996), Appendix; Roger of Hoveden, *Chronica*, ed. William Stubbs (London, 1868–71), vol. II, pp. xxii–xlix, 216–39; Henry Knighton, *Chronicon*, ed. J. R. Lumby (London, 1889), vol. I, pp. 50–1, 78–9; *Knighton's Chronicle, 1337–1396*, ed. G. H. Martin (Oxford, 1995), Introduction; Richard Fitz Nigel, *Dialogus de Scaccario. The Course of the Exchequer*, ed. Charles Johnson, F. E. L. Carter, and D. E. Greenway (Oxford, 1983), p. 63; O'Brien, *God's Peace and King's Peace*, pp. 108–15.

6 *The Anglo-Saxon Chronicle*, trans. G. N. Garmonsway (London, 1954), p. 200. *The Ecclesiastical History of Orderic Vitalis*, ed. Majorie Chibnall (Oxford, 1980), vol. II, pp. 183, 193–5. Douglas, *William the Conqueror*, pp. 248–50, 257. See also *Three Coronation Orders*, ed. J. Wickham Legg (London, Henry Bradshaw Society, 1891), vol. XIX, pp. 54–64; P. E. Schramm, *History of the English Coronation* (Oxford, 1937), p. 34; Janet L. Nelson, "The Rites of the Conqueror," in *Politics and Ritual in Early Medieval Europe* (London, 1986), pp. 375–401; George Garnett, "Coronation and Propaganda: Some Implications of the Norman Claim to the Throne of England in 1066," in *Transactions of the Royal Historical Society*, 5th series, 36 (1986), 91–113, especially p. 93.

7 *The Ecclesiastical History of Orderic Vitalis*, ed. Chibnall, vol. II, p. 257.

ancestor.[8] In turn, this association served as a magnetic focus for political loyalties, imbuing the king's commands with a ring of authority and legitimizing royal policies, especially those that smacked of innovation. Providing the monarchy with an essential measure of stability and anchoring the nascent medieval state at a critical stage of its development, these cults also justified the widening gyre of a more thoroughly centralized government. The cult of the Confessor, in particular, established a model of conciliatory kingship and regnal solidarity in which the ruler safeguarded an ancient past and kept peace within his kingdom.[9]

But it is in the nature of history to defy the control of future generations, and St. Edward's cult proved as easy to manipulate as other monuments of the past. Indeed, its most enduring contributions to English history lay not in its initial enhancement of royal authority but in the very opposite direction: by presenting an ideal of kingship, the cult also established standards against which rulers could be measured. So long as the scrutiny of royal behavior lay solely in the king's own hands, the cult of the Confessor could result in a healthy self-criticism. But if other elements in the kingdom decided that the right to judge royal actions rested in them and not the king alone, then the door opened for a very different use of the cult. This process probably began as early as the late twelfth century, when Thomas Becket and his supporters looked to the Saxon past as a defense against the Constitutions of Clarendon. Certainly it was well underway by the first decade-and-a-half of the thirteenth century, when King John's barons turned to the Confessor for justification of their rebellion. Thus began the re-historicization of the Confessor, a development that stretched through the medieval confirmations of Magna Carta, the new coronation oath of 1308, and finally reached fruition in the century of revolution. Downplaying the miraculous aspects of the cult, early modern English people would thoroughly secularize Holy Edward, transforming him into a purely legalistic icon. The cult of St. Edward thus became the cult of St. Edward's laws.

---

[8] The best study of the cult of the Confessor after 1066 is Paul Binski's *Westminster Abbey and the Plantagenets* (New Haven and London, 1995). I rely heavily on this work in what follows. For cults of kingship on the continent see Amy G. Remensnyder, *Remembering Kings Past. Monastic Foundation Legends in Medieval Southern France* (Ithaca, 1995). See also Emily O'Brien's doctoral dissertation on Edward the Confessor, forthcoming, Oxford University.

[9] Binski, *Westminster Abbey and the Plantagenets*, pp. 6–7.

Yet little about the Confessor's life portended such a prodigious future. The son of King Ethelred the Unready and Emma, daughter of the count of Normandy and a direct descendant of Rollo, Edward hailed from sturdy Anglo-Viking stock. The Danish wars sent him into exile in Normandy, where he lived at the court of his uncle from approximately the age of twelve until his return to England at the age of thirty-five. His mother's later marriage to Cnut made him the step-son of the Danish ruler of England.[10] One particular aspect of Edward's rule caught the contemporary spotlight: even in his own lifetime he enjoyed a reputation for extreme piety and miracle-working. Soon after his death on January 5, 1066, stories of his special powers circulated, and they passed into legend as monastic writers embodied them in works extolling the king's virtuous works.[11] He was said, for example, to be the first of the English kings to touch for the king's evil, and he also received credit for healing the mute and blind and curing infertility and epilepsy. Edward's reputation was further enhanced by his supposedly chaste relationship with his wife Edith, which left him uncorrupted in body as well as spirit.[12]

Other tales celebrated Edward's generosity. One, for example, described him as so moved by his subjects' poverty that he remitted the Danegeld after seeing the devil dancing on a pile of coins,[13] while

---

[10] The standard biography of Edward is Frank Barlow's *Edward the Confessor* (Berkeley, 1970).

[11] *Ibid.*, pp. 256–88. First was the pre-conquest *Life of King Edward who rests at Westminster, attributed to a monk of Saint-Bertin*, ed. and trans. Frank Barlow, 2nd. edn. (Oxford, 1992). This was followed in the early twelfth century by Osbert of Clare's "La vie de s. Eduoard le Confesseur par Osbert de Clare," ed. Marc Bloch, in *Analecta Bollandiana* 41 (1923). In the late twelfth century Ailred of Rievaulx's *Vita Sancti Edwardi Regis et Confessoris* appeared, first published by Sir Roger Twysden in *Historiae Anglicanae Scriptores X* (London, 1652), and reprinted in *Patrologiae curses completus: Patrologia Latina*, ed. J. P. Migne (Paris, 1844), vol. cxcv. Finally came the early thirteenth-century life attributed to Matthew Paris: *La Estoire de Seint Aedward le Rei*, ed. K. Y. Wallace, Anglo-Norman Text Society, 41 (London, 1983). See also Binski, "Reflections on *La estoire de Seint Aedward le rei*: Hagiography and Kingship in Thirteenth-century England," *Journal of Medieval History* 16 (1990), 335–50; D. J. Hall, *English Medieval Pilgrimage* (London, 1965), pp. 166–75; Jonathan Sumption, *Pilgrimage. An Image of Medieval Religion* (Totowa, NJ, 1975), pp. 280–82; Susan Ridyard, *The Royal Saints of Anglo-Saxon England* (Cambridge, 1988), pp. 234–52; Thomas Head, *Hagiography and the Cult of Saints* (Cambridge, 1990), p. 280.

[12] Barlow, "The Vita Aedwardi (Book II); the Seven Sleepers: Some Further Evidence and Reflections," *Speculum* 40 (1965), 385ff. Barlow, *Edward the Confessor*, pp. 257–64, especially pp. 257–8, 259; Barlow, "The Kings Evil," *English Historical Review* 95 (1980), 3–27. Marc Bloch, *The Royal Touch. Sacred Monarchy and Scrofula in England and France* (London, 1973), chapters 1 and 2. The English miracles attributed to Edward number only about half-a-dozen. Shakespeare later publicized his curative powers in *Macbeth*.

[13] *Polychronicon Ranulphi Higden Monachi Cestrensis; Together with the English Translations of John Trevisa and of an unknown writer of the Fifteenth Century*, ed. Joseph R. Lumby (London, 1879),

another recounted how he aided in the escape of a thief whom he had caught looting his treasury.[14] The Confessor's largess was also illustrated in the famous story of his encounter with St. John. According to this tale, Edward, on his way to dedicate a church to the Evangelist at Clavering in Essex, met a beggar who asked for money. Carrying none, Edward took the ring from his finger and gave it to the man, who turned out to be St. John himself. The ring made its way back to the king when the Evangelist later gave it to two English pilgrims whom he encountered on their way to Jerusalem.[15]

Another group of stories, including some especially favored by Stuart dissidents, focused on Edward and his royal office. One, for example, told how an assembly of estates elected him king while he was still in his mother's womb, despite the fact that he had two older brothers. To the compilers of *The Anglo-Saxon Chronicle*, this meant that "the whole nation chose Edward to be king" – a sentiment welcome to seventeenth-century advocates of elective and contractual kingship.[16] The Confessor also enjoyed a reputation as a just judge, an English Solomon, who made no distinction between rich and poor. And he was celebrated both as a guardian of ancient customs and as a great law-maker. Indeed, according to medieval (and early modern) opinion, it was Edward who, with the help of his parliament, scrolled through the various ancient customs, culling the most worthy of them into what would later be called the common law of England.[17] For this he earned the title of author of common law, an appellation that lent credibility to the early modern argument that common law was Saxon law and bolstered the ancient constitutionalist belief in the continuity of English legal institutions.

vol. VI, p. 529. *The Historical Works of Ralph de Diceto, Dean of London*, ed. William Stubbs (London, 1876), p. 189. *The Anglo-Saxon Chronicle*, ed. Garmonsway, p. 173.

[14] *The Life of King Edward*, ed. Barlow, p. xxxviii, n. 107. Lawrence Tanner, "Some Representations of St. Edward the Confessor in Westminster Abbey and Elsewhere," *Journal of the British Archaeological Association* 3rd series, 15 (1952), 9.

[15] Now the story is found only in Ailred's *Vita sancti Edwardi*, but it was probably written by Osbert of Clare. Barlow, *Edward the Confessor*, pp. 272, 282 n. 2. See also *The Life of King Edward*, ed. Barlow, pp. xxxviii, 107, n. 48, 157; E. W. Tristram, *English Medieval Wall Paintings: the Thirteenth Century* (London, 1950), p. 56. The story of Edward and St. John also appeared in *The Golden Legend*, a history of saints written around 1260 in Lombardy by Jacobus de Voraigne. *The Golden Legend or Lives of the Saints as Englished by William Caxton* (London, 1900), pp. 174–6; *The Oxford Dictionary of Saints*, ed. David Hugh Farmer (Oxford, 1978), p. 124.

[16] *The Anglo-Saxon Chronicle*, ed. Garmonsway, p. 163. *The Life of King Edward*, ed. Barlow, pp. 7–8, 60.

[17] Ailred of Rievaulx, *Vita S. Edwardi Regis et Confessoris*, in *Patrologia Latina*, ed. Migne, vol. CXCV, p. 745. O'Brien, *God's Peace and King's Peace*, pp. 47, 224, n. 58.

In the early twelfth century Osbert of Clare, a monk at Westminster, attempted, in true Norman style, to appropriate the Confessor for his own abbey. Toward this end, he launched a campaign to canonize Edward, who had ordered the abbey rebuilt. Osbert eventually persuaded officials to open the king's tomb, where, according to contemporary accounts, they found Edward's body whole and uncorrupted, his crown still on his head, his scepter at his side, and St. John's ring on his finger. In the 1130s Osbert, now a prior at Westminster, stepped up the campaign for canonization by commemorating January 5, the date of his death, with an anniversary mass and preaching on the Confessor's virtues and miracles. Osbert further enhanced Edward's reputation by founding a house of canonesses at Kilburn in Middlesex and charging them to pray for the Confessor's soul.[18] The monk's efforts, reinforced by the strong support of Henry II, culminated in Edward's canonization in 1161. Now enrolled among the saints, his body was translated to Westminster Abbey on Sunday, October 13, 1163, henceforth known as St. Edward's Day. The only king of England to be so honored, his bones, according to legend, have rested since that time in his shrine behind the high altar, which still constitutes the holiest place in Westminster Abbey.[19]

Linked with ruling elites from the very beginning, the cult of the Confessor carried distinct political overtones. Indeed, Frank Barlow describes Edward as a "saint for those interested in the secrets of political power."[20] For Saxons he symbolized all that was English and godly after the Norman conquest. After all, as legend had it, St. Peter himself had told Edward that "the kingdom of the English is the kingdom of God," a sentiment which might well have been in the minds of the jurors in Babergh hundred, south of Bury St.

---

[18] Barlow, *Edward the Confessor*, pp. 265, 272–7, especially p. 274. *The Life of King Edward*, ed. Barlow, pp. 157–63. Ridyard, *The Royal Saints of Anglo-Saxon England*, pp. 20–3. Ridyard notes the "businesslike readiness" of Norman churchmen "to make the heroes of the past serve the politics of the present." *Ibid.*, pp. 251–2. See also Ridyard, "Condigna Veneratio: Post-Conquest Attitudes to the Saints of the Anglo-Saxons," *Anglo-Norman Studies* 9 (1987), 179–206; O'Brien, *God's Peace and the King's Peace*, p. 39.

[19] Barlow, *Edward the Confessor*, pp. 273–83, 325. Ronald Finucane, *Miracles and Pilgrims* (Totowa, NJ, 1977), pp. 36–8. W. L. Warren and M. T. Clanchy suggest that Henry II's motivation to join in the efforts to canonize Edward the Confessor stemmed from a desire to confirm the prestige of his kingship after the anarchy of King Stephen and his mother, the Empress Mathilda. Warren, *Henry II* (Berkeley, 1973), pp. 222–3. Clanchy, *England and Its Rulers 1066–1272*, 2nd. edn. (Oxford, 1998), pp. 88–9.

[20] Barlow, *Edward the Confessor*, p. 284. See also Binski, "Reflections on *La estoire de Seint Aedward le rei*," p. 347; Binski, *Westminster Abbey and the Plantagenets*, p. 3.

Edmunds, who described Edward to the Domesday commissioners as "*rex gloriosus.*"[21]

Association with the Confessor brought many practical advantages to Westminster Abbey. In particular, the community stood to profit from Edward's canonization because the monks needed their own English saint if they were to compete with St. Paul's, St. Albans, and Bury St. Edmunds. Edward fitted the bill, his reputation promising to draw pilgrims to Westminster and thus increase both its fame and its fortune. The Confessor proved valuable for another reason. Like other religious establishments, Westminster Abbey was always in the market for royal charters confirming its rights and privileges as against those of other monasteries. If the Abbey could boast charters from a king who was also a saint, its legal position could prove unassailable. As ill luck had it, however, no such charters existed. Fortunately for Westminster Abbey, this obstacle was easily overcome when Osbert, always ready to serve, took pen in hand and, through feats of what Amy G. Remensnyder terms "imaginative memory," created the necessary documents.[22]

Not surprisingly, kings, too, recognized the advantages of associating with the Confessor. Understandably appreciative of having a saint in the family, they were always eager to bolster their position at home and abroad by evoking the image of the sacred Saxon kingship. Henry I, born not in Normandy but in Oxford, deliberately aligned himself with the English past by marrying Edith, daughter of Margaret of Scotland and a direct descendant of King Ethelred. She, in turn, did her part by obligingly changing her name to Matilda, more respectable because more Saxon. Further, Henry I, seeking to win the support of the Saxons in his struggles with his brother Robert, promised in his famous coronation charter of 1101 that he would keep the *Laga Edwardi* as amended by his father, the Conqueror. By *Laga Edwardi* Henry meant not any particular set of

[21] Barlow, *Edward the Confessor*, pp. 293, 266, n. 6. *Domesday-Book, seu Liber Censualis Willelmi Primi Regis Angliae, Inter Archivos Regni in Domo Capitulari Westmonasterii Asservatus* (London, 1783), vol. II, pp. 415b, 416b, 425. Two abbreviated Domesday Books carried numerous pictures representing events from the Confessor's life. Mercedes Rochelle, *Post-Biblical Saints Art Index* (Jefferson, NC, 1994), p. 87, no. 1174 and no. 1775. See also Tanner, "Some Representations of St. Edward the Confessor in Westminster Abbey and Elsewhere," p. 7.

[22] Remensnyder, *Remembering Kings Past*, pp. 1–15. Barlow records that by 1138 Osbert had honored the Abbey by composing three charters on behalf of Edward. *Edward the Confessor*, p. 274. *The Life of King Edward*, ed. Barlow, p. 157. See also Binski, *Westminster Abbey and the Plantagenets*, p. 122; M. T. Clanchy, *From Memory to Written Record*, 2nd. edn. (Oxford, 1993), pp. 28, 41–2, 148–9, 170–1, 193, 298, 318, and *passim*.

laws but rather, in Bruce O'Brien's words, "the laws and customs that had been observed before and at the time of the Norman conquest."[23] Similar concerns prompted King Stephen, at war with the Empress Matilda, to make the same promise. Henry II followed suit in 1154, issuing a coronation charter in which he affirmed the earlier promise of his grandfather, Henry I.[24] As O'Brien notes, these combined royal efforts made the Confessor's reign "a golden age," an appropriate touchstone for both the conquerors and the conquered.[25]

The cult of the Confessor burgeoned in the thirteenth century, when Henry III (1216–1272) devoted much of his reign and his kingdom's resources to a glorification of St. Edward. Choosing him as his patron saint, Henry re-designed his seal to resemble that of the Confessor. He also named his heir after Edward and selected October 13 – the date of the Confessor's translation – as a day of great celebration, when members of his household gathered in their fine robes to knight the young men in their favor. So profound, in fact, was Henry's devotion that he was said to carry a statue of Holy Edward wherever he traveled.[26] Motivated in part by a desire to Anglicize his rule, Henry recognized the political advantages accruing from association with a king who was born a Saxon but raised a Norman, and, what was more, a king who had been canonized even before St. Thomas, the great enemy of his grandfather, Henry II.[27] But his championing of the Confessor was also inspired by a profound piety which led him to undertake the rebuilding of Westminster Abbey. Going forward entirely in St.

---

[23] O'Brien, *God's Peace and King's Peace*, p. 26. See also Judith A. Green, *The Government of England under Henry I* (Cambridge, 1986), chapter 2, especially p. 98; Holt, "Colonial England, 1066–1215," in *Colonial England, 1066–1215*, pp. 17–18.

[24] Hoveden, *Chronica*, ed. William Stubbs (London, 1868–71), vol. I, p. 157. Roger of Wendover, *Flowers of History*, trans. J. A. Giles (London, 1849), vol. I, p. 446. *The Anglo-Saxon Chronicle*, ed. Garmonsway, p. 236. William of Malmesbury, *Gesta Regum Anglorum, atque Historia Novella*, ed. Thomas D. Hardy (London, 1840), pp. 618–19, 626–7, 767. William of Malmesbury, *Historia Novella*, trans. K. R. Potter (London, 1995), pp. 18–20. Paris, *Historia Anglorum*, ed. Madden, vol. I, pp. 176–81. Paris, *Chronica Majora*, ed. H. R. Luard (London, 1872), vol. II, pp. 40–1, 115–16.

[25] O'Brien, *God's Peace and King's Peace*, p. 17.

[26] Binski, *Westminster Abbey and the Plantagenets*, pp. 1–9, 10–51, and *passim*. Steven H. Wander, "Westminster Abbey: a Case Study in the Meaning of Medieval Architecture" (doctoral dissertation, Stanford University, 1974), p. 56.

[27] Maurice Powicke, *England in the Thirteenth Century*, 2nd. edn. (Oxford, 1962), p. 18. Suzanne Lewis, *The Art of Matthew Paris in the Chronica Majora* (Berkeley, 1987), pp. 496–7, n. 197. Peter Brieger, *English Art 1216–1307* (Oxford, 1968), pp. 106–7. Tanner, "Some Representations of St. Edward the Confessor in Westminster Abbey and Elsewhere," p. 3.

Edward's name, the royal project transmuted the abbey into the physical image of the Confessor's kingship, reifying his cult and forever associating him with Westminster, the new administrative heart of government and now the historical center of the realm. By the end of Henry III's reign in 1272, St. Edward, now literally etched in stone, was on his way to becoming a truly national king – an early, but not the last, invention of tradition in English history.[28]

At the core of Henry III's rebuilding of Westminster Abbey stood a new chapel and a splendid new shrine made of purest gold and precious stones. There, on October 13, 1269, Henry III, along with his sons, his brother, and several leading nobles, deposited the chest containing the Confessor's body and relics.[29] It rested on the tumulus, a mound of earth brought from Jerusalem, which rose some six feet above the ground, its very height testifying to St. Edward's preeminence.[30] Within sight of this holiest of places, the church was now consecrated, this solemn act marking, in Maurice Powicke's words, Henry III's greatest achievement and "the fulfillment of his dearest hopes." From Henry's efforts, too, eventually came the practice of crowning and burying kings and queens in the abbey, the vicinity of St. Edward's shrine constituting the favored spot.[31]

The art and architecture of Henry III's reign, particularly that associated with Westminster Abbey, dramatically celebrated the Confessor and spread his stories among those who visited the precinct, including perhaps ordinary folk drawn to London's

---

[28] See Binski, "Reflections on *La estoire de Seint Aedward le rei*," p. 346; Binski, *The Painted Chamber at Westminster*, Society of Antiquaries, Occasional Paper, n.s. ix (London, 1986), p. 45; Wander, "Westminster Abbey: a Case Study in the Meaning of Medieval Architecture," pp. 45–59, 219–25, and *passim*; Clanchy, *England and Its Rulers 1066–1272*, chapters 9 and 10.

[29] The choice of October 13 as St. Edward's feast day was politically shrewd, since it marked the beginning of the fiscal year, at which time the Exchequer was busy, Westminster filled with petitioners, and the royal council and sometimes parliament were in session. Powicke, *Thirteenth Century England*, p. 18. Lewis *The Art of Matthew Paris in the Chronica Majora*, p. 497, n. 197. Barlow, *Edward the Confessor*, pp. 283–4, n. 6.

[30] Finucane notes that "the bones of really famous saints," such as Edward the Confessor, "were sometimes elevated almost out of reach of the pilgrims." *Miracles and Pilgrims*, p. 27.

[31] Powicke, *Thirteenth Century England*, pp. 18, 159, 161, 205, 224. Alan Harding, *England in the Thirteenth Century* (Cambridge, 1993), p. 16. Binski notes, however, that it was only gradually that Westminster took on the role as royal mausoleum. *Westminster Abbey and the Plantagenets*, 90–4. See also *ibid.*, pp. 10–51 and *passim*; Brieger, *English Art 1216–1307*, pp. 106–34, 200–2; Christopher Wilson, *The Gothic Cathedral. The Architecture of the Great Church 1130–1530* (London, 1990), pp. 178–83. Wilson notes that the Abbey "combined the functions of Reims (coronation church), Saint Denis (royal mausoleum), and the Sainte-Chapelle (relic cult glorifying the monarchy)." *Ibid.*, p. 30.

markets, stalls, fairs, and royal courts. Visitors to the abbey could have noticed sculptures of St. Edward presiding over the transepts.[32] They could also see very near St. Edward's shrine two columns with engravings of the Confessor and St. John. Particularly impressive were the tapestries donated by Abbot Richard of Barking, which depicted more than twenty events from Holy Edward's life on one side of the choir and a corresponding set of Biblical stories on the other.[33] In addition, pictures of St. Edward and St. John adorned the glazed tiles in the floor of the Abbey's chapter house.[34] On the wall arcade in the choir aisles appeared carved and gilded armorial shields, including those of St. Edward, Henry III, benefactors of the Abbey, and leading nobles of the realm.[35]

Henry III's redecoration of the Painted Chamber, his private living quarters at Westminster, also demonstrated his utter devotion to his patron saint. Thus, he commissioned artists to paint the story of St. Edward and St. John on two splays on the eastern-most window, just opposite the royal bed.[36] Behind the bed was a spectacular 10 ft. 8 in. × 6ft. picture of the coronation of the Confessor, elaborately divided by a canopy of five foiled arches, showing him resting majestically on his throne. In his hand he held his sceptre, and on either side stood the two archbishops with his crown. The painting's caption read: "CEST LE CORONEMENT SEINT EDEWARD."[37] The placing of the coronation scene above the royal bed evoked, in Paul Binski's words, "the imagery of just and virtuous

---

[32] For a general discussion of the Abbey's art and architecture see Binski, *Westminster Abbey and the Plantagenets*, chapters 3, 4, and 5. See also Binski, "Reflections on *La estoire de Seint Aedward le rei*," p. 346.

[33] *Ibid.*, p. 337. Binski, "Abbot Berkyng's Tapestries and Matthew Paris's Life of St. Edward the Confessor," *Archaeologia* 109 (1991), 85–100. Tanner, "Some Representations of St. Edward the Confessor in Westminster Abbey and Elsewhere," p. 9. The earliest representation of the story of St. Edward and the beggar may be in the Norman doorway of the church at Wordwell, which dates from the period 1110 to 1140. Robert Halliday, "The Norman Doorways at Wordwell and West Stow Churches," *Proceedings of the Suffolk Institute of Archaeology and History* 37 (1992), 367–9.

[34] Brieger, *English Art 1216–1307*, pp. 120 and n. 1, 133–4, 154. W. R. Lethaby, "Medieval Paintings at Westminster," *Proceedings of the British Academy* 13 (1927), 1.

[35] Brieger, *English Art 1216–1307*, p. 121. Noppen, *Royal Westminster and the Coronation* (New York, 1937), p. 73. Tristram, *English Medieval Wall Painting*, p. 106. W. R. Lethaby, *Westminster Abbey and the King's Craftsmen* (London, 1906), pp. 299–302.

[36] Binski, *Westminster Abbey and the Plantagenets*, pp. 87–9, 127–8. Binski, *The Painted Chamber*, pp. 36, 40. Tristram, *English Medieval Wall Paintings*, pp. 106–8. W. R. Lethaby, "English Primitives. The Painted Chamber and the Early Masters of the Westminster School," *Burlington Magazine* 7 (1905), 259.

[37] Binski, *The Painted Chamber at Westminster*, pp. 33, 38–9. For a critique of Binski and a discussion of the dating of the decorations in the Painted Chamber see Alison Stones's

kingship" and served as a "cogent . . . assertion of Henry's immediate, physical identification with the saint-king." Importantly, the painting and its associations had the most public of reverberations, for the royal bed chamber – the "bed of estate" – functioned throughout the middle ages as a seat of government. Here kings sometimes dispensed justice and received the homage of their subjects. Here, too, parliament occasionally met, the Painted Chamber supplementing the Great Hall and the chapter house of Westminster Abbey.[38]

Henry III also expressed his devotion to the Confessor in more mundane ways. He sponsored St. Edward's fairs, held twice a year at Westminster, commencing on January 5 and October 13 and lasting for three days. During these times, all other fairs throughout England were suspended and London shops were closed. St. Edward's fairs lasted until the fifteenth century, though their business had declined significantly by the mid-fourteenth century.[39]

In addition, Henry III spread the Confessor's reputation among the elite by patronizing the work of Matthew Paris and his school, whose illustrations, paintings, and writings celebrated St. Edward's life. Preeminent among these creations were the illustrations that Paris included in his chronicles. For example, the series of coronation scenes in the *Flores Historiarum* contain ten drawings of the coronations of Arthur, St. Edward, and various Norman kings, the most elaborate depicting that of the Confessor. Carrying sixteen figures, it shows the archbishop of Canterbury anointing Edward with holy oil, while the archbishop of York handed him the scepter.[40] Paris also designed a miniature that featured pilgrims visiting St. Edward's

---

review in *Burlington Magazine* 130 (1988), 142–3. See also Lethaby, "English Primitives," pp. 65, 259; Lethaby, "Medieval Paintings at Westminster," pp. 15–19.

[38] Binski, *The Painted Chamber*, pp. 2, 34–6. The *"lit de justice"* of French kings functioned in a similar way. See Elizabeth A. R. Brown, *The "Lit de Justice": Semantics, Ceremonial, and the Parlement of Paris, 1300–1600* (Sigmaringen, 1994).

[39] Gervase Rosser, *Medieval Westminster, 1200–1540* (Oxford, 1989), pp. 110–11. In 1650 George Walker, writing in defense of the regicide, declared that in these fairs Henry III fleeced his people by shutting Westminster and London shops. *Anglo-Tyrannus, Or the Idea of a Norman Monarch, Represented in the parallel Reignes of Henrie the Third and Charles Kings of England* (London, 1650), p. 26.

[40] Gransden notes that the picture of the coronation of Edward the Confessor is twice as large as the other coronation pictures. "The Continuation of the *Flores Historiarum* from 1265–1327," in *Legends, Traditions, and History in Medieval England*, ed. Gransden (London and Rio Grande, 1992), p. 245 and n. 4. Brieger, *English Art 1216–1307*, pp. 148–9. See also Lewis, *The Art of Matthew Paris in the Chronica Majora*, pp. 6–52.

shrine, where they crawled inside the openings and touched the holy body.[41]

Then there was the illustrated *La Estoire de St. Aedward le Rei*, written for Henry III's wife Eleanor of Provence and usually attributed to Matthew Paris. A French versification of the Latin prose work by Ailred of Rievaulx, it contains a number of pictures of the Confessor, including one showing him meeting with his parliament. According to Binski, Paris's "skilled pictorial glossing of Edward's kingship," along with his accompanying text, presented the Confessor as a ruler for all ages, an ideal king worthy of emulation. Paris particularly applauded St. Edward's sense of justice and fairness, which called to mind Solomon, as well as his willingness to consult with his people in parliament. By ruling through consent and good counsel rather than by arbitrary will and power, the Confessor secured the unity, wholeness, and health of his kingdom – a task which Henry III presumably performed with equal success.[42]

By the end of Henry III's reign in 1272, the cult of the Confessor had clearly come into its own, its power all the greater because its home base was Westminster, where kings now kept their residence, their exchequer, and their courts of law, including the high court of parliament. Moreover, in the precincts of Westminster and London, few people of whatever station could avoid contact of one sort or another with St. Edward. Clerics celebrated his feast days, pilgrims prayed at his shrine, and visitors to the Abbey were barraged by his iconography.[43]

In the fourteenth century, devotion to more militaristic values led kings to elevate St. George and King Arthur to the royal pantheon. But these ancient, mythical heroes never entirely replaced Holy Edward in the kingdom's imagination. On the contrary, his standing among the elite was forever assured and, indeed, institutionalized,

---

[41] Michael Camille, *The Gothic Idol: Ideology and Image-making in Medieval Art* (Cambridge, 1989), pp. 125–6. I owe this citation to Dr. Linda Rouillard.

[42] Binski, "Reflections on *La estoire de Seint Aedward le rei*," pp. 336, 342, 344–7. A modern edition can be found in *La Estoire de Seint Aedward le Rei*, ed. Wallace. Janet Nelson, "Royal Saints and Early Medieval Kingship," *Sanctity and Secularity. Studies in Church History*, ed. D. Baker, 10 (1973), 43–4. David Carpenter, "King, Magnates, and Society: the Personal Rule of Henry III, 1234–1258," *Speculum* 60 (1985), 59–62; Joel T. Rosenthal, "Edward the Confessor and Robert the Pious: Eleventh-Century Kingship and Biography," *Medieval Studies* 30 (1971), 7–20.

[43] B. Spencer, *Souvenirs and Secular Badges* (Salisbury, 1990), part 2. Dillian Gordon, *Making and Meaning. The Wilton Diptych* (London, 1993), p. 54.

by the coronation ceremony. Not only did the ceremony fix St. Edward forever in the royal hall of fame, it also helped transform the cult of the Confessor into the cult of the Confessor's laws.[44] Nothing so magnified St. Edward's preeminence as this development, and nothing so epitomized his symbolic power as his evocation at this most critical of moments in any political society – the transferral of power from one ruler to another. Indeed, the coronation constituted the state's ultimate act of propaganda, dramatizing in a public and spectacular way the king's divine right to govern, his duty to his subjects, and their corresponding obligation to obey.[45] But more than mere public relations was involved, for the ceremony included the anointing of the king with holy oil, an act that made him a *persona mixta*, both *rex et sacerdos*. Nor was the splendid and elaborate imagery limited to the large crowds fortunate enough to witness the ceremony in Westminster Abbey. Chroniclers included accounts of coronations, and participants such as the Cinque Ports took care to preserve records of their involvement. Even the middling political elite, for example, Sir John Paston the elder, Sir John Astley, and the Baron family, owned manuscripts of the coronation liturgy.[46]

It is, then, of profound significance that, by the early fourteenth century, the coronation ceremony went forward almost entirely in St. Edward's name. First, there was the new coronation oath of 1308. Rewritten by Edward II's barons in what Natalie Fryde and J. R. Maddicott call a revolutionary move to control the crown, this oath now appeared in the form which kings would swear for almost four centuries. To the first three clauses, which obliged kings to keep the peace and protect the church, uphold good laws and abrogate old, and dispense equal justice, a fourth was added. This clause came from the London version of St. Edward's laws. Probably

---

[44] Binski notes that St. Edward's incorporation into the coronation ceremony was progressive. *Westminster Abbey and the Plantagenets*, pp. 134–40. See also H. G. Richardson, "Early Coronation Records," *Bulletin of the Institute of Historical Research* 13 (1935–36), 129–45.

[45] Andrew Hughes, "The Origins and Descent of the Fourth Recension of the English Coronation," in *Coronations. Medieval and Early Modern Monarchic Ritual*, ed. Janos Bak (Berkeley, 1990), p. 197. David J. Sturdy, "'Continuity' versus 'Change': Historians and English Coronations of the Medieval and Early Modern Periods," in *ibid.*, p. 235. D. R. Woolf, "The Power of the Past," in *Political Thought and the Tudor Commonwealth. Deep Structure, Discourse and Disguise*, ed. Paul A. Fidler and T. F. Mayer (London, 1992), pp. 27–8.

[46] Sutton and Hammond, *The Coronation of Richard III. The Extant Documents* (New York, 1983), pp. 11–12. However, Binski points out that coronations were rare events. Westminster Abbey was the scene of only two in the thirteenth century and four in the fourteenth century. In his words, "the procedure of a coronation was unlikely to have been recalled in living memory." *Westminster Abbey and the Plantagenets*, p. 128.

written in the years from 1206 to 1215, it required kings to preserve
the rights of the monarchy and to govern by the laws and customs
that the community of the realm "shall choose." It was, moreover,
spoken in French rather than Latin. According to Fryde and
Maddicott, the addition amounted to an attempt to control future
legislation, and, as we shall see, by the mid-seventeenth century it
constituted a major argument in the ancient constitutionalist
arsenal.[47]

For the time being, suffice it to say that generations of English
people heard their kings swear to abide by both the new laws as well
as the old. In this most solemn of ceremonies the archbishop of
Canterbury, after showing the king to the people from the four
corners of the *pulpitum*, asked him:

"Sire, will you grant and keep and by your oath confirm to the people of
England the laws and customs given to them by the previous just and god-
fearing kings, your ancestors, and especially the laws, customs, and liberties
granted to the clergy and people by the glorious king, the sainted Edward,
your predecessor?"
"Sire, do you grant to be held and observed the just laws and customs that
the community of your realm shall determine, and will you, so far as in you
lies, defend and strengthen them to the honor of God?"[48]

To which the king replied, "I grant and promise to keep them." So
swore every king of England, more or less, until the oath was
rewritten at the Glorious Revolution.[49]

Then there was the utter reliance on the Confessor's relics and
regalia during the ceremony. Although a bit daunting, a simple
listing and description of these illustrates St. Edward's omnipresence
during that most significant act of state. According to fourteenth-
and fifteenth-century inventories, the coronation objects included
jewelled crowns, a silver rod, a golden scepter, a paten, a chalice,

---

[47] Fryde, *The Tyranny and Fall of Edward II 1321–1326* (Cambridge, 1979), pp. 16–17. Maddicott, *Thomas of Lancaster 1307–1322. A Study of the Reign of Edward II* (Oxford, 1970), pp. 82ff. Liebermann, ed., *Die Gesetze der Angelsachsen*, vol. 1, pp. 635–6. See also John J. Bruckmann, "English Coronations, 1216–1308" (unpublished doctoral dissertation, University of Toronto, 1964), cited in Sturdy, "Continuity versus Change," pp. 236–38; H. G. Richardson, "The English Coronation Oath," *Transactions of the Royal Historical Society* 4th series, 23 (1941), 129–58; O'Brien, *God's Peace and King's Peace*, pp. 118–19; Holt, *Magna Carta*, pp. 56, 93–5.

[48] Brian Tierney, ed., *The Middle Ages*, vol. 1 *Sources of Medieval History*, 5th. edn. (New York, 1992), p. 300.

[49] Percy E. Schramm, *A History of the English Coronation*, trans. Leopold G. Wickham Legg (Oxford, 1937), pp. 100, 109, 203–11, 218–19. Noppen, *Royal Westminster and the Coronation*, pp. 85–6.

tunics, a golden ring, a pair of gloves, red shoes, a golden comb and spoon, and several swords – almost all associated in one way or another with the Confessor. The coronation chair, probably the most ancient of the items used in the ceremony, was (and remains) closely identified with him. Constructed around 1300 at the command of Edward I, it was allegedly offered by the king at St. Edward's shrine in gratitude for his victory over the Scots. A painting on the back of the chair shows a picture of a king, traditionally taken to be the Confessor, sitting with his feet on a lion. Accordingly, the chair has been known since the early fourteenth century as St. Edward's chair, and, with several exceptions, it has served as the coronation chair since that time.[50]

Also figuring prominently in the coronation were the symbols of secular government, the regalia, with which the king was typically invested after being anointed with the chrism. Indeed, the king's public and outward possession of the kingdom depended on the delivery of St. Edward's regalia in St. Edward's church.[51] The most important of the regalia was St. Edward's crown, said to have been found still on his head when his tomb was first opened in 1102. Worn at coronations from the eleventh century onward, it represented "glory and justice."[52] Also given to the new king at his coronation was the Confessor's scepter, which marked his actual seisin of the kingdom.[53] Then there was St. Edward's ring, traditionally the one he had given to St. John. Now presented to the new king, it was placed on the fourth finger of the right hand, that is, the "marrying finger," signifying his union with his people and the kingdom's devotion to the true faith.[54]

---

[50] Binski, *Westminster Abbey and the Plantagenets*, pp. 135–40. Noppen, *Royal Westminster at the Coronation*, pp. 71–2, 118. See also Lethaby, *Westminster Abbey and the King's Craftsmen*, p. 26 (for a reconstructed picture of St. Edward on the back of the chair); Lethaby, "Medieval Paintings at Westminster," pp. 19–20; Sutton and Hammond, *The Coronation of Richard III*, pp. 38–40, 77, 157; *The Coronation Chair* (London, HMSO, 1953); Brieger, *English Art 1216–1307*, pp. 200, 212–13; Arthur P. Stanley, *Historical Memorials of Westminster Abbey*, 5th. edn. (New York, 1882), pp. 58–9, 78.

[51] Sutton and Hammond, *The Coronation of Richard III*, pp. 228–44. L. G. Wickham Legg, *Coronation Records* (Westminster, 1901), pp. 84, 94–8, 100, 101, 115, 122 and *passim*.

[52] Noppen, *Royal Westminster and the Coronation*, pp. 119–22. Barlow, *Edward the Confessor*, p. 63. St. Edward's crown as it now exists was constructed for the coronation of Charles II in 1661, probably using the circle of the ancient crown, which was broken up during the Commonwealth. Trevor Beeson, *Westminster Abbey*, 8th. edn. (London, 1989), pp. 6–7.

[53] J. A. Armstrong, "The Inauguration Ceremonies of the Yorkist Kings and their Title to the Throne," *Transactions of the Royal Historical Society* 4th series, 30 (1948), 61. Stanley, *Historical Memorials of Westminster Abbey*, p. 44.

[54] Barlow, *Edward the Confessor*, p. 63. Stanley, *Historical Memorials of Westminster Abbey*, p. 44.

In addition, St. Edward's sword figured prominently in the coronation. One of several swords borne in the procession into Westminster Abbey,[55] *Curtana* symbolized, in Matthew Paris's view, the right of the earl of Chester, the sword-bearer, to restrain "the king if he should commit an error."[56] Also present were St. Edward's great stone chalice, from which the archbishop poured the sacramental wine; St. Edward's paten on which he handed the new king the wafer; and St. Edward's comb, with which he smoothed the new king's hair after the anointing. Finally, there was St. Edward's cope, with which the archbishop of Canterbury then covered the king's shoulders, thereby reinforcing in the eyes of the laity the new king's holy nature.[57] Too precious to be taken away from the Abbey, these holy relics of a holy king have remained in its keeping throughout the twentieth century.

Late medieval kings continued to evoke the Confessor's memory in a variety of ways. Edward III (1327–1377), for example, ordered the Confessor's image to be carved over the courts of King's Bench and Common Pleas and over the gate to the Dean's Yard at Westminster, where it could be seen by all who had business at court. He also ordered that sculptures of St. Edward and St. John be placed on the outer wall of St. Stephen's Chapel. In addition, he added hangings depicting the Confessor in the choir and in a window on the south side of Westminster Abbey. Further, his inventories include a retable with pictures of St. Edward handing St. John his ring.[58] His successor Richard II (1377–1399) demonstrated a singular devotion to the Confessor. Indeed, in Nigel Saul's words, he "saw St. Edward as his partner: his mentor in spirituality and guide in matters of government."[59] Thus, he selected the Confessor as his

Sutton and Hammond, *The Coronation of Richard III*, pp. 238–9. Wickham Legg, *Three Coronation Orders*, p. 123.

[55] Binski describes *Curtana* as one of three state swords. *Westminster Abbey and the Plantagenets*, p. 130. The other two were the sword with which the king did justice to the spirituality, and the sword with which he did justice to the temporality. The king's personal sword constituted a fourth. See also Sutton and Hammond, *The Coronation Records of Richard III*, pp. 2, 40, 42, 158, 213, 236–7; Tessa Rose, *The Coronation Ceremony of the Kings and Queens of England and the Crown Jewels* (London, 1992), p. 48.

[56] Matthew Paris, *Chronica Majora*, ed. Luard, vol. III, pp. 337–8. *Matthew Paris's English History*, ed. Giles, vol. I, pp. 8–10. Paris attended the wedding coronation of 1236 where *Curtana* made an appearance. Lewis, *The Art of Matthew Paris in the Chronica Majora*, p. 205.

[57] Sutton and Hammond, *The Coronation of Richard III*, pp. 10, 37, 225, 228, 239, 249. Stanley, *Memorials of Westminster*, pp. 44–5.

[58] Joan Evans, *English Art 1307–1461* (Oxford, 1949), pp. 46–8.

[59] Saul, *Richard II* (New Haven, 1997), p. 311.

patron saint and evoked his name on several occasions during critical moments of his reign. In June of 1381, before meeting with Wat Tyler and the rebels at Smithfield, the young king sought courage by "going to the shrine of the glorious king Edward," where "through the merits of his royal saint" he obtained God's protection. The Confessor also figured in a well-known incident in which the rebels pursued a royal official into the Abbey where he had taken sanctuary, perhaps at the shrine itself. He acted in vain, however, for they caught and killed him, a violation which in turn cost them their lives. This retribution the *Westminster Chronicle* attributed to St. Edward, who, "to the exaltation of his sainthood and the comfort of the realm, was swift indeed to avenge the wrong offered him."[60] Later, during the dangerous days of September, 1397, Richard chose St. Edward's shrine as the spot where the lords spiritual and temporal and the commons took oaths "to uphold and maintain all the statutes, establishments, ordinances and judgments made or given before the said parliament."[61] Moreover, toward the end of his reign Richard moved to alter his own royal arms in a most significant way: he added to them the arms of Edward the Confessor. This newly designed shield he carried into Ireland when he invaded in 1394, motivated, or so one story goes, by the Irish regard for St. Edward.[62] Finally, Richard commissioned a number of works of art depicting the Confessor. Most notable was the Wilton Diptych, which carried a scene of the young king kneeling before the Virgin and child, St. John, St. Edmund, and St. Edward, who held a ring.[63]

---

[60] *The Westminster Chronicles*, ed. and trans. L. C. Hector and Barbara Harvey (Oxford, 1982), pp. 8–11. See also *ibid.*, pp. 450–1, 506–7, 510–11.

[61] *Chronicles of the Revolution 1397–1400. The Reign of Richard II*, ed. and trans. Chris Given-Wilson (Manchester, 1993), pp. 83–5. McKisack, *The Fourteenth Century 1307–1399* (Oxford, 1959), p. 484.

[62] Gordon, *Making and Meaning. The Wilton Diptych* (London, 1993), p. 26, pl. 2, 31, pl. 4. Saul, *Richard II*, pp. 446, 460. Froissart recorded that Richard II evoked the image of the Confessor because the Irish held him in such great esteem, Edward, like they, having struggled mightily against the Danes. Indeed, "the Irishmen loved and dreaded him much more than any other king of England that had been before." Richard's ploy apparently worked, for "the Irishmen were well pleased" and submitted to him "in like manner as their predecessors sometimes did to Saint Edward." *The Chronicle of Froissart*, trans. Sir John Bourchier Lord Berners (New York, 1967), vol. VI, p. 155. However, it is not clear just why the Irish had a soft spot in their hearts for St. Edward, or, for that matter, that they did. Perhaps, as Laura Marin suggests, they liked him because he left them alone.

[63] Gordon, *Making and Meaning. The Wilton Diptych*, p. 26. On the diptych's back were the arms of the Confessor impaled with those of England and France. *Ibid.*, p. 55. Binski, *Westminster Abbey and the Plantagenets*, pp. 199–204. Evans, *English Art 1407–1461*, pp. 102–3. Saul, *Richard II*, pp. 304–5.

The Lancastrian successors exploited St. Edward for all he was worth, seeing in his cult a reliable means of justifying an upstart dynasty. Henry IV, for example, selected October 13, St. Edward's day, as the date for his coronation.[64] The practice of appealing to the Confessor continued throughout the turbulent fifteenth century. Henry V's chantry chapel at Westminster, the first chantry built in England, contained an altar depicting both St. Edmund and St. Edward, and among his tapestries of literary illustrations was one of St. Edward. His son, Henry VI, built a screen showing the Confessor's miracles which he placed in the shrine. Further, as Roy Strong notes, when Henry VI entered London in 1431 after his coronation in Paris, he appealed to St. Edward to reinforce his right to wear the crowns of England and France. As part of the pageantry the city fathers, probably with royal approval, constructed for him a giant genealogical tree that began with St. Louis and St. Edward and coalesced in his father, Henry V.[65]

The poet John Lydgate, perhaps at royal behest, gave voice to Henry's triumphal entry with words that made St. Edward and St. Louis the virtual embodiments of their respective kingdoms. He wrote:

> Twoo green treen ther grewe up-[a]riht,
> The root y-take palpable to the siht,
> Conveyed by lynes be kynges off grete prys;
> In nouther armes ffounde as there no lak,
> Which the sixte Herry many now bere his bak.

Later, at the coronation, the people thanked God

> To se theire Kyng with twoo crovnys shyne,
> From twoo trees trewly ffette the lyne.[66]

Henry VI also commissioned a work portraying himself sitting at the coronation banquet between St. Edward and St. Louis. And in the Coventry pageants of 1474 Queen Margaret was welcomed to the city by a figure representing St. Edward, who offered to pray for her son, Edward.[67]

---

[64] Adam of Usk, *The Chronicle of Adam of Usk A.D. 1377–1421*, ed. Chris Given-Wilson (Oxford, 1997), p. 71. Jacob, *The Fifteenth Century 1399–1485* (Oxford, 1961), p. 18.

[65] Strong, *Art and Power. Renaissance Festivals 1450–1650* (Berkeley, 1984), pp. 8–9.

[66] *The Minor Poems of John Lydgate*, ed. Henry N. McCracken, pt. II, *Secular Poems*, Early English Text Society, no. 192 (London, 1934), pp. 644, 646–7.

[67] Armstrong, "The Inauguration Ceremonies of the Yorkist Kings," pp. 60–72. Evans, *English Art 1307–1461*, pp. 93–4, 111, 181. Sydney Anglo, *Spectacle, Pageantry, and Early Tudor Policy*, 2nd. edn. (Oxford, 1997), p. 56.

ST. EDWARD'S LAWS AND THE DEFACEMENT OF
MEDIEVAL KINGSHIP

By the late fifteenth century the cult of the Confessor had done more than its part to shore up the medieval kingship, covering generations of monarchs with a veil of legitimacy, albeit at times thin and threadbare. But this is not all there was to the Confessor's cult. Ironically, St. Edward lent himself with stunning ease to legitimizing opposition to the English kingship. This phenomenon was observable not only in the century of revolution, when Stuart radicals commandeered St. Edward for their own extremist ends, but as early as the late twelfth and thirteenth centuries, when the enemies of Henry II and King John found the Confessor pertinent to their political purposes. Indeed, in an operative sense the motto *"Ich dien"* applies more readily to Edward the Confessor than to the Black Prince.

It was in the role of law-giver that the Confessor contributed most dramatically to the defacement of the English kingship. It was also in this role that he made his most significant and enduring contribution to the radical face of the ancient constitution. The story of these laws therefore merits close attention, for without an understanding of their provenance and descent, we cannot appreciate their persuasive power in Stuart political discourse.

According to informed opinion from the middle ages to the nineteenth century, the laws came into existence when, in the words of St. Edward's eleventh-century biographer, "this goodly king abrogated bad laws, with his witan established good ones, and filled with joy all of Britain . . ."[68] According to the fourteenth-century chronicler Henry Knighton, "Edward after he was crowned with the council of the barons and others of the kingdom, caused to be reviewed and stablized and confirmed good laws, which for sixty-eight years had slept, and handed over, as it were, to oblivion. Those laws were called the laws of Holy Edward, not because he had first found them but because he had found them neglected from the time of Edgar, who first took in hand the defining of them."[69] A

---

[68] *The Life of King Edward*, ed. Barlow, p. 21. John of Worcester wrote of Edward that "He soon, when he had undertaken the government of the realm, destroyed iniquitous laws, and set about establishing just ones." *The Chronicle of John of Worcester*, ed. Darlington and McGurk, p. 601.

[69] Knighton, *Chronicles*, ed. Lumby, vol. I, p. 50. See also O'Brien, *God's Peace and King's Peace*, p. 257, n. 93.

distillation of past laws, the Confessor's laws were, then, already ancient in his own day and age.

That the figure of Edward the law-giver should loom so large is ironic, since, as we now know, he, unlike many of his predecessors, neither legislated nor codified. Still, a number of Anglo-Norman sources referred to, detailed, and translated into Latin and French laws associated with him and his reign. Some were "impostures," as O'Brien terms them, while others were later descriptions that intended no deception. Whatever the case, all proved helpful to early Norman rulers motivated to govern well their newly conquered land and to ally themselves with a sainted predecessor. Indeed, as O'Brien notes, in this role the St. Edward's laws became the "legal standard" of the age.[70] One of these impostures was the *Decreta* (or *Articuli Decem*) of William I. Dating from the late eleventh or early twelfth century, it was included in Henry of Huntingdon's history and in Roger of Hoveden's *Chronica*. Another imposture, the *Leis Willelme*, dated from the same period and survives in French and Latin versions. Both the *Decreta* and the *Leis* carried William's command "that all shall have and hold the law of King Edward in respect of their lands and all their possessions, with the addition of those decrees that I have ordained for the welfare of the English people."[71] This particular royal promise to maintain the laws of St. Edward carried great weight because it also appeared in the *Textus Roffensis*, a remarkably full collection of charters and legal texts dating from the seventh to the early twelfth century. Housed in the priory of Rochester Cathedral from the middle ages until the present day, this cartulary commanded the respect of generations of English scholars.[72]

The reputation of St. Edward the law-giver was strengthened by the *Leges Henrici Primi*, a private work dating from the early twelfth

---

[70] *Ibid.*, p. 17. In what follows I am indebted to Professor O'Brien for helping me sort out the thorny business of medieval legal texts.

[71] *Ibid.*, pp. 27–8. See also Bruce O'Brien, "The Becket Conflict and the Invention of the Myth of Lex Non Scripta," in *Learning the Law. Teaching and the Transmission of Law in England 1150–1900*, ed. Jonathan A. Bush and Alain Wijffels (London and Rio Grande, Oh., 1999), pp. 1–16. *Cf. English Historical Documents 1042–1189*, ed. David C. Douglas and George W. Greenaway, 2nd. edn. (London, 1981), vol. 1, pp. 431–2; Gransden, *Historical Writing in England*, 287.

[72] The *Textus Roffensis* contains the earliest version of the *Leis Willelme*. *Textus Roffensis*, ed. Peter Sawyer (Copenhagen, 1957), fos. 80–81ᵛ. See also N. R. Ker, ed., *Medieval Libraries of Great Britain. A List of Surviving Books*, 2nd. edn. (London, 1964), p. 295; Southern, "Aspects of the European Tradition of Historical Writing: the Sense of the Past," pp. 253; Green, *The Government of England under Henry I*, p. 97.

century which included references to numerous Anglo-Saxon laws as well as those of Henry I's reign. The *Leges Henrici Primi* also carried that king's coronation charter, or Charter of Liberties, in which, as previously mentioned, Henry I expressly promised the English people that he would "restore to you the law of King Edward together with such emendations to it as my father made with the counsel of his barons." Concerned to give the charter wide publicity, Henry I ordered it sent into every shire, where it might even have been read aloud in the local courts. King Stephen, it will be recalled, issued a similar charter, as did Henry II when he ascended the throne in 1154.[73]

Most important of all in the formation of the ancient constitution were two texts that actually detailed scores of laws allegedly made or collected by St. Edward. One was the *Historia Croylandensis*, supposedly written by Ingulf, abbot of Crowland and "secretary" to William the Conqueror, and the other the *Leges Edwardi Confessoris*, allegedly compiled at William's behest in 1070. As for the first, Ingulf told how, in 1085, William ordered him to bring from London to Crowland the laws of St. Edward,

written in the same idiom in which they were published, and which my lord the renowned king William had proclaimed to be authentic and irrevocable, and had commended to his justices, with an order that they should, under severe penalties, be observed inviolably through the whole kingdom of England. In order, therefore, that it may never befall that either we or any of our body, through ignorance and to our own grievous peril, contravene them, or with rash audacity offend the king's majesty, and improvidently incur the strict censures which are more than once contained in them, I set them out as follows: – These are the laws and customs which king William granted to the people of England after the conquest of the land; being the same which king Edward, his cousin, granted before him.[74]

There followed some fifty-odd chapters of laws and customs that Ingulf attributed to Edward the Confessor and which were, in fact, the longer French version of the *Leis Willelme*.

---

[73] *English Historical Documents*, ed. Douglas and Greenaway, vol. I, p. 434. Liebermann, *Die Gesetze der Angelsachsen*, I, p. 521. See also *Leges Henrici Primi*, ed. L. J. Downer (Oxford, 1972); J. C. Holt, "Colonial England, 1066–1215," in *Colonial England. 1066–1215*, pp. 17–18.

[74] "The History of Ingulf," in *The Church Historians of England*, ed. and trans. by Joseph Stevenson (London, 1854), pp. 691–2. William Fulman, *Rerum Anglicarum Scriptorum Veterum* (Oxford, 1684), pp. 70, 88. Orderic described Ingulf as a monk of St. Wandrille who received the abbey of Crowland from the hand of William I. English by birth, he was said to have been a royal clerk before taking the monk's habit. *The Ecclesiastical History of Orderic Vitalis*, ed. Chibnall, vol. II, p. 345.

The provenance of Ingulf's history is tangled. The earliest extant manuscript dates from the early sixteenth century, but it is merely a transcript. After the dissolution of the monasteries in the 1530s, Crowland Abbey claimed to possess a manuscript autographed by Ingulf himself, which it carefully preserved in a chest locked with three keys. Throughout the sixteenth and seventeenth centuries, scholars mentioned the existence of two other "ancient" manuscripts, one apparently lost in the late Stuart period and the other destroyed in 1731, when fire gutted much of the Cottonian Library. Ingulf's history first appeared in print in 1596, published by the Saxon scholar Sir Henry Savile who dedicated it "to the many who are thirsting for the objects of desire that are found in our antiquities."[75]

As it turned out, those who accepted Savile's invitation drank from a poisoned well, for we now know that Ingulf's history dated not from the period immediately following the conquest but from the early fourteenth century. "A complex tissue of fact and forgery," as Michael Clanchy describes it, parts of the Crowland chronicle were concocted by monks to justify their abbey's title to certain lands and, in time-honored fashion, backdated to increase its persuasive power.[76] In the seventeenth and early eighteenth centuries, scholars such as Spelman, Henry Wharton, George Hickes, and Humphrey Wanley expressed doubts about the history's authenticity, focusing in

[75] Sir Henry Savile, *Rerum Anglicarum Scriptores post Bedam praecipui* (London, 1596). Savile worked from a mutilated copy that did not give the laws themselves. The extant manuscript, which is in B.L. Arundel MSS 178, consists of fifty-four closely written folios. See *The Chronicle of Croyland Abbey by Ingulph*, ed. Walter de Gray Birch (Wisbech, 1883), pp. ii-v; *Ingulph's Chronicle of the Abbey of Croyland with the Continuation by Peter of Blois and Anonymous Writers*, trans. Henry T. Riley (London, 1854), pp. ix, 175; *Ingulf and the Historia Croylandensis*, ed. William G. Searle (Cambridge, 1894), pp. 149–50. Little is known about the two "ancient" manuscripts. In the early seventeenth century Sir Henry Spelman claimed to have examined the autograph at Crowland Abbey, but John Selden attempted in vain to gain access to it. Nor was William Fulman any more successful later in the century, when he tried to examine the autograph before publishing his edition of Ingulf. For his edition, Fulman borrowed an "old" manuscript from Sir John Marsham. Almost nothing is known about this particular manuscript except that it seemed to wind up in the hands of Obediah Walker, Master of University College, Oxford, either because he stole it or because Marsham loaned it to him. In any event, this manuscript has not survived. See Stevenson's preface in "The History of Ingulf," in *The Church Historians of England*, vol. II, pt. II, pp. xix–xxi.

[76] Clanchy, *From Memory to Written Record*, pp. 148–9. See also Mary P. Richards, "Texts and Their Traditions in the Medieval Library of Rochester Cathedral Priory," *Transactions of the American Philosophical Society*, n.s. 78, pt. 3 (1988), pp. 43–59; Patrick Wormald, "*Laga Edwardi*: the Textus Roffensis and Its Context," *Anglo-Norman Studies* 17 (1994), 243–66. *The Ecclesiastical History of Orderic Vitalis*, ed. Chibnall, vol. II, pp. xxvff.

particular on the anachronistic language found in many of the Saxon charters contained therein.[77]

Nevertheless, few early modern writers doubted the story of St. Edward's laws and their confirmation by William I. Indeed, they swallowed the traditional scenario whole, as did the most erudite of sixteenth- and seventeenth-century English people. Moreover, before the late seventeenth and eighteenth centuries Ingulf himself enjoyed the highest of reputations among lawyers and antiquaries, who often described him as the only chronicler to have actually lived through the conquest. As the common lawyer Oliver St. John remarked in 1637, Ingulf was an especially weighty and worthy authority because he "was brought up in England in the Confessor's days, and therefore knew what he wrote."[78] St. John's judgment was shared by John Selden, who relied on Ingulf in his 1623 edition of St. Edward's laws, as well as by John Speed, Sir William Dugdale, William Fulman, Edward Stillingfleet, James Tyrrell, and William Nicholson – a veritable honor roll of early modern antiquaries and scholars.[79]

Also central to the formation of the ancient constitution was the work called the *Leges Edwardi Confessoris*, which claimed to state the Confessor's laws as they were collected by William I in 1070. Described by Wormald as "once the most respected" of medieval legal treatises, the *Leges* began with a prologue declaring, "four years after the acquisition of this country, King William, on the advice of his barons, caused to be summoned from all the counties of the

[77] Spelman, for example, noticed that Ingulf contained pre-conquest charters that used Norman feudal language. However, he explained this anachronism by concluding that the terms in question were translations made after 1066 on behalf of the Normans. H. A. Cronne, "The Study and Use of Charters by English Scholars in the Seventeenth Century: Sir Henry Spelman and Sir William Dugdale," in *English Historical Scholarship in the Sixteenth and Seventeenth Centuries*, ed. Levi Fox (Oxford, Dugdale Society, 1956), pp. 73–91, especially 81. Wharton, in his *Historia de episcopis et decanis Londinensisbus* (London, 1695), also drew attention to anachronisms in eighth- and ninth-century Mercian charters. Wanley, librarian at the Bodleian, levelled similar charges in a letter to Sir Robert Harley and suggested that the history of Crowland was not much older than Henry II's time. See Riley's introduction to *Ingulph's Chronicle of the Abbey of Croyland*, pp. ix–x; Stevenson's preface to "The History of Ingulf," vol. II, pt. 2, p. xxi; and Searle's comments in *Ingulf and the Historia Croylandensis*, pp. 151–2.

[78] *A Complete Collection of State Trials*, ed. T. B. Howell (London, 1816), vol. III, p. 908. See also the papers delivered to the Society of Antiquaries by Camden and Hakewill, discussed in Chapter 3. Hakewill, for example, described the *Textus Roffensis* as "that most famous monument of antiquity." *A Collection of Curious Discourses Written by Eminent Antiquaries upon several Heads in Our English Antiquities*, ed. T. Hearne (London, 1775), vol. I, p. 1.

[79] Searle added to the list of writers who accepted Ingulf's history as genuine Thomas Carte, David Hume, Henry Hallam, Henry Ellis, and John Lord Campbell. *Ingulf and the Historia Croylandensis*, p. 150. *Ingulph's Chronicle of the Abbey of Croyland*, ed. Riley, pp. ix–x.

country English nobles, who were councilors and learned in the law, so that he might hear from them what their customs were." Further, the prologue continued, "When twelve men had been chosen from each county of the entire country, they first of all solemnly affirmed by swearing an oath before him that, as far as they could, they would declare blamelessly their laws and customs, treading the righteous path, omitting nothing, nor altering anything deceitfully."[80]

The result of this nation-wide inquiry, the *Leges Edwardi Confessoris*, then gave thirty-nine laws allegedly promulgated by or somehow associated with St. Edward himself. However, William did not initially select these English laws as those by which he would govern. On the contrary, the thirty-fourth chapter recorded that when he took the testimony of this council he learned that Suffolk, Norfolk, and Cambridgeshire were governed by the laws of the Danes. These he first chose over the English laws because the Danes, like his own ancestors, came from Norway. Their laws would therefore prove more pleasing to the Normans, being "more profound and more honorable" than the laws of the English, Britons, and Picts. His "fellow countrymen," however,

begged him very much to allow them to have the laws and customs with which their ancestors had lived and they themselves were born, because it was hard for them to adopt laws and to judge according to those that they did not know. And they also asked him this for the sake of the soul of King Edward, who had given him the kingdom and whose laws these were, not [those] of other foreigners. Finally, by the counsel and at the request of the barons, he acquiesced. And so the laws of King Edward were authorized.[81]

Just as modern scholars have doubted the provenance of Ingulf's history of Crowland, so do they raise questions about the *Leges Edwardi Confessoris*. According to Bruce O'Brien, the modern authority on this work, the *Leges Edwardi* was probably written at Lincoln Cathedral by an episcopal steward in the early twelfth century.[82] But Wormald, who sees the work as too easily dismissed by modern scholars, suggests that its "authenticity" mattered less than its resonance. Because the *Leges* reflected the communal memory of Saxon law – what Robin Fleming terms "the lived quality of law" –,

---

[80] O'Brien, *God's Peace and King's Peace*, p. 159. In this section I rely on O'Brien's edition of the *Leges Edwardi Confessoris*.

[81] *Ibid.*, pp. 191–3. See also Lambarde, *Archaionomia*; Whelocke, *Archaionomia*; Twysden, *Archaionomia*; Lieberman, *Die Gesetze der Angelsachsen*, vol. 1.

[82] O'Brien, *God's Peace and King's Peace*, pp. 49–61. O'Brien's reasoning, while speculative, is most convincing.

it soon acquired, in Wormald's words, a "talismanic force." And its prologue functioned as a topos, a statement of "what a good king was expected to have done."[83] The *Leges'* popularity is attested by the fact that no less than forty manuscripts survive today. Some, moreover, are pocket-size, indicating that they were made to be used. And chroniclers such as Hoveden, Knighton, and Henry of Huntingdon described William I's meeting of 1070 and carried references to St. Edward's laws in one form or another.[84] The *Leges Edwardi Confessoris* itself went through four redactions in the twelfth and early thirteen centuries and was widely copied as late as the fifteenth century. It was known to Bracton, the noted thirteenth-century jurist and editor of one of the earliest treatises on common law, and it was also cited by lawyers in King's Bench.[85] The work enjoyed an especially high reputation in the sixteenth and seventeenth centuries, and, spurious or not, lawyers and politicians sometimes elevated William I's confirmation to the status of a statute.[86] Equally striking was the tendency throughout the sixteenth and seventeenth centuries to view it as the first Magna Carta, "the groundwork of all that after followed."[87]

On their face, the laws associated with St. Edward yield no hint of such an exalted future. Indeed, taken in their medieval context there is nothing particularly startling about them. Closely resembling continental codes of the same period, most chapters consist of a laundry list of contemporary concerns – the protection of the church, fines for criminal behavior, the payment of tithes and Danegeld, the performance of services, the meeting of folkmoots, and the like. In fact, were it not for two particular sections in the

---

[83] Fleming, *Domesday Book and the Law: Society and Legal Custom in Early Medieval England* (Cambridge, 1998), p. 64. Wormald, *The Making of English Law*, vol. I, pp. 128–9, 409–10.

[84] *Chronica Magistri Rogeri Hovedene*, ed. Stubbs, vol. II, pp. 218–39. Knighton, *Chronicles*, vol. I, p. 78. See also O'Brien, *God's Peace and King's Peace*, pp. 108–11; O'Brien, "The Becket Conflict and the Invention of the Myth of Lex Non Scripta," *passim*; O'Brien, "Forgery and the Literacy of the Early Common Law," *Albion* 27 (1995), 1–18; O'Brien, "The Origin of a Legal Literature of Complaint in England," forthcoming; John Hudson, "Administration, Family and Perceptions of the Past in Late Twelfth-Century England: Richard Fitz Nigel and the *Dialogue of the Exchequer*," in *The Perceptions of the Past in Twelfth-Century Europe*, ed. Paul Magdalino (London, 1992), pp. 75–98.

[85] O'Brien, *God's Peace and King's Peace*, pp. 138–46. Holt, "The Origins of the Constitutional Tradition in England," p. 13.

[86] See, for example, the remarks of Sir Robert Holbourne and Oliver St. John in the Ship Money Case. *A Complete Collection of State Trials*, ed. Howell, vol. III, pp. 894–5, 990.

[87] See, for example, Sir Edward Coke, *La Neufme Part des Reports de Sr. Edw. Coke* (London, 1613), "To the Reader," unnumbered.

Leges and the radical spin given them by people determined to bridle Stuart kings, St. Edward's laws might hold interest only for medievalists. Elevating the Confessor's laws above the commonplace and ensconcing them in the firmament of Stuart political ideology was, first of all, the Prologue itself. Seventeenth-century ancient constitutionalists would find in these words, cited above, two references ideally suited to their political ends. First was the mention of William's "acquisition" of England rather than his "conquest." Then came the description of a national assembly which the new king called to declare the ancient laws. Here was William himself denying the fact of conquest and agreeing to govern with the old English parliament. Surely, later generations would argue, no better proof of institutional continuity could be found.

But of even greater importance to Stuart dissidents was Chapter 17 of the *Leges Edwardi Confessoris*. It read: "The King . . . who is the vicar of the highest King, was established for this, that he rule and defend the kingdom and people of the Lord and, above all, the Holy Church from wrongdoers, and destroy and eradicate evildoers." Then, in language that would resonate throughout seventeenth-century radical literature, the chapter stated that a king who fails in his duty "loses the very name of king." Here the author referred to the story of Pepin and his son Charles. Then mere princes, they wrote to Pope John, inquiring about the authority of the ineffective Childeric, king of France. The pope responded that "those ought to be called kings who vigilantly defend and rule the church of God and His people."[88]

At first sight, Chapter 17, like the rest of St. Edward's laws, sounded a familiar note and seemed to offer little promise of radical elaboration. On one reading, it merely reflected the view that kings had public as well as private obligations – an unstartling notion by the high middle ages. Since antiquity, after all, theorists had insisted that kings were one thing and tyrants another, or, to put it differently, the office of a king was distinguishable from the person of a king. This sentiment had found expression in two ninth-century sources, Einhard's life of Charlemagne and Ado of Vienne's *Chronicon de sex*

---

[88] O'Brien, *God's Peace and King's Peace*, pp. 175–7. Liebermann, *Die Gesetze der Angelsachsen*, vol. I, pp. 642–3. O'Brien notes that the ascription to Pope John was incorrect. Zacharius was the pope involved. Einhard mentioned Pope Stephen II, who confirmed Zacharius' judgment. *Two Lives of Charlemagne. Einhard and Notker the Stammerer*, ed. Lewis Thorpe (London, 1969), p. 55.

mundi actatibus, as well as in Adamar of Chabannes's writings two centuries later.[89]

By the twelfth and thirteenth centuries, a growing body of literature emphasized that the king *qua* king had duties and responsibilities as well as rights and privileges. Thus, the early thirteenth-century forgery of correspondence between the mythical British King Lucius and Pope Eleutherius repeated Chapter 17 of St. Edward's laws almost in its entirety, though without mention of St. Edward himself. The London redaction of the *Leges* gave the Lucius story in Chapter 11.[90] Equally notable, several eminent English jurists included the sentiments of Chapter 17 in influential works. For example, in the thirteenth century Raleigh, Bracton, and the author of Fleta expressed the idea that "A king is a king so long as he rules well; he becomes a tyrant when he oppresses the people committed to his charge . . . The power of wrong is the power of devils, and not God's . . ."[91] They were joined in the fifteenth century by the distinguished jurist Sir John Fortescue, who in his discussion of royal power noted that a king "is obliged to protect the law, the subjects, and their bodies and goods." Toward this end, "he has power . . . issuing from the people, so that it is not permissible for him to rule his people with another power."[92] By the late middle ages this idea had become so pervasive that James Burns describes it as "the ground-bass – or at least an essential note in the ground-bass – of political thinking."[93]

For Stuart radicals the extraordinary value of Chapter 17 of St. Edward's laws lay not only in its expression of the well-known distinction between kings and tyrants, but in the extremist interpretation which the distinction invited. Reasoning that kings were bound

---

[89] Einhard, *Two Lives of Charlemagne*, ed. Thorpe, pp. 55–7. O' Brien, *God's Peace and King's Peace*, pp. 24, 84, 272 n. 58. O'Brien notes that two manuscripts of Ado's work might have been available in twelfth-century England. For the medieval history of this idea see J. A. Watt, "Spiritual and Temporal Powers," in *The Cambridge History of Political Thought*, vol. 1 *Medieval Political Thought c. 350–c. 1450*, ed. J. H. Burns (Cambridge, 1988), pp. 377, 379, 386 and *passim*.

[90] Liebermann, *Die Gesetze der Angelsachsen*, vol. 1, pp. 635–6. For a modern edition of this redaction see O'Brien's forthcoming volume. See also van Caenegem, *The Birth of the English Common Law*, pp. 101–2; John Guy, *Tudor England* (Oxford, 1990), p. 133.

[91] Henry Bracton, *On the Laws and Customs of England*, ed. Samuel E. Thorne (Cambridge, Mass., 1968), Book 1, c. 8 and Book 3, c. 9. The Fleta reference was to Book 1, c. 17.

[92] Fortescue, *Of the Laws and Governance of England*, ed. Shelley Lockwood (Cambridge, 1997), pp. 21–2. I am indebted to James Burns for this citation.

[93] J. H. Burns, *The True Law of Kingship. Concepts of Monarchy in Early-Modern Scotland* (Oxford, 1996), p. 284.

by their office to rule justly and lawfully, seventeenth-century rebels moved deftly to the conclusion that a king who governed otherwise unkinged himself. Now no more than the meanest of subjects, he could be resisted with armed force, deposed, and even executed. As we shall see, the ease with which Chapter 17 lent itself to such causes was demonstrated time and time again in the century of revolution. William Prynne evoked it to justify the civil war, John Milton cited it in defense of Charles I's trial and execution, and William Atwood found in it support for the Glorious Revolution.[94]

Of course, Stuart radicals were not the only early modern theorists to deploy the idea inherent in Chapter 17 against kings and governments. By the sixteenth century Calvinists and Roman Catholics throughout Europe braced their causes with similar theories of resistance.[95] But the Confessor's laws enjoyed an inestimable advantage over these foreign sources. Born and bred in the nation's past, associated with a canonized king and his cult of kingship, and themselves sanctioned by time, St. Edward's laws commanded respect on all sides throughout the early modern period. Equally important, parliamentarian and whig polemicists who sought to dilute or altogether avoid the taint associated with Beza, Hotman, Mornay, Goodman, and Knox, could do so by appealing to St. Edward. This advantage, however, disappeared in 1649 when the regicides evoked Chapter 17 to justify king-killing. From this bloody moment onward, the radical implications of the idea embedded in Chapter 17 and similar sources were too painfully obvious to be ignored. In 1683 the notion received official condemnation in *The Judgment and Decree of the University of Oxford*. Here the king's men denounced as "pernicious," "damnable," and "destructive to the sacred persons of princes" the idea "that if lawful governors become

---

[94] Prynne, *The Treachery and disloyalty of Papists to their Soveraignes, in Doctrine and Practice. Together with the first part of the Soveraigne Power of Parliaments and Kingdomes*, 2nd. enlarged edn. (London, 1643), pp. 51–2, 78. Milton, *A Defence of the English People* (n.p. 1692), pp. 193–5; *Eikonoklastes* (London, 1649), pp. 57–8, 61, 235. Atwood, *The Fundamental Constitution of the English Government* (London, 1690), p. iv. For the medieval roots of this interpretation see Watt, "Spiritual and Temporal Powers," pp. 377–80.

[95] See Quentin Skinner, *The Foundations of Modern Political Thought* (Cambridge, 1978), vol. ii, chapter 9, especially pp. 334–48; J. H. Burns, "Scholasticism: Survival and Revival," in *The Cambridge History of Political Thought*, vol. ii *1450–1700*, ed. J. H. Burns and Mark Goldie (Cambridge, 1991), pp. 132–55; Francis Oakley, "Christian Obedience and Authority, 1520–1550," in *ibid.*, pp. 159–92; Robert M. Kingdon, "Calvinism and Resistance Theory, 1550–1580," in *ibid.*, pp. 193–218; J. H. Salmon, "Catholic Resistance Theory, Ultramontanism, and the Royalist Response, 1580–1620," in *ibid.*, pp. 219–53.

tyrants, or govern otherwise than by the laws of God and man they ought to do, they forfeit the right they had unto their government."[96]

But the political nation did not wait until the early modern period to deploy St. Edward's laws against its kings. Indeed, O'Brien notes that already in late twelfth-century England the idea associated with Chapter 17 signaled to Thomas Becket, archbishop of Canterbury, and his followers that Henry II was limited by ancient Saxon custom, the claims of the Constitutions of Clarendon notwithstanding.[97] Moreover, according to Holt, by the early thirteenth-century King John's barons had also learned well the value of appealing to the Saxon past in general and the Confessor in particular. This time the lesson was taught, interestingly enough, by their own kings as well as by those Englishmen who refused to knuckle under in 1066. That John's opponents had learned from their kings was evident when they chose to base their resistance on the coronation charters of Henry I, King Stephen, and Henry II, all of which carried royal promises to abide by St. Edward's laws as amended by the Conqueror. Further, the barons linked their proposed reforms precisely to King John's failure to abide by St. Edward's laws, and they saw Magna Carta itself as still another in this long line of confirmations.[98] Such was certainly the opinion current in Stuart England, Sir Roger Twysden speaking for generations of historians and lawyers when he wrote that King John's Magna Carta contained "for the most part no other than the ancient rights and customs of the realm, extracted out of the laws of the Confessor and Henry the First."[99]

The prestige of St. Edward's laws, and their reputation for holding kings to account, was further enhanced by Henry III's and Edward I's confirmations of Magna Carta, that of 1297 given pride of place as the first statute in medieval and early modern collections.

---

[96] *Divine Right and Democracy,* ed. David Wootton (Harmondsworth, 1986), p. 121.

[97] O'Brien, "The Becket Conflict and the Invention of the Myth of Lex Non Scripta," pp. 10ff. O'Brien, "The Origin of a Legal Literature of Complaint in England," forthcoming.

[98] Holt, *Magna Carta,* pp. 96–8. Holt, "The Origins of the Constitutional Tradition in England," pp. 13–17. Holt, "The Ancient Constitution in Medieval England," pp. 49–55. See also Clanchy, *England and Its Rulers 1066–1272,* pp. 135–42.

[99] Twysden, *Certaine Considerations upon the Government of England,* ed. Kimball, p. 58. See also Sir Edward Coke, "To the Reader," *La Huict*me *Part des Reports de Sr Edward Coke* (London, 1611); William Petyt, *The Antient Right of the Commons of England Asserted* (London, 1680), p. 32. James Tyrrell, *Patriarcha non Monarcha* (London, 1680), p. 229.

Indeed, by the seventeenth century Magna Carta had been confirmed scores of times. As for the great charter itself, Englishmen could read versions of it in Roger of Wendover and Matthew Paris.[100]

By evoking St. Edward's laws, the barons communicated to King John that they expected him to govern according to the good old laws. In going down this path, they followed in the well-trodden footsteps of their other teachers, those Englishmen who, after 1066, successfully petitioned that William I and his successors abide by Saxon customs. To be sure, kings usually obliged such requests of their own free will and volition. And frequently, of course, they went back on their royal word, considering the confirmations to be in the nature of mere campaign promises and therefore revocable at their pleasure. The Magna Carta of 1215 serves as an obvious example, since John, with the blessing of Pope Innocent III, promptly declared himself free of its provisions soon after he signed it, thus provoking another civil war. Yet the fact that such promises were more honored in the breach than in the observance mattered less than the fact that kings made them at all, for in so doing, they acknowledged that they were, in some sense and for some purposes, under the law, whatever that was. This lesson was as plain to the barons in 1215 as to parliamentarians and whigs in the seventeenth century. Indeed, two of the twentieth-century's leading medievalists, V. H. Galbraith and James Holt, go so far as to suggest that sources such as Magna Carta "presented a Whig interpretation before its time."[101]

Importantly, not all confirmations of St. Edward's laws were voluntary, the Magna Carta of 1215 again an obvious case in point. But here, too, John's opponents could learn from the past, for on more than one occasion the Saxons had forced Norman kings to renew their promises to abide by ancient customs. Here, too, seventeenth-century rebels found a buttress for ancient constitutionalist theorizing, for these forced royal concessions enabled them to play the prescription card: as long as the English refused to submit, long user told for the enemies of the Stuarts. And medieval records fairly bristled with tales of Saxon recalcitrance. Thus, the St. Albans chroniclers told how William I's failure to honor his vows to keep St. Edward's laws led to a renewal of resistance which ended only in

---

[100] Holt, "The St. Albans Chroniclers and Magna Carta," pp. 265–87.

[101] Holt, "The Origins of the Constitutional Tradition in England," pp. 13–14. Holt, "The St. Albans Chroniclers and Magna Carta," in *ibid.*, p. 276. V. H. Galbraith, *Roger of Wendover and Matthew Paris* (Glasgow, 1944), pp. 20–1.

1072. Then, under the leadership of Abbot Frederick, he and the English "came to a second compact and the king gave them satisfaction, reiterated his coronation oath, and swore upon the Holy Evangelists and relics of St. Albans to rule according to Holy Edward's laws." The Conqueror also sought the advice of Archbishop Lanfranc, who told him to pacify the English nobility, "which by all means possible would never cease to molest him in the recovery of their liberty. Here upon therefore, he made means to come to some agreement with them," swearing "a personal oath . . . that he would from thenceforth observe and keep the good and ancient approved laws of the realm, which the noble kings of England his ancestors had made, and ordained heretofore, but namely those of S. Edward, which are supposed to be the most equal and indifferent."[102]

The lesson to be drawn from such tales was that perjury exacted a price, even – or perhaps especially – in the case of kings. Put differently, not only did William fail to subdue the English, their stubborn resistance actually conquered him. At least this was the judgment of seventeenth-century radicals such as Algernon Sidney, who used William's perjury and subsequent re-confirmations of St. Edward's laws to prove that he was no conqueror at all and that he, like the Saxon rulers before him and all kings after, ruled by governmental contract. In Sidney's words, "William the Norman," after swearing "to govern according to their ancient laws, especially those . . . of the famous King Edward," went back on his oath and "pretended to govern according to his own will; but finding the people would not endure it, he renewed his oath" at St. Albans, "which he needed not to have done, but might have departed to his duchy of Normandy if he had not liked the conditions, or thought not fit to observe them."[103]

Still other medieval tales extolled Saxon tenacity and strength in the aftermath of the Norman invasion and in so doing reinforced the ancient constitutionalist belief in institutional continuity. Thus, chroniclers told how William so feared the rebellious English who

---

[102] Paris, *Historia Anglorum*, ed. Madden, vol. I, pp. 14–16. Paris, *Vitae Viginti Truum Abbatum S. Albani* in *Historia Major*, ed. William Wats (London, 1684), pp. 1001–2. Thomas Walsingham, *Gesta Abbatum Monasterii Sancti Albani*, ed. Henry T. Riley (London, 1867), vol. I, pp. 47–8. See also Matthew Westminster, *Flores Historiarum*, ed. H. R. Luard (London, 1890), vol. II, p. 5; Raphael Holinshed, *Chronicles* (London, 1577), II, pp. 303–6.

[103] Sidney, *Discourses Concerning Government* (London, 1698), p. 327 *passim*.

refused his terms that he attempted to woo them with conciliatory grants of land. Witness, for example, the case of Waltheof, earl of Northumberland, who, when offered one-third of England to join Roger of Hereford's and Ralph of Norwich's rebellion, refused because he had already given his fealty to William in return for "great lands." As always, the rebels in the north and west proved particularly ferocious in their opposition, but then, Orderic Vitalis opined, they had never obeyed anyone, not even Edward the Confessor, unless "it suited their ends."[104]

Then there was the story of the valiant men of Swanscombe Down, Kent, who, shortly after the battle of Hastings, surrounded William and his army and forced him to promise that they could keep their ancient laws and customs, especially gavelkind tenure. Exceedingly popular with seventeenth-century dissidents, the tale reinforced the ancient constitutionalist assertion that William I's conquest was limited and incomplete because Saxon customs survived. The story, usually attributed to the thirteenth-century writer William Sprott and repeated by William Thorne, went like this. After learning that William was marching south from London to subdue the rest of the country, Archbishop Stigand, Abbot Egelsin, and the elders of Kent summoned "the whole population of the whole of Kent" and explained the dangers facing them. The people, "choosing rather to end their unhappy lives than submit to the unwanted yoke of slavery, by unanimous vote decided to oppose Duke William, and fight with him for their ancestral rights."[105]

On the appointed day the entire population met at Swanscombe near Gravesend, where the men hid in bushes to await William's arrival. Carrying boughs as protection, they closed off all escape routes. When the duke arrived the next day, he "found with astonishment that in the fields . . . the whole county was ranged around him in a circle, like a moveable wood . . . approaching him at a slow pace." In great fear he and his men "stood astounded, and he who thought he held the whole of England in the hollow of his hand was now anxious about his own life." At this point, however, the English offered to spare the lives of the Normans in return for retaining their "ancestral laws and customs." If William refused their offer, they stood ready "to die here rather than sink into

---

[104] *The Ecclesiastical History of Orderic Vitalis*, ed. Chibnall, II, pp. 183, 195.
[105] Quoted in Holt, "The Origins of the Constitutional Tradition in England," pp. 9–12. See also Holt, "The Ancient Constitution in Medieval England," pp. 53–5.

slavery." Left with no choice, William, "more prudently than willingly," agreed, knowing that if he lost Kent he lost England.[106]

Although the story is false, generations of English people accepted it as gospel. Raphael Holinshed, Samuel Daniel, John Stow, John Speed, and Sir Richard Baker repeated the tale. Lambarde included it in his *Perambulation of Kent* as well as in *Archaionomia*, and Michael Drayton told the story in *Poly-Olbion*. Richard Tottell even incorporated the story into his *Magna Charta cum Statutis* (1556), the first published version of the statutes of the realm.[107] Small wonder, then, that seventeenth-century dissidents found it worth citing as proof that the conquest remained incomplete; their ancestors had never surrendered their rights to overmighty sovereigns.

One other tale from William's reign underlined the essential continuity of Saxon law and thus found a welcome home in seventeenth-century ancient constitutionalist lore. Ironically, however, this story turned on a rather different note, namely, that the endurance of St. Edward's laws depended not on English recalcitrance but rather on early and easy submission to the new regime. The basis of the story was a brief account in Little Domesday Book about a piece of land in Norfolk which changed hands shortly after the conquest. As later told in a manuscript belonging to Sir Henry Spelman, the Saxon Edwin of Sharnborn complained to William I that, in the aftermath of Hastings, he had lost his land and castle to William of Warren, the new king's favorite and close companion. In court Edwin claimed that the dispossession was unjust because he himself had early submitted to the Conqueror and therefore did not deserve to lose his lands. William agreed and, according to Spelman's manuscript, ordered Warren to return the estate to Edwin.[108]

---

[106] Quoted in Holt, *ibid*. Holt, "The Origins of the Constitutional Tradition in England," pp. 9–12.

[107] Holt, "The Ancient Constitution in Medieval England," p. 55. The tale is known only through William Thorne, who claimed to have seen Sprott's earlier work on which he based his own writings. Sprott was, however, a somewhat mysterious figure, and neither the sixteenth-century antiquary John Leland nor Twysden could ever find his manuscript, which was supposed to have been at Canterbury. However, John Joscelin, secretary to Matthew Parker, Archbishop of Canterbury, claimed to have seen both Sprott's and Thorne's work, both of which he copied. Thorne's manuscript is known only through Twysden, who included it in his *Decem Scriptores* of 1652. See Holt, *ibid*., pp. 9–10 and n. 20; *William Thorne's Chronicles of Saint Augustine's Abbey Canterbury*, ed. A. H. Davies (Oxford, 1934).

[108] *Domesday-Book*, vol. ii, p. 213a. Bodleian Library, Oxford, Ashmolean MSS 1141. v. 7362. Spelman, *Archaeologus. In Modum Glossarii ad rem antiquam posteriorem* (London, 1626), under

The polemical power of Sharnborn's case was all the greater because it often appeared in the company of similar tales found in *Domesday* and medieval chronicles. Particularly welcome to seventeenth-century radical ancient constitutionalists were reports of a trial held sometime in the 1070s at Penenden Heath in Kent. Here an assembly consisting of both Norman and English suitors ruled that the liberty and land of the church at Canterbury belonged, by ancient Saxon custom, not to William I's brother, Odo, bishop of Bayeux and now earl of Kent, but to Archbishop Lanfranc. Present at the hearing was the Saxon Aethelric, formerly bishop of Chichester, "a man of great age and very wise in the law of the land, who by the king's command was brought to the trial in a waggon in order that he might declare and expound the ancient practice of the laws."[109]

Such stories lent support to radical ancient constitutionalist claims of historical continuity. As William Petyt wrote in one of the most influential whig polemics of the late seventeenth century, "'Tis true indeed King William I gave away the estates of several of those who were in arms against him, to his adventurers and followers, but the rest of the English (as well by his coronation oath, as by a solemn ratification of St. Edward's laws in a parliament in his fourth year) were to enjoy their estates and the benefit of those laws."[110] The words of the republican Henry Neville were equally pertinent. Noting that the Normans entered England

by treaty, it was obvious there was no conquest made upon any but Harold; in whose stead William the first came, and would claim no more than his victory, than what Harold enjoyed: excepting; that he might confiscate (as

"Drenges." See also Janelle Greenberg and Laura Marin, "Politics and Memory: Sharnborn's Case and the Role of the Norman Conquest in Stuart Political Thought," in *Politics and the Political Imagination in Later Stuart Britain. Essays Presented to Lois Green Schwoerer,* ed. Howard Nenner (Rochester, NY, 1997), pp. 121–42.

[109] Douglas, "William the Conqueror: Duke and King," p. 205. Douglas, *William the Conqueror,* pp. 171–2, 306–8. The texts associated with the proceedings are printed in John La Patourel, "The Reports on the Trial on Penenden Heath," in *Studies in Medieval History Presented to F. M. Powicke* (Oxford, 1948), pp. 15–26. See also David R. Bates, "The Land Pleas of William I's Reign: Penenden Heath Revisited," *Bulletin of the Institute of Historical Research* 51 (1978), 1–19; Fleming, *Domesday Book and the Law,* pp. 56, 72ff. 83–4. For the persuasive force of such anecdotal evidence see Annabel Patterson, "Foul, his Wife, the Mayor, and Foul's Mare: The Power of Anecdote in Tudor Historiography," in *The Historical Imagination in Early Modern Britain: History, Rhetoric, and Fiction, 1500–1800,* ed. Donald R. Kelley and David Harris Sacks (Cambridge, 1997), pp. 159–78.

[110] Petyt, *The Antient Right of the Commons of England Asserted; or, A Discourse Proving by Records and the best Historians, that the Commons of England were ever an Essential part of Parliament* (London, 1680), pp. 35–6.

he did) those great men who took part with the wrong title; and Frenchmen were put into their estates. Which though it made in this kingdom a mixture between Normans and Saxons, yet produced no change, or innovation in the government: the Norman peers being as tenacious of their liberties, and as active in the recovery of them to the full, as the Saxon families were.[111]

If radical ancient constitutionalists had only St. Edward's laws and the tales of their survival with which to assault the Stuart kingship, they would have been armed to the teeth. But it was their good fortune to possess two other medieval sources which, though not enjoying a completely untarnished reputation among seventeenth-century scholars, nevertheless commanded deep respect and rendered credible the basic tenets of ancient constitutionalism. These were the *Modus tenendi Parliamentum* and the *Mirror of Justices*. The allure of these two works, like that of St. Edward's laws, stemmed from the fact that they reinforced the unbroken links between Saxon and Stuart England and, when "properly" interpreted, subordinated the king to parliament and people.

The *Modus*, whose proem delcared that it was written in the Confessor's time, actually dated from Edward II's reign in the early fourteenth century. As for the purposes for which it was created, modern opinions vary. It could have been compiled by a lawyer as a manual of parliamentary procedure and as a description of how parliament ought to work.[112] Or, as Maddicott suggests, the *Modus* might well have been written by someone close to Thomas of Lancaster in order to draw supporters away from the Despencers – in which case it functioned as "both a manifesto and a political broadside."[113] Existing in some thirty mcdieval as well as in numerous sixteenth-century copies, it boasted a most distinguished pedigree. It was, for example, referred to in the draft of the Protestation of the Speaker either in the parliaments of 1487 or 1504. Then, perhaps as a guide to procedure, it was transcribed in the journal of the House of Lords in 1510, when the journal began. Further, throughout the sixteenth and early seventeenth centuries the clerk of parliament and speaker of the House of Commons

---

[111] Henry Neville, "Plato Redivivus, or, A Dialogue Concerning Government c. 1681," in *Two English Republican Tracts*, ed. Caroline Robbins (Cambridge, 1969), p. 121.

[112] John Taylor, *English Historical Literature in the Fourteenth Century* (Oxford, 1987), pp. 212–13. *Parliamentary Texts of the Later Middle Ages*, ed. Nicholas Pronay and John Taylor (Oxford, 1980), pp. 1–21.

[113] Maddicott, *Thomas of Lancaster*, p. 291.

turned to it for advice about parliamentary procedure.[114] First published in 1572 by John Hooker alias Vowell, the *Modus* was included in the second edition of Holinshed's *Chronicles* published in 1587. In 1641 it again appeared in print by order of the Long Parliament, this time in a version edited by the noted lawyer-antiquary William Hakewill. In 1569 *A Discourse upon the Exposicion and Understandinge of Statutes*, written by Thomas Egerton (later Lord Chancellor Ellesmere), made use of it; and Henry Elsyng, clerk of the parliaments during the 1620s, turned to it for his own *Manner of Holding Parliaments of England*. Frequently cited by members of the Society of Antiquaries in the late sixteenth and early seventeenth centuries, the *Modus* was in Cotton's library from whence it circulated among his colleagues.[115] It also found its way into parliamentary debates in 1593, 1610, and 1621. Indeed, in 1628 Sir John Eliot probably read from it during the debates on the Petition of Right.[116] Moreover, Sir Edward Coke included the proem of the *Modus* in the famous preface to the *Ninth Reports*, and he even linked it to Henry I's coronation charter and Magna Carta, whose authors, Coke insisted, were familiar with its contents.[117]

The *Modus* was, then, a work of singular prominence in the late middle ages and early modern period. Although Selden before the civil war and Prynne after attacked it as a manufactured text, it was

---

[114] Taylor, *English Historical Literature in the Fourteenth Century*, pp. 215, 216. *Parliamentary Texts of the Later Middle Ages*, ed. Pronay and Taylor, pp. 51–9, 199–201, 202–15. For the history of the *Modus* see *ibid.*, pp. 13–63; John Taylor, "The Manuscripts of the *Modus Tenendi Parliamentum*," *English Historical Review* 83 (1968), 673–88; Maude V. Clarke, *Medieval Representation and Consent* (London, 1964). There was also an Irish version of the *Modus*, which Henry II allegedly introduced as a model for an Irish parliament. However, it lacked the "Proem" in which St. Edward's laws were mentioned. Taylor, *English Historical Literature in the Fourteenth Century*, pp. 213–4. Clarke, *Medieval Representation and Consent*, pp. 86–8, 91–5. G. O. Sayles, "Modus Tenendi Parliamentum: Irish or English," in *England and Ireland in the Later Middle Ages*, ed. J. F. Lydon (Dublin, 1981), pp. 111–52. Elizabeth Read Foster, "The Painful Labour of Mr. Elsyng," *Transactions of the American Philosophical Society* n.s. 62, pt. 8 (1972) 29, 38, 44–5, 52, 53, 58, and *passim*.

[115] See for example, B.L. MS Stowe. 366. fo. 47ᵛ.

[116] *Parliamentary Texts of the Later Middle Ages*, ed. Pronay and Taylor, pp. 51–9. Vernon F. Snow, ed., "The Order and Usage of the Keeping of a Parlement in England . . . collected by John Vowell alias Hooker," in *Parliament in Elizabethan England: John Hooker's Order and Usage* (New Haven, 1977). Thomas Egerton, *A Discourse upon the Exposicion and Understandinge of Statutes*, ed. Samuel E. Thorne (San Marino, Ca., 1942), p. 113. Foster, "Mr. Elsyng's Painful Labour." Annabel Patterson, *Reading Holinshed's Chronicles* (Chicago, 1994), pp. 124–6. G. L. Harriss, "The Formation of Parliament," in *The English Parliament in the Middle Ages*, ed. R. G. Davies and J. H. Denton (Philadelphia, 1981), pp. 40–9.

[117] Coke, Preface to *Ninth Reports* (London, 1613). *The Fourth Part of the Institutes of the Laws of England* , pp. 9, 12. *The Second Part of the Institutes of the Laws of England*, pp. 7–8.

highly esteemed by Stuart dissidents who continually pressed it into service in a wide variety of circumstances. And they did so with great success, if the tory writer Fabian Philipps can be believed. Commenting on its ideological power with typical hyperbole, he called the *Modus* "a machine of the devil" and attributed the coming of the civil war to its persuasive force. More than this, he continued, the work served as a "complete directory" to rebellion in the days of Jack Cade and Wat Tyler. The royalist poet John Cleveland settled for labelling it "that *Larva antiquitas*."[118] Appearing at first glance rather benign, the *Modus* itself concentrated on such matters as who should be called to parliament, the seating arrangements of members, and the order of business. But its proem, especially favored by parliamentarians and whigs, strongly reinforced the notion that William I was no conqueror because he agreed to govern by Saxon laws and institutions, and parliament in particular. It read:

> Here is described the manner in which the parliament of the king of England and of his Englishmen was held in the time of King Edward, the son of Ethelred. Which manner was related by the more distinguished men of the kingdom in the presence of William duke of Normandy, Conqueror and king of England: by the conqueror's own command, and through his approval it was used in his times and in the times of his successors, the kings of England.[119]

The *Modus* suited seventeenth-century dissidents for other reasons. Although carrying no set of laws, it strongly implied that in certain circumstances parliament stood above the king and, moreover, that the House of Commons outranked the Lords. Thus, in a section devoted to the resolution of conflicts within government, the *Modus* suggested that when king, lords, and commons reached an impasse, the earl marshal, steward, and constable ought to appoint a council of twenty-five, to be selected from "all the peers of the kingdom." This council, which because of its number might well have reminded rebels of the Council of Twenty-five charged with enforcing Magna Carta, included a number of "equals," as the author defined "peers": two bishops and three proctors from the clergy, two earls and three barons, five knights of the shires, five citizens, and five

---

[118] Phillips, *The Established Government of England, Vindicated from all Popular and Republican Principles and Mistakes* (London, 1687), pp. 689–91. Cleveland, *Majestas Intemerata. Or, the Immortality of the King* (n.p., 1649), p. 34.

[119] William Hakewill, *Modus tenendi Parliamentum: the Old Manner of holding Parliaments in England. Extracted out of our Ancient Records* (London, 1641), p. 1. Snow, ed., "The Order and Usage," pp. 125, 144.

burgesses – in other words, a council in which fifteen of twenty-five members sat in the House of Commons. If this body proved unable to resolve a particular dispute, its members were to choose successively smaller groups until only one remained. His decision in the matter would be passed on to the king and his advisers, who might amend it "in full parliament, and by the consent of the parliament, and not contrary to the parliament."[120]

But it was not left entirely to seventeenth-century dissidents to draw revolutionary conclusions from this predominance of commoners in the government of the kingdom. Indeed, according to Maddicott and J. R. Roskell, the *Modus* was intended for precisely such use in the reign of Edward II, when his enemies sought support by broadening the composition of the lower house to include "the middling people of the shires."[121]

The *Modus* also had something to say about the order of parliamentary business. War, should there be one, took precedence, followed by matters concerning the royal family. Next in order of importance came "the common business of the kingdom, as in making laws, when there shall be lack of original, judicial, or executing of particular persons." Finally, parliament dealt with the business of private persons, such as petitions. According to the *Modus*, the importance of this last-named task prevented the king from dissolving parliament so long as individual petitions pended.[122] Since, in Maddicott's view, Edward II's enemies themselves intended this section to limit the royal power, it should come as no surprise to find seventeenth-century rebels using it to usurp the king's traditional right to control the sitting of parliament. Milton, for example, referred to this part of the *Modus* in his authorized answer to the *Eikon Basilike*. Here he wrote that the king must insure that "parliaments were not to be dissolved till all petitions were heard [and] all grievances addressed . . ." Indeed, "the old Modi calls it flat perjury if he dissolves them before."[123] The *Modus* came in handy for the

---

[120] Hakewill, *Modus tenendi Parliamentum*, pp. 19–20. In the 1641 edition two bishops were left out, probably as a result of the dispute over the presence of the bishops in the House of Lords. For the correct number see Hooker's version of the *Modus* in Snow, ed., "The Order and Usage," p. 135.

[121] Maddicott, *Thomas of Lancaster*, p. 291. Roskell, "A Consideration of Certain Aspects and Problems of the English *Modus Tenendi Parliamentum*, *Bulletin of the John Rylands Library* 1 (1968), 415.

[122] Hakewill, *Modus tenendi Parliamentum*, p. 21. Snow, ed., "The Order and Usage," pp. 135–6, 143.

[123] Milton, *Eikonoklastes*, pp. 44–5.

same reason when Charles II and James II tried to stifle opposition by depriving their enemies of a public forum, as during the Exclusion crisis and the Glorious Revolution.[124]

The *Modus* also commented on the status of the various members of parliament, and, in a passage that gave delight and comfort to anti-court elements in both the fourteenth and the seventeenth centuries, exalted the commonalty of the realm over the nobility. "We must understand," its author began, "that two knights which come to parliament for the shires and county . . . have a greater voice in parliament to grant than the greatest Earl in England." Proof of the Commons' dominance lay in the fact that "the king may hold parliaments with the commonalty and the commons of the kingdom without bishops, earls, and barons, yet so as they be summoned to the parliament, although no bishop, earl, or baron come according to their summons, because in times past, neither was there bishop, earl, nor baron, and yet even then kings kept their parliament." Therefore, "all things which are to be affirmed or informed, granted or denied, or to be done by Parliament; must be granted by the commonalty of the parliament."[125]

Nor was this all in the *Modus* that appealed to seventeenth-century dissidents. A section entitled "Touching the King's Absence from Parliament" stated that "the king is bound by all means possible to be present" unless he is sick. Even then, a committee from parliament must visit him to confirm his illness.[126] This part of the *Modus* proved utterly indispensable throughout the civil war, when Charles I, after abandoning Westminster for York and Oxford, condemned the two houses for carrying on business without him. It served a similar turn at the Glorious Revolution when James II fled the kingdom.[127]

Finally, the *Modus* provided ammunition for radical causes by defining the power of parliament in shockingly high language. In particular, the work described parliament's jurisdiction as including "all weighty and great causes," namely, reforming and regulating religion, levying aids and subsidies "for the preservation of the king

---

[124] See, for example, "Vox Populi: Or, The People's Claim to their Parliaments' Sitting, to Redress Grievances . . . .," in *State Tracts: Being a Collection of Several Treatises Relating to the Government* (London, 1689), vol. II, p. 222.

[125] Hakewill, *Modus tenendi Parliamentum*, pp. 24–6. Snow, ed., "Of the Order and Usage," pp. 181–2.

[126] Hakewill, *Modus tenendi Parliamentum*, pp. 18–9. Snow, ed., "The Order and Usage," p. 140.

[127] See, for example, Prynne, *The Treachery and Disloyalty of Papists to their Soveraignes*, pp. 42–3.

and public estate," "establishing the succession," and deciding matters such as royal marriages and war and peace. Moreover, the power of parliament encompassed "the making and establishing of good and wholesome laws, or the repealing and debarring of former laws, as whose execution may be hurtful or prejudicial to the estates of the prince or commonwealth."[128] Such descriptions of parliament were understandably welcome to subjects bent on placing their kings under the authority of a sovereign parliament. Prynne, for one, cited this portion of the *Modus* as a justification for making war on Charles I, since, in his understanding, the language meant that parliament could "oblige both king and subject."[129]

The *Mirror of Justices* joined the *Modus* and St. Edward's laws in advancing the cause of radical ancient constitutionalism. Emphasizing the continuity of law and legal institutions from the Saxon period down to the seventeenth century, it located the origins of kingship in the community and endowed parliament with the right to judge the king. Existing in only one medieval manuscript, the *Mirror* was first published in law French in 1642 – a year which also saw the outbreak of civil war between king and parliament – and in an English translation in 1646.[130] Claiming to rely on laws that "have obtained since the time of King Arthur," the anonymous author purported to describe the workings of government in ancient times. He told, for example, how King Alfred "ordained as a perpetual usage" that parliament should assemble at London twice a year, and more often if necessary[131] – a passage much to the liking of generations of Stuart dissidents who turned to it when their kings refused to summon parliament.[132] Equally valuable was the portion of the *Mirror* that described the king as holding his office by virtue of an election by the forty Saxon rulers whom God had made victorious over the Britons. Importantly, at his coronation his people

---

[128] Snow, ed., "The Order and Usage," pp. 146–7.
[129] Prynne, *The Treachery and Disloyalty of Papists to their Soveraignes*, p. 46.
[130] *La Somme appelle Mirroir Des Iustices vel Speculum Iusticiariorum, Factum per Andream Horne* (London, 1642). *The Booke Called, The Mirrour of Justices: Made by Andrew Horne. With the Book, called, The Diversity of Courts, And Their Jurisdictions. Both translated out of the old French into the English Tongue* (London, 1646).
[131] *The Mirror of Justices*, ed. William Joseph Whittaker, with an introduction by Frederic William Maitland, Selden Society, vol. VII (London, 1895), p. 3.
[132] See, for example, Bulstrode Whitelocke, *Notes Uppon the Kings Writt for Choosing Members of Parlement XIII Car. II. Being Disquisitions on the Government of England by King, Lords, and Commons* (London, 1766), vol. II, p. 154.

"made him swear that he would maintain the Christian faith with all his power and would guide his people by law without respect of any person . . . and would be obedient to the holy Church, and would submit to justice and would suffer right like any other of his people." Indeed, "the first and most sovereign abuse is that the king" claim the right to act "beyond the law, whereas he ought to be subject to it, as is contained in his oath."[133]

Most valuable of all to the radical ancient constitutionalist cause was the portion of the *Mirror* that could be read as sanctioning the use of force against a ruler. Regarding the right relationship between king and people, the author of the *Mirror* insisted that, although the king "should have no peer in his land," if he "should by fault sin against any of his people," neither he "nor any of his commissioners could be judge, he being also party." In such cases the law demanded "that the king should have companions to hear and determine in parliaments all the writs and plaints concerning wrongs done by the king, the queen, their children, and their special ministers, for which wrongs one should not otherwise have obtained common right." This meant, in turn, that the king "was obliged to suffer right as well as his subjects."[134] Beginning in 1642, opponents of the Stuarts lost no time in operationalizing the lesson inherent in this passage. Prynne, for one, deployed it in his incendiary *Soveraigne Power of Parliaments and Kingdomes* to prove that parliament, in which the king's "companions" sat, authorized the kingdom "to restrain and bridle the king when he casts off the bridle of the law, and invades the subjects' liberties."[135]

Despite its claim of antiquity, the *Mirror*, like the *Modus*, dated from the post-conquest period. And also like the *Modus* its authenticity was questioned by Selden and later Prynne. Too, modern scholars argue over its authorship and the purposes for which it was written. Maitland treated it as a fanciful and satirical creation whose author, "in Paradise or wherever else he may be . . . was pleasantly surprised" when seventeenth-century Englishmen "repeated his fictions as gospel truth, and erudite men spoke of him in the same

---

[133] *The Mirror of Justices*, ed. Whittaker, pp. 6, 155.
[134] *Ibid.*
[135] Prynne, *The Treachery and Disloyalty of Papists to their Soveraignes*, pp. 3, 36–7, 54, 56. *The Soveraigne Power of Parliaments and Kingdomes: Divided into Foure Parts. Together with an Appendix* (London, 1643), p. 9. *The Third Part of the Soveraigne Power of Parliaments and Kingdomes* (London, 1643), p. 3.

breath with Glanvill and Bracton."[136] Sometimes attributed to the Londoner Andrew Horn, an evaluation by E. F. J. Tucker suggests that the *Mirror*'s author was a forerunner of reformers such as John Wycliff, William Langland, and John Ball, who championed the cause of local communities against the incursion of the central government.[137] Whatever its provenance, to seventeenth-century rebels it presented more proof, if proof were needed, of the central tenets of ancient constitutionalist thought. Milton, for one, used it to good effect, and it certainly frightened royalists such as Fabian Philipps, who attacked it as a "grand imposture."[138]

By the early sixteenth century, the basic building blocks of the ancient constitution were firmly in place. The cult of the Confessor had been joined by the cult of the Confessor's laws. These laws, reinforced by a community of highly revered and widely known texts, encouraged a belief in the essential continuity of past and present. And this conviction led in turn to the historical view at the heart of ancient constitutionalism: while William had conquered Harold and those Saxons who supported him, he had not conquered Saxon law and legal institutions. Not only had these survived the Norman invasion but they passed intact to the people of England, who might justly deploy them to hold kings to account. On this trusty and solid medieval foundation Tudor writers would build the early modern version of the ancient constitution.

---

[136] *The Mirror of Justices*, ed. Whittaker, p. xlviii. See also Harold G. Reuschlein, "Who Wrote the *Mirror of Justices?*" *Law Quarterly Review* 58 (1942), 265; J. Cato, "Andrew Horn: Law and History in Fourteenth-Century England," in *The Writing of History in the Middle Ages: Essays Presented to Richard William Southern*, ed. R. C. Davis and J. M. Wallace-Hadrill (Oxford, 1981), pp. 367–91.

[137] Tucker, "*The Mirror of Justices*: Its Authorship and Preoccupations," *The Irish Jurist* 9, n.s., pt. 1 (1974), 99–109.

[138] Milton, *Eikonoklastes*, pp. 41, 45, 234. Philipps, *The Established Government of England*, p. 589.

CHAPTER 3

"Divers and sundry ancient histories and chronicles": the articulation of the ancient constitution in the Tudor period

INTRODUCTION

If the middle ages saw the creation of an ancient constitution that Stuart rebels later deployed against their kings, the sixteenth century witnessed its more precise articulation. Indeed, throughout the Tudor period writers of different political persuasions repeated and elaborated on precisely those sources and stories that carried the ancient constitutionalist version of the past. Although they sometimes quibbled about certain details, virtually all found the essential institutions of English government flourishing in the Saxon age or earlier. And virtually all associated the common law with St. Edward and traced the survival of the ancient constitution through the conquest and the following centuries. That they did so suggests that seventeenth-century radicals deserve more credit for historical accuracy than they often receive. While they frequently put their own spin upon sources and stories, they nevertheless built on a tradition that descended to them through highly respected Tudor historical and legal writings. This chapter will examine the Tudor literature to which they were heir.

The literature itself was the product of an unprecedented inquiry into the nation's past, inspired by a confluence of ideas, events, and technology. Ironically, much of the initiative for this examination of early English history came from the Tudor monarchy, as it contested with the papacy for control of the English church. In order to legitimize the break with Rome, reformers, under royal sponsorship, probed historical records for proof that the English church represented the one, true religion that papists had long ago corrupted. The Reformation also increased the country's self-consciousness and fostered a nationalist fervor which, in turn, imparted a new urgency and vitality to the study of the past. It mattered, too, that the

79

England of Elizabeth was a time of military victory abroad and, for some, rising prosperity at home. According to May McKisack, these circumstances "tended to arouse new interests in family ties, appreciation of ancient monuments, [and] curiosity. . . about how Britain and British institutions came to be as they are."[1] Add to this atmosphere the influence of the common lawyers, whose daily bread consisted of custom and case law, and the immersion of literate English people in their history seems foreordained.

The preoccupation with the past was associated with several developments of far-reaching influence and long-lasting impact – all of which helped to shape and perpetuate the theory of the ancient constitution. First came the publication in the mid- and late sixteenth century of the chronicles of Bede, Matthew Paris, William of Malmesbury, Henry Knighton, Henry of Huntingdon, and Roger Hoveden. The *Leges Edwardi Confessoris* and the *Modus tenendi Parliamentum* also appeared in print for the first time.[2] A second decisive event – the dissolution of the monasteries from 1535 to 1539 – loosed a flood of medieval manuscripts into a market driven by collectors and scholars eager to capitalize on the growing interest in the origins of English institutions. John Leland, John Bale, Sir Henry Savile, and Archbishop Matthew Parker accumulated impressive collections of manuscripts, and in so doing helped save monastic libraries for future generations.[3]

The most successful collector was Sir Robert Cotton, who managed to acquire the greatest private library in early modern England. The pupil of William Camden and a client of the earl of Northampton, Cotton assembled a wide array of medieval sources, including those most closely associated with the ancient constitution. Notable among the manuscripts circulating from his library were the Saxon laws, the *Modus,* and the *Red Book of the Exchequer,* as well as the chronicles of Paris, Knighton, Hoveden, Malmesbury, Wendover, Sprott, and de Diceto. As Cotton's loan lists indicate, his customers

---

[1] McKisack, *Medieval History in the Tudor Age* (Oxford, 1971), Introduction. John N. King, *English Reformation Literature* (Princeton, 1983), pp. 76–121 and *passim.*
[2] For the publication of the medieval chronicles see Elizabeth C. van Houts, "Camden, Cotton and the Chronicles of the Norman Conquest of England," *British Library Journal* 18 (1992), 148–62.
[3] F. J. Levy, *Tudor Historical Thought* (San Marino, Ca., 1967), pp. 126–30. McKisack, *Medieval History in the Tudor Age,* pp. 1–74. H. McCusker, "Books and Manuscripts Formerly in the Possession of John Bale," *The Library* 16 (1935), 144–65. C. E. Wright, "The Dispersal of the Monastic Libraries and the Beginnings of Anglo-Saxon Studies," *Transactions of the Cambridge Bibliographical Society* (1951), 208–37.

constituted a veritable honor roll of late sixteenth- and early seventeenth-century lawyers and scholars, including Sir Roger Owen, Sir Henry Spelman, William Hakewill, Francis Tate, William Camden, Arthur Agarde, and Francis Thynne. Nor were borrowers limited to the scholarly and legal community. Politicians and governmental officials such as the earl of Manchester, the earl of Arundel, Attorney General Edward Coke, and Recorder of London William Fleetwood also found the Cotton library useful.[4]

The wider availability of medieval sources and the increasing interest in the national past transformed English culture in several ways. Especially noteworthy was the appearance of a new kind of discourse, the popular history of the sort associated in the Tudor period with John Foxe, Richard Grafton, Raphael Holinshed, and John Stow, and in the seventeenth century with John Speed, Samuel Daniel, William Martyn, and Richard Baker. Appealing to an audience that extended beyond the educated elite, these works popularized medieval history among wealthy merchants and landed gentry who looked to the past for stories of English heroes and historic deeds. In addition, the spread of literacy in both town and country meant that more and more people could cultivate an interest in their national past, especially as depicted in writings of the popular variety. A less literate clientele was served by Stow's and Grafton's abridged pocket books, John Taylor's annotated woodcuts of English kings, and William Elderton's broadsides.[5]

Finally, curiosity about how things used to be mobilized a small band of Englishmen to associate for the purpose of examining the nation's history. Formed around 1586, this organization, the Society of Antiquaries, devoted itself for almost two decades to discovering the origins of English institutions such as parliament, the common law, and the church. More than any other entity, this society rendered canonical the major sources of ancient constitutionalism,

---

[4] Cotton's loan lists can be found in B.L. Harl. MSS 6018. fos. 152–190. See also Kevin Sharpe, *Sir Robert Cotton 1586–1631. History and Politics in Early Modern England* (Oxford, 1979), especially pp. 48–81; Linda Levy Peck, *Northampton: Patronage and Policy at the Court of James I* (London, 1982), chapter 6 *passim*; Graham Parry, *The Trophies of Time. English Antiquarians of the Seventeenth Century* (Oxford, 1995), chapter 3.

[5] Margaret Spufford, *Contrasting Communities. English Villagers in the Sixteenth and Seventeenth Centuries* (Cambridge, 1974), pp. 171–218. Annabel Patterson, *Reading Holinshed's Chronicles* (Chicago, 1994), pp. xii–xiii. R. S. Schofield, "The Measurement of Literacy in Pre-Industrial England," in J. R. Goody, ed., *Literacy in Traditional Societies* (Cambridge, 1968), pp. 310–25. Lawrence Stone, "The Educational Revolution in England, 1560–1650," *Past and Present* 28 (1964), 49–80.

especially St. Edward's laws and the *Modus*, and guaranteed their high reputation within the scholarly, political, and legal world.

The importance of the literature associated with sixteenth- and early seventeenth-century antiquaries and chroniclers can scarcely be overstated, for in teaching a wider English audience about their national history, it validated the tales central to ancient constitutionalist thought and imparted a ring of truth to what would later be called the whig version of history. Some of the writings, as we will see, contained ambiguous descriptions of the early English past and directed readers' attention to historical discontinuities as well as continuities. Still, within the multitudinous pages of Tudor literature, radical ancient constitutionalists would find virtually every argument central to their cause, in particular, the antiquity of parliament and the common law and their survival throughout the centuries. In addition, sixteenth-century writers often described William I as entering England not as a conqueror but as the heir of his cousin Edward the Confessor and by acceptance of the nation.

Tudor chroniclers and antiquaries paid special homage to St. Edward's laws, and for the first time we see the body of Saxon laws taking precedence over the cult of his kingship. Indeed, the vast majority of references to the Confessor concerned his practical and earthly political achievements rather than his miraculous and magical prowess. Equally important, Protestant writers increased the respectability of that precise section of St. Edward's laws that carried the most potential for radical elaboration. This was Chapter 17, which stated that a king who misruled thereby lost the name of king. The person most responsible for the re-historicization of the Confessor was the renowned martyrologist John Foxe. He provided immense aid to the rebel cause by interpreting Chapter 17 in much the same way as would Stuart dissidents, that is, as sanctioning insurrection against a king who abandoned his office. Indeed, more than any other event since Magna Carta and the new coronation oath of 1308, Foxe's treatment transformed St. Edward's laws into an ideological argument and, in the process, elbowed the cult of kingship into the background.

THE HISTORICAL LITERATURE OF THE TUDOR PERIOD

The staying power of ancient constitutionalist sources in sixteenth-century historical thought is perhaps surprising, given the advances of Renaissance humanism. The new scholarship, after all, alerted English people to the concept of anachronism and encouraged them to evaluate sources more critically. As a result, some Tudor scholars raised doubts about the authenticity of the Brut and Arthur legends and questioned the credibility of sources such as Gildas and Geoffrey of Monmouth.[6] Looking at the past through more critical eyes might also have diminished the power of the miracles associated with Holy Edward. However, even the most sophisticated and up-to-date historians never doubted the authenticity of the central ancient constitutionalist texts. Nor did they question the essential continuity of law and legal institutions from the Saxon period down to their own day. Throughout the period, the place of Edward the Confessor as the founder of common law and the survival of his laws into the Norman period and beyond enjoyed the widest acceptance. So, too, did the existence of parliament before 1066, though writers might dispute the precise date at which kings began regularly to summon the House of Commons.

The tone of much Tudor historical writing was set by Henry VIII himself. Concerned to prove his imperial right to govern the English church, he well understood the power of the ancient constitutionalist version of the past. Indeed, as early as 1519 he demonstrated that he knew his Saxon sources. In a case involving a plea of sanctuary for an appeal of murder, Henry spoke against the appellee in the Star Chamber: " 'I do not suppose that St. Edward, King Edgar, and other kings and holy fathers who made the sanctuary ever intended the sanctuary to serve for voluntary murder . . . ' "[7] Particularly useful for legitimizing the break with Rome was an entire collection of Saxon materials, the "Collectanea satis Copiosa." This array of ancient sources included English chronicles and Anglo-Saxon laws that Thomas Cranmer and the bishop of Hereford, Edward Foxe, compiled in support of the Boleynist faction. Since, according to John Guy, the king himself read and even glossed these sources, we can speculate that one in particular caught his eye. This was the

---

[6] Levy, *Tudor Historical Thought*, pp. 56, 57, 58, 64–8, 125–6, 130–3, 145–6, 172. D. R. Woolf, *The Idea of History in Early Stuart England* (Toronto, 1990), pp. 33, 59, 69, 95, 117, 203.

[7] Quoted in John Baker, ed., *The Reports of Sir John Spelman*, Selden Society, vol. XCIV (London, 1978), vol. II, pp. 342–3. See also John Guy, "Thomas Cromwell and the Intellectual Origins of the Henrician Revolution," in Alastair Fox and John Guy, eds., *Reassessing the Henrician Age. Humanism, Politics and Reform, 1500–1550* (Oxford, 1986), pp. 166–7; Colin Kidd, *British Identities Before Nationalism. Ethnicity and Nationhood in the Atlantic World, 1600–1800* (Cambridge, 1999), chapter 5.

alleged correspondence between the mythical King Lucius, supposedly the first Christian ruler of Britain, and Pope Eleutherius.[8] In the second century AD Lucius had written to the pope, requesting that he send him the Roman laws so that he could better rule the British people. But the pope declined, reminding Lucius "that all nations are not of like conditions, and therefore those constitutions that are beneficial to one, may now and then be prejudicial to another." In fact, the pope explained, King Lucius already possessed a perfectly good set of laws, the *lex Britanniae*, which insured his supremacy in both church and state. All that God required of him was that he rule according to divine law and the laws of Britain. Then, in words virtually identical to those of Chapter 17 of St. Edward's laws, the pope explained to Lucius that he was "vicar of God in your kingdom . . . A king is named by virtue of ruling and not for having a realm. You shall be king while you rule well, but if you do otherwise the name of king shall not remain upon you, and you will lose it. The omnipotent God grant you so to rule the kingdom of Britain that you many reign with him eternally, whose vicar you are in the said realm."[9]

We now know, and have since the nineteenth century, that the story is false. There was no King Lucius, and the alleged correspondence was manufactured in the early thirteenth century to combat a feared incursion of Roman law from the continent.[10] But it carried the imprimatur of the London version of the *Leges Edwardi Confessoris*, where it had appeared as Chapter 11. And the Lucius legend quickly passed into the vocabulary of sixteenth-century thought, as Henry VIII's apologists drew from its words a papal guarantee of royal supremacy in state and church. John Jewell, bishop of Salisbury, found the correspondence relevant to his defense of the English church, citing it along with the story of Pope Zacharius, Pepin, and

---

[8] Guy, *Tudor England* (Oxford, 1990), pp. 110, 128, 133, 144. Guy, "Thomas Cromwell and the Intellectual Origins of the Henrician Reformation," pp. 151–78. The "Collectanea" was discovered and identified by Dr. Graham Nicholson. *Ibid.*, p. 157. I am indebted to Guy's accounts for much that follows. See also Virginia Murphy, "The Literature and Propaganda of Henry VIII's First Divorce," in *The Reign of Henry VIII. Politics, Policy and Piety*, ed. Diarmaid MacCulloch (New York, 1995), pp. 146–7.

[9] B.L. Cott. Ms. Cleo. E. VI. fos. 74ᵛ-75ᵛ. I have used Guy's translation. "Thomas Cromwell and the Henrician Revolution," pp. 158–9.

[10] Raoul C. van Caenegem, *The Birth of the English Common Law*, 2nd. edn. (Cambridge, 1988), pp. 101–2. John Guy and John Morrill, *The Tudors and the Stuarts* (Oxford, 1992), p. 25. Guy, *Tudor England*, p. 133.

Childeric.[11] Bishop Foxe utilized the letters for the same purpose, throwing in for good measure the laws of Ethelred, Edgar, Ine, Alfred, and Cnut.[12] Indeed, the correspondence soon entered the historical and legal literature of the period, appearing, for example, in Lambarde's *Archaionomia* and in Holinshed's *Chronicles*, discussed more fully below.[13] The point made in the letters even found its way into the Act in Restraint of Appeals of 1533. Its preamble supported the king's "imperial" kingship by reference to "sundry old authentic histories and chronicles" that described ancient English rulers as empowered by God with plenary power to govern in both church and state.[14] Moreover, as we shall see, the correspondence played especially well in radical ancient constitutionalist circles in the following century.

Writing in the shadow of Henry VIII and his Protestant heirs, Tudor chroniclers and antiquaries functioned as the secular counterparts of Reformation polemicists. Just as religious scholars rummaged through medieval records for proof that their church had always been pure and free from papal domination, so did secular writers scurry to provide England with a "cultural longevity" to match.[15] It was in this atmosphere that Saxon studies became a major preoccupation of the scholarly community, spawned by fear of foreign domination and fueled by a growing national self-consciousness. It was also within this atmosphere that the ancient constitution became a Saxon as well as a Protestant constitution: England's

---

[11] "The Defence of the Apologie of the Church of England, conteining an Answer to a certaine Booke lately set forth by M. Harding, and entituled, A Confutation of etc.," in *The Works of John Jewell, Bishop of Salisbury*, ed. John Ayre (Cambridge, Parker Society, 1850), pt. VI, p. 974. Jewell used the story of Zacharius, Pepin, and Childeric to prove that the pope sometimes interferred inappropriately in secular matters. His opponent, Thomas Harding, cited the story to prove the great power of the papacy to depose kings and emperors. *Ibid.*, pt. IV, pp. 672, 680–1.

[12] Edward Foxe, *The true Dyfferences betwen y regall power and the Ecclesiasticall power translated out of Latyn by Henry lord Stafforde* (London, 1548), Sig. lxxxi^L–lxxxvi^R. This was a reprint of Foxe's *De Vera Differentia Regiae Potestatis et Ecclesiasticae* published in 1534. This literature is discussed in Guy, "Thomas Cromwell and the Henrician Revolution," *passim*; O'Day, *The Debate on the English Reformation* (London, 1986), pp. 12–15.

[13] Holinshed, *Chronicles* (London, 1587/1807), vol. I, pp. 23–5. In this book I use both the 1577 edition and the 1587 edition that was reprinted in 1807, since early modern Englishmen themselves used both. See also Lambarde, *Archaionomia*, fos. 131–31v; John Caius, "Historiae Cantegrigiensis," in *The Works of John Caius* (London, 1574), pp. 18–19.

[14] Guy, "Thomas Cromwell and the Henrician Revolution," pp. 151–2.

[15] Linda van Norden, "Celtic Antiquarianism," in *Essays Dedicated to Lily B. Campbell* (Berkeley and Los Angeles, 1950), p. 65. Joan Evans, *A History of the Society of Antiquaries* (Oxford, 1956), p. 11.

historical uniqueness could now be found in its glorious Germanic past, where the origins of its most precious institutions, secular as well as religious, lay.[16]

Toward this end, the lawyer–antiquary William Lambarde, with the blessings of Archbishop Matthew Parker and the noted Saxonist Laurence Nowell, published *Archaionomia* in 1568. The centerpiece of the Saxonist revival, it contained Latin translations of the laws associated with Ine, Alfred, Edward the Elder, Aethelstan, Edmund, Edgar, Cnut, and Ethelred, as well as the *Leges Edwardi Confessoris* and the *Leis Willelme*.[17] Although later scholars criticized Lambarde's work for inaccuracies in spelling and translation, *Archaionomia* commanded the utmost respect from generations of Elizabethan and Stuart Englishmen.[18] The Saxon laws became even more accessible when, in 1596, Sir Henry Savile published the chronicles of Ingulf, Henry Huntingdon, and Roger Hoveden, all of which included extensive portions of and references to the Confessor's laws.[19]

In constructing a version of the past that grounded both church and state firmly in the mists of antiquity, Tudor writers often deployed precisely those medieval tales that emphasized the central tenet in ancient constitutionalist thinking, namely, the continuity of law and institutions across the great divide of 1066. Although few (if any) sixteenth-century historians approached the Norman conquest as a polemical issue, intent on proving that William did or did not reign as a conqueror, their versions of Anglo-Norman history typically confirmed the basic tenets of ancient constitutionalist thought: like their medieval predecessors, Tudor writers depicted William as defeating the English army but not the English laws. Even though he frequently reneged on his promises and replaced some of St. Edward's laws with foreign customs, the Saxons endured. And by refusing to knuckle under they forced William to buy them off with further restorations of St. Edward's laws. The fact that their strength obliged him to keep backing down meant that

---

[16] Levy, *Tudor Historical Thought*, pp. 136–40.

[17] Lambarde, *Archaionomia*. St. Edward's laws begin at fo. 126ᵛ, William I's at fo. 124. See also Levy, *Tudor Historical Thought*, pp. 136, 141; Philip Styles, "Politics and Historical Research in the Early Seventeenth Century," in *English Historical Scholarship in the Sixteenth and Seventeenth Centuries*, ed. Levi Fox (London, 1956), p. 51; Samuel L. Kliger, *The Goths in England* (Cambridge, Mass., 1952), pp. 21–5.

[18] Levy, *Tudor Historical Thought*, pp. 117–20, 136–8. McKisack, *Medieval History in the Tudor Age*, pp. 78–80.

[19] Sir Henry Savile, *Rerum anglicarum scriptores post Bedam praecipui* (London, 1596).

they kept alive their prescriptive right to be governed by the ancient laws of the kingdom. That is, no temporary eclipse of Saxon laws could stand as a legal precedent so long as the English were on record as objecting. Indeed, medieval history demonstrated that they wound up conquering the Normans. Witness, for example, Henry I's restoration of St. Edward's laws in his coronation charter of 1101, as well as the myriad of confirmations that followed. At best – or worst – then, William managed only a brief and transient muffling of St. Edward's laws, which descended to Tudor England in the form of the common law.

And so it was, sixteenth-century writers continued, with parliament. Originating long before 1066, its centrality in the life of the kingdom insured its survival after the Norman invasion. On this issue most Tudor chroniclers agreed completely. Take, for example, the Italian humanist Polydore Vergil. Employed by Henry VII and Henry VIII to justify the new dynasty at home and abroad, he wrote the *Historia Anglica* for his masters. A measure of the *Historia's* impact was its inclusion, sometimes word for word, in works such as Richard Grafton's continuations of John Hardyng's *Chronicle*, Edward Hall's history of Edward V, and Holinshed's *Chronicles*.[20] Polydore's account of St. Edward's laws and their survival after 1066 followed the usual medieval line. In 1054, he wrote, Edward the Confessor,

having gotten peace and quietness both on sea and on land, and foreseeing no less the safety of his people then himself, as a man naturally bent to the loving of all men, which is the very ground of right and foundation of the law, he minded above all things to make such laws as he thought good and expedient at that time, surely were many lost in ure, made first of the Britons, then of the Saxons, and last of all of the Danes; so that many men measuring all things according to their private commodity oftentimes applied for their purpose inequity in the stead of justice. Wherefore King Edward, out of the abundance of laws, picked forth every most wholesome and necessary decree, ordering only certain selected to be used as indifferent rules and prescripts of good life unto all degrees, which by the posterity were termed common laws.[21]

However, the Confessor's laws, already ancient when codified, fell on hard times soon after the Norman invasion, when William I

---

[20] Levy, *Tudor Historical Thought*, pp. 172–5. Denys Hay, *Polydore Vergil. Renaissance Historian and Man of Letters* (Oxford, 1952), pp. 79–128. McKisack, *Medieval History in the Tudor Age*, pp. 98–104. Parry, *The Trophies of Time*, pp. 2, 27–8.

[21] *Polydore's English History*, vol. 1. *Containing the First Eight Books, Comprising the Period Prior to the Norman conquest*, ed. Sir Henry Ellis (London, Camden Society, 1846), p. 292.

cancelled them and instituted customs from France. But this action, far from subduing the Saxons, only provoked them to take up arms for "the better part of their life" and to plague "such kings as denied to ratify them [the Saxon laws] with their pristine power . . ." Polydore thus raised the spectre of a discontinuity in early English history. But it was a discontinuity limited in scope and duration, a partial interruption that lasted only until Henry I brought the Confessor's laws back to life in his Charter of Liberties of 1101. And alive they remained in Polydore's own day, when they were known as the common law of England.[22] William I's victory over English law appeared, then, as an aberration that in no way threatened the ultimate survival of Saxon law down to the Tudor period.

Other Tudor chroniclers presented views of the English past equally suited to ancient constitutionalist tastes. Importantly, these authors, unlike Polydore, wrote in English, and their works were frequently republished throughout the period. One of the most commonly cited was Robert Fabyan, an affluent London draper who served the city as alderman and sheriff. His *New Chronicles of England and France*, first appearing in 1516 and reprinted in 1533, 1542, and 1559, emphasized the continuity of laws from Brutus through Dunwallo and eventually the Norman rulers. Meriting special mention was Henry I, who insured the survival of these laws when at his coronation he "made the holy church free and used Saint Edward's laws, with the amendment of them." A century later King John provoked a falling out with his barons because "he would not hold the laws of Saint Edward."[23] Interested readers could find the same stories in Thomas Lanquet and Thomas Cooper's *An Epitome of Cronicles*, considered sufficiently fashionable to be copied by Robert Crowley in 1559.[24] The tales of St. Edward's laws and their various confirmations in the Norman period also appeared in John Rastall's *Chronycles of Englande* and *A breviat Chronycle, contayning all the Kynges, from Brute to thys Day*.[25]

[22] Polydore Vergil, *Urbinatis Anglicae historiae libri uigintisex* (Basil, 1546), book ix, fos. 150–55.
[23] Fabyan, *The New Chronicles of England and France* (London, 1516, repr. London, 1811), pp. 20–1, 25, 165, 253, 320. The 1811 reprint is a collation of all editions. See also Levy, *Tudor Historical Thought*, pp. 19–20, 24, 26, 57, 175, 179–80; McKisack, *Medieval History in the Tudor Age*, p. 95.
[24] Lanquet, *Cooper's Chronicle* (London, 1560), pp. 198, 203a, 219. Levy, *Tudor Historical Thought*, pp. 177–8, 187, 189. McKisack, *Medieval History in the Tudor Age*, p. 104.
[25] John Rastall, *The Chronycles of Englande and of dyvers other realmes* (London, 1530), under the reigns of Henry I and King John. *A Breviat Chronycle, contayning all the Kynges, from Brute to thys Day* (London, 1560), pages unnumbered. See also Peter C. Herman, "Rastell's *Pastyme of*

Elizabethan writers such as Richard Grafton and John Stow repeated the stories. Grafton, King's Printer and publisher of the English Bible, described in his *Chronicle at Large* (1568 and 1569) how William I altered "the whole state and government," replacing Saxon laws with grievous Norman customs written in the French tongue.[26] Still, while the Normans "conquered and quietly possessed" England, certain segments of the population retained the right to be ruled by St. Edward's laws. Telling the story of the men at Swanscombe Down who were prepared to give up their lives rather than "depart from their ancient laws and customs," Grafton noted that William had been compelled to accede to their demands, thus guaranteeing the existence "even to this day" of gavelkind tenure.[27] William also granted that the city of London could retain the liberties it had enjoyed under St. Edward.[28] This concession was extended throughout the entire realm by Henry I in his Charter of Liberties. In Grafton's words, "no one thing moved the whole realm more to agree upon him, than the faithful promise he made to abolish his father's laws, which were deemed of the people to be both against equity and conscience" and to restore "St. Edward's laws with the amendments of them, besides the reformation and amendment of sundry and diverse other abuses in the commonwealth."[29] The same story line characterized Stow's two major histories – *The Chronicles of England, from Brute unto the present year*, published in 1580 and 1587, and *The Annales of England*, which appeared in 1592, 1605, 1606, 1614, and 1631. Summaries and abridgments of both were printed throughout the late sixteenth and seventeenth centuries, insuring that this particular view of the past reached a very wide audience indeed.[30]

Just as sixteenth-century writers found Saxon laws surviving the conquest, so, too, did they note the endurance of that other pillar of

---

People: Monarchy and the Law in Early Modern Historiography," *Journal of Medieval and Early Modern Studies* (forthcoming). Professor Herman graciously made his manuscript available to me.

[26] Grafton, *A Chronicle at large and Meere History of the Affayres of Englande and Kinges of the Same, Deduced from the Creation of the Worlde, unto the First Habitation of Thys Yslande* ([London], 1568), vol. II, p. 7, vol. I, p. 188.

[27] *Ibid.*, vol. I, pp. 2–3.

[28] *Ibid.*, vol. II, p. 18.

[29] *Ibid.*, vol. II, p. 32.

[30] Stow, *The Chronicles of England, from Brute unto this present Yeare 1580* (London, 1580), pp. 42–3, 146, 149–52, 158, 160, 177, 245. Stow, *The Annales of England* (London, 1605), pp. 122–3, 136–7, 144, 146, 149, 172, 190, 257.

the ancient constitution, parliament. According to Polydore Vergil, parliaments existed both before and after the Norman invasion. However, in words that later earned him the gratitude of royalists and the animosity of ancient constitutionalists, Polydore raised doubts about the regular presence of the Commons before 1116. In his opinion, "kings before that date were used not to consult the assembly of the people or only to do so very occasionally; so that one may correctly attribute its establishment to Henry – and so thoroughly was it established that its foundations stand firm even to this day."[31]

Although the question of parliament's early composition took on intense and sustained ideological significance only in the early seventeenth century, Polydore's dating encountered pointed criticism from Tudor and early Stuart antiquaries. Neither his high opinion of parliament nor his acknowledgment that early kings occasionally summoned the Commons made up for what many considered his dismissive attitude toward the lower house. William Fleetwood, noted common lawyer and member of the Society of Antiquaries, referred to the Italian's "magnificent error," while fellow members Francis Tate and Sir John Dodderidge described him as "much deceived." Their colleague Sir Henry Spelman dismissed some of Polydore's historical views on the ground that, as a mere "alien in our commonwealth," he was not well schooled in English antiquities.[32] Still, notwithstanding the criticism that later writers directed at Vergil, much of his account of early English history reinforced the foundation of ancient constitutionalism: both the common law and parliament were immemorial, dating from beyond the Normans and descending to the people of sixteenth-century England.

Readers who disputed Vergil's chronology of parliamentary development had only to turn to those Tudor writers who found full parliaments, complete with a House of Commons, meeting regularly before the Norman conquest as well as after. Thus, John Hardyng

---

[31] Polydore Vergil, *Historia Angliae*, p. 188. Hay, *Polydore Vergil: Renaissance Historian and Man of Letters*, p. 137. E. Evans, "Of the Antiquity of Parliaments in England: Some Elizabethan and Early Stuart Opinions," *History* 23 (1938), 206–7.

[32] Fleetwood, An historicall and Legall discourse upon a case taken out of the 26: des: Pla: 60 (1575). B.L. Stowe MS 423. fo. 133v. Dodderidge, The several opinions of . . . Antiquaries touching the Antiquitie . . . of the high court of Parliament in England. B.L. Add. MS 48. 102A. fo. 7. Spelman, "Of the Antiquity and Etymology of Terms and Times for Administration of Justice," in *A Collection of Curious Discourses Written By eminent Antiquaries upon several Heads in Our English Antiquities*, ed. T. Hearne (London, 1775), vol. II, pp. 343–4, 369.

suggested that such a parliament was present even before the Roman invasion, and he believed that it continued to meet throughout the British, Saxon, and Norman periods.[33] Other chroniclers wrote generally of pre-Norman parliaments but without commenting on their precise composition. Fabyan, for example, noted that Cnut called a parliament at Oxford and that the Confessor, too, held a parliament in which he outlawed Godwin and his sons.[34]

FOXE'S *ACTS AND MONUMENTS* AND HOLINSHED'S *CHRONICLES*

The success of the above works notwithstanding, the ancient constitutionalist gospel received its most powerful enunciation in two of the most celebrated and widely read histories of the early modern era – the great chronicle associated with the name of Raphael Holinshed and John Foxe's best-selling *Acts and Monuments*. Serving as major conduits through which ancient constitutionalist tales penetrated Stuart political life, these works were deployed by parliamentarians, republicans, and whigs throughout the century of revolution. More than this. One of the sources, Foxe's *Acts and Monuments*, bestowed upon Stuart dissidents a full-blown theory of resistance constructed squarely upon St. Edward's laws. Although Protestant writers such as John Ponet, John Knox, and Christopher Goodman contributed significantly to the effort, Foxe's preeminence in the radicalization of St. Edward's laws stands uncontested. After all, in a work considered second only to the Bible in popularity, he interpreted St. Edward's laws, and Chapter 17 in particular, as sanctioning rebellion against an unjust ruler. No contemporary had ever gone this far. Indeed, earlier in the Tudor century the idea embedded in Chapter 17 was more likely to be used to champion kings than to denigrate them. By presenting St. Edward's laws in this glaring new light, and by drawing attention to their most radical implications, Foxe re-historicized the Confessor and helped transform the cult of his kingship into the cult of his laws. This is a fact of the greatest importance, for the most difficult ideological task faced by Stuart rebels was that of convincing the nation of the legality of

---

[33] *The Chronicle of Jhon [sic] Hardyng* (London, 1543), pp. xxxiii, cxii, cxix. However, Hardyng described William as obtaining the throne by "conquest" and "victory without title of right."

[34] Fabyan, *The New Chronicles of England and France*, pp. 217, 226.

resistance, deposition, and regicide. To have the "proper" interpretation of one of their chief polemical weapons handed to them by a
Protestant historian and hero of the first order was almost too good
to be true.

The story of Foxe's re-interpretation of Chapter 17 is a complex
one, requiring an extended telling. It is itself part of a much larger
scenario involving the Reformation and Counter-Reformation and
the religious wars that these movements occasioned. The story
begins with the successes of the Catholic Counter-Reformation,
which had by mid-century recaptured the thrones in England and
Scotland and threatened to silence Protestant voices on the continent. Faced with a resurgence of Catholic power, Protestant
polemicists began to re-think the doctrine of non-resistance as
preached by Luther and Calvin. The result of their efforts was the
articulation of a theory that not only justified the withholding of
allegiance from Catholic princes but also sanctioned the use of force
against them.[35]

Protestants in England and Scotland played a particularly critical
role in the development of this new line of thought, contributing
arguments that helped radicalize early modern political theory. They
began with the Lutheran and Calvinist belief that human magistracy
was of divine origin. According to Luther and Calvin, because God
had ordained rulers to govern, subjection to them was absolute. This
was the meaning of St. Paul's injunction in Romans 13:1: "Let every
soul be subject unto the higher powers. For there is no power but of
God: the powers that be are ordained of God." Although Luther
and Calvin had flirted with the notion that inferior magistrates, who
were also ordained of God, might in some circumstances resist
tyrants, they never completely abandoned their devotion to the
Pauline doctrine of non-resistance.

However, as Protestant fortunes declined in the 1550s, theorists
drew the conclusion from which Luther and Calvin had shrunk:
since God could not be conceived of as condoning evil, the proper
office of a king was to do only good. Therefore, a ruler who governed

[35] This discussion is based on Quentin Skinner, *The Foundations of Modern Political Thought*
(Cambridge, 1978), vol. II, pp. 189–238. See also Francis Oakley, "Christian Obedience and
Authority, 1520–1550," in *The Cambridge History of Political Thought, 1450–1700*, ed. J. H.
Burns and Mark Goldie (Cambridge, 1991), pp. 159–92; Robert M. Kingdon, "Calvinism
and Resistance Theory, 1550–1580," in *ibid.*, pp. 193–214. See also James H. Burns, *The
True Law of Kingship. Concepts of Monarchy in Early Modern Scotland* (Oxford, 1996), chapter 4
and Conclusion.

contrary to God's will – that is, a Catholic king – could not possibly be ordained of God. Such a king, in fact, unkinged himself. In Christopher Goodman's words, the ruler who abandoned his godly office became "a felonious private citizen" whom both the people and their elected representatives must resist. Indeed, God himself "gives the sword" into their hands.[36] Nor was this duty to resist merely theoretical, for history brimmed with examples of its implementation. Thus John Ponet, in a chapter entitled "Whether it be lawfull to depose an evil governor, and kill a tyrant," noted that both Edward II and Richard II had been dispatched because they ruled contrary to God's ordinance. Moreover, popes themselves had sanctioned such behavior. Witness, Ponet continued, how Pope Zacharius had deposed Childeric, king of France, "because he was said to be a lecherous person, and an unprofitable governor of the realm: and forced him to be a monk, and made Pipine (father of Charles) king of France."[37]

But while Ponet, Knox, and Goodman proved immensely serviceable in the Protestant cause, none of them gained a firm and conspicuous foothold in parliamentarian and whig political thought. None of the three appealed to the cult of the Confessor's laws, and two of them – Goodman and Knox – were probably too closely associated with Scotland for English comfort. Instead, parliamentarians and whigs turned to Foxe's much more popular and easily accessible *Acts and Monuments*.[38] This massive work, running to more than a thousand pages, was the premier chronicle of the English Reformation. More clearly than any other early modern treatise, it demonstrated the wedding of religion, politics, nationalism, and history. A measure of its influence can be found in its publication history throughout the sixteenth and seventeenth centuries. Intended

---

[36] Goodman, *How Superior Powers Oght to be Obeyd* (Geneva, 1558, published by the Facsimile Text Society, New York, 1931), pp. 184–5. See also pp. 60, 110, 149–50, 166–7, 185, 187–90. A proclamation of Phillip and Mary ordered that any "rebel" found with this work in his possession was to be executed. Robert Steele, ed., *A Bibliography of Royal Proclamations of the Tudor and Stuart Sovereigns* (Oxford, 1910), no. 488. See also John Knox, "The First Blast of the Trumpet Against the Monstrous Regiment of Women," in *Works of John Knox; Collected and Edited by David Laing* (New York, 1966), vol. IV, pp. 399, 413–16. This work was first published in 1558.

[37] Ponet, *A Short Treatise of Politic Power* (Menston, Yorkshire, 1970), pp. Giii–iii[v]. The work was published in 1556.

[38] See, for example, William Prynne, *The Soveraigne Power of Parliaments and Kingdomes* (London, 1643), pp. 6, 94, and *passim*; *A Collection of the Rights and Priviledges of Parliament* (London, 1642), pp. 4–5; *Vox Popupli: Or the Peoples Humble discovery of Their own Loyaltie, And His Majesties ungrounded Iealousies* (London, 1642).

as a polemic against the Catholic Mary Tudor, from whose persecutions Foxe had sought refuge on the continent, the work was first published in Latin in 1554 and 1559. It appeared in an English version in 1563, and in 1570 in an expanded and corrected version entitled *The Ecclesiasticall history contaynyng the Actes and Monumentes of thynges passed in every kynges tyme in this Realme . . . from the primitive tyme till the reigne of K. Henry VIII.* Other editions followed in 1576, 1583, and 1596, with the last becoming known as *The Book of Martyrs.* Still further versions appeared in 1610, 1631–32, 1641 and 1684, and abridgments and excerpts were published in 1576, 1589, 1598, 1615, 1651, 1676, and 1677. By the late seventeenth century, as many as ten thousand copies had probably been sold. Foxe's work became even more widely available when Convocation ordered that the corrected edition of 1570 be placed in all cathedral churches. In addition, many parish churches owned copies, and local clergymen read it aloud from the pulpit and recommended its purchase to their parishioners. Indeed, so great was the work's popularity that in many Protestant households it constituted the sole authority for church history, providing an arsenal of arguments with which to protect Protestantism against Rome.[39] Nor was the influence of *Acts and Monuments* limited to the British shores, Christopher Hill noting that all East India ships sailed with copies of both the Bible and Foxe's work.[40]

In writing *Acts and Monuments*, Foxe aimed at nothing less than convincing the English people of their historical uniqueness: because they had preserved the pure religion longer than any other nation, they deserved credit for the Reformation, the continued success of which rested squarely on their shoulders.[41] Recognizing the necessity

---

[39] McKisack, *Medieval History in the Tudor Age*, pp. 113–15. William Haller, *Foxe's Book of Martyrs and the Elect Nation* (London, 1963), especially pp. 110–86. O'Day, *Education and Society in Britain, 1500–1800* (London, 1982), pp. 9–24. Patrick Collinson, "Truth and Legend: the Veracity of John Foxe's *Book of Martyrs*," in *Clio's Mirror: Historiography in Britain and the Netherlands*, ed. A. C. Duke and C. A. Tamse (Zutphen, 1985), pp. 31–54. Collinson, "Truth, Lies, and Fiction in Sixteenth-Century Protestant Historiography," in *The Historical Imagination in Early Modern Britain. History, Rhetoric, and Fiction, 1500–1800*, ed. Donald R. Kelley and David Harris Sacks (Cambridge, 1997), pp. 37–68. Christopher Hill, "The First Century of the Church in England," in *Collected Essays*, vol. ii *Religion and Politics in Seventeenth Century England* (Hassocks and Amhurst, 1986). Paul Christianson, *Reformers and Babylon: English Apocalyptic Visions from the Reformation to the Eve of the Civil War* (Toronto, 1978). Catherine Firth, *The Apocalyptic Tradition in Reformation Britain, 1530–1645* (Oxford, 1979).

[40] Hill, *The English Bible and the Seventeenth-Century Revolution* (London, 1993), p. 18.

[41] O'Day, *The Debate on the English Reformation*, pp. 16–26. Levy, *Tudor Historical Thought*, pp. 98–101.

of grounding the English church firmly in the nation's history, Foxe constructed a narrative that was thoroughly ancient constitutionalist as well as Protestant in nature. In his telling, the origins of both secular and ecclesiastical institutions lay in the early English past. Foxe's account became especially trenchant in the editions published after he returned from exile. In the 1570 version of *Acts and Monuments*, which, as previously noted, was sent throughout the country, he included material not present in all earlier editions. This was Chapter 17 of St. Edward's laws, which he knew from the fourth London redaction. Playing a particularly vital role in his Protestant narrative, this chapter appeared in its entirety and for the first time in English. Equally noteworthy, Foxe discussed the chapter in the context of William I's broken promises to abide by St. Edward's laws and linked it to Saxon rebellions. In so doing he transformed Chapter 17 from a support of imperial kingship, which form it had taken during the Henrician Reformation, into a convincing historical justification for resistance.

The explanation for this addition to the 1570 version of *Acts and Monuments* probably lies in the crisis of the Elizabethan succession, when the plots to bring the Catholic Mary Queen of Scots to the throne threatened Protestant fortunes. By inserting this most critical section of St. Edward's laws, Foxe invited his readers to look favorably upon the deposition of rulers who had fallen from the straight and narrow path of Protestantism and the ancient law. Monarchs who so behaved lost the very name of king and thereby deposed themselves. This truth, he implied, should reassure those who feared a Catholic coup every bit as much as it had comforted the Saxons who rebelled against William the Conqueror. Because Foxe's words reached the widest possible audience in late sixteenth- and seventeenth-century England, and because they had such special resonance for Stuart radicals, I will discuss his treatment at length.

After listing the Saxon rulers from the fifth century down to the reign of Edward the Confessor, Foxe described early English laws in the usual fashion, crediting Edward the Confessor with compiling from the various laws of the realm "one universal and common law for all people." "So just, so equal, and so serving the public profit and wealth of all estates" were these laws that the people deemed them worth fighting for. Indeed, when rulers abrogated St. Edward's laws "the people did long after rebel . . . to have the same laws again . . ."

However, their rebellions did not always meet with permanent success. A case in point was the reign of William the Conqueror, who first at his coronation and then on other occasions "did swear and practice the same good laws of Edward, for the common laws of this realm." Thus the Saxon laws survived the Norman conquest, at least for a time. However, after William had secured his new kingdom "he foreswore himself, and placed his own laws in their room, much worse and obscurer than the other were."[42]

So far Foxe's account contained nothing new or startling. Both medieval and other Tudor chroniclers had written exactly the same thing. But at this point he departed from the usual story line. Immediately on the heels of his description of William's perjury, Foxe inserted Chapter 17 of St. Edward's laws. This he then linked to the coronation oath, the reciprocal promises made by king and people, and finally to the possibility of armed resistance should a king fail to do his duty. As Foxe put it, "notwithstanding" William's perjury,

among the said laws of Edward . . . this I find among the ancient records of the Guildhall in London; The office of a King, with such other appurtenances as belong to the realm of Britain set forth and described in the Latin style; which I thought here not unmeet to be expressed in the English tongue, for them that understood no Latin. The tenor and meaning whereof thus followeth.

The king, because he is the vicar of the highest king, is appointed for this purpose, to rule the earthly kingdom, and the Lord's people, and above all things to reverence his holy church . . . which unless he do, the name of a king agreeth not unto him, but he loseth the name of a king . . .

To this Foxe added the story of the pope, Pepin, and Childeric.[43]

In all likelihood, contemporaries understood the meaning of associating William's failure to abide by his oath with the fate that befell kings who refused to live up to the terms of their office. But Foxe did not let the matter rest there. He shared with his readers the rest of the Confessor's words from Chapter 17:

A king, saith he, ought above all things to fear God, to love and to observe his commandments, and cause them to be observed through his whole kingdom. He ought also to keep, cherish, maintain and govern the holy church within his kingdom, with all integrity and liberty, according to the

---

[42] Foxe, *The First Volume of the Ecclesiasticall history contaynyng the Actes and Monumentes of thynges passed in every kynges tyme in this Realme* (London, 1570), pp. 215–16.

[43] *Ibid.*, p. 216.

constitutions of his ancestors and predecessors, and to defend the same . . . He ought also to set up good laws and customs, such as be wholesome and approved: such as be otherwise, to repeal them, and thrust them out of his kingdom.[44]

Lest his readers miss the point, Foxe reminded them that these words formed part of the coronation oath to which kings swore before they were crowned. Returning once again to the story of William's promise and perjury, he emphasized the reciprocal nature of the coronation ceremony, noting that only after kings had sworn to abide by their office did subjects give their allegiance. Importantly, he implied that a breach of the coronation oath could result in the use of popular force. In his words, "After the duty and office of princes thus descried, consequently followeth the institution of subjects, declared in many good and necessary ordinances very requisite and convenient for public government. *Of which laws William Conqueror was compelled through the clamor of the people to take some* . . . [emphasis added]."

William did not, however, keep his promises. "Contrary to his own oath at his coronation," he omitted some of these laws, "inserting and placing the most of his own laws in his language, to serve his purpose: which as yet to this present day in the Norman language do remain."[45] Moreover, William changed "the whole state of the governance of this commonwealth; and obtained new laws, at his own pleasure, profitable to himself, but grievous and hurtful to the people, abolishing the laws of King Edward, whereunto notwithstanding he was sworn before, to observe and maintain them." Thus, the Normans "conquered and altered the whole realm after their own purpose."[46]

But this was by no means the end of Foxe's story, for the English declined once again to give the conqueror his due. Refusing to acquiesce to Norman rule, they raised "great commotions and rebellions . . . (as histories record) to have the said laws of King Edward revived again."[47] These laws, Foxe continued, found renewed life after the death of William Rufus in 1100, first when Henry I "reduced again King Edward's laws, with emendation thereof," and then during the anarchy of Stephen and Matilda, when the Londoners "made great suit" to the Empress Matilda "to have and to use again Saint Edward's laws." Upon her refusal, they

---

[44] *Ibid.*, p. 216. [45] *Ibid.*, p. 216. [46] *Ibid.*, pp. 216–17. [47] *Ibid.*, pp. 221–2.

and the men of Kent joined King Stephen.[48] Finally, Foxe described how King John promised that the church could enjoy the privileges granted to it by St. Edward.[49] In the end, St. Edward's laws triumphed because the Saxons exercised their right to resist kings who failed to fulfill their holy office. This meant that the conquerors were themselves conquered.

Although any interpretation of these portions of *Acts and Monuments* must be tentative, I suggest that Foxe intended his readers to connect Saxon resistance in general and St. Edward's laws in particular with resistance against unjust and ungodly rulers such as Mary Queen of Scots. But, as the Henrician Reformation had demonstrated, the sentiments embodied in Chapter 17 were nothing if not malleable. Indeed, they proved equally valuable after the threat to Elizabeth had waned, since in the case of godly, that is, Protestant rulers, Chapter 17 could just as easily be interpreted as commanding absolute obedience. St. Edward's laws were truly laws for all seasons.

The *Chronicles* associated with Holinshed proved almost as valuable as Foxe's momentous history. As Annabel Patterson demonstrates, the work offered a provocatively political and Protestant reading of English history, one in which parliament, and the House of Commons in particular, possessed a well-founded ancient right to control over-mighty sovereigns. The target might well have been Elizabeth I herself, who could govern as oppressively as her father when she deemed it necessary.[50] The *Chronicles* carries its own complex history. As Patterson notes, Holinshed himself served as major editor and compiler of the 1577 work, while the edition of 1587 was the effort of Abraham Fleming, William Harrison, Francis Thynne, John Stow, and John Hooker alias Vowell. Thus, the *Chronicles* can be seen as "a giant interdisciplinary project" that resulted from the collaborative work of a syndicate consisting of "free-lance antiquarians, lesser clergymen, members of parliament with legal training, minor poets, publishers and booksellers."[51]

In one sense, however, it is somewhat surprising that the *Chronicles* should prove so attractive to Stuart radicals, since the work some-

---

[48] *Ibid.*, p. 260.   [49] *Ibid.*, pp. 326–7.

[50] Patterson, *Reading Holinshed's Chronicles*. The following discussion is largely based on Patterson's work.

[51] *Ibid.*, pp. vii–viii. Abraham Fleming also helped with the edition of 1577. The work will be referred to as Holinshed's *Chronicles* despite its multiple authorship. See also Cynthia Susan Clegg, *Press Censorship in Elizabethan England* (Cambridge, 1997).

times depicted William as an outright conqueror who treated the English and their laws with great severity. For example, Holinshed wrote that William "seized into his hands most part of every man's possessions, causing them to redeem the same at his hands again, and yet retained a property in the most of them; so that those should afterwards enjoy them, should acknowledge themselves to hold them of him." Then, "abrogating in manner all the ancient laws used in times past, and instituted by the former kings for the good order and quietness of the people, he made new, nothing so equal or easy to be kept; which nevertheless those that came after (not without their great harm) were constrained to observe."[52] Indeed, "so cruelly bent" were the Normans on "our utter subversion and overthrow, that in the beginning it was less reproach to be accounted a slave than an Englishman, or a drudge in any filthy business than a Briton."[53] As for parliament, Holinshed followed Polydore Vergil, suggesting that before the reign of Henry I "the kings of England used but seldom to call together the states of the realm after any certain manner or general kind of process, to have their consents in matters to be decreed."[54]

But other accounts of the English past lurked within the multitudinous pages of the *Chronicles*. Added in 1587, this material reinforced the story line essential to Stuart ancient constitutionalists. There was, for example, a version of the *Modus tenendi Parliamentum* included in the new edition of Holinshed. Its pages would have exposed generations of readers to an account of the high authority of parliament, especially the House of Commons, and to the survival of this institution after 1066.[55] Moreover, both editions included the stories of King Lucius, Pope Eleutherius, Pepin, and Childeric, which carried the message of Chapter 17 of St. Edward's laws.[56]

Equally pertinent were the *Chronicles*' stories of Saxon strength and determination which ultimately conquered the conquerors. According to Holinshed, on numerous occasions the English, refusing to bend to the Norman sword, launched "mutinies and rebellions for the retaining of St. Edward's laws," later "called the common laws."

---

[52] Holinshed, *Chronicles* (1587/1807), vol. II, pp. 13, 52. Patterson notes that this passage was added in 1587.

[53] *Ibid.* (1587/1807), vol. I, p. 13.

[54] *Ibid.*, vol. II, p. 65.

[55] Patterson, *Reading Holinshed's Chronicles*, pp. 124–6.

[56] Holinshed, *Chronicles* (1587/1807), vol. I, pp. 511–12. *Ibid.* (1577), vol. I, p. 74.

First came William's capitulation to the men of Swanscombe Down, who compelled him to enter into a covenant with them.[57] Then came the rebellion of 1072, when Edwin and Morcar raised a great army against him. Realizing that the Saxons "would never cease to molest him in the recovery of their liberties," the Conqueror once again promised to "thenceforth observe and keep the good and ancient approved laws of the realm, which the noble kings of England his ancestors had made, and ordained heretofore, but namely those of S. Edward, which were supposed to be the most equal and indifferent." In so doing William recognized the strength of his enemies, "whose power without doubt so long as it was united could not possibly be overcome as he thought."[58]

And so it went with the Conqueror's successors, who, whenever "they sought to purchase the people's favor," promised "to abolish the laws ordained by their father, [and to] establish other more equal, and restore those which were used in S. Edward's days." Indeed, this "kind of purchasing favor was used" regularly in Norman and Angevin England.[59] Witness, Holinshed directed, the confirmation of Henry I in his Charter of Liberties. Here the 1587 edition made a slight but telling alteration: it omitted the words in which Henry I swore to abide by the Confessor's laws with his father's "emendations." This substantive deletion removed from the Charter any mention of legal changes enacted by the Conqueror and so seemed to expunge entirely the stain of conquest. And, of course, it was precisely Henry I's promise that King Stephen, Henry II, and King John swore to abide by.[60]

Continuing his story, Holinshed wrote that the Normans, having learned their lesson, "fell in with a desire to see by what rule the state of the land was governed in time of the Saxons." That accomplished, "they not only commended their manner of regiment, but also admitted a great part of their laws (now current under the name of S. Edward's laws, and used as principles and grounds)."[61]

---

[57] *Ibid.* (1587/1807), vol. I, pp. 747–8, vol. II, pp. 1–3. *Ibid.* (1577), vol. I, pp. 290–1.
[58] *Ibid.* (1587/1807), vol. II, pp. 15–16. *Ibid.* (1577), vol. I, p. 306.
[59] *Ibid.* (1587/1807), vol. II, pp. 13–14. *Ibid.* (1577), vol. I, p. 304.
[60] *Ibid.* (1587/1807), vol. II, pp. 47–8, 91–3. *Ibid.* (1577), vol. II, pp. 336–7.
[61] *Ibid.* (1587/1807), vol. I, p. 298. It was added in 1587. In addition to the common law, the *Chronicles* noted that other legal institutions dated from the Saxon period. For example, feudal wardship and marriage existed in Edward the Confessor's reign, as did a free woman's right to her dower estate upon her husband's death. These institutions, too, descended to Tudor England. *Ibid.* (1587/1807), vol. I, p. 206. *Ibid.* (1577), vol. I, p. 44.

Thus, the common law, which consisted of "practice confirmed by long experience," was "fetched even from the course of most ancient laws made far before the conquest, and thereto the deepest reach and foundations of reason, are ruled and adjudged for law."[62]

Holinshed's accounts of the origins of French influence in England also suited seventeenth-century ancient constitutionalists. Far from ascribing this phenomenon entirely to the Norman conquerors, the 1587 edition of the *Chronicles* properly credited Emma and Edward the Confessor, thus diminishing once again the effects of 1066. In this view, "the first footing that ever the French did set in this island, since the time of Ethelbert and Sigebert, was with Emma, which lady brought over a train of French gentlemen and ladies with her into England."[63] Later the Confessor himself returned from his exile with "diverse Normans . . . which in time of his banishment had showed him great friendship." Moreover, so "bewitched [was] the Confessor with their lying and boasting" that he elevated them "to the greatest offices in the realm," thereby reinforcing the French in "their lordly and outrageous demeanor" and "kindl[ing] the stomachs of the English nobility against them . . . "[64] Here was a ready and convincing retort to those seventeenth-century royalists who pointed to the Norman conquest as the means by which the French influence entered England.

The *Chronicles* also presented the "proper" view of the title by which William I governed England. In addition to describing him as ruling by "plain conquest," Holinshed depicted the king as the lawful successor of his kinsman, Edward the Confessor. Because the Confessor and his subjects distrusted Harold Godwinson, the king demised the crown in his will to the duke of Normandy and his heirs, who were, after all, his blood relatives. This made William "heir by title, and not by conquest, albeit that mistrust of other titles, and partly for the glory of his victory, he challenged in the end, the name of conqueror, and hath been so written ever since the time of his arrival."[65] In other words, William only pretended to rule by title of conquest; in point of fact, he took the throne as the lawful and legitimate successor of his cousin, Edward the Confessor.

---

[62] *Ibid.* (1587/1807), vol. I, p. 303. This, too, was added in 1587. See also "The Preface to the Reader," *Chronicles*, 1587/1806, vol. II.

[63] *Ibid.* (1587/1807), vol. I, p. 12.

[64] *Ibid.*, vol. I, pp. 12, 747. See also Stow, *The Annales of England*, p. 123.

[65] Holinshed, *Chronicles* (1587/1807), vol. I, p. 206. *Ibid.* (1577), vol. I, p. 44.

When the time came, rebels would have ready at hand both Foxe and Holinshed with which to justify their causes. Throughout these much-read pages were the stories of Pepin and the pope, the Lucius–Eleutherius correspondence, and Chapter 17 of St. Edward's laws. All told how a king who violated his office by ruling in an ungodly and unjust fashion lost the name of king. This early modern Englishmen had on the word of two ancient kings, one British and one Saxon, and two bishops of Rome.

THE SOCIETY OF ANTIQUARIES AND ANCIENT CONSTITUTIONALIST THOUGHT

If Tudor chroniclers disseminated ancient constitutionalist tales to a general reading public, members of the Society of Antiquaries guaranteed their acceptance among those interested in history, politics, and law. Founded around 1586 by William Camden, a master of Westminster, and his pupil Robert Cotton, this organization devoted itself to historical study until 1607, when its inquiries into the origins of parliament earned the enmity of James I. Attempts to revive the Society in 1614 failed, this time the king taking "a little mislike" to the group because he feared it would meddle in matters of state.[66] By then, however, some of the most respected and erudite lawyers and scholars of early modern England had placed their seal of approval on the ideas and literature supporting the ancient constitution. In their various writings, parliamentarians and whigs would find ample evidence of an immemorial parliament and common law which descended from the Saxon period, or earlier, down to their own day and age. Here, too, they would find unequivocal depictions of Norman acquiescence to Saxon laws and institutions.[67]

The founding of the Society of Antiquaries owed much to the appearance of Camden's *Britannia*, though Patterson adds that the publication of Holinshed's *Chronicles* might just as easily have served as catalyst. Camden's work, first published in 1586, was a chorogra-

---

[66] Sir Henry Spelman, *The English Works of Sir Henry Spelman, Kt. Published in his Life-Time; Together with his Posthumous Works, Relating to the Laws and Antiquities of England; First Publish'd by the Present Lord Bishop of Lincoln, in the Year 1695* (London, 1723), vol. IV, pp. 69–70.

[67] Linda van Norden, "Sir Henry Spelman on the Chronology of the Elizabethan College of Antiquaries," *Huntington Library Quarterly* 13 (1949–50), 131–60. McKisack, *Medieval History in the Tudor Age*, chapter 7. Sharpe, *Sir Robert Cotton*, chapter 1. Parry, *The Trophies of Time*, pp. 43–4 and *passim*.

phical study based on the author's numerous fact-finding trips to various parts of the island. Immensely influential, *Britannia* went through numerous editions and printings, appearing in Latin in 1586, 1587, 1590, 1594, 1600, and in 1607, and in English in 1610, 1637, and 1695. Camden followed this work with *Remains concerning Britain*, published in 1605, 1615, and 1623.[68]

In addition to earning the patronage of Lord Burleigh and Queen Elizabeth herself, Camden's scholarship placed him at the center of a group of men who admired his skills and shared his interests.[69] As mentioned earlier, included among the membership of the Society of Antiquaries were Arthur Agarde, William Lord Compton, Sir John Davies, Sir John Dodderidge, William Fleetwood, William Hakewill, Michael Heneage, Joseph Holland, William Lambarde, Sir James Ley, Sir Henry Spelman, Francis Tate, Francis Thynne, and Sir James Whitelocke. Nor were the members of the Society cloistered intellectuals with the luxury to indulge a quaint interest in the past. Many worked in the legal profession, and a number achieved positions of political prominence. Thus, Davies served as attorney-general of Ireland, while Dodderidge sat on King's Bench. Ley achieved the position of chief justice of King's Bench. Hakewill served as a master of Chancery and solicitor general. Other members held political office. Fleetwood, Tate, Ley, and Compton, for example, sat in the House of Commons, while Fleetwood also served as recorder of London, and Compton sat as a member of the privy council.[70]

The Society especially benefited from the association of antiquaries who worked actively in governmental records and archives. Agarde, for example, spent decades in the Elizabethan Exchequer, eventually becoming deputy-chamberlain; and Heneage served for more than twenty years as keeper of the records in the Tower.

---

[68] Patterson, *Reading Holinshed's Chronicles*, p. 100. See also Parry, *Trophies of Time*, chapter 1. Derek Hirst suggests that Camden wrote *Britannia*, as well as the *Annals*, "in reaction to the providentialism beloved of John Foxe." *Authority and Conflict. England, 1603–1658* (Cambridge, Mass., 1986), p. 88.

[69] McKisack, *Medieval History in the Tudor Age*, pp. 150–4. Levy, *Tudor Historical Thought*, pp. 148–61, 165, 190–1, 223. Sharpe, *Sir Robert Cotton*, pp. 11–12, 13, 17–47, 84–6, 95–109, 196–8. Stan A. E. Mendyk, *"Speculum Britanniae." Regional Study, Antiquarianism, and Science in Britain to 1700* (Toronto, 1989), pp. 23–4, 49–55, 57–8. Parry, *The Trophies of Time*, pp. 22–48.

[70] McKisack, *Medieval History in the Tudor Age*, pp. 66–8, 78. Evans, *A History of the Society of Antiquaries*, pp. 6–13. Parry, *The Trophies of Time*, pp. 5, 19, 43–4, 72–3, 105, 114, 209–10, 217, 363–4.

Lambarde, too, had ready access to archives, serving Elizabeth as keeper of the records at the Rolls Chapel and keeper of the records at the Tower. Dethick and Thynne were heralds, and in 1597 Camden himself became Clarenceau Knight of Arms.[71]

Given the overwhelming proportion of common lawyers who participated in the Society, some might be tempted to dismiss it as representing the narrow and esoteric interests of the over-specialized legal mind. But as the above description of the members' credentials indicates, nothing could be further from the truth. The reach of common lawyers was long and deep in the early modern period, when the Inns of Court constituted a third university, and many gentlemen spent time studying common law. To examine the views of the antiquaries is, then, to tap some of the broadest and most cultivated scholarly minds of the late sixteenth and early seventeenth centuries. As Graham Parry puts it, "they had a power over the past, for they were able to determine what parts of it were vital and should be held in respectful attention; they were judges of what was authentic and what was fabulous."[72]

The Elizabethan antiquaries worked from a number of published and unpublished sources. Cotton's library proved particularly useful, providing the usual medieval chronicles as well as various other collections of Saxon laws, the *Modus tenendi Parliamentum*, and the *Mirror of Justices*. Camden, Agarde, Lambarde, Stow, and Thynne also collected manuscripts that circulated among the members, while Fleetwood, Holland, Thynne, and Tate amassed collections of manuscripts, charters, and coins. In addition, the Elizabethan antiquaries had at their disposal a growing number of recently published sources, including Matthew Paris, William of Malmesbury, and Henry of Huntingdon, as well as Savile's editions of Hoveden, Knighton, and Ingulf. They also relied heavily on Lambarde's *Archaionomia*.

Members of the Society of Antiquaries made full use of this abundant array of medieval works, diligently plumbing their depths for stories of the English past. These sources formed the basis of the papers which members wrote for presentation at their bi-weekly meetings in London. Many of the papers presented in the years from the late 1580s to 1603 have survived, providing a precious glimpse

---

[71] McKisack, *Medieval History in the Tudor Age*, pp. 78–9, 85. Parry, *The Trophies of Time*, pp. 43–4.

[72] *Ibid.*, pp. 15–16.

into how some of the greatest scholars of the Elizabethan and early Stuart age viewed their national past.[73] Of utmost significance is the sturdy thread of ancient constitutionalism that runs through their historical reconstructions. Whatever the topic under discussion, most members made clear their belief in the immemorial nature of English law and legal institutions and their continuity from Saxon times, if not earlier, to the present. Importantly, by confronting the issue and meaning of the Norman conquest more directly than any earlier group of writers, the antiquaries laid much of the groundwork for later ideological disputes. Indeed, they articulated the very arguments that radical ancient constitutionalists later directed at the Stuart kings.

It is not entirely clear why the antiquaries wrote so pointedly about 1066. Perhaps their intense and explicit interest in the origins of English institutions necessarily focused their attention on the Norman invasion. Then, too, they wrote in the shadow of Arthur Hall's case, a messy dispute over the origins of parliament. Revolving around parliamentary privilege, the conflict involved Hall, a member of the House of Commons in the parliament of 1576. He had attracted attention when he wrote a tract justifying his attempt to save his servant from arrest during a parliamentary session. In pleading his case, Hall attacked the immemorial nature of the lower house, describing it as "a new person in the trinity." Indeed, he wrote, the first knights and burgesses were summoned only in the reign of Edward III. All earlier assemblies, such as that called by William the Conqueror in 1070 for the purpose of confirming St. Edward's laws, consisted only of the nobility and those learned in the law. The composition of parliament should occasion no surprise, since, Hall reminded his readers, "great conquerors do not commonly grant such large freedoms to subjects, to have interest with them in their commonwealth, neither yet do bind themselves to so hard extremes, to establish nothing without the consent of the other two estates." The house which he disparaged did not take kindly to his words. After excoriating his work as "dangerous and lewd," the Commons voted to disable him and send him to the Tower.[74] Hall's

---

[73] The Society of Antiquaries met some thirty-eight times from November 27, 1590 to June 21, 1607. Apparently no meetings took place during 1598 and 1599, when London was threatened by the plague. Evans, *A History of the Society of Antiquaries*, p. 10.

[74] *A letter sent by F. A. touchying the proceedings in a private quarell and unkindnesse, betweene Arthur Hall, and Melchisedech Mallerie Gentlemen, to his very friende L. B. being in Italie. With an admonition to the*

"libel" provoked heated controversy, and contemporaries, including members of the Society of Antiquaries, criticized his views throughout the early modern period.

But stimulus for the antiquaries' interest in 1066 could just as easily have been the controversy over the succession. As Queen Elizabeth approached the end of her life, the identity of her successor understandably became a matter of great concern. The most likely candidate was her cousin James Stuart, who, as King James VI, governed the kingdom of Scotland.[75] At Elizabeth's death in 1603, James did indeed succeed. Not content to unite the crowns of the two kingdoms in his person, he launched a campaign to bring about a full and complete union. As the next chapter will discuss, the debates over the proposed union of England and Scotland brought the matter of conquest sharply to the fore. This focus followed from the fact that contemporaries on both sides of the border viewed title by conquest as the only theory capable of uniting two independent and sovereign kingdoms. At that time, several members of the Society of Antiquaries contributed tracts aimed at protecting English law from the incursions of Scottish civil law.

Although the most extensive debates over union occurred after James I rode south, the matter of the succession received a preliminary airing in the late sixteenth century. During its last decade, in an atmosphere heavily influenced by Reformation and Counter-Reformation polemics, contemporaries discussed the advantages and disadvantages of having a Stuart and a Protestant on the throne of England. In some of these discussions, the issue of conquest in general and the Norman conquest in particular arose.[76] James VI himself may have focused attention on conquest theory when, in *The Trew Law of Free Monarchies* (1598), he put forward an absolutist view

---

Father of F. A. to him being a Burgesse of the Parliament, for his better behavior therein (1579), "Admonition." The case is discussed in G. R. Elton, "Arthur Hall, Lord Burghley and the Antiquity of Parliament," in *Studies in Tudor and Stuart Government and Politics* (Cambridge, 1983), vol. III, pp. 254–73; J. E. Neale, *Elizabeth I and Her Parliaments, 1559–1581* (London, 1953), pp. 407–10; H. G. Wright, *The Life and Works of Arthur Hall of Grantham, Member of Parliament, Courtier, and first Translator of Homer into English* (London, 1919), pp. 68–75.

[75] For the history of the succession in the early modern period see Howard Nenner, *The Right to be King. The Succession to the Crown of England 1603–1714* (Chapel Hill, 1995), chapters 1–3.

[76] See, for example, Robert Parsons, *A Conference About the Next Succession to the Crowne of England* (London, 1594), pt. 2, chapter 2, p. 12. Parsons was a Jesuit who wrote under the name R. Doleman. He used ancient constitutionalist arguments in order to prove that William was no conqueror but reigned instead by consent. He attacked the proposed union from this position, opposing it because the union of two Protestant nations would have harmed the Catholic cause.

of kingship that included a pointed reference to conquest. Noting that in all free monarchies kings shared their sovereignty with no earthly institutions, James cited as one of his proofs the early history of England. In his words, "when the bastard of Normandy came into England, and made himself king, was it not by force, and with a mighty army? Where he gave the law, and took none, changed the laws, inverted the order of government" was it not by conquest? Indeed, the English "laws, which to this day they are ruled by, are written in his language, and not in theirs."[77]

These words in praise of conquest and an absolute sovereignty vested in kings cannot have escaped the attention of the antiquaries, whose readings of medieval records ran in a different direction. In the late sixteenth and early seventeenth centuries members of the Society countered such arguments with unequivocally ancient constitutionalist views of 1066, parliament, and the common law. William Hakewill, for one, gave a paper entitled "The Antiquity of the Laws of the Island." He first considered "the ancient grounds, from whence they have been derived"; and, second, "the long time, during which they have been used by the same state or kingdom." Citing sources such as Matthew Paris and "that most famous monument of antiquity," the *Textus Roffensis*, he concluded that English law was ancient on both counts: not only did it agree "with the written law of God, the law of primary reason, and the old laws of Greece (of all laws human the most ancient in very many points,)" but it was also of "long continuance within this island."[78]

For Hakewill, the antiquity of English law was perfectly compatible with the fact that the island had been conquered several times, in particular by the Romans, the Saxons, and the Danes. Indeed, "so absolute and victorious" was the Saxon conquest that many of their laws, as collected by Edward the Confessor, remained "extant among us at this day."[79] For proof that these institutions "were used here in England before the conquest of the Normans," Hakewill turned to Henry I's Charter of Liberties, where, as "all the

<hr/>

[77] "The Trew Law of Free Monarchies," in *King James VI and I. Political Writings*, ed. Johann P. Sommerville (Cambridge, 1994), p. 74. See also Burns, *The True Law of Kingship*, chapters 7 and 8.

[78] *A Collection of Curious Discourses*, ed. Hearne, vol. 1, p. 1. These papers were published later in 1657, 1671, and 1679. *The Several Opinions of sundry Antiquaries*, in *The Antiquity and Power of Parliaments in England. Written by Mr. Justice Doddridge and several other Learned Divines* (London, 1671).

[79] *A Collection of Curious Discourses*, ed. Hearne, vol. 1, pp. 4–6.

writers agree," that king "did again restore the laws of Edward the Confessor." Admittedly, the Normans had altered Saxon laws, but only slightly. "So," Hakewill concluded, "I am of opinion, (wherein nevertheless I do always submit me to better judgment) that the British laws were altered by the Romans; theirs by the Saxons; and theirs again much altered by the Danes, which mingled with some points of the Saxon law, and fewer of the Norman law, is the common law now is use."[80] In other words, the common law of his own day and age was a melange, of which Norman law constituted but a lesser part.

For Sir John Dodderidge, a justice of King's Bench, the antiquity of the common law and parliament went hand-in-hand. Thus, "the ancient laws of the Britains, which (to the honor of our common laws) have their use to this day, were composed in their common counsels." Indeed, even the Druids held parliaments. Although the Roman conquest eclipsed British institutions, the Saxons resumed the practice of making law in parliament, and the Danes followed suit. Moreover, although these assemblies were called by different names in the reigns of Ine, Alfred, Cnut, and Edward the Confessor, they nevertheless possessed "all the parts of our parliaments," including the Commons.[81]

Nor, according to Dodderidge, did the Normans significantly alter the structure of government. As for the common law, William I himself confirmed the laws of St. Edward. Parliament, too, found life after 1066. This was true despite the fact that William I and William Rufus held parliaments without the Commons. In Dodderidge's words, the first two Normans "reigned with their swords in their hands, absolutely of themselves; not admitting the former general assemblies of the states, but permitting only provincial synods of the clergy for compounding of the ecclesiastical causes." Then, with a nod to the doctrine of prescription, Dodderidge noted that the assembly of clergy "sat as precedents" and thus kept the full institution alive. From this he drew a significant conclusion: "the Conqueror himself did not challenge to himself so absolute a conquest, but summoned to himself the English nobility as well as those learned in the law" to teach him about the Saxon laws, which he then confirmed. Further, William II also called not only the "archbishops, bishops, etc. but *procerum Regni, Londini Palatio Regis*" –

---

[80] *Ibid.*, vol. 1, p. 7.   [81] *Ibid.*, vol. 1, pp. 283–6.

by which term Dodderidge meant the representatives of the kingdom.[82] This evidence led him to conclude that Polydore Vergil erred when he wrote that only in 1116 did a full parliament assemble for the first time. Although Dodderidge admitted that "the Commons were not called" in the wake of the conquest, the interruption was only temporary. In no way did it compromise his conclusion that "the great antiquity of this high court delivered . . . from before the Romans; but never so dignified, as since Queen Elizabeth's time."[83]

Dodderidge then introduced the *Modus tenendi Parliamentum* as proof of his position. Discussing its contents in detail, he highlighted precisely those sections that parliamentarians and whigs later cherished. According to the *Modus*, the Commons was the essential element of any parliament. Indeed, the king could hold a parliament with only the Commons, "for there was a parliament before there was any barons." However, "if the Commons do not appear, there can be no parliament, though all the great peers of the realm were present with the king: for the proctors, knights, citizens, and burgesses of the realm do represent the whole commons of the realm; but the great peers of the realm are present only for themselves, and for no others." Nor, Dodderidge continued from the *Modus*, could the king dissolve parliament "as long as any bill remains undiscussed," for such an action amounted to perjury. Further, he described the process by which, in cases of disagreement, a council of twenty-five, most from the Commons, could steadily reduce their number until only one was left to treat with the king.[84]

Arthur Agarde and Francis Tate expressed similar views. Agarde, for example, noted the existence of Saxon parliaments containing not only the great men of the kingdom but *omni populi* as well. And he found William I and his successors continuing the practice of summoning full parliaments.[85] Tate affirmed Dodderidge's judgment that William "challenged not so absolute a conquest of this land" because he ruled with parliament. He also agreed that Polydore was "much deceived" in his description of the composition of early parliaments. However, Tate pointed out that even the Italian scholar had admitted that kings sometimes consulted the Commons before

---

[82] *Ibid.*, vol. 1, pp. 283–6.
[83] *Ibid.*, vol. 1, pp. 286–7, 289.
[84] *Ibid.*, vol. 1, pp. 291–2.
[85] *Ibid.*, vol. 1, p. 297. *The Antiquity and Power of Parliaments in England*, pp. 40–54.

the reign of Henry I, and, as far as he himself was concerned, the practice had been typical in all times. At this point Tate introduced Hall's case, suggesting an explanation for the M.P.'s error concerning the history of parliament. In words that found echoes in seventeenth-century ancient constitutionalist thought, he suggested that Hall had misunderstood the meaning of words used in medieval records, assuming, for example, that "barons" and "magnates" included only the great men of the kingdom. But, Tate insisted, this was not so, for, as Hoveden had noted, "the word *magnate* comprehended the people."[86]

Camden, too, found full parliaments before the Norman conquest. He held to this position despite the fact that the "ancientest summons" he had seen dated from 49 Henry III, that is, 1265. He further acknowledged that there was "no certainty" in the assembling of the estates until the reign of King John. He admitted, too, that William I and William Rufus "reigned with their swords in their hands, absolutely of themselves," and that they refused to hold assemblies of state. But, like Dodderidge, Camden believed that the provincial synods of the clergy served "nevertheless, as precedents." And his reading of Hoveden and Ingulf supported the claim that William I himself made laws "by the counsels of the barons . . . nobles and *sapientes*, and *sua lega eruditos*," that is, wisemen and those learned in the law.[87]

Camden further discussed these issues in his *Britannia*. On the one hand, he credited William the Conqueror with "an insolent and bloody victory" and "a notable alteration and change . . . in the kingdom of England." He also noted that as a "trophy for this conquest" William "abrogated some part of the positive laws of England, brought in some customs of Normandy, and by virtue of a decree commanded, That all causes should be pleaded in the French tongue." Moroever, Camden told how William dispossessed the English of their lands, which he then gave to his own followers. On the other hand, the passage that immediately followed gave heart to radical ancient constitutionalists. Noting that William now undertook "to govern the state by excellent laws," Camden, citing Gervase of Tilbury and Ingulf, told how the king ordered that "all the laws of England" be laid before him. After rejecting some, he

---

[86] *Ibid.*, pp. 59–73. *A Collection of Curious Discourses*, ed. Hearne, vol. I, pp. 302–3, vol. II, p. 78.
[87] *Ibid.*, vol. I, pp. 304, 306. *The Antiquity and Power of Parliaments in England*, pp. 74–80.

allowed others, adding those of Normandy to the mix. Moreover, Camden reiterated his belief that parliament had existed in Saxon England, where it was known as the witanagemot, or assembly of the wise.[88]

Equally useful for ancient constitutionalist purposes was Camden's account of William's coronation, where he laid claim to his new kingdom not by conquest but "by God's providence appointed, and by virtue of a gift from his lord and cousin King Edward the Glorious granted."[89] Further, Camden found the origins of French influence not in conquest but in St. Edward's taste for all things French. In his words,

Many approved customs, laws, manners, fashions, and phrases have the English always borrowed of their neighbors the French, especially since the time of Edward the Confessor, who resided long in France, and is charged by some historians of his time, to have returned from thence wholly Frenchified; than by the Norman conquest which immediately ensued.[90]

Other antiquaries, for example, Agarde, Tate, and Hakewill, agreed, Hakewill writing that Edward "brought into this land sundry of the Norman laws (as one who had been brought up in Normandy)."[91]

Finally, Camden took Polydore Vergil to task for crediting the Normans with introducing trial by jury. "Nothing," Camden wrote, "is more false," since the laws of Ethelred had provided for precisely such an institution.[92] Thus, on the vital matter of legal continuity, Camden remained on what Stuart ancient constitutionalists considered the side of the angels: Saxon laws and legal institutions survived 1066 intact.

Despite his later writings on the introduction of feudal tenures in 1066, Sir Henry Spelman's papers to the Society of Antiquaries reinforced a critical part of the ancient constitutionalist story. Thus, when he wrote about the history of the law terms he cited St. Edward's laws as proof that they had existed in Saxon England. He

---

[88] Camden, *Britain*, trans. Philemon Holland (London, 1610), pp. 152–3. See also Camden's remarks in *A Collection of Curious Discourses*, ed. Hearne, vol. I, pp. 152–3, 177.

[89] Camden, *Britain*, pp. 145–6.

[90] Camden, *Remains concerning Britain*, ed. R. D. Dunn (Toronto, 1984), p. 139. The *Remains* was published in 1605, 1614, and 1623. Dunn used the 1605 edition as the basic text, incorporating Camden's revisions and additions from the two later editions.

[91] *A Collection of Curious Discourses*, ed. Hearne, vol. I, pp. 7, 173, vol. II, p. 309. See also Lambarde, *A Perambulation of Kent: Containing the Description, Hystorie, and Customes of that Shire* (London, 1576), p. 318.

[92] Camden, *Britain*, p. 153.

took particular issue with Polydore Vergil, that "alien in our commonwealth," who falsely credited the Normans with their origin. Nor did the Normans change the dates of the terms, for "this constitution of Edward the Confessor was, amongst his other laws," confirmed by William the Conqueror as the *Leges Edwardi Confessoris* stated. His successors Henry I, King Stephen, and Henry II did the same.[93]

Finally there was William Lambarde, legal antiquary *extraordinaire*, whose scholarly efforts Queen Elizabeth rewarded with appointment as keeper of the Tower records. Although I have not found any papers that he gave at Society meetings, his views on the early history of English institutions appeared in several works written during the period – *Archaionomia, Archeion,* and the *Perambulation of Kent*. The result of a lifetime of study in Saxon sources, these treatises, in and of themselves, carried all the evidence necessary to sustain the basic tenets of ancient constitutionalism. Lambarde's research convinced him that the most vital of Tudor institutions – the common law and parliament – enjoyed a history that stretched back at least as far as the Saxon period. *Archaionomia* itself stood as proof positive of a common law that existed long before and after the Normans arrived. Here, in the preeminent work of the sixteenth-century Saxonist revival, Englishmen could read for themselves the laws of St. Edward and his various predecessors. Here, too, they could find the prologue in which William I, after "acquiring" England, called together members of the Saxon community to confirm the laws of St. Edward. If this were not enough, they could peruse the alleged correspondence between King Lucius and Pope Eleutherius.[94] As for the events of 1066, Lambarde told in his *Perambulation of Kent* how William himself reviewed the Saxon laws, kept some, altered others, and imposed the Norman language on the entire realm. He also included the story of the men of Kent and their victorious confrontation with William at Swanscombe Downs. Appearing in 1570, 1576, 1596, and by 1640 in a fourth edition, this work in and of itself would have familiarized generations of Englishmen with just the "right" stories.[95]

---

[93] Spelman, *A Collection of Curious Discourses*, ed. Hearne, vol. II, pp. 343–4, 369. Spelman wrote this paper in 1604.

[94] For early Saxon laws, such as those of Ine, Alfred, Ethelred, and Cnut see *Archaionomia*, fos. 1–123. The correspondence between King Lucius and Pope Eleutherius is in fos. 131–31ᵛ.

[95] *A Perambulation of Kent*, pp. 5, 22–3, 318, 390.

In *Archeion, or, a Discourse upon the High Courts of Justice in England*, Lambarde continued to show his indelible Saxon colors. Although not printed until 1635, *Archeion* was completed by the early 1590s. Not surprisingly, the work located the origins of parliament in the Saxon period, even though Lambarde agreed with Polydore Vergil that the word "parliament" entered with the Normans and was first used in the reign of Henry I. Still, Lambarde well understood that the institution itself was much older. As the *Modus tenendi Parliamentum* proved, it had existed in Saxon England, where it was called synoth, micle, micel-gemot, witena-gemot, and "*commune concilium regni*, the common council of the realm." As for the composition of the body, it contained all of the "nobility and commons . . . or wisemen."[96]

Lambarde's Saxonist inclinations did not prevent him from viewing William I as a conqueror of sorts. Thus, he noted that during the reigns of both William and his son Rufus "the ordinary course of justice was greatly disturbed, as well by reason of the intestine and foreign wars, as also because that these two princes governed by a mere and absolute power, as in a realm obtained by conquest." But Lambarde would also have been aware of the prescriptive power of the many Saxon rebellions. He recognized, too, that the courts, including the high court of parliament, persevered, albeit "put to silence for a season." And, finally, he believed that they "had continuance afterwards, and do yet (as they may) bear life amongst us."[97]

Thanks to Lambarde, members of the Society of Antiquaries were also familiar with the idea contained in Chapters 11 and 17 of *Archaionomia*. At least this seems to be a reasonable inference from the fact that Dethick, Camden, and Hakewill cited the correspondence between Lucius and the pope in which the notion was expressed.[98] Members also commented upon the relationship between English and Norman law. Although they recognized the similarities between the two legal systems, they typically turned to explanations other than conquest to account for them. Hakewill and Spelman, for example, directed attention to the Scandinavian influence, which long preceded the arrival of William the Conqueror. Indeed, in Hakewill's words, "the great affinity of our laws with the

---

[96] Lambarde, *Archeion or, a Discourse upon the High Court of Justice in England*, ed. Charles H. McIlwain and Paul L. Ward (Cambridge, Mass., 1957), pp. 124–5, 128–32.
[97] *Ibid.*, p. 17.
[98] *A Collection of Curious Discourses*, ed. Hearne, vol. II, pp. 165, 167, 170–1.

customs of Normandy" stemmed from the Danish invasion. The Danes, by introducing trial by jury, tenures, wardship, dower of a third part, and descent by primogeniture "achieved the agreement of our common law with the law of Denmark in fundamental points, wherein it differeth from the laws of all the world else."[99] Spelman concurred, noting that England and France descended from a single heritage. In his words, because "the Western nations are for the most part deduced from the Germans, so in ancient times there was a great agreement and affinity in their laws." Indeed, Spelman even reversed the flow of influence, suggesting that the Norman had "received the customs of . . . his country from . . . ours, by the hand of Edward the Confessor, as in the beginning of their old customary, themselves do acknowledge" – a conclusion that would have made good sense to contemporaries.[100]

Of course not all sources lent themselves to an ancient constitutionalist interpretation. Indeed, certain Tudor writers presented a picture of the Normans as conquering the land entirely and completely, omitting all mention of the saving grace of St. Edward's laws. The Elizabethan Richard Crompton, for one, wrote in this vein,[101] as did the anonymous author of "A Discourse of the Lawes of England." As expressed in this latter tract, "the common law is that which the last conqueror planted, and is called a law of necessity, for that the people were forced to receive it before this *Arbitria principu[m] pro Legibus habebantur.*"[102] Moreover, even those sources that acknowledged the long stream of royal confirmations of Saxon laws admitted of more than one interpretation. Thus, in the late seventeenth-century the royalists Robert Brady and William Dugdale viewed the many and varied confirmations of St. Edward's laws as evidence of an absolute kingship, not as support for an independent parliament and common law. Indeed, to them the drumbeat of confirmations signaled that kings themselves made law, although they agreed of their own free will and volition to do so in consultation with the kingdom.

But, as the subsequent chapters will show, their particular reading of English history never quite caught fire. Too much of the medieval

---

[99] *A Collection of Curious Discourses*, ed. Hearne, vol. I, p. 7.
[100] *Ibid.*, vol. II, pp. 343–4, 369.
[101] Richard Crompton, *The Mansion of Magnanimitie* ([London], 1599), pages unnumbered.
[102] "The Course of the Lawes of England and the abuses of the ministers thereof, laid open." B.L. Add. MSS 41. 616. fo. 81ᵛ.

and Tudor literature confirmed the central premises of seventeenth-century ancient constitutionalism: although William I introduced some alterations, he achieved at most a temporary and incomplete interruption of Saxon laws and legal institutions. Indeed, historical evidence amply demonstrated that he himself preserved ancient customs and practices, both voluntarily and under compulsion. Thus, Saxon institutions survived 1066 essentially intact and descended directly to the people of early modern England. The credit for this continuity lay both with Saxon rebels, who refused to give in, and with Norman kings, who admitted defeat or curried favor by continually confirming St. Edward's laws. That kings made these promises with crossed fingers mattered far less, both to contemporaries and future generations, than that they made them at all.

CHAPTER 4

"By lex terrae is meant the laws of St. Edward the Confessor": the footprints of the Saxons in the early seventeenth century

INTRODUCTION

The ancient constitutionalist vision of the past and the sources upon which it rested continued to be nourished by early seventeenth-century chroniclers, antiquaries, and the most erudite scholars of the era. Indeed, according to Glenn Burgess, this was the heyday of the ancient constitution.[1] Occasionally, to be sure, writers differed as to whether it originated with the Britons or the Saxons, or whether each and every institution of Stuart government began in antiquity. Still, many learned Englishmen traced the essentials of their polity to the pre-1066 period, and many insisted that these survived the conquest intact as a result of consecutive royal promises. Their differences appear, then, as mere variations upon the theme of historical continuity from pre-conquest times to the seventeenth century.

Moreover, during the early Stuart period the ancient constitutionalist version of the past retained its plasticity. As in the middle ages and Tudor period, it was used to justify different, even antithetical, political ends. Indeed, so malleable was the ancient constitution of the pre-civil war period that it could accommodate a belief in divine right monarchy as well as a reverence for an immemorial parliament and common law. In Derek Hirst's words, the early modern mind was capable of conceiving "of both a sovereign king and a sovereign common law," of both "absolute royal prerogatives and absolute rights to property."[2] The ease with which it did so is apparent in the writings of the oracle of the common law, Sir Edward Coke. His enthusiastic, indeed hyperbolic, praise of the ancient constitution

---

[1] Burgess, *The Politics of the Ancient Constitution* (University Park, Pa., 1992), pp. 117–19, 212.
[2] Hirst, *Authority and Conflict. England, 1603–1658* (Cambridge, Mass., 1986), p. 87.

also included descriptions of England as an "absolute monarchy" ruled by a king who was "the only supreme governor" empowered "immediately of almighty God" – a position he occupied not only by divine command but according to the ancient laws of the realm. Sir John Davies can be read to the same effect. Further, Coke and Davies, like other common lawyers, readily acknowledged that the king possessed a discretionary power which allowed him to dispense with parliamentary statutes when he deemed it necessary for the welfare of the kingdom.[3]

However, in the early decades of the century cracks appeared in the ancient constitutionalist facade. Despite widespread agreement about the nature of royal power and the proper relationship between the king and his parliament, the political nation began to quarrel about the legality of certain royal policies. Especially provocative were James I's proposed union of Scotland and England and his and his son's attempts to raise money in extra-parliamentary ways. With both supporters and opponents of these policies looking to their own national history for polemical inspiration, a battle for control of the past began. The struggle focused increasingly on the meanings and implications of the ancient constitution in general and St. Edward's laws in particular. The playing field was not, however, an even one. The lessons and tales carried by St. Edward's laws, the *Modus tenendi Parliamentum*, and the *Mirror of Justices* provided a more effective ideological cover for dissidents than for supporters of the monarchy.

No contemporary went so far as to interpret the medieval sources as sanctioning resistance. This drastic step came only in 1642. Still, the nascent politicization of the ancient constitution in these early years gave the three texts valuable publicity and familiarized later generations with their ideological possibilities. Of the three, the Confessor's laws turned out to carry an especially explosive payload, and their successful launching at this time did much to transform a cult of kingship into a cult of law. This chapter seeks to illuminate the increasingly long shadow of St. Edward's laws, as well as the ideological potential of the *Modus* and the *Mirror*, in the early decades of the seventeenth century. First, I will examine the political

---

[3] Coke, *Caudrey's Case, The Fifth Part of the Reports of Sir Edward Coke* (London, 1826), pp. 8b, 10a, 21a, 39b, 40b. *Magdalen College Case, Eleventh Part of the Reports of Sir Edward Coke* (London, 1826), p. 72a. *The Third Part of the Institutes of the Laws of England*, ed. Francis Hargrave (London, 1797), p. 18. *Case of Non Obstante, The Twelfth Part of the Reports of Sir Edward Coke* (London, 1826), p. 18. Davies, *The Question concerning Impositions* (London, 1656), pp. 30–2.

atmosphere in which the battle for the past initially began, that is, the controversy over the union of the two kingdoms. Next, I will explore the early seventeenth-century historical and scholarly literature that kept the ancient constitutionalist version of history front and center. Finally, I will deal with the legal and parliamentary disputes that fueled the battle for the English past.

The following discussion takes place within an historiographical framework articulated by the so-called revisionists and their critics. The revisionist "school" emerged as a reaction against the views put forward in the late nineteenth century by Samuel R. Gardiner.[4] Gardiner had interpreted the period from 1603 to 1640 as one in which an increasingly aggressive House of Commons led the fight for English liberties as against an aggrandizing Stuart monarchy, which, if left to its own devices, would have instituted an absolutist form of government.

Turning Gardiner's whiggish account on its head, revisionists constructed a very different reading of the early Stuart century. In this view, James I and Charles I emerge as progressive monarchs who promoted change in the face of tradition-bound, backward-looking factions concerned primarily with their own selfish interests and local politics. Although certain political and religious issues led to the occasional disagreement, no dispute proved sufficiently disruptive to cause a deep and long-lasting fissure in the body politic. Indeed, during most of their reigns, James I and Charles I worked well with various elements in parliament, with whom they shared common goals and political principles. True, Charles I later dissipated much of the trust which the political nation placed in him. But even then he might have ridden out the storm had it not been for the crisis of the three kingdoms which forced upon him the necessity of raising an army to deal with Catholics in Ireland and Presbyterians in Scotland. And it was over the control of the militia that the nation finally went to war in 1642. Thus, in Geoffrey Elton's much-quoted phrase, there was no "high road" to civil war, and no long-term causes for the taking up of arms against Charles I. In this view, the history of the early Stuart century reads as one of consensus, not conflict.[5]

---

[4] Gardiner, *History of England from the Accession of James I to the Outbreak of the Civil War, 1603–1642* (10 vols., New York, 1908).

[5] See G. R. Elton, "A High Road to Civil War?," in *Studies in Tudor and Stuart Politics and Government* (Cambridge, 1974), vol. II, pp. 164–82; Elton, "The Stuart Century," in *ibid.*,

This reinterpretation has contributed much to our understanding of the period. We now know, for example, that the House of Lords played a role at least as significant as the Commons in parliamentary politics and probably more so. We have also learned that much that transpired in these years can be understood only by taking account of the ties between the center and the localities. Indeed, so compellingly have the revisionists rewritten early Stuart history that they themselves occupy the historiographical mainstream. But despite, or rather because of, their notable success, this interpretation has itself fallen under attack from scholars who think it goes too far. "Post-revisionists" urge that the civil wars of the 1640s did indeed have origins that stretched back into the century. Moreover, included among these origins were matters relating to political principle and ideology.[6] My treatment of early seventeenth-century England falls within the post-revisionist camp and supports its findings.

THE PROPOSED UNION OF THE TWO KINGDOMS AND THE CONTROVERSY OVER THE MEANING OF THE NORMAN CONQUEST

The great utility of St. Edward's laws, the *Modus*, and the *Mirror* became apparent very early in James I's reign, when he launched his

pp. 155–63; Conrad Russell, "Parliament in Perspective, 1604–1629," *History* 51 (1976), 1–27; Russell, *Parliaments and English Politics 1621–1629* (Oxford, 1979); Russell's essays reprinted in *Unrevolutionary England, 1603–1642* (London, 1990); Kevin Sharpe, "Introduction: Parliamentary History In or Out of Perspective?," in *Faction and Parliament: Essays on Early Stuart History*, ed. Kevin Sharpe (Oxford, 1978), pp. 1–42; J. S. Morrill, *The Revolt of the Provinces* (London, 1980); Morrill, *The Nature of the English Revolution* (New York, 1993); Mark Kishlansky, "The Emergence of Adversary Politics in the Long Parliament," *Journal of Modern History* 49 (1977), 617–40. For general analyses of the historiography of the period see Ann Hughes, *The Causes of the English Civil War* (London, 1991); Richard Cust and Ann Hughes, "Introduction: After Revisionism," in *Conflict in Early Stuart England: Studies in Religion and Politics 1603–1642*, ed. Cust and Hughes (London, 1989); R. C. Richardson, *The Debate on the English Revolution Revisited*, 2nd. edn. (London, 1988); Howard Tomlinson, ed., *Before the English Civil War* (London, 1983).

[6] Hirst, "Revisionism Revised: the Place of Principle," *Past and Present* 92 (1981), 79–102. T. K. Rabb, "Revisionism Revised: Two Perspectives on Early Stuart Parliamentary History," *ibid.*, 55–78. Rabb, *Jacobean Gentleman. Sir Edwin Sandys, 1561–1629* (Princeton, 1998). J. H. Hexter, "The Early Stuarts and Parliament: Old Hat and *Nouvelle Vague*," *Parliamentary History* 1 (1981), 181–215. Hughes, *The Causes of the English Civil War*. Cust and Hughes, eds., *Conflict in Early Stuart England*. Christopher Hill, "Parliament and People in Seventeenth-Century England," *Past and Present* 92 (1981), 100–24. Lawrence Stone, *The Causes of the English Revolution 1529–1642* (London, 1972). Linda Popofsky, "The Crisis over Tonnage and Poundage in Parliament in 1629," *Past and Present* 126 (1990), 44–75. Thomas Cogswell, *The Blessed Revolution* (Cambridge, 1989). Johann P. Sommerville, *Politics and Ideology in England, 1603–1640* (London, 1986).

plan to unify the two kingdoms. Coloring the political atmosphere of the first decade of the century, the campaigns for and against unification depended heavily on the early histories of Scotland and England. James I himself fired the first salvo by calling on the image of St. Edward to increase his legitimacy in his new kingdom. Presenting himself as a latter-day Edward the Confessor, a ruler of mixed blood who governed justly, James added to the Great Seal the arms of St. Edward and Cadwaldr, the last two uncontested rulers of Saxon England and Celtic Britain. As Bruce Galloway has written, this move symbolized his recognition that "a union of hearts and minds" was essential to the success of his cause.[7] Moreover, records of James's coronation noted his use of St. Edward's scepter, his wearing of St. Edward's crown and robes, and his pre-ceremonial preparations in St. Edward's chapel.[8] Such public displays of devotion to the Saxon past remind us that the cult of the Confessor continued to have a hold on the English nation, especially where the matter of political legitimacy was concerned.

All in all, James I's initial moves were shrewd ones, given that English fears of an inundation of Scottish civil law constituted a major impediment to his plan. Indeed, he could not have found better ways to alleviate this threat than by evoking the image of the very founder of English common law. The new Great Seal and the coronation ceremony broadcast in a most public and official way that the new king intended to honor the ancient laws of his new kingdom. Still, these bows to St. Edward could not in and of themselves counteract the negative forces which the plan for unification unleashed. By provoking numerous inquiries into the English past, the project interjected the general issue of conquest into political debate and, in so doing, forced Englishmen to hone their arguments about the constitutional effects of the Norman conquest. Indeed, for the first time the nature and consequences of that event became a matter of protracted and heated political debate.

This assertion contradicts the views of those modern scholars who suggest that only in the 1620s, 1640s, or 1680s did the meaning of 1066 emerge as a topic of controversy, and who further assert that it was not until the civil war that Englishmen reasoned from a Norman

[7] Galloway, *The Union of England and Scotland 1603–1608* (Edinburgh, 1986), pp. 16, 49. See also *Historical Manuscripts Commission, Salisbury Manuscripts* (London, 1930), vol. xv, p. 69.

[8] John Nichols, *The Progresses, and Public Processions, of Queen Elizabeth . . . to Which are subjoined some of the Early Progresses of King James* (London, 1705), vol. iii, pp. 35–9.

conquest to Stuart absolutism.[9] In my view, however, the matter needs to be reexamined in light of the debates over union with Scotland. This literature suggests that the political meaning of 1066 stood at the center of the controversy between unionists and their opponents. Moreover, the whole tenor of debate, both within and without the parliament at Westminster, strongly hints that contemporaries themselves made a link between a conquest in 1066 and royal absolutism in the early seventeenth century. In fact, English anti-unionists often assumed as a matter of course that if William I had conquered Saxon laws, both he and his Stuart successors reigned as absolute monarchs.

The story of the proposed union of Scotland and England has been well told by James Burns, Bruce Galloway, Brian Levack, Roger Mason, and Jenny Wormald, with Annabel Patterson and Daniel Woolf elucidating its role in early seventeenth-century drama and historiography.[10] From the very beginning prospects for union were poor, since James faced dogged opposition from both sides of the border. The Scots, for their part, feared that union would leave their country at the mercy of the English parliament and destroy Scottish sovereignty, an apprehension fueled by James I's talk of making Scotland "be as Wales was."[11] Then there was the English propensity, bordering on racism, to view the Scots and all things Scottish as inherently inferior. Indeed, the English claimed that this lowly position was formalized in law when Scottish kings did homage to their English counterparts, as in the case of Malcolm and Edward the Confessor. For many Scots, then, James's proposal for union threatened to bring the very subordination that their neighbors to the south had failed to achieve through the centuries, though not for want of trying.[12]

---

[9] See, for example, Brooks and Sharpe, "History, English Law and the Renaissance," *Past and Present* 72 (1976), 133–42; Skinner, "History and Ideology in the English Revolution," pp. 151–78; Pocock, *The Ancient Constitution and the Feudal Law,* pp. 282–3.

[10] Burns, *The True Law of Kingship. Concepts of Monarchy in Early-Modern Scotland* (Oxford, 1996), chapter 8. Galloway, *The Union of Scotland and England, 1603–1608.* Levack, *The Formation of the British State* (Oxford, 1987). Mason, "Imagining Scotland: Scottish Political Thought and the Problem of Britain 1560–1650," in *Scots and Britons. British Political Thought and the Union of 1603,* ed. Roger A. Mason (Cambridge, 1994), pp. 3–13. Wormald, "The Union of 1603," in *ibid.,* pp. 17–40. Patterson, *Censorship and Interpretation. The Conditions of Writing and Reading in Early Modern England* (Madison, Wis., 1990), pp. 58–73. Woolf, *The Idea of History in Early Stuart England* (Toronto, 1990), pp. 55–64.

[11] *Political Works of James I,* ed. C. H. McIlwain (Cambridge, Mass., 1918), p. 202. Levack, *The Formation of the British State,* p. 34.

[12] See, for example, Roger A. Mason, "Scotching the Brut: Politics, History and National

English anti-unionists also feared for their constitution. In particular, they dreaded the prospect of a supreme Scotland, whose civil law would first contaminate and eventually eclipse their most precious legal institutions. Such a consequence followed inevitably if a Scottish king and his Scottish favorites governed in the interests of their native country. James's initial rush to appoint Scots to positions of power in England fed this fear and, equally troublesome, raised the specter of an expansion of the royal prerogative. Rebuffing parliamentary attempts to circumscribe his authority, James claimed an unlimited power to naturalize his fellow countrymen for service in his government. As Levack notes, here "in concrete form was an illustration of the fear expressed in the Form of Apology and Satisfaction of 1604, that 'the prerogatives of princes may easily and do daily grow.' "[13]

Closely connected to English trepidations about an expanding royal prerogative was concern over the political principle by which the union was to be legitimized. Many anti-unionists warned that a theory of conquest constituted the only means of justifying a new British kingdom consisting of two sovereign and independent nations. Even the creation of a new name – Great Britain – raised the specter of conquest theory. In the words of the House of Commons committee charged with examining prospects for unification, "we find no precedent, at home or abroad, of uniting or contracting the names of two several kingdoms or states into one name, where the union hath grown by marriage or blood; and that those examples which may be alleged, as far as we can find, are but in the case of conquest." But if conquest constituted the sole authority by which the union of the two kingdoms could be achieved, then a frightening conclusion ineluctably followed: England was " 'a kingdom conquered, and then may the king add

Myth in Sixteenth-Century Britain," in *Scotland and England 1286–1815*, ed. Roger A. Mason (Edinburgh, 1987), pp. 60–84; Mason, "The Scottish Reformation and the Origins of Anglo-British Imperialism," in *Scots and Britains*, ed. Mason, pp. 161–86; Wormald, "The Union of 1603," *ibid.*, pp. 224–30; Wormald, "The Creation of Britain: Multiple Kingdoms or Core and Colonies," *Transactions of the Royal Historical Society*, 6th series, 2 (1992), 179–80.

[13] These fears also surfaced in 1607, when parliament debated the naturalization clauses of the Instrument of Union of 1604. James I had permitted an addition to the Instrument limiting the service of Scots in the judiciary and the English parliament until the union was achieved. He insisted, however, on a saving of the royal prerogative that allowed him to make denizations and appointments at his pleasure. Levack, *The Formation of the British State*, pp. 36–8.

and alter laws at his own pleasure.' "[14] Thus, according to many
members of parliament, the proposed union threatened to introduce
royal absolutism into the English government.

Given James I's propensity for describing the union in the
language of conquest, they had cause for concern, as did the Scots.
As noted in the previous chapter, before coming to the English
throne James had made clear his affinity for conquest theory.[15]
Moreover, in 1607 he told the parliament at Westminster to think of
the union with Scotland "as if you had got it by conquest, but such a
conquest as may be cemented by love, the only sure bond of
subjection or friendship: that as there is over both but *unus Rex*, so
there may be in both but *unus Grex* and *una Lex*." England and its
parliament, he continued, "are to be the husband, they the wife; you
conquerors, they as conquered." It mattered little that the conquest
was to be "not by the sword, but by the sweet and sure bond."[16]
English fears appeared the more credible when unionists such as Sir
John Hayward, Sir Thomas Craig, and Edward Ayscu defended
James's proposal in language that struck at the heart of ancient
constitutionalism. In pleading the cause of unification, they attempted to show the essential similarity of English and Scottish law.
At first sight, this line of reasoning made sense. However, at the
heart of their argument stood the claim that the affinity of the two
legal systems stemmed from a Norman conquest which obliterated
both Saxon and Scottish legal institutions. Not surprisingly, this
tactic, far from assuaging English fears, actually heightened them. It
could hardly have been otherwise, given that the picture presented
by many unionists directed attention to a flawed and discontinuous

[14] Quoted in *ibid.*, p. 38. See also Conrad Russell, "English Parliaments 1593–1606: One
Epoch or Two?," in *The Parliaments of Elizabethan England*, ed. D. M. Dean and N. L. Jones
(Oxford, 1990), pp. 207–13. Although unionist tracts often mentioned conquest in general
and the Norman conquest in particular, writers typically denied that the union of Scotland
would be accomplished in that way. See, for example, Sir Henry Savile, "Historical
Collections," in Galloway and Levack, *The Jacobean Union*, p. 196; Sir John Dodderidge, "A
Breif Consideracion of the Unyon," in *ibid.*, p. 150; Sir Henry Spelman, "Of the Union," in
ibid., p. 165.

[15] For a discussion of James I's commitment to an absolutist form of government see Burns,
The True Law of Kingship: Concepts of Monarchy in Early Modern Scotland (Oxford, 1996), chapters
7 and 8 *passim*; Johann P. Sommerville, ed., *King James VI and I. Political Writings* (Cambridge,
1994), "Introduction" and *passim*; Sommerville, "English and European Political Ideas in
the Early Seventeenth Century: Revisionism and the Case of Absolutism," *Journal of British
Studies* 35 (1996), 168–94.

[16] *Political Works of James I*, ed. McIlwain, pp. 292, 294. Levack, *The Formation of the British State*,
p. 27. Linda Levy Peck, "Kingship, Counsel and Law in Early Stuart Britain," in *The
Varieties of British Political Thought, 1500–1800* (Cambridge, 1993), pp. 84–7.

English history. Sir John Hayward, for example, wrote several unionist tracts in which he took aim at the ancient constitutionalist version of the English past. Trained as a civilian, he enjoyed the patronage of Thomas Howard, earl of Arundel, as well as the king himself. He also served as tutor to Prince Henry. His words, then, likely reflected opinions at court and carried great weight.

Hayward wrote in response to the English Jesuit Robert Parsons, who opposed union because the uniting of two Protestant kingdoms would impede the progress of the Counter-Reformation. Arguing against James VI's indefeasible right to inherit the English throne, Parsons launched an attack based squarely on the ancient constitutionalist version of history. English history, he claimed, demonstrated that kings were often elected by their people, with whom they therefore enjoyed a contractual agreement. William I was a case in point. Here Parsons took special aim at conquest theory. Noting that William's confirmations of St. Edward's laws proved that there was none, he pointed to Chapter 17 to demonstrate that subjects owed allegiance to their rulers only so long as kings governed well. The story of Childeric and Pepin, which he knew from this chapter, nailed the point down.[17]

Hayward responded with a withering attack on the ancient constitutionalist view of 1066. Although he knew that some Englishmen believed "that the laws of England were never changed since the time of Brutus," not by the Romans, the Saxons, the Danes, or the Normans, such "hyperbolical praises" of the common law were "now out of season."[18] In fact, William I "came to the Crown by dint of sword," abrogating St. Edward's laws which he replaced with new laws written in a new language. In conquest, then, "we find of the beginning of laws." Not only did the common law derive from the Norman sword, so, too, did parliament, Henry I calling the first such assembly at Salisbury in 1116.[19]

Interestingly and understandably, when Parsons and Hayward wrote later under different circumstances, they deployed different arguments. Proving that the ancient constitutionalist version of

---

[17] Parsons, *A Conference about the Next Succession to the Crowne of Ingland* (n.p., 1594). Parsons wrote under the name R. Doleman.

[18] Hayward, *A Treatise of Union of the Two Realmes of England and Scotland* (London, 1604), Sig. AIᵛ, pp. 11, 14.

[19] *An Answer to the First Part of a Certaine Conference, Concerning Succession, Published not long since under the name of R. Dolman* (London, 1603), pp. 33–4.

history was nothing if not flexible, Hayward, as will be discussed below, wrote a history of early England in which St. Edward's laws triumphed in 1066. In 1606 Parsons interpreted the Confessor's laws as proving that the Normans conquered both England and its laws. This time he wrote in answer to Sir Edward Coke's *Fifth Part of The Reports* (1605), where Coke had argued the right of the king, as the head of the English church, to punish Catholics. Coke based his case upon the king's ancient ecclesiastical authority, an authority guaranteed, he claimed, by St. Edward's laws which William I confirmed and which existed still. Mocking Coke for his "egregious hyperbole," Parsons turned the Confessor against him. Far from proving the antiquity of the royal ecclesiastical authority, St. Edward's laws told the very opposite story. Chapter 17, for example, demonstrated the pope's, not the king's, right to control the English church, since Pope John gave Pepin the right to depose Childeric. As for English law itself, William obliterated it in 1066. The common law that Coke now extolled was "brought in principally by conquest, and a conqueror, and such a one as intended to bridle the English by that means, and to bring them under" by imposing new laws. This Parsons knew from "old histories," which told how the people and nobility were reduced to begging for the restoration of St. Edward's laws. There was more. Not only, he continued, did the laws of England lack prestige, they lacked the basic sense of justice that characterized Roman law countries such as Scotland, Spain, France, and Italy (readers, of course, would recognize three of the four as Catholic). For example, common law denied counsel to the defendant in a capital case. And then the court left the judgment "to a jury of unlearned men" that must give their verdicts openly.[20] Antiunionists in England would have thought that with friends like Parsons, they had no need of enemies.

The Scottish civilian Sir Thomas Craig supported union by accepting that William I had conquered England, Scotland, and their laws. Arguing for a union of equals, he noted that the legal systems of the two kingdoms were basically similar. The cause of this affinity lay in the events of 1066, when William I not only subdued the English rebels but "as the last indignity, introduced his own laws into the ancient English system." This was the feudal law of Lombardy, which the Conqueror also imposed on Scotland and

[20] Parsons, *An Answere to the fifth part of reports of Sir Edward Coke* (n.p., 1606), pp. 12–15, 100ff.

which was in force in "all the sovereign states of Europe at the present time, by reason of its equity." While Craig acknowledged the survival of St. Edward's laws after 1066, he failed to draw the usual ancient constitutionalist conclusion. Whatever their power, they could not remove the stain of total conquest.[21]

In taking this position, Craig knew that he crossed swords with those Englishmen who "profess to believe that their laws are of purely indigenous growth" and "unlike those of other countries."[22] Not only were they wrong but, more to the point, their misreading of their own history led them to glorify the fruits of French conquest and obscured the fact that William I's title, because it flowed from force and violence, was flawed, notwithstanding "the sanction of almost six centuries continuance."[23] Rather than criticizing the proposed union, the English should rejoice that the crown "has reverted to its lawful heir and possessor," now "purged of any flaw in title." Indeed, James VI – as he was in Scotland – "centers the titles" of the Romans, the Saxons, the Danes, and the Normans, all of whom had conquered England. Thus, in Craig's view, James's succession to the two kingdoms represented "the resumption of a condition previously existing" and brought "the healing of a division" rather than "the institution of something new."[24]

Then there was Edward Ayscu's *A Historie Contayning the Warres, Treaties, Marriages, and other occurrents between England and Scotland*, which appeared in 1606 with a dedication to Prince Henry. Noting the common history of the two kingdoms, whose inhabitants had descended from the same stock, Ayscu pointed out that by 1066 "two absolute kings" reigned in both Scotland and England. To the north was Malcolm, to the south William, who, "taking upon him the part of a Conqueror, performed the same in his right kind: for abrogating the ancient laws and customs of the land, he established others, such as either he had brought out of Normandy, or that he thought more

---

[21] Craig, *De Unione Regnorum Britanniae Tractatus*, ed. C. Sanford Terry (Edinburgh, 1909) pp. 310–11. Craig, *Scotland's Sovereignty Asserted*, trans. George Ridpath (London, 1695), pp. 266–7. Craig, *The Right of Succession to the Kingdom of England* (London, 1703), p. 161. For discussions of Craig's legal and political thought see Burns, *The True Law of Kingship*, pp. 255–6, 263–5; Brian Levack, "Law, Sovereignty and the Union," in *Scots and Britons*, ed. Mason, pp. 217–23, 227–30, 234–7; J. G. A. Pocock, "Two Kingdoms and Three Histories? Political Thought in British Contexts," in *ibid.*, pp. 305–6; Pocock, *The Ancient Constitution and the Feudal Law* (Cambridge, 1987), pp. 79–90, 91–2, 243–4.
[22] Craig, *De Unione*, pp. 311, 322.
[23] *Ibid.*, pp. 266–8.
[24] *Ibid.*, pp. 268, 402–3.

fit for the present government of the English nation." Not content with this measure, William dispossessed the English of their lands and possessions, which he then bestowed upon "his followers and partakers in his conquest, at his own will and pleasure." In addition to trashing the ancient constitutionalist version of history, Ayscu went after St. Edward himself. In his view the Confessor was a king "who through a vainglorious show of religious chastity, took no more care to raise up seed unto himself." Surely, Ayscu implied, such a ruler was undeserving of adoration.[25]

Even when unionists refrained from directly attacking the antiquity of English laws and legal institutions, the very tenor of much of their literature emphasized the fundamental discontinuity and imperfection of English history. Indeed, in his very first speech to parliament in March of 1604, James I himself hinted at this point. Discussing the proposed union, he declared that it would constitute an entirely new entity that surpassed the two separate kingdoms in perfection and glory. In his view, unification served the same purpose as the consolidation of the seven kingdoms under the house of Wessex, or the merger of the various French duchies, "one after another conquered by the sword," into a new kingdom. In fact, the people both north and south of the border should rejoice, "for even as little brooks lose their names by their running and fall into great rivers, and the very name and memory of the great rivers swallowed up in the ocean," so would the torrent of union give birth to a grander and more splendid entity.[26] This speech, highly publicized throughout the country, established, in Patterson's words, "the Jacobean discourse" in which the new king made "available to the reading public in a highly dramatic form a representation of the king's character."[27] That their new king spoke with such ease and zeal of improving on this already best of constitutions, tried by time and the experience of generations of their ancestors, could not have endeared him to all of his new subjects.

Their uneasiness must have been heightened by the tone of other

---

[25] Ayscu, *A Historie Contayning the Warres, Treaties, Marriages, and other occurents betweene England and Scotland, from King William the Conqueror, untill the happy Union of them both in our gratious King James* (London, 1606), pp. 44, 45, 47. See also Woolf, *The Idea of History in Early Stuart England*, pp. 58–61.

[26] "A Speech, As It Was Delivered in the Upper House of Parliament to the Lords Spirituall and Temporall, and to the Knights, Citizens and Burgesses there assembled," in Sommerville, ed., *King James VI and I. Political Writings*, pp. 136–7 and *passim*.

[27] Patterson, *Censorship and Interpretation*, pp. 65–6.

works written to promote the union. Listen, for example, to the words of Edward Forset, who in 1606 described how "the whole island of Britannia, being a body perfectly shaped, rounded, and bounded with an invironing sea," was for "a long time . . . dissevered, and disfigured . . . until at the last the mighty and only wonder working hand of God, wiping away the deformity (not by any violent cutting off, but by a new molding as it were of the two heads into one) hath restored it again to his first right, imperial, and most monarchical greatness."[28] And so it went in any number of works which found the history of England characterized by similar gaping wounds.[29]

Not all unionist writers disparaged the ancient constitutionalist view of the past. Such was its malleability in the early seventeenth century that it could also be turned to the task of supporting the union. Thus, John Lewis earned James I's approval with his *History of Great Britain*, in which he chronicled the continuity of laws from Dunwallo through William the Conqueror.[30] Then there was George Saltern's *Of the Ancient Laws of Great Britaine*, a blatantly ancient constitutionalist defence of the union which James himself probably saw and approved. A Bristol lawyer with connections to Middle Temple, Saltern wrote to calm English fears of a catastrophe should the proposed union materialize. England's safety lay, he suggested, in the fact that Scottish and English laws were equally ancient, which meant in turn that neither country need fear inundation by the other. Citing Lambarde's *Archaionomia*, Camden's *Britannia*, and medieval chroniclers, Saltern traced both legal systems back to the Britons and noted their similarities across the centuries. According to his version of English history, Lucius, king of the

---

[28] Forset, *A Comparative Discourse of the Bodies Natural and Politique* (London, 1606), p. 58.

[29] See John Thornborough, *A Discourse Plainely Proving the evident utilitie and urgent necessitie of the desired happie Union of the two famous Kingdomes of England and Scotland: by way of answer to certaine objections against the same* (London, 1604), pp. 5–8, 23–8; *The Ioiefull and Blessed Reuniting of the two mighty kingdomes* (Oxford, 1604), pp. 29, 36, 45; "A Treatise of the Happie and Blessed Union," in Galloway and Levack, eds., *Six Tracts of 1604* (Edinburgh, 1985), pp. 126. n. 77, 144; William Herbert, *Prophecie of Cadwallder* (London, 1604); [Sir William Cornwallis], *The Miraculous and Happie Union of England and Scotland* (London, 1604); John Gordon, *The Union of Great Brittaine* (London, 1604). Plays and pageants also emphasize this theme. See, for example, Anthony Mundy, *The Triumphes of a re-united Britania* (London, 1605), B1ᵛ, B2, B2ᵛ. Here James I was depicted as a second Brute who reunited England, Scotland, and Wales into "one happy Britannia," thereby restoring the island's "peace and quietness."

[30] Lewis, *The History of Great-Britaine from the First Inhabitants Thereof.* Though not published until 1729, the work was written between 1605 and 1612. See Woolf, *The Idea of History in Early Stuart England*, p. 62.

Britons, deserved credit for creating the ancient laws. Saltern also told the story of Lucius and Pope Eleutherius, which he explicitly linked to Chapter 17 of St. Edward's laws, throwing in for good measure the similar passage from Bracton. The ancient laws of the kingdom, which had their origin in the laws of God, Edward the Confessor "reduced to one common law." Known in Saltern's own day and age as St. Edward's laws, they contained "the secret footsteps of the ancient British constitution."[31]

Nor, in Saltern's opinion, had these footsteps been interrupted, not even by William the Conqueror. Indeed, the Normans honored the ancient laws "transmitted to us by St. Edward" through confirmations and coronation oaths. "How true it is," Saltern concluded, "that our ancient common laws were begun in the time of the first Britains, grounded upon the laws of God, printed in nature and Scripture, continued by the Saxons in their judgment books, and transmitted to us by St. Edward and the Conqueror." And so it was with parliaments, which had met, complete with the Commons, as early as Ine's reign. Indeed, even King Arthur and King Alfred held parliaments – probably a reference to the *Mirror of Justices*. The antiquity and continuity of English institutions moved Saltern to recall the words of Fortescue: although "this land hath been possessed by Britains, Romans, Saxons, Danes, and Normans," it "was still ruled with the self-same laws and customs."[32] In Johann Sommerville's opinion, such talk made Saltern an "ignorant populizer."[33] Perhaps. But, as we shall see, he had plenty of company in the early Stuart period.

The works of Lewis and Saltern demonstrate once again the utility and flexibility of ancient constitutionalist sources. But these two authors had very little company among those who supported the union of the two kingdoms. Most of James I's backers, especially influential writers such as Hayward and Craig, unintentionally fed English fears by attacking the very foundation of ancient constitutionalist thinking. That contemporaries recognized the threat appeared from the unequivocal language used in parliament and

---

[31] Saltern, *Of the Ancient Laws of Great Britaine* (London, 1605). Because pagination is unreliable, I am using my own numbering. See pp. 2–3, 4, 5–6, 10, 12, 13–24, 29, 38, 39–40, 48, 49, 60–6. See also Woolf, *The Idea of History in Early Stuart England*, pp. 61, and n. 35, 282; Colin Kidd, *British Identities Before Nationalism. Ethnicity and Nationhood in the Atlantic World, 1600–1800* (Cambridge, 1999), pp. 61–2, 83–4, 195.

[32] Saltern, *Of the Ancient Laws of Great Britaine*, pp. 10, 14, 18–24, 29, 38, 39–40, 42–3, 48.

[33] Sommerville, *Politics and Ideology in England, 1603–1640*, p. 91.

quoted above: union could be achieved and justified only by a theory of conquest, from which it followed that the king could make laws at his own pleasure. And if this were the case, then what need had James I, or any king, for parliament?

The danger was likewise acknowledged by antiquaries such as William Camden and Sir Roger Owen, who did much to acquaint the political nation with the link between conquest theory and royal absolutism. They picked up the gauntlet by publicizing a relatively unknown law case from the early years of William I's reign. We know about this case because Camden included it in the 1607 edition of *Britannia*, written at the height of the controversy over unification. Here he told the tale of Sharnborn vs. the earl of Warren, having omitted it from all previous editions and printings of *Britannia*. Although we cannot say with any certainty, it is surely possible that Camden mentioned it now because he considered it highly relevant to the current debates. In his description of Norfolk, he explained how, shortly after the Norman invasion one Edwin, a Saxon lord, brought a case against the earl of Warren in the king's court. As mentioned in chapter 2, Edwin alleged that he had been disseised of lands in Sharnborn, which the king then bestowed upon Warren. The disseisin had been unjust, Edwin argued, because he himself had supported William from the very beginning and therefore deserved to keep his lands. William, the story goes, accepted his plea and ordered Warren, a close favorite, to return the lands to the Saxon.[34]

This case, briefly mentioned in *Little Domesday* and more fully told in a manuscript belonging to Sir John Spelman, became a standard weapon in the arsenal of radical ancient constitutionalists. In their reading it proved that William did not reign as a conqueror because Saxon laws and institutions survived the conquest. The first to give the story in published form, Camden imbued it with a ring of truth sufficiently resounding to impress the greatest scholars of the period. The eminent Saxonist scholar Sir Roger Twysden went so far as to include it in his 1644 edition of *Archaionomia*, where he enshrined it with St. Edward's laws; the *Leis Willelme*, in which the Conqueror

---

[34] Camden also included the story in the first English edition of *Britannia*, published in 1610, as well as in the 1637 printing. See also Janelle Greenberg and Laura Marin, "Politics and Memory: Sharnborn's Case and the Role of the Norman Conquest in Stuart Political Thought," in *Politics and the Political Imagination in Later Stuart Britain: Essays Presented to Lois Green Schwoerer*, ed. Howard Nenner (Rochester, NY, 1997), pp. 121–42.

confirmed the Confessor's laws; and Henry I's Charter of Liberties. Then, with full understanding that he followed in the footsteps of King John's barons, Twysden linked Magna Carta to these Saxon and early Norman laws. In so doing, he figuratively and physically associated Sharnborn's case with precisely those legal works that seventeenth-century antiquaries and lawyers most revered.[35] Similarly, Sir Matthew Hale accepted the story unquestioningly, including it in his highly respected *History of the Common Law,* where he referred to the case as "that excellent monument of antiquity."[36]

According to Camden, the area of Sharnborn deserved mention in the 1607 edition of *Britannia* both because of

Felix the Burgundian who brought these East Englishmen to the Christian faith and state of perpetual felicity . . . as also because it is verily thought and that by faithful testimony of the old deeds and evidences, that an old Englishman lord of this place before the coming of the Normans, by virtue of sentence given judicially in open court by William Conqueror himself, recovered his lordship against Warren, unto whom the Conqueror had given it.

Camden concluded his description of Sharnborn's case by noting that its "argument they enforce hard who would prove that the said William entered upon the possession of England by covenant and agreement, and not by right of war and conquest."[37] Although I can only speculate, his words can be read as intimating that contemporaries now discussed the Norman conquest in terms that concerned the nature of kingship. Further, by contrasting rule by compact with rule by the sword, Camden hinted that some Englishmen linked conquest with absolutism. Michael Drayton's *Poly-Olbion,* a 1612 versification of *Britannia,* told the story to the same effect.[38]

Similar testimony came from Camden's fellow antiquary, Sir Roger Owen. A barrister at Lincoln's Inn, Owen was also an active politician, serving in parliament in the reigns of Elizabeth and James I. Not only was he well positioned to observe the currents of political and legal discourse, he also participated actively in the debates over the union of the two kingdoms. Around 1615 Owen wrote a frequently cited tract entitled "Of the Common Lawes of England,"

---

[35] *Archaionomia* (Cambridge, 1644), fos. 154–6.

[36] Sir Matthew Hale, *The History of the Common Law of England,* ed. Charles M. Gray (Chicago, 1971), pp. 47–71, especially pp. 61–4.

[37] *Britannia* (London, 1607), p. 350. Philemon Holland's English translation is used here. *Britain* (London, 1610), p. 480.

[38] Drayton, *Poly-Olbion* (Oxford, 1933), vol. IV, p. 343.

in which he presented a thoroughly ancient constitutionalist version of English history.[39] Owen's work will be discussed in greater detail later in this chapter. For the time being, suffice it to say that in his extended discussion of Saxon law and its survival after 1066, he cited Sharnborn vs. Warren in order to "put an end to the modern argument that our laws were abolished by the Normans" and that William therefore reigned as a conqueror.[40]

The case received even wider publicity when the prominent common lawyer and antiquary Sir John Davies found it relevant to the question of conquest. Davies, too, was well situated to comment on such matters. An esteemed common lawyer and early member of the Society of Antiquaries, he served James I as solicitor-general and attorney-general for Ireland. In 1612 he wrote a tract that raised the question of why the English had never truly conquered Ireland. The answer he found in England's failure successfully to implant its own legal system into its westernmost colony – a failure which he contrasted with the Norman achievement in 1066. Readily acknowledging that the Normans conquered England in some sense, he told how William the Conqueror made French the language of the law "as a mark and badge of conquest." Davies further noted that "he oppressed the English nobility very sore." Nevertheless, the Conqueror "governed all, both English and Normans, by one and the same law; which was the ancient common law of England, long before the conquest."[41] Put differently, William did not rule as a conqueror, for he permitted "any Englishman (that submitted himself unto him)" to keep his lands. As specific proof Davies cited "the notable controversy between Warren the Norman," a man "of the best rank, and in greatest favor," and Sharnborn, of Sharnborn Castle in Norfolk. Although William had given the castle to Warren,

yet when the inheritor thereof, had alleged before the king, that he never bore arms against him; that he was his subject as well as the other, and that he did inherit and hold his lands, by the rules of that law, which the king had established among all his subjects; the king gave judgment against

---

[39] Owen wrote the manuscript in 1615 or 1616. See William Klein, "The Ancient Constitution Revisited," in *Political Discourse in Early Modern Britain*, ed. Nicholas Phillipson and Quentin Skinner, (Cambridge, 1993), pp. 23–44.

[40] Of the Common Lawes of England. B.L. Landsdowne MSS 646. fos. 229ᵛ-230ᵛ.

[41] Davies, *Discovery of the True Causes why Ireland was never Entirely Subdued* (London, 1612, reprinted Shannon, 1969), pp. 127–8. For Davies's career and legal thought see Hans Pawlisch, *Sir John Davies and the Conquest of Ireland* (Cambridge, 1985).

Warren, and commanded that Sherborn [sic] should hold his land in peace.

By this means, Davies concluded, William "obtained a peaceable possession of the kingdom within a few years; whereas, if he had cast all the English out of his protection, and held them as aliens and enemies to the crown, the Normans (perhaps) might have spent as much time in the conquest of England, as the English have spent in the conquest of Ireland."[42] In other words, governing by St. Edward's laws was William's way of winning the hearts and minds of the English people.

While neither Camden, nor Owen, nor Davies explicitly linked conquest theory or Sharnborn's case to fears of Stuart absolutism, all were surely aware that debates and resolutions in parliament did precisely that. Owen, after all, sat in the lower house, and he, Camden, and Davies were long-time associates in the Society of Antiquaries. All were familiar with the view that if the king of England governed by conquest, then he could make laws at his will and pleasure. All could have valued Sharnborn's case because it provided a counterweight to a line of argumentation that reasoned from a Norman conquest of Saxon laws to a Stuart absolutism. More than an historical anecdote with mere antiquarian appeal, the story soon became a permanent part of radical political discourse because its message sounded loud and clear: just as William I had not reigned as a conqueror and therefore an absolute sovereign, neither did his seventeenth-century successors.

Thus, it seems worth considering that the debate over the union of the two kingdoms focused attention as never before upon the constitutional meaning of 1066 and its relevance to seventeenth-century law and politics. These new polemical circumstances greatly increased the value of any sources that pointed to a survival of Saxon laws after the Norman invasion. Hence the overwhelming purchase of St. Edward's laws, the *Modus*, the *Mirror*, and now Sharnborn's case, all of which took on a powerful political relevance and significance. But radical ancient constitutionalists found much more in the early seventeenth century with which to bolster their particular version of the English past. Indeed, the historical and legal materials of the period resounded with references and interpretations that would well serve their ideological goals.

---

[42] Davies, *A Discovery of the True Causes*, pp. 127–8.

ANCIENT CONSTITUTIONALISM IN EARLY SEVENTEENTH-
CENTURY HISTORICAL AND LEGAL LITERATURE

By and large, writers who commented on the early English past followed in the footsteps of their Tudor predecessors: they emphasized important elements of historical continuity, while sometimes allowing for a temporary eclipse of certain legal and political institutions. Moreover, they told the story of 1066 and its aftermath in ways that invited contemporaries to apply the common law doctrine of prescription to modern legal and political situations. In particular, early seventeenth-century writers reinforced the notion that the English people possessed a prescriptive right to be governed by St. Edward's laws. It mattered, too, that the best published of these writers ranked among the favorites of radical ancient constitutionalists. Take, for example, John Speed, whose *History of Great Britaine* was one of the most popular works of the period. First published in 1611, it was reissued, eventually in two new editions, in 1614, 1623, 1632, and 1650. A staunch Protestant, Speed enjoyed the friendship of Sir Robert Cotton, who supplied him with medieval manuscripts and chronicles.[43] From these sources Speed constructed a version of the medieval past that proved eminently useful to enemies of the Stuart kingship. This was true despite the fact that, as Woolf notes, Speed viewed the pre-Norman era as a "labyrinth of ambiguity." His skepticism led him to question the Brutus legend and to criticize other stories, including some of those that surrounded Edward the Confessor. Noting that more things were said about that particular king than could be safely believed, Speed raised questions about the veracity of the tales concerning Edward's miraculous healing powers and his being elected king while still in his mother's womb. Indeed, the unquestioning acceptance of such stories reflected badly on his fellow countrymen, leading "the worthy French historian" Phillipe de Commynes "to tax the English with over much credulity that way."[44]

While Speed's well-placed scepticism might well have diminished St. Edward's cult of kingship, it did not save him from embracing the

[43] David Howarth, "Sir Robert Cotton and the Commemoration of Famous Men," *British Library Journal* 18 (1992), 26. Graham Parry, *The Trophies of Time. English Antiquarians of the Seventeenth Century* (Oxford, 1995), p. 75.
[44] Speed, *History of Great Britaine* (London, 1611), vol. 1, p. 398.

usual sources and stories associated with the cult of St. Edward's laws. Thus, he credited St. Edward with creating the common law from the various customs of the Mercians, West Saxons, Danes, and Northumbrians. Although the Normans altered "the forms of pleading and process," St. Edward's laws remained "the fountain of those, which at this day we term the common law." Speed also echoed the antiquaries' belief that Norman custom had much in common with both Saxon and Danish laws, "being a branch of the same root."[45] Thus, whatever changes they introduced could not have resulted in profound alterations.

Turning to the Norman conquest and its aftermath, Speed described how Duke William, in spite of his promises to the men of Swanscombe Down and at his coronation, nevertheless harrassed the Saxon rebels, whose "unquenched desire of liberty he daily dreaded." Not content with enacting such repressive policies, "the ancient laws of the kingdom he abrogated for the most part, ordaining new," and these "written in the harsh Norman tongue." Still, the Saxons refused to relent, and William, "fearing to lose the crown with shame, which he had gotten by the effusion of so much blood," met with Abbot Frederick at St. Albans, where he swore "to observe and inviolably to keep the ancient laws of this land; and most especially those compiled by King Edward the Confessor."[46]

Once again, Speed continued, William went back on his word, and it remained for Henry I to restore English liberties, promising in his coronation charter "to frame just laws grounded on those of Saint Edward (than which nothing more was desired)." Thus it was that the Conqueror's son, "to the greatest contentment of the people . . . gave power and strength unto King Edward's laws," and so ingratiated himself "into the loves of all that with a general concurrence he was saluted king."[47] King Stephen followed suit, acknowledging that he too possessed the crown by election.[48] Still, St. Edward's laws did not rest forever secure, for King John strayed from the lawful path. His barons responded by presenting him with Henry I's coronation charter and forcing from him an oath "for restoring good laws, and antiquating bad," so that they might recover "those liberties which long they had lost."[49] For radical ancient constitutionalists, the bottom line of such stories was not that

[45] *Ibid.*, pp. 399, 411.   [16] *Ibid.*, pp. 415–18.   [47] *Ibid.*, pp. 418, 434–5.
[48] *Ibid.*, p. 446.   [49] *Ibid.*, p. 501.

kings reneged on their promises, but that the English refused to surrender. By fighting the good fight, they retained a prescriptive right to be governed by St. Edward's laws.

Speed's account of the history of parliament followed Polydore Vergil. To Henry I belonged the credit for "laying the first foundation of our high court of parliament," earlier kings being but "seldom" inclined to seek "the joint advice of their peoples; saving at the beginning of their government, and in time of war."[50] Now, however, "the subject, best understanding his own grievances, hath both liberty in choice of their knights and burgesses, as also free voice to complain thereof in that honorable assembly." Still, Speed believed that even though Saxon kings and their predecessors called parliaments infrequently, the Commons was sometimes present at such assemblies, as, for example, at Gloucester, when the Confessor "called an assembly of estates" that included the lower house.[51]

Peter Heylyn, chaplain to Archbishop Laud and Charles I, also wove an ancient constitionalist narrative into his immensely popular *Microcosmus, or A Little Description of the Great World*. First published in 1621 with a dedication to Prince Charles, it was reprinted in 1625, 1627, 1629, 1630, 1633, 1636, 1639, and in an eighth edition in 1652. As part of Heylyn's larger *Cosmographie*, it reappeared in an enlarged ninth edition in 1652, and in 1682 it was published in its thirteenth edition. In *Microcosmus* Heylyn sang the praises of an immemorial common law. Although recognizing the spurious character of the Brute and Trojan fable, he perpetuated the story of St. Edward, who "collected out of the Danish, Saxon, and Mercian laws, one universal and general law; whence our common law is thought to have had its original." But, Heylyn continued, this was true only of the written laws, "not of the customary and unwritten laws; these being certainly more ancient." Indeed, this common law, which he deemed "appropriate only to this kingdom," possessed "greater antiquity and indifference than the civil" law.[52] As for the Norman conquest, Heylyn acknowledged that William, "pretending a donation of Edward the Confessor," invaded and "possessed himself of the kingdom: using such policy in his new conquest, that he utterly disheartened the English from hopes of a better future."[53]

[50] *Ibid.*, p. 409.   [51] *Ibid.*, p. 399.

[52] Heylyn, *A Little Description of the Great World. Augmented and Revised* (Oxford, 1625), pp. 457, 463, 478, 480, 483.

[53] *Ibid.*, p. 486.

Especially well suited for radical argumentation was Richard Verstegan's thoroughly Saxonist history entitled *A Restitution of Decayed Intelligence* (1605). A Catholic activist in Elizabeth's reign, he dedicated the work to James I, probably in the hope of securing the new king's toleration.[54] Although the Gun Powder Plot put paid to this plan, Verstegan succeeded in producing a history of England sufficiently well received to merit reprintings in 1628, 1634, 1652, 1655, and 1673.[55] In his work he went to great lengths to establish the superiority of the Saxons over all other inhabitants of the island. Critical of those who confused the English with the British peoples, he explained that the Saxons derived from the Germanic tribes of the continent, whom he praised as simple people "without fraud and subtlety."[56] History itself showed their great staying power, as they bested the British and survived the Danish and Norman invasions. As for the latter, although the Normans conquered the land and dispossessed many Englishmen of their wealth, the Saxons resisted their tyranny and soon recouped their losses, acquiring land, offices, and benefices. Soon, too, the French adopted the Saxon tongue and customs. In the end, then, the English stood as the dominant people – "the corps and body of the realm." Verstegan singled out for special praise "noble Kent," which, to its "everlasting honor," defied the Conqueror and "reserved unto itself both lands and liberties."[57]

That radical ancient constitutionalists throughout the century made use of these particular histories occasions no surprise. However, they also drew heavily and frequently on two early seventeenth-century works which seemed, at first sight, to offer little hope of extremist elaboration. Written by Samuel Daniel and William Martyn, these histories depicted William as conquering the

[54] A. G. Petti, "Richard Verstegan and the Catholic Martyrologies of the Later Elizabethan Period," *Recusant History* 5 (1959–60), 64–90. Parry, *The Trophies of Time*, chapter 2 and *passim*.

[55] Verstegan, *A Restitution of Decayed Intelligence: In Antiquities. Concerning the most noble and renouned English nation* (Antwerp, 1605). All later editions were published in London. See also Woolf, *The Idea of History in Early Stuart England*, pp. 202–4; R. Schoeck, "Early Anglo-Saxon Studies and Legal Scholarship in the Renaissance," *Studies in the Renaissance* 5 (1958), 102–10; Parry, *The Trophies of Time*, pp. 51–69; Kidd, *British Identities Before Nationalism*, pp. 61–3, 77, 86–7, 111, 194, 218–22.

[56] Verstegan, *A Restitution of Decayed Intelligence*, Sig. 4r, p. 56.

[57] *Ibid.*, pp. 155, 178–9, 182–7, 203. See also *An Introduction to a Breviary of the History of England* (London, 1693). Wrongly attributed to Sir Walter Raleigh, this work, which was written earlier in the century, also carried many of the usual ancient constitutionalist stories. *Ibid.*, pp. 13, 28, 33, 36–7, 41–4, 57–9, 66, 69.

Saxon laws as well as the Saxon army. In his *Collection of the History of England*, published in 1612, with later editions and reprintings appearing in 1613, 1618, 1626, 1634, and 1650, Daniel described the common law as a Norman innovation imposed by the Conqueror.[58] To be sure, William I, Henry I, Henry II, and King John promised on a number of occasions to abide by the laws of St. Edward, which Daniel described as the first "universal law of the kingdom." But kings made these promises in order to quiet the people "with a show of the continuation of their ancient customs and liberties." In fact, however, the Normans instituted "a great innovation both in the laws and government of England." In particular, the common law rested upon a thoroughly French foundation, "though there might be some veins issuing from former originals." Moreover, these Norman laws "bred most heavy doleances, not only in this king's time, but long after," in part because they were written in a language which the Saxons did not understand.[59]

On the other hand, Daniel's view of the origins of parliament proved less threatening to an ancient constitutionalist reading of early English history. At least this was true of the amended account found in all editions of his history except the first, which was published in 1612 and 1613. As Woolf notes, originally Daniel had included a gloss in which he described Henry I's parliament of 1116 as the "first" such assembly of estates – a definition which made parliament a Norman innovation.[60] However, he apparently changed his mind about the matter, because in the 1618 edition he altered the gloss to read "the first parliament, after the conquest." Daniel further noted that from this time forward the assembly of the three estates was known by the name parliament, in accordance with Norman practice. The reprintings of 1626 and 1634 also carried the later wording.[61] This alteration mattered, for it left open the possibility that an assembly consisting of both Lords and Commons originated before 1066 and was merely revived and renamed by

[58] The first volume, which ended with the anarchy of King Stephen's reign, was entitled *The First Part of the Historie of England* and appeared in 1612 and was reprinted in 1613. In 1618 Daniel carried the story forward to the end of Edward III's reign in *The Collection of the History of England*, which was reprinted in 1626, 1634, and 1650. The 1626 work is used here. See Woolf, *The Idea of History in Early Stuart England*, pp. 77–104.

[59] Daniel, *The Collection of the Historie of England* (London, 1626), pp. 36–7.

[60] Daniel, *The First Part of the Historie of England* (London, 1612, 1613), p. 194. Woolf, *The Idea of History in Early Stuart England*, p. 99.

[61] Daniel, *The Collection of the Historie of England* (London, 1618), p. 56. *Ibid.* (London, 1626), p. 56. *Ibid.* (London, 1634), pp. 66–7.

Henry I – a version of parliamentary history perfectly compatible with an ancient constitutionalist reading. Speculating on the reasons for the altered gloss, Woolf suggests that Daniel might have uncovered more information about Saxon parliaments, perhaps in the writings of Selden. Or, perhaps Daniel feared that the policies of James I threatened parliament's position within the state and so changed the wording to strengthen its hand.[62] Whatever the case, the fact that all but the first version of Daniel's history described the assembly of 1116 as the first after the *conquest* and the first to be *called* parliament made his work acceptable to radical ancient constitutionalists, who cited it throughout the Stuart period.

Daniel wrote less equivocally about the fate of other Saxon institutions after 1066, especially those concerned with "the government and security of the kingdom." Thus, the administrative division of England into shires, hundreds, boroughs, and villages, and the tithing, all of which Daniel knew from Lambarde's *Archaionomia*, remained intact. These institutions functioned as links in a chain, holding "the whole frame of the state together in peace and order, as, all the most politic regiments upon earth, all the interleagued societies of men, cannot show us a straighter form of combination." Ironically, these Saxon institutions worked to the benefit of the Normans. Rendering the Saxons "law-bound hand and foot," they enabled William to conquer the country easily and quickly.[63]

Ancient constitutionalists could also take heart from Daniel's discussion of the title by which William held the kingdom. Disdaining the name of conqueror, William I never claimed "any power by conquest, but as a regular prince," submitting "himself to the orders of the kingdom" and "desirous rather to have his testamentary title (howsoever weak) to make good his succession, rather than his sword." To be sure, "the style of conqueror by the flattery of the time, was after given him." Nevertheless "he showed by all the course of his government he assumed it not."[64] Equally cheering to ancient constitutionalists was Daniel's inclusion of the story of the men of Kent and his description of the making of Magna Carta,

---

[62] Woolf, *The Idea of History in Early Stuart England*, p. 99.
[63] Daniel, *The Collection of the Historie of England*, p. 38. Thus was William able "to turn all this ordinance upon the state, and batter herself with her own weapon . . . The Conqueror, without this, had not made it the work of one day. . . . " *Ibid.*, pp. 38–9.
[64] *Ibid.*, p. 31.

which he linked firmly to St. Edward's laws through Henry I's coronation charter.[65]

As for the Saxons themselves, Daniel had words of highest praise. He admired, for example, their laws and legal practices, and, indeed, the Saxon character, which he contrasted favorably with that of the Normans. The Normans were, in his opinion, "a people more inured to litigation, and of spirits more impatient, and contentious, than were the English." In fact, this character trait explained why William introduced "new terms, new constitutions, new forms of pleas, new offices, and new courts," all of which presumably made it easier to fly to law. In contrast, and to their credit, the English enjoyed "laws and constitutions" that were "plain, brief, and simple, without perplexities" and disputes. Further, "their grants and transactions" were "brief and simple," thus showing them "a clear-meaning people, retaining still the nature of that plain realness they brought with them, uncomposed of other fashion than their own, and unaffecting imitation."[66] Daniel also admired the tenacity of the English language, which the conquerors attempted unsuccessfully to extirpate. In fact, the French tongue was itself incorporated into the English "as rivers to the ocean, that changed not it, but were changed into it."[67]

William Martyn's *Historie, and Lives, of the Kings of England*, published in 1618 and reprinted in 1638, contained similar elements of historical continuity and discontinuity. A member of Middle Temple and recorder of London from 1607 to 1617, Martyn depicted William I as ruling England "as a conqueror, with more policy than by profitable laws; and with more severity than did become the gracious disposition of a favorable king." William also "enacted and established straight and severe laws, and published them in his own language," leading many to transgress through ignorance – though the valiant men of Swanscombe Down retained their ancient customs.[68] The situation changed, however, when Henry I came to

---

[65] *Ibid.*, pp. 39, 118–19.
[66] *Ibid.*, p. 37. The Saxon approach to legal matters resulted, Daniel suggested, from the fact that they were often at war and, therefore, a spirit of unity and good fellowship prevailed in their private lives.
[67] *Ibid.*, p. 36.
[68] Martyn, *The Historie, and Lives, of the Kings of England; From William the Conqueror, unto the end of the Raigne of King Henrie the Eight* (London, 1615), pp. 2, 3, 4. Martyn added that William "rather practiced the licentious power of an insolent conqueror, than the gracious kindness of an anointed king." *Ibid.*, p. 6.

the throne, for he "mitigated the rigor of the former new laws, and promised restitution of the old." King Stephen did likewise, his hand strengthened when the Londoners, "desiring the restitution of King Edward's laws," refused to support the Empress Matilda who had declined their request.[69] Not only did Henry I restore the laws of St. Edward, his marriage to Maud, herself of English descent, brought the restoration of "Saxon blood" with the accession of Henry II.[70] Later, however, St. Edward's laws faded once again, leading the kingdom to draw up Magna Carta. The Great Charter demanded the restoration of "the ancient laws of King Edward . . . to their former vigor and strength," these laws being "both easeful and commodious to the common people."[71]

Antiquaries and common lawyers also provided radical ancient constitutionalists with valuable ammunition. Of all the writers whose name we invariably associate with this tradition, none is better known than Sir Edward Coke's. And none was more esteemed by radical ancient constitutionalists throughout the century of revolution. This was true despite the fact that Coke, at least early in his career, appeared to be just as comfortable attributing absolute prerogatives to the king as he was championing the privileges of parliament. Coke himself was a man of unusual parts, enjoying a political and legal career scarcely equalled in the late sixteenth and early seventeenth century. Active in government at one level or another for nearly forty years, he entered public life in the 1580s, holding the positions of recorder of Norwich, justice of the peace in Norfolk, and recorder of London. In the 1590s he began an association with the queen's government, which led to his appointment as solicitor general, speaker of the House of Commons, and attorney general. Coke continued as attorney general after James I's succession in 1603, and in 1606 the king rewarded him with an appointment as chief justice of the court of Common Pleas. Before the decade was out, however, Coke's relationship with the king soured, and in 1613 James I moved him to chief justice of King's Bench – prestigious but unprofitable. His fortunes bottomed out in 1616, when he was stripped entirely of judicial office, in part at least

---

[69] *Ibid.*, p. 29.
[70] *Ibid.*, p. 31, where the marginal gloss reads: "Saxon blood restored. See the descent of Henry I."
[71] *Ibid.*, p. 63.

because of anti-monarchical views he had expressed in his law reports.

However, Coke continued to serve in parliament. He sat in the Commons in 1621, 1624, 1625, and finally in 1628, where he played a major role in drafting the Petition of Right. By then Coke's version of the ancient constitution had changed from one that guaranteed both royal and parliamentarian privileges to one weighted in favor of parliament. Charles I considered him dangerous enough to merit imprisonment in the Tower, and the power of his pen caused the government such concern that the king commanded that his study be searched and his papers seized. The Long Parliament returned the favor by ordering the *Second*, *Third*, and *Fourth Parts* of Coke's *Institutes of the Laws of England* published posthumously in 1642 and 1644.[72]

Of all Coke's voluminous writings, radical ancient constitutionalists valued most highly the prefaces to his case reports and his *Institutes on the Laws of England*.[73] Indeed, in Richard Helgerson's words, the prefaces "constitute a running defense of England's native legal system," in which Coke "transformed a largely unreflective cultural practice into an ideological weapon."[74] Serving as teaching materials for young men studying at the Inns of Court and supplying generations of lawyers and politicians with legal argumentation, these works led contemporaries to label him "the great God Pan of the Legal Oracles."[75] It therefore mattered that Coke depended heavily on St. Edward's laws, the *Modus*, and the *Mirror* to make his case for the ancient constitution and against the first two Stuarts. To Coke these proved beyond the shadow of a doubt that Stuart liberties and institutions originated long before the conquest and survived virtually unchanged until his own day and age. Coke

---

[72] For Coke's life and early career see Stephen D. White, *Sir Edward Coke and "The Grievances of the Commonwealth," 1621–1628* (Chapel Hill, 1979), Introduction.

[73] *Les Reports de Edward Coke* consisted of thirteen volumes, eleven of which appeared in the years from 1600 to 1615, and the last two of which were published in 1656 and 1659. The *First Institute* appeared in 1628. See White, *Sir Edward Coke*, pp. 10–11 and n. 41 and n. 43; Alan Cromartie, "The Constitutional Revolution: The Transformation of Political Culture in Early Stuart England," *Past and Present*, 163 (1999), 84ff; Charles M. Gray, "Parliament, Liberty, and the Law," in *Parliament and Liberty from the Reign of Elizabeth to the English Civil War*, ed. J. H. Hexter, (Stanford, 1992), pp. 155–200.

[74] Helgerson, *Forms of Nationhood. The Elizabethan Writing of England* (Chicago, 1992), pp. 78–88, especially p. 85.

[75] See William Prynne's remarks in *Brief Animadversions on, Amendments of, and Additional Explanatory Records to, the Fourth Part of the Institutes of the Lawes of England* (London, 1669), "To All Ingenuous Readers," p. 3.

stated this position with particular force in the prefaces to the *Third*, *Eighth*, and *Ninth Parts* of his *Reports*. In the *Third*, for example, he noted that "the common law of England had been time out of mind of man before the conquest, and was not altered or changed by the Conqueror."[76]

However, in making this claim Coke was not necessarily suggesting that the common law had literally always existed, or that it had literally never changed. On the contrary, as mentioned in chapter 1, like all common lawyers he readily acknowledged that parliamentary statutes had altered common law in substantial ways. Equally to the point, his *First Institutes*, published in 1628, firmly established his familiarity with Littleton's association of time out of mind with 1189. So in describing English law in this fashion, Coke merely reiterated the standard position: what mattered was that common law existed in pre-conquest times, which was indeed before the date of legal memory. Generations of writings had established as much. To be sure, Coke understood that because so little in the way of records survived from the pre-conquest period, he could not say with any certainty exactly when particular institutions began. Still, even in the absence of records Coke knew a way to recover those laws, for they were "the same which the Norman conqueror then found within this realm of England." Citing Ingulf, the *Modus*, and the *Mirror* as his authorities, he told how William the Conqueror had summoned juries from every county to swear as to the content of St. Edward's laws, which he then confirmed. These laws constituted "a Magna Carta (the ground work of all those that after followed)." Although William Rufus "misruled," Henry I "restored the law of King Edward . . . with those amendments, which his father added by the advice of his barons." Similar confirmations followed at the hands of King Stephen, Henry II, King John, and Henry III. These, too, merited the title "Great Charters." With regard to King John's Magna Carta, Coke wrote that the ancient laws and liberties contained therein came from St. Edward's laws, "not that King Edward the Confessor did institute them, but that he out of the huge heap of the laws, etc. chose the best and reduced them into one."[77]

---

[76] Coke, *Le Tierce Part Des Reportes del Edward Coke* (London, 1602), "To the Reader," pages unnumbered.

[77] *Ibid.* Coke, *La Huict^{me} Part des Reports de Sr. Edw. Coke* (London, 1611), "To the Reader," pages unnumbered. See also Coke, *The First Part of the Institutes of the Laws of England*, 7th. edn. (London, 1670), pp. 110–13. *The Second Part of the Institutes of the Laws of England* (London,

Not only did Coke find the common law in existence long before
as well as after the conquest, he also found evidence of parliament's
early origins and survival. Here he turned to the *Mirror of Justices*, in
which "appeareth the whole frame of the ancient common laws of
this realm." In this treatise he and his fellow Englishmen could read
of parliaments summoned as early as the reign of King Arthur, and
also of King Alfred, who "ordaineth for a usage perpetual" that such
assemblies meet at least twice a year, and more often if necessary.
And so kings had done throughout the Saxon period as well as after
the Norman conquest.[78] Coke knew that some of his contemporaries
believed that William the Conqueror, whose "hand was always upon
the hilt," failed to summon parliament. But they were wrong, since
ample evidence existed of parliaments "assembled and holden
according to the common laws of England in William the Conquer-
or's time." Witness, for example, the *Modus tenendi Parliamentum*,
approved by the Conqueror himself. Its proem, stunningly apt for
Coke's case, read:

Here is described the manner in which the parliament of the king of
England and of his Englishmen was held in the time of King Edward, the
son of King Ethelred, which manner was related by the more distinguished
men of the kingdom in the presence of William, duke of Normandy,
conqueror and king of England: by the Conqueror's own command, and
through his approval it was used in his times and in the times of his
Customary usage had been observed since William and his successors had
held parliament in the manner of the Confessor.[79]

In addition to demonstrating the continuation of parliaments after
1066, Coke's medieval sources proved another point vital to ancient
constitutionalists: early parliaments included the Commons as well
as the Lords. According to the Saxon laws, which he knew from
Archaionomia, kings such as Ine, Ethelbert, Alfred, Ethelstan, Edgar,
Ethelred, and Cnut, summoned assemblies that included all the
sapientes, that is, the wisemen, of the kingdom. Following Lambarde,

---

1797), vol. I, pp. 7–8, 11, 28, 100, 115, 268 and *passim. Ibid.*, vol. II, p. 498. Coke, *La Neuf^me Part
des Reports de Sr. Edw. Coke* (London, 1613), "To the Reader," pages unnumbered.

[78] Coke, *La Neuf^me Part des Reports de Sr. Edw. Coke*, "To the Reader." *The First Part of the Institutes
of the Laws of England*, pp. 110, 111a. See also Coke, *The Second Part of the Institutes of the Laws of
England*, vol. I, pp. 28 and *passim*; *The Third Part of the Institutes of the Laws of England: Concerning
High Treason and other Pleas of the Crown* (London, 1797), Proem, pp. 16, 62, 111, 118, 221, 222
and *passim*.

[79] *Ibid.* Coke gave the proem in Latin. I have used Nicholas Pronay and John Taylor's
translation in *Parliamentary Texts of the Later Middle Ages* (Oxford, 1980), p. 80. See also the
Fourth Part of the Institutes of the Laws of England (London, 1797), pp. 1–12 and *passim*.

Coke read this term as referring to the Commons as well as the Lords in parliament.[80] The *Modus*, too, demonstrated that parliaments both before and after 1066 included both houses, "which manner continued to this day."[81]

Sir John Davies, Coke's fellow jurist and antiquary, wrote similarly of early English history. Singing the praises of an immemorial common law, Davies, whose familiarity with Sharnborn's case has already been noted, cited Ingulf to demonstrate that "the Conqueror changed them not."[82] Moreover, he criticized writers like Polydore Vergil for calling William "our lawgiver." Such could not have been the case, since the Conqueror confirmed England's ancient laws. These laws William himself found "so honorable, and profitable, both for the prince and people, as that he thought it not fit to make any alteration in the fundamental points or substance thereof." Admittedly, Davies continued, William introduced one particular change: he "altered some legal forms of proceeding, and to honor his own language, and for a mark of conquest withall, he caused the pleading of divers actions" to be in French. But this change pertained only to *formulis iuris*, not to the substance of the law. And, in any event, the imposition of French did not prove a hardship to the Saxons, for law French was easily learned.[83]

The common lawyers' understanding of early English history was also well articulated in Sir Roger Owen's "Of the Common Lawes of England," written around 1615. Although never published, the work enjoyed a high reputation among scholars and common lawyers and was frequently cited throughout the century.[84] As previously noted, Owen was a member of the Society of Antiquaries and an active parliamentarian politician. He, like Coke and Davies, found all manner of Stuart institutions in existence before the conquest. Working from sources such as Lambarde's *Archaionomia*, Ingulf, *Domesday Book*, and the *Textus Roffensis*, he noted "that the High Court of Parliament, the Chancery, the King's Bench, the Common

---

[80] *La Neuf*ᵐᵉ *Part des Reports de Sr. Edw. Coke*, "To the Reader."

[81] *Ibid.* Coke, *The Fourth Part of the Institutes of the Laws of England*, pp. 1–12 and *passim*.

[82] Davies, *A Perfect Abridgment of the Eleauen Bookes of Reports of the Reverend, and Learned Kt. Sr. Edw. Cook* (London, 1651), "To the Reader," A2.

[83] Davies, *Le Primer report des Cases & Matters en Ley resolues & adiuges en les Courts del Roy en Ireland* (Dublin, 1615), "A Preface Dedicatory."

[84] See, for example, Bulstrode Whitelocke, *Notes Uppon the Kings Writt* (London, 1776), vol. 1, p. 412; George Lawson, *Politica Sacra et Civilis* (London, 1660), pp. 76, 151, 161; James Tyrrell, *Bibliotheca Politica: Or an Enquiry into the Ancient Constitution of the English Government* (London, 1692–4), p. 739.

Place; the Exchequer, the sheriff and his county courts, the bailiff and their hundred courts, the lords of manors and the court barons and leets, that the same quantity of estates, tenants for years, for life, in tail in fee simple were afore the conquest."[85]

And so it was with the common law. Resting on "the glorious pyramid of . . . antiquity," it was undisturbed by the arrival of the Normans. Indeed, Owen found "the same common laws . . . in practice now as was before the Conq[est]," William claiming England "not *jure gladii*, but as heir to the Confessor." As if to underline his utter commitment to this viewpoint, Owen wrote that he stood upon this argument "as the children of Israel did upon the last Passover they celebrated in Egypt," with "their loins girded." His determination seems to have been prompted by the "modern" argument that "our laws were abolished by the Normans."[86] But Owen's medieval sources told him otherwise. For proof of the antiquity of common law and its survival throughout the centuries, he cited Sharnborn's case and *Domesday Book*, both of which proved that William allowed many Saxons to keep the land which they had held before 1066. Indeed, the "subjects of England and Englishmen, notwithstanding the conquest, by virtue of their English blood, in the time of King William the Conqueror did inherit land as if no conquest had been made." Not only did Englishmen enjoy "their own inheritance, but also the very privileges they had before the conquest . . ."[87] Thus, the continued existence of St. Edward's laws, which William and his successors confirmed, demonstrated to Owen's satisfaction that "Duke William did not reign by conquest or altered [sic] our laws."[88]

But, in Owen's view, the endurance of Saxon laws through the centuries protected more than ordinary Englishmen. Their survival also guaranteed that kings would continue to enjoy the same powers over the church that they knew before 1066. Indeed, governing the church properly constituted one of the duties of kingship. Demonstrating once again the flexibility of St. Edward's laws, Owen cited

[85] Quoted in Klein, "The Ancient Constitution Revisited," pp. 36–7. See also Owen, Of the Common Lawes of England, B.L. MS Landsdowne 646, fos. 1–43, 201, 206ᵛ, 208ᵛ, 210ᵛ–11, 220–1.

[86] *Ibid.*, fo. 229ᵛ.

[87] *Ibid.*, fos. 229–32, 238–9.

[88] *Ibid.*, fos. 27ᵛ, 64, 232–6.

Chapter 17, which stated that a king who misruled "loseth the name of a king."[89]

Even the two greatest scholars of the period, Sir Henry Spelman and John Selden, succumbed to an ancient constitutionalist view of the past. Spelman, the older of the two, was a member of the Elizabethan Society of Antiquaries who received his education at Trinity College, Cambridge, and Lincoln's Inn. He was also well schooled in practical politics, serving in his native Norfolk as a justice of the peace and sheriff, as well as representing Castle Rising and Worcester in the parliaments of James I.[90] At first sight, situating Spelman in the ancient constitutionalist camp seems questionable, since we now typically credit him with being one of the first contemporaries to appreciate that William I imposed feudal tenures on the defeated English kingdom. This meant that the major features of land law – knights service, hereditary fiefs, reliefs, feudal escheat, and fines for alienation – were of Norman origin. Nothing of the sort had ever existed in Saxon England. Spelman further noted that "the Conqueror not only generally dispossessed the Saxons" but "gave the lands to his Normans and others."[91] In recognizing the imposition of a foreign body of law upon the English, Spelman verged on concluding that the Norman conquest, by wiping out Saxon law and legal institutions, introduced a deep and abiding fissure in English history. From here it would have been but a short step to depicting William I as a genuine conqueror whose will was law. Such was certainly the conclusion that royalists and tories later drew from his words.

However, as Burgess and Pocock have noted, Spelman himself did not make the link between conquest, the imposition of feudal tenures, and the transformation of Saxon society. On the contrary, he continued to assert the continuity of laws and legal institutions into the Norman period and well beyond, leading to the conclusion that his views therefore had much in common with those of his fellow antiquaries and common lawyers.[92] Spelman's Saxonist in-

---

[89] *Ibid.*, fos. 229, 239–9ᵛ, 251ᵛ-2, 253.

[90] See Edmund Gibson, "Life of Sir Henry Spelman," in *Reliquiae Spelmanniae. The Posthumous Works of Sir Henry Spelman Kt. Relating to the Laws and Antiquities of England* (Oxford, 1698); Parry, *The Trophies of Time*, pp. 157–81.

[91] Spelman, "The Original, Growth, Propogation and Condition of Feuds and Tenures by Knights-Service, in England," in *Reliquiae Spelmanniae*, ed. Gibson. Although not published until 1698, this was written in 1639 in response to a law case in which Spelman was involved. See Pocock, *The Ancient Constitution and the Feudal Law*, pp. 100ff.

[92] *Ibid.*, pp. 288–9. Burgess, *The Politics of the Ancient Constitution*, pp. 69–70.

clinations appear readily from an examination of volume 1 of the *Archaeologus* (1626), described by Stan A. E. Mendyk as an "historical dictionary of legal and ecclesiastical terminology, remarkable for its historiographical significance."[93] Relying on sources such as Ingulf, whom he believed to be William I's clerk, the *Modus*, and Lambarde's *Archaionomia*, Spelman included within its pages a number of entries that reinforced important historical continuities across the divide of 1066. Thus, under the heading *"Ius Commune"* Spelman associated the founding of the common law with ancient Saxon kings, and St. Edward in particular. And under *"Laga"* and *"Lex Hen. I"* he linked Magna Carta to the confirmations of St. Edward's laws in Henry I's and Henry II's coronation charters, thus reinforcing the centuries-old belief in a direct link between Saxon and contemporary liberties. Indeed, throughout this volume Spelman indicated an unquestioning acceptance of the authenticity of the Confessor's law. He cited them, for example, in his discussions of the offices of constable and justiciar, the *Lex Anglorum* in Britain and Germany, and Danish and Norwegian law.[94] Finally, as earlier mentioned, Spelman likely served as the source for Sharnborn's case, since among his papers in the Bodleian Library is a manuscript detailing the history of the Sharnborn family, including the case of Edwin vs. the earl of Warren.[95]

Spelman's colleague, John Selden, proved equally useful to the ancient constitutionalist cause. Perhaps the most eminent legal scholar of the century, Selden trained at Clifford's Inn and Inner Temple. After achieving success as a conveyancer, he turned his considerable scholarly talents to the study of English history, in particular, its legal and ecclesiastical institutions. His close association with Camden, Cotton, and Archbishop James Ussher gave him access to a wide range of manuscript materials which he put to good use in his historical studies. Actively involved in politics during the

---

[93] Mendyk, *"Speculum Britanniae". Regional Study, Antiquarianism, and Science in Britain to 1700* (Toronto, 1989), pp. 273–4, n. 60.

[94] Spelman, *Archaeologus. In Modum Glossarii ad rem antiquam posteriorem* (London, 1626), pp. 182, 183, 208, 399, 400, 422, 429, 435–6, 437, 438, 439–40. This first volume covered letters "A" through "L," while the second part, published in 1664, dealt with the rest of the alphabet. See also Spelman's statements in *The English Works of Sir Henry Spelman, Kt. Published in his Life-time; Together with his Posthumous Works, Relating to the Laws and Antiquities of England; First Publish'd by the Present Lord Bishop of Lincoln, in the Year 1695* (London, 1723), part I, p. 130; part II, Preface and pp. 49–56, where he credited the Confessor with turning the various Saxon laws into the common law of England.

[95] Bodleian Library, Ashmolean MSS 1141. v. 7362, fos. 1–16v.

reigns of James I and Charles I, Selden entered parliament in 1624 and participated in the impeachment of the marquess of Buckingham in 1626 and in the drafting of the Petition of Right in 1628. A member of the Long Parliament summoned in 1640, Selden continued his opposition to the Stuart monarchy, retiring from public life in December of 1648.[96]

Although steeped in continental humanism, Selden located extensive portions of his writings comfortably within the ancient constitutionalist tradition: he accepted that major political and legal institutions existed at least as early as the Saxon period and survived from 1066 down to the seventeenth century. But Selden also recognized the presence of discontinuity in early English history. Take, for example, his *Jani Anglorum Facies Altera*, first published in 1610 and in an English translation in 1683. Described by Paul Christianson, the modern authority on Selden, as a "persuasive historical account of the English constitution" that remained influential far into the century, this work came close to admitting that 1066 constituted a catastrophic break with the English past. Here Selden wrote that William the Conqueror introduced changes, particularly in tenure and land-holdings.[97] His later works sometimes sounded the same note. Thus, in *The Historie of Tithes* (1618) he acknowledged that Saxon laws were "abrogated" at the conquest.[98] In his commentary on Michael Drayton's *Poly-Olbion* (1612) he described William as utterly conquering the Saxons, while in *Titles of Honor* (1614) he credited the Normans with introducing the military fief.[99] But Selden's most damaging blow to the ancient constitution came in his attacks on the antiquity of the *Mirror of Justices* and the *Modus tenendi Parliamentum*. Neither, in his view, served to prove continuity from Saxon down to Stuart times because both dated from the later

[96] Selden's life and career are discussed in Paul Christianson, "Young John Selden and the Ancient Constitution, ca. 1610–1618" *Proceedings of the American Philosophical Society,* 128 (1984), 271–315; Christianson, *Discourse on History, Law, and Governance in the Public Career of John Selden, 1610–1635* (Toronto, 1996); Pocock, *The Ancient Constitution and the Feudal Law, passim*; Parry, *The Trophies of Time,* chapter 4; White, *Sir Edward Coke and "The Grievances of the Commonwealth," 1621–1628,* chapter 7 *passim*.

[97] Selden, *Jani Anglorum Facies Altera, rendered into English, with large Notes thereupon, by Redman Westcott, Gent.* (London, 1683), pp. 47–8, 52, 55, 57–8. See also Christianson, "Young John Selden and the Ancient Constitution," pp. 279, 283.

[98] Selden, *The Historie of Tithes* (London, 1618), p. 484.

[99] Drayton, *Poly-Olbion,* ed. Hebel, vol. IV. Selden, *Titles of Honor* (London, 1614), pp. 228–9. Christianson, "Young John Selden and the Ancient Constitution," pp. 283–6, 289 90, notes 57, 58, 109, 110, 111.

middle ages. Indeed, the *Modus* was "an old book, which pretends to more antiquity by far than it ought." Although "many men have copies of it . . . none hath ever been seen very ancient." Selden repeated this opinion in the 1614 and 1631 editions of *Titles of Honor*, where he charged that the *Modus* had led many men astray.[100]

But Selden also understood that there was much more to the story. Indeed, his reading of impeccably reliable sources such as Lambarde's *Archaionomia*, Malmesbury, and Ingulf assured him that critical Saxon political and legal institutions survived the Norman conquest relatively intact. "There are," he wrote, "a great many laws of King Ine, Alfred, Edward, Athelstan, Edmund, Edgar, Ethelred, and Cnut the Dane, written in the Saxon language; which have lasted till these very times." To these laws people now "swear in the name of King Edward; not that he appointed them, but that he observed them."[101] The Confessor's laws endured because after the Norman invasion, William was "prevailed upon by the barons, to govern according to King Edward's laws, and at S. Albans takes his oath to do so. Yet some new laws were added to the old ones." This meant that "however those laws are attributed to the Confessor; it is certain that they are not without many mixtures of somewhat later transcribers."[102] Henry I and Henry II also confirmed the Saxon laws, together with the emendations of William I. King John followed suit in 1215.[103]

Selden's reading of early English history also taught him that parliament-like bodies existed as far back as the Druids, who met "to explain the laws in being, and to make new ones as occasion required . . . as now at this very time all matters of law go to be decided . . . at Westminster Hall in England . . ." And so it was with the Saxons, who made their laws "in the general assembly of the states or parliament." As for the membership of these bodies, Selden cited the preamble to the eighth-century laws of King Ine, who stated that he made his laws "by the advice and order of Kenred my father and of Hedda and Erkonwald my bishops, and all of my aldermen and of the elders and wise men of my people." This

---

[100] Selden, *Jani Anglorum*, p. 94. Selden, *Titles of Honor*, p. 274. *Titles of Honor*, 2nd. edn. (London, 1631), p. 691. See also Christianson, "Young John Selden and the Ancient Constitution," p. 312, n. 48.

[101] Selden, *Jani Anglorum*, p. 38.

[102] *Ibid.*, pp. 47, 48–50. Selden, *The Historie of Tithes*, pp. 224–5.

[103] Selden, *Jani Anglorum*, pp. 60–2, 69. Christianson, "Young John Selden and the Ancient Constitution," pp. 285–6.

practice, Selden continued, seems to have derived from the ancient Germans, for Tacitus described how their rulers dealt with matters of great concern by consulting "all the whole body of men." The practice continued under the Normans, who coined the name parliament.[104]

Selden's views on the origins of government also fitted comfortably into an ancient constitutionalist framework. In the 1614 edition of *Titles of Honor* he wrote that civil society first began in families, which grouped together in cities and towns and governed themselves in a democratic fashion. Democracy, then, preceded monarchy, meaning that the king's powers derived from the people. The nature and extent of the royal power was determined by the original contract between ruler and ruled, which agreement Selden elucidated by turning to ancient sources. In Sommerville's view, Selden probably "regarded these ancient records as relics of the original contract by which the people had transferred power to the king."[105]

Other writers with an antiquarian bent used the familiar narrative of historical continuity from Saxon to Stuart times. Edmund Bolton, for one, depicted the English as swallowing up the Norman invaders. Acknowledging the existence of an "English Revolution" which lasted from 1066 to the accession of James I, he explained that it was confined to the royal succession and lineage. The Normans never subdued the English themselves, who "still carried the general opinion, face and body of the nation."[106] The lexicographer John Minsheu also provided valuable evidence of the ancient constitutionalist view of the past. In his dictionary, first published in 1617 and in a second edition in 1625, he noted under his entry for "Parlament" that an assembly of the Lords and Commons had been present in the Confessor's time. Citing that "monument of antiquity," the *Modus tenendi Parliamentum*, Minsheu told how William the Conqueror

---

[104] *Ibid.*, pp. 93–4. Selden, *The Historie of Tithes*, pp. 195ff. See also Parry, *The Trophies of Time*, pp. 104–5; Christianson, "Young John Selden and the Ancient Constitution," pp. 275–6.

[105] Selden, *Titles of Honor*, pp. 2–5. Sommerville, "John Selden, the Law of Nature, and the Origins of Government," *Historical Journal* 27 (1984), 444–5. Christianson, "Young John Selden and the Ancient Constitution," pp. 286–7. Christianson and Sommerville also discuss the changes that Selden made in the second edition of *Titles of Honor*, published in 1631.

[106] Bolton, *Hypercritica or a Rule of Judgement for Writing or Reading our History's* (Oxford, 1722), pp. 224–5. Daniel Woolf has established that this work was written in 1621. "Edmund Bolton, Francis Bacon and the Making of *Hypercritica*, 1618–1621," *The Bodleian Library Record* 11 (1983), 162–8. But *cf.* Sharpe's reading of Bolton. *Sir Robert Cotton 1586–1631* (Oxford, 1976), p. 23, n. 44.

had examined and approved its contents. This meant that full parliaments existed before 1066 and continued to meet afterwards. Minsheu acknowledged that Polydore Vergil had dated this assembly from the reign of Henry I, but, he emphasized, even the Italian confessed "that it was used before, though very seldom."[107]

In the works of these common lawyers and antiquaries, radical ancient constitutionalists would later find a veritable gold mine. Despite the fact that none of these writers drew from the various medieval sources a right of resistance, their words nevertheless increased the persuasive power of this version of English history, authenticating and publicizing its leading sources. But common lawyers and antiquaries were not the only scholars who elevated the sources upon which radical ancient constitutionalists based their theories of resistance. Even civilians got into the act. Thus, John Cowell, Cambridge professor of civil law, found ancient constitutionalist sources, especially the *Modus*, the *Mirror*, and St. Edward's laws, acceptable enough to include them in his *Institutiones* (1605) and *Interpreter* (1607). This is perhaps surprising, given that the *Interpreter* earned Cowell a reputation for absolutism and resulted in a dressing down by James I. The work's influence even reached into the civil wars, when parliamentarian pamphleteers condemned it as too friendly by far to the Stuart kingship.

However, by mid-century Cowell's reputation had undergone something of a change. The royalist poet John Cleveland, for example, accused him of damaging Charles I's cause by making "an authority" of the *Modus*,[108] while one of Cromwell's supporters praised him as a "good . . . commonwealthman." Indeed, in 1651 the *Institutiones* was translated into English by order of parliament.[109] A perusal of the work shows that much of what Cowell wrote depended on the trinity of medieval sources and the standard ancient constitutionalist tales that they carried.[110] Thus, his reading

---

107 Minsheu, *Ductoris in Linguas, The Guide into the Tongues* (London, 1617), p. 349. *Ibid.* (London, 1625), p. 526.

108 Cleveland, *Majestas Intemerata. Or, The Immortality of the King* (n.p., 1649), p. 34.

109 *Institutes of the Laws of England . . . Translated into English According to Act of Parliament for the Benefit of All* (London, 1651), Preface. Cromwell deemed it helpful to the cause of union with Scotland.

110 For references to Lambarde's *Archaionomia* and St. Edward's laws see *Institutes of the Laws of England*, under "abjuration"; "Danegeld"; "Domesday"; "earl"; "freehold"; "leet"; "manumission"; "non terme"; "Peter's Pence"; "pledge"; "team"; "thridborow"; "toll"; "uncouth"; and "wapentake." References to the *Mirror of Justices* can be found under "abjuration"; "frankpledge"; "mahim"; "mainprise"; "naam"; "toll"; and "utlawrie."

of Lambarde's *Archaionomia* led him to credit St. Edward with establishing the common law by compressing the various laws of the kingdom into one body. From these William the Conqueror "chose the best and to them adding of the Norman laws, such as he thought good . . . ordained laws for our kingdom, which we have at this present, or the most of them."[111] Cowell even included the story of the men of Swanscombe Down, whose refusal to bend their knees to the Conqueror accounted for the continued existence of gavelkind tenure.[112]

Cowell also found parliament to be of ancient origin, though he knew that Polydore Vergil credited Henry I with its institution. Still, he noted, even Polydore admitted that previous kings had summoned it, and it surely existed in Saxon times. So much was proven by the *Modus tenendi Parliamentum*, that "monument of antiquity" which "was delivered by the discreeter sort of the realm unto William the Conqueror, at his commandment, and allowed by him." Cowell then quoted the *Modus*' proem at length.[113]

The civilian Sir John Hayward shared many of Cowell's views. Although he had earlier attacked ancient constitutionalist theorizing when defending the union of Scotland and England, he returned to the idiom when writing *The Lives of the III. Normans, Kings of England* (1613). There he described William as claiming the crown not as conqueror but as rightful successor of Edward the Confessor and "as an universal successor of former kings, in all the rights and privileges which they did enjoy." Further, Hayward told how at William's coronation, when he took an oath to govern church and people justly, the English "received [William] king by general consent." In addition, Hayward presented William's victory over Saxon laws and institutions as incomplete because he permitted the Dane-law, which closely resembled Norman customs – "both being derived from one common head" – to continue in Norfolk, Suffolk, and Cambridge-shire. William also granted that the city of London could continue to use St. Edward's laws, and, under pressure from the men of Kent, he

---

Cowell also mentioned St. Edward's sword, *Curtana*, and noted that it was the first sword carried before the king at his coronation. However, he remarked that it was said "that the point is broken: which may argue an emblem of mercy." See under "curteyn (curtana)."

[111] Cowell, *The Interpreter: or Booke Containing the Signification of Words* (Cambridge, 1607), under "Law" and "Merchenlage."

[112] *Ibid.*, under "gavelkind."

[113] *Ibid.*, under "Parliament."

promised that county that it could retain its ancient customs.[114] Thus, in one form or another, Saxon laws survived the conquest.

Hayward's account of the origins of the French influence in early medieval England struck a similarly familiar chord. In his view, the Normanization of England was limited and gradual, occurring "with the silent approbation of the English; who have always been inclinable to accommodate themselves to the fashions of France."[115] In fact, the Confessor himself initiated this process. Returning from Normandy more French than English, he inspired his subjects to abandon "the ancient usages of their country, and with great affection or affection rather," to conform "themselves to the fashions of France." To the Confessor also went credit for advancing Frenchmen to positions of power in England, a development which made William's domination all the easier.[116] Here, then, was a civilian in the employ of James I inadvertently supplying Stuart rebels with the perfect answer to a question frequently asked by royalists: from whence did the Norman influence derive if not from conquest?

On the other hand, Hayward depicted William as deserving of the name of conqueror because, his various promises to obey St. Edward's laws notwithstanding, he changed the "greatest part, and brought in the customs of Normandy in their stead," also ordering that legal proceedings go forward in the Norman tongue, a "barbarous and broken French, not well understood of the natural French, and not at all of the vulgar English."[117] Moreover, Hayward told how William stripped the Saxons of their wealth and advanced Normans in their place, so that "scarce any noble family of English blood did bear either office or authority within the realm." Indeed, the severity of Norman law "laid upon the English as fetters upon their feet [and] a ponderous yoke upon their necks."[118] However, this frightful condition lasted only a short time, for successive confirmations of St. Edward's laws soon softened the impact of Norman custom. Thus, William Rufus and Henry I, "being desirous to win the favor of the people did fill them with fair promises, to abrogate the laws of King William their father and to restore to them the laws of K. Edward."[119] King Stephen, Henry II, King John, followed suit, as did Henry III, whose promise "remained in

---

[114] Hayward, *The Lives of the III. Normans, Kings of England*, pp. 32, 43, 96–7, 122–3.
[115] *Ibid.*, pp. 123–4.   [116] *Ibid.*, p. 46.   [117] *Ibid.*, pp. 44, 96, 100.
[118] *Ibid.*, pp. 100–2.   [119] *Ibid.*, pp. 241–2.

force," presumably in the form of Magna Carta. Indeed, such was the practice that whenever Norman kings "were willing to give contentment to the people: who desired no other reward for all their blood spent in the service of their kings, but to have the laws of K. Edward restored," the laws of the land "afterwards . . . became, not only tolerable, but easy and sweet, and happily not fit to be changed."[120]

The accession of Henry I and his marriage to Matilda proved especially significant in Hayward's version of early English history, since it reinforced the continuity between Saxon and Norman England by uniting the two peoples "both in blood and title to the crown." Indeed, more than any other event this union endeared Henry to the whole English nation, for the people "saw the blood of their Saxon kings restored again to the possession of the crown."[121] To Henry I also went credit for instituting "the form of the high court of parliament, as now it is in use." Before his time, kings summoned only the nobility and clergy.[122]

Significantly, for all of his talk about Norman oppression of the native Saxons, Hayward was nevertheless able to write that "no essential change" followed in the aftermath of 1066. In his words, "the state still remained the same, the solid body of the state remained still English: the coming in of many Normans, was but as rivers falling into the ocean; which change not the ocean, but are confounded with the waters thereof."[123] For Hayward, then, the ancient constitution and St. Edward's laws could be used for various purposes. As to what he exactly "believed," we cannot say. But it is undeniable that under one set of circumstances he thought the ancient constitutionalist view of the past worth strong repudiation, and under another he felt comfortable arguing within its framework.

Finally, even middle-class Englishmen knew of this particular historical construction and the sources that supported it. William Whiteway, for one, found the ancient constitutionalist version of the past familiar. Serving in parliament in 1626, when Buckingham was impeached, this Dorchester burgess was familiar with the Petition of Right and with Sir John Eliot's attack on tunnage and poundage in 1629. In 1623 he wrote in his commonplace book, under the heading "Materials for the History of the Raigns of K. J. and K. C.," these

---

[120] *Ibid.*, pp. 100–2.   [121] *Ibid.*, p. 236.
[122] *Ibid.*, pp. 283–4.   [123] *Ibid.*, pp. 123–4.

words: "K. Edward the 3. before the conquest confirmed the laws now called the common laws. These were for the most part made before by K. Edgar" and other predecessors of St. Edward.[124] Moreover, as Patterson notes, Whiteway also found the 1578 edition of Holinshed worth quoting, in particular, extracts from John Hooker's version of the *Modus*. Citing what Patterson describes as "the most tendentious" part, he wrote that " 'If the lords of the Parliament be [not] present the King and the Commons may make laws. But the King and Lords cannot do so without consent of the Commons.' "[125]

A more obscure Englishman also manifested an interest in the ancient Saxon laws in general and St. Edward in particular. This was William Blundell, whom Woolf describes as "a struggling minor gentleman" of the Catholic faith. Living in a small village in Lancashire in the early decades of the seventeenth century, Blundell came into possession of some Saxon coins. In attempting to prove his right to keep them, he turned to ancient laws such as St. Edward's, which he probably knew from Ingulf.[126]

As this chapter has so far shown, the debate over the unification of Scotland and England precipitated barbed attacks on the continuity of English history and focused unparalleled attention on the link between the Norman conquest and royal absolutism. These attacks forced many politically articulate Englishmen to rethink and sharpen their views of the Norman conquest. The debate over the union also spurred them to defend their version of 1066 with special vigor. Writers of general histories of England, for their part, hewed to the course laid down by their Tudor predecessors, highlighting both the continuities and discontinuities of early English history. Still, the pages of these works echo with the traditional stories of Saxon strength and tenacity, which kept alive St. Edward's laws and preserved the prescriptive rights of the English people to be governed by the same. Predictably, radical ancient constitutionalists would later find these early seventeenth-century materials extremely helpful in justifying opposition to Stuart kings. But they also received

---

[124] Cambridge University Library, Dd. xi. 73. 191.b. 195.a.

[125] Annabel Patterson, *Reading Holinshed's Chronicles* (Chicago, 1994), pp. 270–1.

[126] D. R. Woolf, "Little Crosby and the Horizons of Early Modern Political Culture," in Donald R. Kelley and David Harris Sacks, eds., *The Historical Imagination in Early Modern Britain. History, Rhetoric, and Fiction, 1500–1800* (Cambridge, 1997), pp. 104–5. Blundell might also have known of St. Edward's laws through Foxe's *Acts and Monuments*, with which he was also familiar. *Ibid.*, p. 97.

inspiration from another source, namely, those political disputes which, in the early seventeenth century, provoked pointed controversy about the nature of the legal relationship between king and subject.

THE ROLE OF MEDIEVAL SOURCES IN EARLY STUART LEGAL DISPUTES: EXTRA-PARLIAMENTARY TAXATION AND ARBITRARY IMPRISONMENT IN THE REIGNS OF JAMES I AND CHARLES I

Ancient constitutionalist sources saw protracted duty in early seventeenth-century parliaments and courts of law, when they were forcefully pressed into service against royal policies that many deemed threatening to the polity. While some historians suggest that the theory of the ancient constitution began to wane during Charles I's reign, when it proved inadequate to a new set of political and polemical circumstances, I will argue, rather, that it took on a new and even more vigorous life. Indeed, it was at this time that its ideological potential was first fully realized – a development not lost on radical ancient constitutionalists later in the century, who frequently turned to this period for ammunition and inspiration. True, no contemporary went so far as to suggest that St. Edward's laws, the *Modus tenendi Parliamentum*, or the *Mirror of Justices* sanctioned resistance. Nevertheless, the uses to which early seventeenth-century dissidents put these sources prepared the way for the full articulation of resistance theory in 1642.

The disputes in question concerned the proper boundary between the king *solus*, on the one hand, and the king in parliament, on the other. On certain occasions James I and his son Charles I chose to act alone when many in the political nation preferred, indeed, insisted, that they act through parliament. Especially troubling were royal policies that sought to raise money outside of parliament.[127] Since the middle ages the power of taxation had resided primarily in the king and his Commons. When he needed supply, he summoned parliament. This practice enabled the two houses, and the Commons in particular, to keep the monarch abreast of grievances affecting members, their constituents, and the commonwealth itself.

---

[127] Thomas Cogswell, "A Low Road to Extinction? Supply and Redress of Grievances in the Parliaments of the 1620s." *Historical Journal* 33 (1990), 283–303. Cogswell, "War and the Liberties of the Subject," in *Parliament and Liberty*, ed. Hexter, pp. 225–51. Richard Cust, *The Forced Loan and English Politics, 1626–1629* (Oxford, 1987).

On occasion, the early seventeenth-century Commons attempted to influence royal policy by linking supply to the redress of grievances. Occasionally, too, the Stuarts short-circuited this process by resorting to extra-parliamentary forms of taxation such as impositions, benevolences, forced loans, and tunnage and poundage. Equally problematic was the royal inclination to adjourn and dissolve parliament when the two houses rose up in opposition. To many politically articulate Englishmen, such policies not only threatened their pocket books but also jeopardized the very institution of parliament. And without parliament kings might too easily ignore their interests, political, economic, and otherwise.

This matter arose early in James I's reign, when he levied an imposition on currants, a move that drew strong objections from merchants and some members of parliament. After the decision in *Bate's Case* (1606) validated his right to collect such a levy, his government extended the tax to any number of imports. In 1610 the two houses debated the matter at length. The arguments adduced by both sides resonated throughout the century, leading Elizabeth Read Foster to suggest that the debates deserve to be read "in the larger context of the development of parliament and the constitutional issues" of the period.[128] By and large, the king and his opponents agreed that the right to tax resided either in king or parliament and was authorized either by common law, statute, or even reason of state. For both sides, then, history mattered. The king's men argued that monarchs must have possessed the power to tax because, according to the common law, kings had custody of ports along with the right to restrain subjects and their goods from coming and going. From this it necessarily followed that James I could lawfully lay impositions upon imports. Some also noted that, as keeper of the kingdom, James I possessed an absolute prerogative which permitted him to supplement the ordinary laws of the land when the public welfare was at stake.[129]

Before mounting a full response, the House of Commons appointed a committee to search the records in the Tower, parliamentary rolls, year books, close rolls, patent rolls, and royal charters for precedents concerning impositions. The committee included

---

[128] Foster, ed., *Proceedings in Parliament 1610* (New Haven, 1966), vol. I, p. xii.
[129] *Ibid.*, vol. I, pp. xi–xvi; vol. II, pp. 50, 88, 202ff, 226. Samuel R. Gardiner, ed., *Parliamentary Debates in 1610*, Camden Society, vol. LXXXI (London, 1862), pp. 62–3, 85–8, 91, 98–102.

several members of the Society of Antiquaries, in particular, Francis Tate, Sir Roger Owen, and Sir Robert Cotton, as well as James Whitelocke, Heneage Finch, and Nicholas Fuller.[130] Their search of the records, which Foster describes as conducted "with impressive industry and accuracy," told them that neither common law nor statute law supported James I's right to impose without parliamentary consent. As for the particular records which this committee found apt, case reports from the middle ages through the reign of Elizabeth I were deemed worth citing in the debates. In addition, the king's opponents referred to Magna Carta, which, in good antiquarian fashion, they interpreted as declarative of ancient custom, that is, St. Edward's laws.[131]

The *Modus tenendi Parliamentum* and St. Edward's laws proved particularly useful in the debates. Finch, for one, found the *Modus* well suited to answer the case put forward by Sir Francis Bacon, the king's solicitor general. Bacon had supported the royal cause by arguing that the origins of impositions lay in the king, and not in parliament or people. This must be so because in early times parliaments were not "so stirring" as to be able to place limitations upon the monarch. It therefore stood to reason that kings, not parliaments, had originally taxed, though over the course of time they eventually permitted the Commons to participate. In response, Finch admitted that neither side could demonstrate the exact origins of the power to levy impositions. But his reading of early English history differed markedly from Bacon's. Far from being weak institutions which only later developed into formidable bodies, "parliaments are as ancient as the law and a part of the fundamental constitution of the common law." The *Modus tenendi Parliamentum*, "extant in many hands," proved as much. William the Conqueror himself saw, and presumably approved of, this work, which meant in turn that parliament existed before the conquest as well as after. The *Modus*, then, gave the lie to those "ignorant chroniclers [who] write that Henry I was the first king that called a parliament." Finch understood the source of the chroniclers' error: because they could not find proof of a parliament more ancient, they concluded there was none. For Finch, however, the *Modus* was proof enough. In his view, parliaments, which existed before the conquest, must have

---

[130] Foster, ed., *Proceedings in Parliament 1610*, vol. I, pp. xv–xvi; vol. II, p. 74.
[131] For references to case reports see *ibid.*, vol. II, pp. 182, 230, 231. References to Magna Carta can be found in *ibid.*, pp. 162, 190, 227.

possessed the right to tax. After all, "'tis improbable that kings in those times, when subjects were fain to fight for their just and ancient liberties, would thrust such a liberty on the people as a negative voice in making or altering of laws."[132]

Owen also deployed the Saxon past against James I. In proof of his contention that neither the common law nor the constitution of the kingdom granted the king a right to impose outside of parliament, Owen referred to the practice in ancient England. Noting that the Britons had paid taxes to the Romans, he reminded his listeners that this ended with the conquest of the Saxons, who altered the laws, the language, and the religion. Therefore, "we must prove our customs to proceed from the Saxons," which Owen proposed to do by reference to St. Edward. In the Confessor's time, monies went to the lords of the ports by prescription, that is, to private persons and not to the king. But no charges attached to merchandise. The message, then, was clear: because Saxon kings could not levy such a tax, neither could the Stuarts.[133]

Then there was William Hakewill's celebrated speech, delivered at the end of the last session of parliament. Existing in numerous copies and widely read, the Long Parliament considered it sufficiently germane to warrant publication in July of 1641 under the title *The Libertie of the Subject*. In that same year Hakewill brought out his own edition of the *Modus*, which he had probably completed as early as 1610. It therefore occasions no surprise to find him basing his opposition to extra-parliamentary levies, at least in part, on Saxon history. Summarizing the arguments of the king's supporters, he noted their claim that royal levies must have begun "either by the king's absolute power or by a legal assent of the people, which can be no where but in parliament." Yet such assent "must appear of record," and, the king's men concluded, because no such record existed, the right could only have originated "by the king's absolute power" which "same power remains still." "How," they asked, "began that custom . . . if not by the king's absolute power? And when was that power taken away?"[134]

---

[132] *Ibid.*, vol. II, p. 231. See also Gardiner, ed., *Parliamentary Debates in 1610*, p. 63, where Montague also cited the *Modus*.

[133] *Ibid.*, pp. 114–15.

[134] Hakewill, *The Libertie of the Subject: Against the Pretended Power of Impositions. Maintained by an Argument in Parliament An, 7. Jacobi Regis* (London, 1641), pp. 125–7. This version of his speech is the one which Hakewill himself edited and allowed to be published because the

Hakewill's answer consisted of several parts. First, he countered, the issue could be illuminated by extending the question of origins to include many rights and practices other than taxation. Instead of merely inquiring into the beginnings of imposts, why not explore the history of a wide range of usages, such as original writs, trial by twelve jurors, the age of majority for men and women, and the limitation of a year and a day? Where lay the origins of these practices? For that matter, "who reduced all the known grounds of the common law to that certainty that they now are?" Just because Hakewill and his colleagues could not ascertain exactly when or how these practices arose, the king's men were not entitled to "therefore conclude that they began by the king's absolute power, and infer, that by the same reason, they may be changed at his pleasure." Admitting that the origins of many practices lay in obscurity, Hakewill settled for concluding that they began "by a tacit consent of king and people, and the long approbation of time beyond the memory of man."[135] In other words, by prescription. Such practices therefore had a life of their own independent of the royal authority.

Hakewill knew another answer to the king's argument in favor of an absolute power to impose. "Though no man can directly affirm," most of the above usages "might begin by act of parliament, though now there be no records extant of such ancient parliaments." He well understood that making such a suggestion flew in the face of those who saw parliament as a late-comer to the political scene. He had in mind both those chroniclers who found Henry I summoning the first parliament, as well as those whose search of the records pointed to Henry III as its progenitor. But these views availed nought, because Hakewill knew of an unimpeachable source that told a different story. This was William I's set of laws, which included his confirmation of St. Edward's laws and which Hakewill knew from Lambarde's *Archaionomia*. These told him that "William the Conqueror held parliaments, for what can be else understood by these words, *Per commune consilium totius Regni nostri stabilitum fuit*." Nor, of course, was William the first to summon this body. "Nay, long before him," in 712, Ine summoned parliaments. Moreover, these ancient parliaments contained all the elements of the modern institution, as Lambarde made clear when he decribed laws as made

earlier printed version contained mistakes. "To the Reader." See also Rabb, *Jacobean Gentleman. Sir Edwin Sandys*, p. 158.
[135] Hakewill, *The Libertie of the Subject*, pp. 126–7.

"*per commune consilium & assensum Procerum, Cominum, omnium Sapientium, Seniorum, Populorum totius Regni* . . . which are the same in Latin which ours is in English, *By the King, the Lords Spiritual and Temporal, and the Commons.*" Why, Hakewill asked rhetorically, could not imposts have been "first granted at one of these parliaments, as well as to have . . . first begun by the king's absolute power?"[136]

As for the absence of parliamentary records, Hakewill again had a ready and convincing answer: "most of the ancient records," he noted, were burned in the Exchequer fire in Henry II's time. It was wrong, of course, to "conclude therefore that there were never any such."[137] Finally came his ultimate response to the argument that the king enjoyed an absolute right to impose by common law: even if that were true, parliament had at numerous times curtailed and limited it, indeed, had utterly taken it away. Witness Magna Carta, that "most ancient statute law . . . won and sealed with the blood of our ancestors," and confirmed scores of times in parliament.[138]

These arguments carried the day, and in July of 1610 the lower house passed a measure, without any negative voice, declaring that by the laws of England no impositions could be lawfully laid by the king upon the subjects' goods but by consent in parliament.[139] But the nation had by no means seen the end of the issues raised in this "Long Parliament," as one contemporary called it. James I persisted in looking for ways to raise money by extra-parliamentary means, and his opponents persisted in opposing such moves. The issue once more surfaced in the parliament of 1621, when James I's wholesale selling of patents of monopoly led to the impeachment of several of the worst offenders. James's foreign policy also drew fire. Frightened that the successes of the Counter-Reformation boded ill for Protestants at home and abroad, some in parliament pushed James to pursue war actively against Spain, a major Catholic player in the Thirty Years' War. From James's point of view, the implementation of this plan would not only prove expensive, it would also put a crimp in his scheme to marry Prince Charles to the Spanish infanta. When the king prohibited the lower house from discussing such matters of state, it responded with a "protestation" declaring its right to debate whatever issues touched on the welfare of the kingdom. Further, the Commons, reiterating an earlier petition to

---

[136] *Ibid.*, pp. 128–9.   [137] *Ibid.*, p. 129.   [138] *Ibid.*, pp. 98–100.
[139] Foster, *Proceedings in Parliament 1610*, vol. II, pp. 258–71, 283–6.

the king, claimed that "the liberties, franchises, privileges and jurisdictions of parliament are the ancient and undoubted birthright and inheritance of the subjects of England." James responded swiftly and forcefully. Having recently told the house that its rights derived not from their ancestors but "from the grace and permission" of his own forebears, he ordered the Commons to adjourn. Then, at a meeting of the Privy Council, he saw to it that the Protestation was officially ripped from the journal of the House of Commons.[140]

James could scarcely have acted in a more threatening way: by raising money outside of parliament and using his prerogative to adjourn and dissolve parliament, he left his opponents wondering about the future role of the two houses in the government of the kingdom. That the members themselves fully understood the threat appears from proceedings in parliament. The first clash came when the Commons attempted, of its own and without the Lords, to judge and punish one Edward Floyd. A Roman Catholic lawyer already imprisoned in the Fleet, Floyd had made derogatory remarks about James's daughter Elizabeth and her husband, Frederick V, elector of the Palatine, who was then fighting the good Protestant fight on the continent. While few doubted the Commons' right to exercise jurisdiction over its own members and to participate with the House of Lords in the impeachment process, questions arose about its power to proceed in this matter. The king himself postponed Floyd's punishment and then, along with the Lords, directly attacked the juridical power of the Commons. In particular, the king questioned whether the house constituted a court of record, as it must if it had the power to punish, and if it could proceed without sworn testimony. If the Commons could so prove, James wondered whether its judisdiction extended beyond its own members to subjects such as Floyd. The king introduced as evidence a case found for him in the Tower, the precedent of 1 Henry IV, which stated "*Que les communes ne soient parties a judgements.*" If this were true, "we have been misled by those who affirmed the power of this house to judge alone." In other words, parliamentary judicature was limited to the Lords and the king.[141]

As Stephen White notes, this position called into question not only

---

[140] Quoted in J. P. Kenyon, ed., *The Stuart Constitution*, 2nd. edn. (Cambridge, 1986), pp. 27, 42.

[141] *Commons Debates, 1621*, ed. Wallace Notestein, Frances Relf, and Hartley Simpson (New Haven, 1935), vol. IV, pp. 286–7, 290–1. See also White, *Sir Edward Coke and "The Grievances of the Commonwealth," 1621–1628*, pp. 155–9, especially 156; Rabb, *Jacobean Gentleman. Sir*

the Commons' earlier proceedings against James's monopolists but also its general right to judge its own members and to protect its own privileges.[142] Such a challenge could not go unanswered. But the Commons found its case difficult to make. Hakewill, for one, admitted that he could find no precedents supporting a claim of judicature in cases such as Floyd's, a view shared by the common lawyer William Noy.[143] Other members, however, turned to medieval records that described the Commons' centrality in the government of the kingdom. One of them, Sir Edward Peyton, found the *Modus* well suited to his purposes. According to his reading of the work, the consent of the Commons was essential to any judgment in parliament, "for else there might be a parliament of the Lords without the Commons." But this, he continued, "could not be," since the *Modus* established that the lower house was such an essential part of parliament that the king could hold a meeting with only the Commons in attendance. This precedent Peyton offered at the conference between the two houses, when the Lords pressed the Commons for proof of its claims.[144]

Some in the lower house also deployed the *Modus* against the king's right to adjourn parliament – an undoubted royal prerogative if ever there was one. Upon hearing the news that James planned to send them home, Edward Alford told the house that the king could not do so, since the *Modus* bound him to continue parliament's sitting "till bills be passed." This Alford took to mean "that the king could not dissolve a parliament when we have things in the forge of moment till they were finished." On the other hand, the *Modus* proved that "the Commons may end a parliament, and continue a parliament."[145] Although no other speaker in 1621 is recorded as using the *Modus* in this way, the lesson was clear: even this most indisputable of prerogatives might fall prey to the ancient constitutionalist version of English history. Indeed, throughout the century whenever dissidents sought to encroach upon the king's traditional

Edward Sandys, pp. 241–8; Robert Zaller, *The Parliament of 1621: a Study in Constitutional Conflict* (Berkeley, 1971), pp. 104–15.

[142] *Commons Debates, 1621*, ed. Notestein, Relf, and Simpson, vol. IV, pp. 286–7, 290–1. White, *Sir Edward Coke and "The Grievances of the Commonwealth," 1621–1628*, pp. 155–9, especially 156.

[143] *Commons Debates, 1621*, ed. Notestein, Relf, and Simpson, vol. III, pp. 137–8; vol. IV, p. 291. White, *Sir Edward Coke and "The Grievances of the Commonwealth," 1621–1628*, p. 156.

[144] *Commons Debates, 1621*, ed. Notestein, Relf, and Simpson, vol. II, pp. 352–3; vol. III, pp. 191, 192.

[145] *Ibid.*, vol. II, pp. 352–3, 403; vol. III, p. 340; vol. IV, p. 388.

control over the summoning and sitting of parliament, they drew on the same passage of the *Modus* that attracted Alford's attention.

Problems relating to supply and religion proved even more vexing to Charles I than they had to his father. At odds with Spain and committed to aid Protestants on the continent, the king needed money which parliament, however devoted to the cause, declined to provide. From its point of view, the duke of Buckingham's failed attempt to rescue French Huguenots was all too typical of the mismanagement of the military. And to make matters worse, the costly fiasco brought England to the brink of war with France. When parliament refused in 1626 to vote supply for war, Charles levied forced loans on an enormous scale, imprisoning many who refused to pay without cause shown. The decision in *Darnel's Case*, handed down by King's Bench in 1627, declared that such prisoners were not bailable.[146] This ruling, combined with Charles's billeting of soldiers on civilians and his placing of wide areas under martial law, set the stage for the Petition of Right, forced upon the king by parliament in 1628. In these proceedings the two houses depended heavily upon medieval history in general, and upon the canonical medieval sources in particular.

For many in parliament, the Petition of Right carried the message that the royal prerogative was limited by the *lex terrae*. The law of the land protected the subjects' "ancient and fundamental liberties," in particular their liberty of person and proprietary interest in their goods and property as against royal interference. Where could this *lex terrae* be found? Undoubtedly in Magna Carta, confirmed some thirty times since the thirteenth century. But the great charter itself merely declared an even more ancient law. In fact, the *lex terrae* was synomomous with St. Edward's laws. This point, along with the related belief in the continuity of these laws down to Stuart times, lay at the heart of the straightforward remarks of John Williams, bishop of Lincoln. Chaplain to Lord Ellesmere and James I as well as James's lord keeper, Williams would later serve as archbishop of

---

[146] See Paul Christianson, "John Selden, the Five Knights' Case, and Discretionary Imprisonment in Early Stuart England," *Criminal Justice History* 6 (1985), 65–87; J. A. Guy, "The Origins of the Petition of Right Reconsidered," *Historical Journal* 25 (1982), 289–312; Linda Popofsky, "Habeas Corpus and 'Liberty of the Subject:' Legal Arguments for the Petition of Right of 1628," *The Historian* 41 (1979), 257–75; Cust, *Forced Loans and English Politics*, pp. 55–62, 236–8; Burgess, *The Politics of the Ancient Constitution*, pp. 190–94. But *cf.* Mark Kishlansky, "Tyranny Denied: Charles I, Attorney General Heath, and the Five Knights' Case," *Historical Journal* 42 (1999), 53–83.

York. Despite his earlier associations, Charles I considered Williams so untrustworthy that he tried, unsuccessfully, to keep him out of the House of Lords in several parliaments, including that of 1628. Indeed, on two occasions Charles even imprisoned him in the Tower.[147] In 1628 Williams entertained no doubts whatsoever about the definition of the law of the land. "By *lex terrae*," he stated simply, "is meant the laws of St. Edward the Confessor."[148]

Sir Dudley Digges discoursed at greater length on the matter. Selected by the Commons to help present its case at a conference of the two houses, he too stated plainly that the laws of England dated "from the Saxon days, notwithstanding the injuries and ruins of time." Moreover, "they have continued in most parts the same," as the survival of the laws of Ethelbert, Ine, Offa, and Alfred indicate. Admittedly, Digges continued, the Danes put these laws to rest and stilled English customs. But "by the blessing of God a good king, Edward, commonly called St. Edward, did awaken those laws," repairing those that he had reawakened and embellishing those he had repaired, and confirming those he had embellished. To these laws "William the Conqueror and all his successors since that time have sworn unto." This explained, Digges continued, why "many cases frequent in our modern laws strongly" concur "with those of the ancient Saxon kings." For example, just as contemporary England knew court barons, court leets, and sheriffs' courts, so too did Saxon England. Moreover, "as we have now, they had their parliaments where new laws were made *cum consensu praelatorum, magnatum et totius communitatis*; or, as another writes, *cum consilio praelatorum, nobilium, et sapientum laicorum*" – that is, with the consent of the prelates, the nobles, the wise laymen, indeed, of the whole community.[149] Digges's words reached a much wider audience when they appeared in the 1642 tract *A Conference Desired by the Lords and Had by a Committee of both Houses, concerning the Rights and Privileges of the Subjects.* By then, however, Digges was leaning in the direction of the king's camp and would soon, as we shall see, turn his pen against the Long Parliament.

---

[147] See Elizabeth Read Foster, *The House of Lords 1603–1649* (Chapel Hill, 1983), pp. 17–18, 35–7, 145–6; Sommerville, "Parliament, Privilege, and the Liberties of the Subject," pp. 72–3.

[148] *Commons Debates 1628*, ed. Robert C. Johnson and Maija Jansson Cole, assisted by Mary Frear Keeler and William B. Bidwell (New Haven, 1977), vol. II, p. 333; vol. V, pp. 172, 321.

[149] *Ibid.*, vol. II, pp. 333–4. See also the remarks of Charles I's secretary of state, Sir John Coke, who traced the common law "from the Saxons, yea from the Romans." *Ibid.*, vol. III, pp. 137, 140.

The continuity of Saxon laws and legal institutions also mattered to the common lawyer Richard Creswell, who attacked royal policies by emphasizing the antiquity of the subject's rights to his person and property. "The kings of England," he told the Commons, "have a 'monarchical' state, not a 'seignoral'; the first makes freedom, the second slavery." This had long been the case. Witness, Creswell continued, Sharnborne's case, in which the Conqueror, by voiding his own grant to the earl of Warren, submitted himself to Saxon customs. "Why then, claiming so ancient a right, may we not stand for that which is as old as the conquest." Or – for this was the point of story – even older.[150]

Coke, whom Hirst calls "the most important of all parliament men,"[151] likewise cited the Saxon laws, which William the Conqueror himself had confirmed. Referring readers to Lambarde's *Archaionomia*, Coke noted William's promise to allow free men to hold their lands in peace without any tallage except that granted by common consent.[152] John Pym underlined Coke's remarks. Freedom from imprisonment without cause shown was an ancient right of Englishmen confirmed by the Conqueror himself, who, "though he conquered the kingdom, conquered not the law."[153] The *Modus* also proved pertinent. During the April 4 debates over taxation, Sir John Eliot carried it into the House of Commons where he might have read from it.[154]

After debating their grievances at length, the two houses, with the Commons taking the lead, agreed on a Petition of Right. The measure committed the king to end extra-parliamentary taxation, imprisonment without cause shown, billeting, and martial law. On June 7, 1628, Charles I accepted the Petition of Right, though not without trying to gut it. After promising the House of Commons that he would publish the Petition with his second, less ambiguous reply, he then reneged. Ordering all copies of the Petition destroyed, he produced a new edition which included his exceptions and qualifications to the document. Then, in a move designed to strike fear into the hearts of his opponents, he ordered Eliot to be imprisoned in the

---

[150] *Ibid.*, vol. II, p. 154.

[151] Hirst, "The Place of Principle," p. 90.

[152] *Commons Debates, 1628*, ed. Johnson and Cole, vol. II, p. 64. See also Mr. Prynne's 1st Lecture on ye Petition of Right made in Parl. March 17 An. Dmi. 1627. 3 Car. 1. B.L. Stowe MSS 302. fos. 47–79, especially 57ᵛ–70.

[153] *Commons Debates, 1628*, vol. II, p. 106.

[154] *Ibid.*, vol. II, pp. 306–7. See also B.L. Stowe MSS 366. fo. 47ᵛ.

Tower for seditious conduct. There Eliot died rather than submit to the royal authority.[155] Charles soon dissolved parliament, determined not to call another if he could possibly avoid it. He then resumed the very practices that the Petition had condemned.

Still, the Petition of Right mattered. After all, the Commons, joined by the upper house, had united in order to safeguard liberty and property from the royal absolute prerogative. And they had justified their cause primarily by pressing the ancient constitution into service – a fact that did not escape the king's supporters. One was Sir Francis Kynaston, an esquire to Charles I, who responded with a withering attack on the line of historical reasoning behind the Petition. In his answer he put a monarchical twist upon both St. Edward's laws and the common law doctrine of prescription. Kynaston was moved to take pen in hand by a recent work entitled *The Priviledges and Practices of Parliaments in England*. Written around 1620 by Ralph Starkey, this tract was first published in 1628 and reprinted in 1640, 1641, and 1680 as germane to the work of the Short and Long Parliaments as well as to the exclusion controversy.[156] It sorely offended Kynaston by resorting to English history to pump up the king's opponents while giving the royal authority decidedly short shrift. Indeed, Starkey had gone so far as to describe parliament as the proper guardian of both "private and public tranquility," empowered to "look into the necessity of public condition, and so to foresee reasonable remedy." In language that antimonarchical elements would have found most welcome in 1621 and 1628, Starkey noted that parliaments had played this role at least since Saxon times, and perhaps under the Britons. The arrival of the Normans saw the name changed from Miclegemot to parliament, but "the frame or jurisdiction of this court" remained the same as before the conquest and indeed "continued . . . to this day." As

---

155 B.L. Stowe MSS 366. fo. 47ᵛ. See Sommerville, *Politics and Ideology in England 1603–1640*, pp. 163–73; Burgess, *The Politics of the Ancient Constitution*, pp. 190–4; Guy, "The Origins of the Petition of Right Reconsidered," pp. 289–312; Michael B. Young, "The Origins of the Petition of Right Reconsidered Further," *Historical Journal* 27 (1984), 449–52; White, *Sir Edward Coke and "The Grievances of the Commonwealth"*, pp. 213–74; Popofsky, "Habeas Corpus and 'Liberty of the Subject,'" pp. 257–75; Elizabeth Read Foster, "Petitions and the Petition of Right," *Journal of British Studies* 14 (1974), 21–45; Frances H. Relf, *The Petition of Right* (Minneapolis, 1917).

156 Sommerville, "English and European Political Ideas in the Early Seventeenth Century," pp. 192–3. Sommerville, "Parliament, Privilege, and the Liberties of the Subject," pp. 81–3.

proof he cited Coke's preface to the *Ninth Part* of his *Reports*, which also served to demonstrate the presence of "all the communality of the land" in that body.[157]

Kynaston, however, would have none of this nonsense about parliaments which were "coeternal with the world, [or] at least with the kingdom." Such talk made it appear that only parliaments deserved extended discussion, whereas kings received only perfunctory treatment.[158] In point of fact, Kynaston continued, history suited the king's needs as well as his opponents. For example, there was no way of knowing if Edward the Confessor held parliaments, because no parliamentary rolls or statutes survived from his time. It was clear, however, "that the Conqueror, who altered the laws and the tenures, and made new ones," also likely altered Saxon courts such as parliament. Indeed, the best records show that the modern parliament began in Henry II's time. Although he acknowledged that the Saxons held great assemblies consisting of the nobility, the clergy, and commons, Kynaston would not accept "that these meetings were parliaments, in such a sense as we call parliaments nowadays."[159] In fact, all known evidence belied the existence of parliaments in ancient times, "where the sword solely conquered and governed" and "the king's will, was his law, and the advice, counsel or consent of the people was never asked, (or) regarded." In the early days, "laws were made by the sole power and command of our Saxon kings." Witness, for example, "the practice of St. Edward the Confessor, who we read called not his people to the making of laws, but did wisely collect and choose" the best of the ancient laws. This body of laws "are at this day in the Tower, and are our fundamental and principal laws."[160]

Kynaston now proceeded to plead the doctrine of prescription, on which his opponents relied so heavily, on the behalf of the king. Admitting that the author of *Priviledges* had a point when he suggested that the Commons had often been summoned to parlia-

---

[157] *The Priviledges and Practice of Parliaments in England. Collected out of the Common Lawes of the Land. Seene and allowed by the Learned in the Lawes. Commend to the High Court of Parliament now Assembled* (London, 1628), pp. 1–2.

[158] Kynaston, A True Presentation of Foremost Parliaments, to the view of present Times and Posteritie, B.L. Landsdowne MS 213. fos. 147–47ᵛ. See also Cromartie, "The Constitutional Revolution," pp. 105–6.

[159] A True Presentation of Foremost Parliaments, fos. 150 3.

[160] *Ibid.*, fos. 153–53ᵛ.

ment, Kynaston denied that the lower house therefore enjoyed a prescriptive right. His evidence rested on the fact that its right had been interrupted and intermitted because kings sometimes summoned only the Lords. The Commons could not, therefore, "allege and prove constant usage, without intermission." Moreover, according to common law, nothing could be prescribed for when records showed "the beginning of a thing." But many records pointed to Henry II as first summoning the Commons. This evidence of a beginning thus negated a claim to a prescriptive right.[161]

Kynaston now presented his own view of English government. Although the king permitted his subjects a role in framing laws, "the essential form of laws" derived from the royal will for the good government of the people. This held true not only for the present king but for William the Conqueror, who made whatever laws he wanted "by the power and prerogative of his sword." Then, however, he deigned to summon the barons and wisemen to London, where he confirmed the laws of St. Edward. Finally, Kynaston exhorted the king's enemies to understand that even the most vicious and wicked tyrant, be he a conqueror or a rightful heir, reigned nevertheless as God's vicegerent. Therefore, no subject or assembly possessed the right to judge him. Indeed, parliaments "have their origination, their essence, being, and continuation from the king's absolute prerogative and pleasure."[162]

The Case of Ship Money

Charles I's own view of his relationship with parliament no doubt echoed Kynaston's, and, loath to call another parliament to raise money, he proceeded to levy the infamous ship money. This levy was in the nature of a service which port cities traditionally paid for the defense of the realm in time of emergency. Charles I now greatly extended the levy. Objections came from all sides, especially on the ground that no emergency existed. Prynne, for example, vigorously attacked the policy in *An Humble Remonstrance Against Ship-money Lately*

---

[161] *Ibid.*, fos. 158–58ᵛ. Since the reign of Henry II was outside legal memory, that is, 1189, Kynaston's words might seem to support Burgess's approach to time immemorial, not mine. But common law doctrine held that if a charter existed, litigants had to plead it, not prescription.

[162] *Ibid.*, fos. 167, 170. See also fos. 156 and 158, where Kynaston refers to Henry I's coronation charter and Magna Carta as restorations of St. Edward's laws.

imposed. Written in 1636, it was published without his permission in 1641 and again by order of the House of Commons in 1643. Initially, or so Prynne claimed, the work so frightened the privy council that it tried to suppress it.[163] In this tract he argued the illegality of extra-parliamentary levies, in particular ship money, by championing the high power of parliament as against kings. Such taxation was, on its face, "directly contrary to the fundamental laws and liberties" of this land. For his first proof Prynne turned to "the ancient law of Edward the Confessor, and William the Conqueror (ratified by all our kings by their very coronation oath)" and registered by Lambarde and Selden in their collections of Saxon laws.[164] In particular *Archaionomia* made it clear that the king's supporters erred when they claimed that the Saxon tax called Danegeld was levied without consent of parliament. On the contrary, this tax was imposed "not by the king's absolute prerogative . . . but granted and imposed by the parliament, with the people's consent."[165]

Evoking the persuasive power of the doctrine of prescription, Prynne further noted that when kings levied the Danegeld in times of peace, the complaints of the people caused them to relent. The first to do so was "that good and gracious prince king Edward the Confessor." Although William the Conqueror and William Rufus renewed it, Henry I and later King Stephen released the English people by ratifying St. Edward's laws. Such evidence led Prynne to conclude that ship money ran directly against precedent, "yea, against the law of King Edward the Confessor, which our kings," including William I, "are sworn to observe."[166]

The *Mirror of Justices* also figured in Prynne's attack, since it carried the maxim that a man could not be a judge in his own case. Citing Chapter 2 of the *Mirror*, Prynne warned Charles I that the royal tax collectors might levy more than necessity required, thus depriving subjects of security of "goods, lands, [and] liberties." Prynne left it for the reader to judge the injustice of a situation in which subjects had to petition the king, whose coffers their hard-earned labors filled, for redress.[167]

---

[163] Prynne, *An Humble Remonstrance Against Ship-money Lately imposed: Laying Open the Illegality, Injustice, Abuse, and Inconvenience thereof* (London, 1643), "To the Reader."
[164] *Ibid.*, pp. 1–2, 3.
[165] *Ibid.*, pp. 19–23, 26, 29.
[166] *Ibid.*, *passim*.
[167] *Ibid.*, p. 8.

Matters came to a head when John Hampden refused to pay ship money. After imprisoning him, Charles I sought a judgment in the Exchequer Chamber confirming his right to do so during an emergency. Both sides relied on a variety of arguments and sources, including *jus gentium* and Roman law tags such as "necessity knows no law." Both sides also called on medieval sources to prove either that kings anciently levied ship money without parliamentary consent, or that they had done no such thing. In this contest for control of the English past, St. Edward's laws proved particularly apt, since certain provisions dealt directly with the Dangeld and could be read both as supporting and opposing the king's position. Thus, Sir Robert Holbourne, one of Hampden's lawyers, made much of the Confessor's condemnation of the Danegeld, a tax levied in defense of the kingdom against Danish invasion. Moreover, when William confirmed St. Edward's laws, he too gave up Danegeld. After all, the Conqueror promised his subjects that he would take only what he was entitled to by tenure, and this did not include extra grants such as Danegeld. Importantly, Holbourne reminded the court, William's promise was "not a charter between the king and his tenants," that is, a narrow feudal arrangement, but an agreement "betwixt the king and the kingdom." Holbourne acknowledged that this charter could not be found in the parliament rolls. But no such records existed until early in Edward III's reign in the fourteenth century. Indeed, much of the common law depended on records now lost. However, this dearth was due not to the fact that no such records had ever existed but rather to the fires and other accidents that befell governmental archives from time to time.[168]

Fortunately, Holbourne told the court, other compelling evidence existed, namely, William I's statute confirming Saxon laws. "This law," which "was but the law of the Confessor," helped prove that neither before nor after the conquest could kings tax their subjects without their approval in parliament. Magna Carta, which embodied the common law, and its many confirmations put the matter beyond dispute. For his information about Saxon laws, Holbourne relied on Ingulf who lived at the time of the conquest, as well as on the writings of Lambarde, Camden, and Owen. Admittedly, he continued, kings after 1066 levied Danegeld without parliamentary

---

[168] *A Complete Collection of State Trials*, compiled by T. B. Howell (London, 1816), vol. III, pp. 980ff.

approval, the last time being Edward III's levy in 1377. However, the doctrine of prescription precluded such royal moves from becoming lawful customs. Because the people always objected to such extra-parliamentary levies, royal actions never grew into precedents. In his words, "the people did decry it and it was not such a practice as could bring in a law." Reiterating the common law definition of customary usage, Holbourne told the court that for the practice of levying taxes outside of parliament to become part of the law of the land, it must meet certain criteria. First, it had to receive the tacit assent of the realm. Second, it must be general over all the kingdom. Third, it must be reasonable, and finally it must be consistently and constantly exercised. "It is not enough," he argued, "to be at some times and seldom, but it must be *semper eadem*." Moreover, even when parliaments voluntarily granted supply, they attached protestations so "that those things should not be drawn into example." In sum, the royal right to levy ship money did not meet the common law definition of customary usage, nor was it sanctioned by statute. It must, therefore, be an unlawful practice.[169]

Holbourne's co-counsel, Oliver St. John, argued similarly. He too considered that William I gave up the Danegeld when he confirmed St. Edward's laws in the fourth year of his reign. This "act of parliament" was drawn up according to the "common counsel of all the realm." For confirmation of his judgment, St. John vouched Camden's *Britannia*, Lambarde's *Archeion*, and Spelman's *Glossary*: all agreed that when the Conqueror took Danegeld, it was only by parliamentary grant. Moreover, by agreeing to and confirming Magna Carta, later kings renewed the promise not to tax except with the consent of parliament.[170] Now St. John too looked to the doctrine of prescription to drive his point home. By failing to object to the levying of taxes only in parliament, kings and queens thereby gave their tacit consent to this practice. Indeed, their "non-claims" should be taken "as so many *le voets* and declarations of their general consents." Put differently, in such great matters as concerned the subjects' liberty and property, the maxim *nullum tempus occurrit Regi* – time does not run against the king – did not protect the king.[171]

[169] *Ibid.*, vol. III, pp. 981–3, 984, 987, 990, 1001, 1008, and *passim*.
[170] *Ibid.*, vol. III, pp. 887, 894–6, 898, 908. Like Holbourne, St. John's took his proof from Ingulf and Selden's *Eadmerus*, as well as from the *Red Book of the Exchequer* and Coke's preface to the *Eighth Part* of his *Reports*.
[171] *Ibid.*, vol. III, p. 923.

Arguing for Charles I, attorney general Sir John Banks found ancient constitutionalist sources equally supportive of his cause. Indeed, he attempted to construct an ancient constitutionalist argument for royal authority. The origins of the English government, he told the justices assembled in the Exchequer, indicated that "kings were before parliaments." This meant in turn that the king, as an absolute ruler, possessed the right, given him by both God and the law, to provide for the defense of the realm by levying ship money. Indeed, kings before and after the conquest had provided for the safety of the kingdom in precisely this manner, even though it meant infringing upon the property rights of the subject. The *Mirror of Justices* proved as much, since it placed the dominion of the sea squarely in the king's hands. Further, the power to decide the necessity of such a move rested solely with the king, although he might choose to take the advice of others. Thus, before 1066 kings consulted with the lords and wisemen when the realm was in danger, and William I did the same. So much appeared from his confirmation of the "*antiquas leges et consuetudines Angliae.*" "So then," Banks concluded, "if these were the laws, and this was the power that the ancient kings of England had before his time, he did ratify and confirm it, but not diminish it."[172]

This argument brought him to Holbourne's charge that because kings had not issued writs for ship money since the reign of Edward III, the right, even if it had ever existed, was now extinct. Not so, Banks retorted, for discontinuance of time could not take away the king's right which was inherent in the crown. "No prescription," he told the court, "can invade the king's profit." Nor could disusage constitute a precedent, for time did not run against the king. Moreover, this held for Saxon kings such as Alfred as well as for all subsequent monarchs. In other words, in both Saxon times and after the conquest, the *lex terrae* guaranteed the monarch's exercise of this absolute prerogative. Put differently, "originally, by the institution of the laws of this realm, what was once in his hand, and was never granted from him, is still in him."[173]

The king's solicitor general, Sir Edward Littleton, citing Lambarde's *Archaionomia*, echoed Banks's arguments, though in a softened form. He insisted that St. Edward's laws proved that kings had

---

[172] *Ibid.*, vol. III, pp. 1016, 1018, 1019, 1020, 1021, 1023, 1025–6, 1047, and *passim*.
[173] *Ibid.*, vol. III, pp. 1039–40, 1047, 1051–2, 1064, and *passim*.

levied Danegeld before the conquest. Then, commandeering one of the Confessor's legends, Littleton described how William I renounced the Danegeld after seeing a devil dancing on a pile of money. As for William ruling as a conqueror, such was surely not the case; "for after he came in, men did recover the lands which were their ancestors." A good thing, too, continued Littleton, for "take our laws, and take our lives."[174]

By a narrow margin of seven to five, the judges in the *Ship Money Case* ruled in the king's favor. Generally speaking, those who favored the royal position did so on the ground that ship money was not a tax but rather a service owed the king for defense of the realm in emergency situations. In the view of Sir Robert Berkeley, a justice in King's Bench, St. Edward's laws meshed perfectly with a theory of royal absolutism. The simple fact of the matter was that anciently, kings raised money without parliamentary consent because originally parliaments did not exist. This meant that Charles I could do likewise. As an absolute monarch, he alone could provide for the defense of the realm because the "*jura summae magestatis*" was vested solely in him and not in "his high court of parliament." After all, that body owed its very existence to the king, who summoned it when he wanted and sent it home when he had finished with it.[175] As sovereign governor of the realm, he might also, when he deemed it meet for the welfare of the kingdom, dispense with parliamentary statutes. Moreover, in this same capacity he enjoyed the benefit of the *nullum tempus occurrit Regi* maxim, which guaranteed, despite Holbourne's and St. John's arguments to the contrary, that "disuage [was] no precedent."[176]

Continuing, Berkeley noted that the king enjoyed these rights, which were inherent in the crown and therefore untouchable by parliament, because St. Edward's laws guaranteed them. When monarchs swore to keep and observe the laws, customs, and liberties that "the glorious king Edward granted the clergy and people," they thereby confirmed their rights as absolute sovereigns. Regarding Holbourne's and St. John's claims that the king could act only with parliament, Berkeley reminded the court that "the law knows no such king-yoking policy. The law is of itself an old and trusty servant of the king's . . . I never read nor heard, that *Lex* was *Rex*; but it is

[174] *Ibid.*, vol. III, pp. 931, 944.
[175] *Ibid.*, vol. III, pp. 1090, 1098–9, 1101–2, 1106, 1115, and *passim*.
[176] *Ibid.*, vol. III, pp. 1102, 1115.

common and most true, that *Rex* is *Lex*, for he is '*lex loquens*,' a living, speaking, an acting law." Once again St. Edward's laws, which William swore to keep, proved relevant. Far from derogating from the royal authority, these laws acknowledged the king's right to collect Danegeld without parliamentary consent.[177] As for Holbourne's and St. John's usage of Magna Carta against Charles I, Berkeley agreed with Banks that it came from a period of rebellion and therefore lacked legitimacy. Nor did it even merit the name of statute. For Berkeley, then, neither common law nor statute told against the king's right to collect ship money.[178]

The other six judges who sided with the crown put forward similar arguments on behalf of Charles I. Sir George Vernon, justice of Common Pleas, supported the royal policy on the ground that England had been a monarchical state since Brute.[179] Sir John Finch, lord chief justice of Common Pleas, argued that the king possessed the right to raise money outside of parliament because "certainly there was a king before a parliament, for how else could there be an assembly of king, lords and commons?" Moreover, the king was not bound to call parliament unless he pleased, and it sat only as long as he wished. As for ship money itself, Charles I's policy rested on a solid legal foundation. Witness, in particular, William I's confirmation of St. Edward's laws, which sanctioned the collection of the Danegeld. Admittedly, the Conqueror's grant had freed the subject from unjust taxes. But ship money was just.[180]

Those justices who ruled in Hampden's favor also found ancient constitutionalist sources relevant to their cause. Thus, Sir Humphrey Davenport, lord chief baron of the Exchequer, admitted that kings could mount a defense of the kingdom without calling parliament when danger was imminent. However, because no emergency now existed, the king ought to have summoned parliament. His levy was, then, illegal. In this sense the present situation differed greatly from that in 1588 or 1066, when English monarchs had insufficient time to asssemble the two houses. Before he finished his argument, Davenport paused to comment on the Norman conquest. In his view, "William I (not the Conqueror, for he did not conquer the kingdom, he conquered the king of the kingdom)" came in, as Lambarde

---

[177] *Ibid.*, vol. III, pp. 1091–4, 1097, 1098–9, 1105.
[178] *Ibid.*, vol. III, p. 1106ff.
[179] *Ibid.*, vol. III, pp. 1125–6.
[180] *Ibid.*, vol. III, 1226, 1228, 1230, and *passim*.

described, "not in *per conquestum*, but *per acquisitionem*." Indeed, so far was William from ruling as a conqueror that he went to the trouble of sending commissioners to every county to learn exactly "what the ancient laws of England were." According to these laws, which were, of course, the Confessor's laws, Danegeld was a lawful tribute which the king could demand by writ under the Great Seal. But only "when the danger is instant." Then subjects must pay. On all other occasions, however, he must summon parliament – and this by the charters of William I, which confirmed St. Edward's laws, as well as by the Magna Cartas of King John and Henry III.[181]

According to Sir George Crooke, justice of King's Bench, Charles I could not collect ship money without parliamentary consent because Saxon laws, which William the Conqueror confirmed, prohibited such levies. As these laws, as well as Magna Carta, demonstrated, ancient kings could lay no charge upon the subject except by common consent of the realm. Indeed, Crooke reminded the court, "the law did always account the parliament able to provide and to give sufficient aid, and most fit to consult *de arduis regni*; and there is a consent of and grant of the Commons to what is done, they are actors in it." So critical in fact was parliament to the governing of the realm that a law in King Alfred's day mandated it meet at least twice a year – an obvious reference to the *Mirror of Justices*.[182] To Sir Richard Hutton, a justice in Common Pleas, Magna Carta, "an ancient and great statute," told for Hampden as against the king, for it prohibited proceeding against a free man except by the law of the land. And these laws protected subjects in their liberty and property. As for the *nullum tempus* prerogative which some of his brethren had cited in Charles I's favor, it was indeed a great power. Nevertheless, it did not rank among those inseparable prerogatives of the crown, which neither the king could give away nor parliament take. Thus, both the statute 25 Edward III, c. 1 and a case from 11 Henry IV, fo. 7 deprived the king of the use of the *nullum tempus* prerogative where the lapse of a presentation to a church was concerned. Moreover, in Hutton's judgment, statutes of Edward I and Edward III mandated that no impositions could be levied without parliament. Nor, indeed, did kings collect ship money since these reigns, which meant in turn – or so Hutton implied – that

---

[181] *Ibid.*, vol. III, pp. 1214–15.
[182] *Ibid.*, vol. III, pp. 1129–30, 1135, 1147, 1159.

discontinuance had negated whatever right to extra-parliamentary taxation kings had previously enjoyed. Put differently, the king did not possess a prescriptive right to ship money, but, or so Hutton implied, his subjects enjoyed a prescriptive right to be taxed only in parliament.[183]

The debate over ship money took place on a polemical battlefield in which the king's supporters and his opponents battled over the meaning of early English history. And the decision in favor of Charles I brought him victory. At least for a time. Still short of funds, he was forced in April of 1640 to summon another parliament. This body, the Short Parliament, met from April 13 to May 5, when the king angrily sent it home. Its importance appears readily from the fact some of its leaders, for example, John Pym and Sir Walter Erle, had seen duty in 1620s and would also appear among the leadership in the Long Parliament. Moreover, many of the political arguments used against Charles I in the 1640s had seen duty in early seventeenth-century parliaments and court cases. Equally significant, from the beginning to the end of his reign Charles's opponents reinforced these arguments by reference to St. Edward's laws, the *Modus* and *Mirror*. Here, then, were the vital links between the political disputes of the early seventeenth century and the civil war. Here, too, was the continuity that some scholars claim did not exist.

The *Modus* figured conspicuously in the Short Parliament, providing support for the political ideas that distinguished its proceedings. Indeed, several members, for example, Lord Saye and Sele and William Glanville, speaker of the House of Commons, possessed their own copies of the *Modus*. Others knew it by association. Thus, the son of Sir John Eliot, who had carried the *Modus* into the Commons in 1628, served in the Short Parliament. John Pym, the future leader of the Long Parliament, also had a thorough knowledge of the work through his acquaintance with Sir Edward Coke. In addition to serving with Coke in the parliament of 1628, Pym knew his printed works and even possessed some of his unpublished manuscripts. The latter he had rescued from Coke's study before the king's men had a chance to seize them. The earl of Northumberland also had a first hand acquaintance with the *Modus*. As the patron of William Hakewill, he supported the antiquary's publication of that

---

[183] *Ibid.*, vol. III, 1192, 1194–8, 1200–1, and *passim*.

work in 1641, where the *Modus* appeared in its second English translation.

The value of the *Modus* in promoting the anti-Stuart cause became unmistakably evident when Pym found it relevant to his assault on the king's power to call and dissolve parliament. In his lengthy and well-known speech of April 17, 1640, Pym included this particular royal prerogative among the main grievances against Charles I. Taking aim at the king's habit of dismissing any parliament that refused to do his bidding, Pym found the practice detrimental to the welfare of the kingdom. Referring to the session of 1629 when members held the speaker of the Commons in his chair, he excoriated Charles for sending parliaments home when "there were petitions left not heard." Such actions took "away the last will of a dying man" and prevented "us of our last sighs and groans to his majesty." In Pym's view, sending parliament packing before it had concluded its business constituted the greatest punishment it could possibly suffer. Indeed, "the breaking up of parliament" was tantamount to killing it.[184] Benjamin Rudyard, who had also seen parliamentary service in 1628 and 1629, likewise criticized Charles's use of the power of dissolution. Associating the discontinuance of parliaments with "papists," he told the lower house that the "breakings of parliaments makes dangerous wounds in the body politic and if these splinters be not pulled out with a gentle hand, we may hereafter dispair of cure." Other members spoke to the same effect.[185] But this particular grievance was not the only one that weakened "the soul of the body politic," as Rudyard called parliament. In words that would have reminded contemporaries of the *Mirror* and Edward III's statutes prescribing annual parliaments, Pym charged that "the intermission of parliaments have been a true cause of all these evils to the commonwealth, which by law should be once every year." To many in the Short Parliament, such grievances "have altered the happy and healthful constitution" of the kingdom and breached "our liberties and privileges."[186]

Charles I himself acknowledged the ideological power of ancient constitutionalist sources. After dissolving the Short Parliament in

---

[184] *Proceedings of the Short Parliament of 1640*, ed. Esther S. Cope with the collaboration of Willson H. Coates, Camden Society, 4th series, vol. XIX (London, 1977), pp. 149–50, 245, 254.

[185] *Ibid.*, pp. 113, 138–9, 163, 174, 245, 248–9.

[186] *Ibid.*, pp. 138, 148–9. But *cf.* Kevin Sharpe, "Crown, Parliament and Locality," in *Politics and Ideas in Early Stuart England* (London, 1989), pp. 98–9.

May of 1640, he ordered the arrest of Lord Saye and Sele, one of the peers who supported Pym's arguments. In addition, the king ordered that Saye and Sele's library be searched for seditious materials. Heading the list of subversive literature recovered in the lord's study was the *Modus*, followed by a manuscript proving that the kings of England had always consulted with their parliaments – perhaps a reference to the *Mirror*.[187]

In the period following the dissolution of the Short Parliament in May, Charles I confronted crises both in Ireland and Scotland. Especially troublesome was his defeat in the Second Bishops' War which had come about as a result of his efforts to impose the Book of Common Prayer upon the Scottish Presbyterians. With Scottish forces occupying Northumberland and Durham, the king had little choice but to summon the Long Parliament. Its early proceedings contain further evidence that control of parliament's sitting continued to be of utmost importance. In February of 1641 the two houses passed the Triennial Bill, which contained a clause stating that parliament, which must meet at least once every three years, could not be dissolved "within fifty days at least after the time appointed for the meeting thereof." In May came "The Act against Dissolving the Long Parliament without its Own Consent." In December the question of royal control over parliament's sitting surfaced again, this time when the Commons presented the Grand Remonstrance to the king. A primary means through which Pym appealed to the country, it carried a long list of grievances. Included among them were several which struck at the king's power of dissolution. Revolutionary in their implications, these measures attacked the heart of the royal prerogative as exercised for centuries.[188] How convenient that Charles's opponents had at their disposal "an ancient manuscript" – the *Modus* – which made the radically new appear traditional.

When the complete breakdown of government finally came in August of 1642, Charles I's enemies already had at their disposal a powerful version of the medieval past eminently well suited to their ideological interests. Not only was it sustained by a trinity of texts

---

[187] Bodleian Library, Tanner MSS 88. fos. 115–15ᵛ. See also J. S. A. Adamson, "The Baronial Context of the English Civil War," *Transactions of the Royal Historical Society*, 5th series, 40 (1990), 97, n. 24.

[188] J. P. Kenyon, ed., *The Stuart Constitution*, 2nd. edn. (Cambridge, 1986), p. 213. Sharpe, "Crown, Parliament and Locality," p. 97.

and the cult of St. Edward's laws, its stories had already been given the "proper" spin during the early years of the Stuart period. Now it remained for Charles I's enemies to formulate a full-fledged theory of resistance.

CHAPTER 5

"You shall be king while you rule well": the radical ancient constitution in the civil wars and interregnum

Ideas unlike events are never unprecedented.

Hannah Arendt

INTRODUCTION

The revolutionary potential of St. Edward's laws, the *Modus tenendi Parliamentum*, and the *Mirror of Justices* was first fully realized during the period from 1642 to 1660, when rebels of all stripes deployed them to justify rebellion, regicide, and republicanism. Modern scholars, as has already been noted, sometimes suggest that in the civil war period "political rationalism" and natural law theories began to rival ancient constitutionalist argumentation and eventually to supplant it.[1] While it is true that other idioms of political thought appeared in parliamentarian discourse, I suggest in this chapter that the suppleness of the medieval canon has been greatly underestimated. Not only did St. Edward's laws, the *Modus*, and the *Mirror* remain central to dissident theorizing, their value even increased. Indeed, they gave rebels familiar and convincing historical arguments with which to counter the royalists' powerful defense of the king. More particularly, the three sources served as ballast for a new line of anti-royalist argumentation. This was the doctrine of coordination, which the Long Parliament and its supporters fashioned from Charles I's *Answer to the XIX Propositions*.

To appreciate the critical role of St. Edward's laws, the *Modus*, and the *Mirror*, we must first get the lay of the ideological land. By mid-century, two divergent views of political society shaped the political thought of Stuart England. The first was the royalist "order" theory

---

[1] See, for example, Glenn Burgess, *The Politics of the Ancient Constitution* (University Park, Pa., 1992), pp. 221–7; J. G. A. Pocock, *The Ancient Constitution and the Feudal Law* (Cambridge, 1987), chapter 7 *passim*, p. 304.

of kingship, built on the early seventeenth-century theorizing of James I, civilians such as Alberico Gentili and Calybute Downing, and clergymen such as Roger Maynwaring and Peter Heylyn. This absolutist view of monarchical power located sovereignty in a king who reigned by virtue of a direct grant from God. According to such theorizing, kings exercised a reserve of power, a discretionary authority analogous to God's miracle-working power and the father's discretionary power within the family. As God's vicegerent and sovereign governor of the realm, the monarch had no equal within the kingdom. Moreover, as the earthly source of political authority, he stood at the center of the body politic and political society, his position unrivaled by that of any person, agency, or aggregate of powers. From these tenets it followed that subjects owed unconditional obedience to their king. Under no circumstances could they resist his rule, not even if he degenerated into the worst of tyrants.[2]

Antithetical to the order theory was the parliamentarian view of government. According to this ideology, God directly empowered the "people," who might then institute whatever form of government they pleased. That is, as parliamentarians were fond of saying, while government in general was from God, the particular form came from the people. Many parliamentarians went on to suggest that, in England, the people had at some distant point in time instituted a mixed or limited monarchy in which sovereignty resided in the three coordinate and coeval estates of King, Lords, and Commons. This division of power gave the numerically superior two houses, as the representative of the kingdom, the upper hand. Other parliamentarians pleaded their case without reference to the theory of coordination, speaking more generally of a scheme of government in which the people chose the king on condition that he govern according to those rules enumerated in the coronation oath. Whatever the approach, most parliamentarians theorized that the king's relationship with his people was contractual, which meant in turn that their obedience was conditional. Indeed, a king who broke the terms of the agreement by

---

[2] See Corinne C. Weston and Janelle Greenberg, *Subjects and Sovereigns: the Grand Controversy Over Legal Sovereignty in Stuart England* (Cambridge, 1981), chapters 1 and 2; J. H. Burns, *The True Law of Kingship. Concepts of Monarchy in Early-Modern Scotland* (Oxford, 1996), chapter 7; Johann P. Sommerville, "English and European Political Ideas in the Early Seventeenth Century: Revisionism and the Case of Absolutism," *Journal of British Studies* 35 (1996), 168–94; John Sanderson, "Conrad Russell's Ideas," *History of Political Thought* 14 (1993), 85–102; Sanderson, *"But the People's Creatures": the Philosophical Basis of the English Civil War* (Manchester, 1989), chapters 2 and 3.

which he held his crown thereby freed his subjects from allegiance. Now, unfettered by legal and moral bonds, they could dispose of him and replace him with another ruler more to their liking.[3]

Royalists and parliamentarians also had their own views of English history. No mere scholarly dispute, the battle for control of the past lay at the heart of a heated and protracted ideological feud that lasted throughout the century. Many royalists constructed a version of medieval history which depicted kings as predating parliament and the common law. This meant that whatever authority these legal institutions possessed, they possessed by virtue of the king's largesse. Or, to put it differently, while the king's power was original, the power of parliament and the common law was derivative.[4] The distinction between an original and a derivative power mattered greatly in Stuart England, since contemporaries of various political persuasions often viewed the former as inherently superior to the latter. This notion Englishmen expressed in the classical maxim, "*Quod efficit tale, id ipsum est magis tale*" – that which maketh another such, it is itself much more.[5] Other royalists, to be sure, reasoned differently, acknowledging, for example, that the people might well have constituted the original human source of authority and might even have chosen and endowed the first king. However, once made, the grant of power was irrevocable, and once chosen, the king reigned as God's vicegerent on earth. Whatever the royalist view of the origins of government, virtually all the king's men believed that parliament and the common law had no life independent of the monarchy.

The age and longevity of governmental institutions also mattered in the royalists' approach to 1066. Many, though certainly not all, of the king's supporters showed a passing acceptance of conquest theory when they dealt with conquests in general and the Norman

---

[3] See Weston and Greenberg, *Subjects and Sovereigns*, chapter 3.

[4] See, for example, David Jenkins, "Lex Terrae; or, Laws of the Land," in *Somers Tracts*, ed. Walter Scott, 2nd. edn. (London, 1810), vol. v, pp. 103, 104 and *passim*; *The True Law of Free Monarchy, Or the reciprocall and mutuall duty betwixt a free King and His naturall Subjects* (London, 1642), pp. 10–11; Charles Dallison, *The Royalists Defence* (n.p., 1648), pp. 4, 7, 12, 93.

[5] See, for example, Samuel Rutherford, "Lex, Rex (1643)," in *The Presbyterian's Armoury* (Edinburgh, 1843), p. 83; John Doughty, *The Kings Cause Rationally, briefly, and plainly debated, as it stands Defacto* (n.p., 1644), p. 36; *Maximes Unfolded* (London, 1643), p. 39. Not all polemicists agreed with this line of reasoning. See, for example, Dudley Digges, *The Unlawfulnesse of Subjects taking up Armes Against Their Soveraigne* (n.p., 1644), p. 113; Philip Hunton, "A Treatise of Monarchy (1643)," in *The Harleian Miscellany*, vol. vi (London, 1810),p. 331; this is the 1689 edition.

conquest in particular. To such royalists, William I reigned as an absolute conqueror, obliterating Saxon laws and planting Norman institutions in their place. Indeed, parliament and the common law, far from originating in the distant past, were relative newcomers to the political scene, summoned into existence by a conqueror and his successors who manipulated them for their own purposes. This version of history, then, emphasized the disjuncture and discontinuity of England's past. At the same time, it provided support for the argument that, just as William the Conqueror reigned absolutely, so too did his heir and successor Charles I.

The parliamentarian version of history, on the other hand, led to a very different pattern of power. Drawing on the historical tradition articulated by Tudor and early Stuart antiquaries and chroniclers, the king's enemies often argued that the kingdom, parliament, and common law were at least as old as, and perhaps older than, the kingship. This meant that they were equal or superior to the monarchy and in any event enjoyed an existence independent of the king. Predictably, given the Tudor and early Stuart writers whose lead they followed, parliamentarians placed great emphasis on institutional continuity from the Saxon period down through the seventeenth century. Indeed, the king's enemies usually insisted that their scheme of government dated back at least as far as Saxon times, survived the Norman conquest intact, and descended to Stuart Englishmen in much the same form.

In putting forth this claim, parliamentarians made use of the doctrine of prescription, which members of early seventeenth-century parliaments had forcefully pressed into service against James I and his son. Because the earliest records depicted King, Lords, and Commons as sharing equally in the government of the kingdom before 1066 or at least by 1116 – both dates safely outside legal memory –, their right to do so was prescriptive. To be sure, sometimes rulers such as William I and William Rufus attempted to alter this arrangement. But on such occasions the English people always entered protests, thus preserving their prescriptive right to be governed by the ancient laws.

CIVIL WAR IDEOLOGIES TAKE SHAPE

Both royalist and parliamentarian theories of government appeared compatible with the outward forms of the English government. Both rested on ideas that were deeply rooted in English history. And both drew on a wide range of historical, legal, religious, and classical sources. Their full articulation dated from the extended quarrel between Charles I and the Long Parliament in the months pre-ceeding and following the outbreak of civil war in August of 1642. At that time, royalists and parliamentarians waged a war of words aimed at monopolizing the ideological high ground. Indeed, in Nigel Smith's words, "never before in English history had written and printed literature played such a predominant role in public affairs, and never before had it been felt by contemporaries to be of such importance."[6] There is no overestimating the importance of this part of the struggle, for its purpose was to win the hearts and minds of the English people.

Both sides therefore placed the highest premium on presenting their causes in the best possible light. As defenders of God's anointed and the government as established by law, royalists enjoyed a decided advantage. Parliamentarians, on the other hand, had to convince themselves and others that making war against the king of England – under whom they and their ancestors had lived for generations – was necessary, just, and lawful. This meant reframing the question of obedience in such a way as to soothe troubled consciences. It was in this high-stakes atmosphere that St. Edward's laws, the *Modus tenendi Parliamentum*, and the *Mirror of Justices* came in so handy, for they emboldened rebels to refute centuries of legal learning and religious teaching. It was also in this atmosphere that the cult of the Confessor's laws completely overwhelmed and displaced his cult of kingship. Moreover, with several notable exceptions, these laws now became the monopoly of Stuart dissidents and would remain so for the rest of the century. This community of texts encouraged the king's enemies to present the most radical of actions as sanctioned by those ultimate authorities, God and time immemorial.

Initially parliamentarians faced an uphill battle, given that their enemies could readily assemble a wide array of familiar religious and legal materials in support of Charles I. A plethora of Biblical verses, for example, seemingly proved that God enjoined unconditional allegiance to kings. Favorite royalist citations included Proverbs 8.15: "By Me kings reign"; Psalms 105.15: "Touch not mine anointed"; Romans 13.1–2: "Let every soul be subject unto the higher powers.

---

[6] Smith, *Literature and Revolution in England, 1640–1660* (New Haven, 1994), p. 1.

For there is no power but of God: the powers that be are ordained of God"; and 1 Peter 2.13: "Submit yourselves to every ordinance of man for God's sake."[7] Charles I himself found comfort in scriptural supports of monarchy when he listed among his reasons for denying the jurisdiction of the High Court of Justice a verse from Ecclesiastes: "Where the word of a king is, there is power; and who may say unto him, what doest thou?"[8]

Royalists also found scripture relevant to their claim that conquest conferred legitimacy upon kings and gave them absolute power over the vanquished. In making this suggestion I take issue with modern scholars who find little or no evidence that royalists appealed to conquest theory. However, many of Charles I's supporters clearly believed it relevant to their cause. Thus, Henry Ferne, the king's chaplain and his choice to preach the sermon before his execution, pointed to the Holy Scriptures as sanctioning rule by conquest. It was, after all, one of God's ways of "disposing of people."[9] With regard to English history, the descent of the crown was "often settled by conquest in the lines of the Saxons, Danes, and Normans."[10] In fact, these conquests explained how Ferne and his fellow countrymen had become subjects in the first place. "Was it any otherwise than by

[7] See, for example, Henry Ferne, *The Resolving of Conscience* (Cambridge, 1642), pp. 15–16; Ferne, *A Reply unto Severall Treatises Pleading for the Armes now taken up by Subjects in the pretended defence of Religion and Liberty* (Oxford, 1643), pp. 67ff; *A Pious and Learned speech Delivered in the High Court of Parliament, 1 Henry 4. by Thomas Mercks then Bishop of Carlisle* (London, 1642), pp. 4–5 by my numbering; John Spelman, *The Case of Our Affairs, in Law, and Religion, and other Circumstances briefly examined, and Presented to the Conscience* (Oxford, 1643), pp. 17–20; *A Sermon Preached in the Citie of London By a Lover of Truth* (London, 1643); *The Grand Question concerning Taking up Armes against the King answered* (n.p. 1643); *The Public Confider* (Oxford, 1643), pp. 2–3; Peter Heylyn, "The Rebel's Catechism (1643)," in *The Harleian Miscellany*, vol. VII (London, 1811), pp. 461–79; John Bramhall, "The Serpent-Salve: Or, a Remedy for the Biting of an Aspe" (1643), in *The Works of the Most Reverend Father in God, John Bramhall* (Dublin, 1676), p. 527.

[8] Ecclesiastes 8:4. "His Majesty's Reasons against the Pretended Jurisdiction of His Sacred Majesty of the High Court of Justice," in *Eikon Basilike. The Portraiture of His Sacred Majesty in His Solitudes and Sufferings*, ed. Philip A. Knachel (Ithaca, NY, The Folger Shakespeare Library, 1966), p. 189.

[9] Ferne, *A Reply unto Severall Treatises*, p. 19. For the view that royalists did not depend heavily on conquest theory see Pocock, *The Ancient Constitution and the Feudal Law*, pp. 149, 169; Peter Laslett, *Locke's Two Treatises of Government* (Cambridge, 1960), pp. 403–4; Quentin Skinner, "History and Ideology in the English Revolution," *Historical Journal* 8 (1965), 151–78. John Wallace, however, writes that conquest theory was both explicit and implicit in royalist thinking. *Destiny His Choice: the Loyalism of Andrew Marvell* (Cambridge, 1968), pp. 22–30.

[10] Ferne, *The Resolving of Conscience*, p. 19. See also Griffith Williams, *Jura Majestatis, the Rights of Kings both in Church and State* (Oxford, 1644), pp. 39–40: kings were accountable only to God "because they have their crown immediately from God, who first gave it to the conqueror through his sword, and since to succeeding kings, by the ordinary means of his succession."

force and arms" that "the Saxons, Danes, and Normans made themselves masters of this people . . . ?"[11] Surely English history proved that the succession "sprang up by conquest," which meant in turn that the people's rights derived from the royal largesse. Indeed, whatever privileges the people and parliament possessed "came into existence by degrees (and not at the very institution of government) and by the condescension of kings."[12]

Other royalist clergymen also acknowledged the validity of conquest. Thus, John Bramhall, one time archbishop of Armagh and a close associate of both Archbishop William Laud and the king himself, suggested that "just conquest in a lawful war" gave "right of dominion, as well as possession." This opinion "is . . . consonant to the universal opinion and practice of all nations, yea, to the infallible and undoubted testimony of Holy Scripture."[13] Griffith Williams, bishop of Ossory, also wrote of God as sanctioning conquest. In fact, God "hath oftentimes thrown down" tyrants from their seat, and "this he doth most commonly by the power of the sword, when the conqueror shall make his strength to become the law of justice, and his ability to hold it, to become his right of enjoying it."[14] As for the kings of England, Williams wrote that "they have their crown immediately from God, who first gave it to the Conqueror through his sword, and since to the succeeding kings, by the ordinary means of hereditary succession."[15] To John Maxwell, variously bishop of Killala, Anchory, and Tuam, "a kingdom acquired by a lawful conquest . . . is good," and in such cases "the good and benefit of the conqueror is the prime thing and principal. The conqueror may dispose of [his conquest] at pleasure and for his own good."[16]

Charles I's secular supporters echoed this line of reasoning. In a

[11] Ferne, *A Reply unto Severall Treatises*, pp. 19, 21.

[12] *Ibid.*, pp. 26–7, 46–7. See also Ferne's remarks in *The Resolving of Conscience*, p. 19: The English crown "not only descends by inheritance, but also has so often been settled by conquest in the lines of Saxons, Danes, and Normans."

[13] Bramhall, "The Serpent-Salve," p. 537. See also p. 527, where Bramhall wrote that some kings "were named immediately by God: Those whose predecessors or themselves have attained to sovereignty by the sword, by conquest in a just war, claim immediately under God."

[14] Williams, *Jura Majestatis*, p. 17. See also pp. 16, 27.

[15] *Ibid.*, p. 40.

[16] Maxwell, *Sacro-Sancta Regum Majestas: or, The Sacred and Royall Prerogative of Christian Kings* (Oxford, 1644), p. 158. See also pp. 110–11, where Maxwell wrote that "Scripture is clear and full for the lawful title of a sovereign by conquest. Otherwise we must deny David's title over Aram." For Maxwell's authorship see Mendle, *Henry Parker and the English Civil War: the Political Thought of the Public's "Privado"* (Cambridge, 1995), pp. 123–4.

much-cited treatise first published in 1644 and reprinted in 1647 and 1662, his close adviser Sir Dudley Digges acknowledged the validity of conquest. A member of the opposition in early Stuart parliaments, Digges went over to the king's side before the civil war began. Labeled a "constitutional royalist" by modern scholars, he now deployed the political idiom with which he earlier would have had little sympathy. In his words, "The original [of the English government] was conquest (as it is of almost all the kingdoms in the world)." Indeed, "the whole land was the conqueror's."[17] This simple fact explained why Digges cared so little about English history before 1066. It was irrelevant, since William I "inverted the government, altered the laws, disposed of his possessions to his Norman followers (whose blood runs in the veins of our most ancient gentry) and made all, as well English as his native subjects, feudaries to him." The necessary proof of the Norman conquest rested in the fact "that the laws given us by him, and which we are to live by now, are written in his language."[18]

Although royalist writers often admitted the legitimacy of rule by conquest, few agreed with Maxwell, who suggested that even "without the consent of the people" conquest conferred legitimate title.[19] According to many of the king's supporters, victory by sword must be ratified by the consent of the community. But "consent" had many meanings, some extremely favorable to the royalist cause. Ferne, for example, denied that the kings of England could actually rule as conquerors – "God forbid" – , since they bound themselves by covenants with their people. This meant, in turn, that subjects consented to be governed by a conqueror. Importantly, however, Ferne's apparent concession turned out to be negligible, for he allowed that "a forced consent will suffice."[20] Digges agreed that conquest alone did not suffice to engage subjects' allegiance. Although conquest might give the conqueror a "lawful way of acquisition," only consent could create "a moral bond" between king and subject. And "the will is not capable of being forced."

---

[17] Digges, *The Unlawfulnesse of Subjects taking up Armes*, p. 118. See also Mendle, *Henry Parker and the English Civil War*, p. 185; David L. Smith, *Constitutional Royalism and the Search for Settlement, c. 1640–1649* (Cambridge, 1994).

[18] Digges, *The Unlawfulness of Subjects taking up Armes*, pp. 116–17. See also *Britannia, Passionately and Historically, Remembering her Majesty and Happiness in former Ages* (London, 1644), p. 3; *The True Law of Free Monarchy*, p. 10; Dallison, *The Royalists Defence*, p. 19.

[19] Maxwell, *Sacro-Sancta Regum Majestas*, p. 158.

[20] Ferne, *A Reply unto Severall Treatises*, pp. 18–23.

However, this did not mean that the people empowered the king. As Digges put it, the "consent of the people was not an adequate cause, but a necessary qualification" to prepare the conqueror to receive his commission from God.[21] And how did the king secure his subjects' consent? By limiting his own power. That is, in order to "sweeten their subjection . . . he restrains his absolute right by compact, and bestows some liberties and some privileges upon the people." Importantly, however, "these acts of grace he confirms unto them by such security as should not endanger his person nor regal authority."[22]

In addition to viewing conquest as one means by which government was established, many royalists readily acknowledged that election sometimes played a role in empowering kings. Thus, on occasion, especially when kingdoms had dissolved into anarchy or when there was no heir, the people elected their rulers. However, unlike their enemies in parliament, royalists concluded that in these cases God, and not the people, actually conferred power on the king and ordained his rule. Not even in elective kingdoms, then, did the people possess constitutive power and the king merely commissionary authority. On the contrary, the king remained, as Ferne put it, the fountain and original of power, immediately ordained by God, who could either give power directly to a ruler or confirm the people's act. Further, once they consented to the conqueror's rule, they themselves were now unconditionally bound to the agreement that they made.[23]

Equally important, many of Charles I's supporters asserted that after electing a king, the people relinquished once and for all their power to meddle with his government. Putting a decidely monarchical spin on the classical *lex regia*, royalists typically insisted that in elective kingdoms, once the people had chosen their ruler and conveyed their power to him, they could not revoke the grant. As Digges wrote, "after a people hath by solemn contract divested itself of the power, which was primarily in them, they cannot upon what

---

[21] Digges, *The Unlawfulnesse of Subjects taking up Armes*, pp. 76–7.
[22] *Ibid.*, p. 117. See also Dallison, *The Royalists Defence*, p. 19.
[23] Digges, *An Answer to a Printed Book, Intituled, Observations upon some of His Majesties Late Answers and Expresses* (Oxford, 1642), pp. 1–6. See also Ferne, *The Resolving of Conscience*, pp. 16, 18, 19–20; Williams, *Jura Majestatis*, pp. 16–17, 38, 40, 120, 179; Maxwell, *Sacro-Sancta*, pp. 13–14; Bramhall, "The Serpent-Salve," p. 527; [John Spelman], *A Review of the Observations upon some of his Majesties late Answers and Expresses* (Oxford, 1643), p. 4. For the authorship of this work see Mendle, *Henry Parker and the English Civil War*, pp. 104–5.

pretence soever, without manifest breach of divine ordinance, and violation of public faith, resume that authority, which they have placed in another." That is, once the people conveyed their power to the king, he had it and they did not. From this it followed that the king remained "the only fountain of all power and justice," his election notwithstanding.[24]

Whether royalists viewed the kings of England as ruling by virtue of conquest or election, virtually all agreed that subjects possessed no right to rebel should kings disregard whatever promises they made to the people. Even tyrants must be obeyed. As one anonymous author wrote, "A rebel is worse than the worst prince, and rebellion worst than the worst government of the worst prince that hitherto hath been." To rebel against the prince, he concluded, was to rebel against God.[25]

Nor did any breach of the contract implied in the coronation oath empower subjects to judge errant rulers. This followed from the fact that God's vicegerent on earth voluntarily restrained his power "by promise and oath, and not by giving to his subjects legal power to un-king him, if he should not perform [the] covenant."[26] As Griffith Williams explained, royal grants and promises "neither transferreth any power of sovereignty unto the parliament, nor denieth the monarch to be absolute, nor admitted of any resistance against him." Rather, kings chose to limit themselves much as God did, as when, for example, he promised David that he would not fail him.[27] Writing in the same vein was Charles I's trusted adviser, John Spelman, sometimes considered another constitutional royalist. The son of the great antiquary and a scholar in his own right, Spelman

---

[24] Digges, *An Answer to a Printed Book*, pp. 1–2, 4, 5. See also Ferne, *A Reply unto Severall Treatises*, pp. 79–80; Ferne, *The Resolving of Conscience*, pp. 16, 18, 19–20; John Cleveland, *Majestas Intemerata. Or, The Immortality of the King* (n.p., 1649), pp. 22, 96, 99, 100, 101; Maxwell, *Sacro-Sancta*, pp. 12, 18–22; Doughty, *The Kings Cause Rationally, briefly, and plainly debated*, p. 36.

[25] *The Doctrine of the Church of England, Established by Parliament against Disobedience and wilful Rebellion* (London, 1642), pp. 5–7. See also Ferne, *The Resolving of Conscience*, pp. 14–23 *passim*; *The Whipper Whipt* (London, 1644), pp. 33–6; Williams, *Jura Majestatis*, pp. 139–40, 149, 154, 176 *passim*; Maxwell, *Sacro-Sancta*, pp. 40, 102–3; *A Pious and Learned speech*, p. 5 (by my numbering), where the author wrote that subjects must endure the faults and imperfections of kings just as they endure the weather. See also Burns's discussion of Scottish writers such as Ninian Wiznet: *The True Law of Kingship*, pp. 210–11; Burns, "George Buchanan and the Anti-Monarchomachs," in *Political Discourse in Early Modern Britain*, ed. Nicholas Phillipson and Quentin Skinner (Cambridge, 1993), pp. 3–23.

[26] Digges, *The Unlawfulnesse of Subjects taking up Armes*, pp. 116–17. Dallison, *The Royalist's Defence*, pp. 19ff.

[27] Williams, *Jura Majestatis*, p. 179.

attended Charles I in his "private council" in Oxford and was on his way to becoming secretary of state when camp fever struck him down in 1643. In his opinion, when kings voluntarily subjected themselves to the law, they remained sovereign governors of the realm, just as Christ remained king of kings when he acted similarly. To call either "subjects" incurred the wrath of God.[28]

Then there were the common law and statutory supports of monarchical government, including the statute 25 Edward III defining treason as "a levying of war against our sovereign lord the king."[29] The legal maxim "the king can do no wrong" also provided support for Charles I's cause. This medieval truism prohibited even legal actions – never mind outright rebellion – against the monarch. Understandably and predictably royalists enlisted the maxim to counter parliamentarian attempts to justify making war on Charles I. As the royal justice David Jenkins wrote in 1647 from his imprisonment in the Tower, "The law saith the king can do no wrong; that he is *medicus regni, pater patriae, sponsus regni* . . . The king is God's lieutenant, and is not able to do an unjust thing." This meant that "the justices and ministers of justice are to be questioned and punished if the laws be violated; and no reflection to be made on the king."[30] Charles I also cited the maxim when he repudiated the legitimacy of the High Court of Justice.[31]

Other royalist polemicists combined English law and history to produce an account of government in which the king reigned as an absolute sovereign. One was Sir Robert Filmer, alleged author of the *Free-holder's Grand Inquest*, published first in 1648 and then during the exclusion crisis in 1679. Here Filmer cited medieval sources to prove the king's precedence and power over parliament in general and the

---

[28] Spelman, *The Case of Our Affaires*, pp. 11–12. See also Spelman, *Certain Considerations upon the Duties both of Prince and People* (London, 1643), p. 20.

[29] See, for example, Heylyn, "The Rebel's Catechism," p. 463; Spelman, *The Case of Our Affaires*, p. 16; Jenkins, "Lex Terrae," pp. 101–4 *passim*.

[30] *Ibid.*, pp. 102, 108. See also Ferne, *A Reply unto Severall Treatises*, p. 11; George Bate, *The Regal Apology. Or, The Declaration of the Commons, Feb. 11, 1647. Canvassed* (n.p., 1647), pp. 9–10, 43; *The Public Confider*, p. 6; Bramhall, "The Serpent-Salve," p. 556. For a discussion of the various meanings and history of "the king can do no wrong" see Clayton Roberts, *The Growth of Responsible Government* (Cambridge, 1966); Janelle Greenberg, "Our Grand Maxim of State, 'The King Can Do No Wrong,'" *History of Political Thought* 12 (1991), 210–28; Joyce Lee Malcolm, "Doing No Wrong: Law, Liberty, and the Constraint of Kings," *Journal of British Studies* 38 (1999), 161–86.

[31] "His Majesty's Reasons against the Pretended Jurisdiction of the High Court of Parliament," p. 189.

Commons in particular.[32] According to the *Free-holders*, the royal superiority stemmed from the fact that the kingship antedated the existence of a modern parliament. Filmer knew that both Coke and Prynne believed otherwise, but neither had understood the medieval sources from which they worked. Articulating an argument that would characterize royalist theorizing until the end of the century, the *Free-holders* put its own spin on Tudor writers. As Polydore Vergil had acknowledged, the Commons was seldom called before 1116. Moreover, Filmer continued, it did not become a regular part of parliament until 1265, the date of the earliest extant writ of summons.[33] In other words, that body was not immemorial because 1265 lay within legal memory – 1189. This meant in turn that the Commons had no prescriptive right to share in the government of the kingdom. The constitutional royalist Sir Edward Hyde, earl of Clarendon, would later construct an ancient constitutionalist case for the king. Readily acknowledging that St. Edward's laws survived the conquest through repeated royal confirmations, he read them as confirming the high authority of the monarchy, not the right of the two houses to make war upon the king.[34]

Royalists could, then, draw on respected religious, legal, and even historical traditions to prove that those who fomented rebellion merited the name of traitor and incurred divine damnation. The king's command of the legal high ground thus confronted parliamentarians with a daunting challenge: they must convincingly refute centuries of legal learning and religious teaching. For many the answer lay in the ancient constitutionalist version of history, which parliamentarians now expanded to encompass Charles I's unexpectedly relevant *Answer to the XIX Propositions*. Penned for the king by Sir John Colepeper, chancellor of the exchequer, and Lucius Viscount Falkland, secretary of state, the document quickly became a touchstone for both royalists and parliamentarians. The *Answer* carried the

---

[32] Weston suggests that Sir Robert Holbourne was its author, while James Daly, Peter Laslett, and Johann Sommerville attribute it to Sir Robert Filmer. See Weston, "The Authorship of the *Free-holders Grand Inquest*," *English Historical Review* 95 (1980), 74–98; Weston, "The Case for Sir Robert Holborne Reasserted," *History of Political Thought* 8 (1987), 435–60; Daly, "Some Problems in the Authorship of Sir Robert Filmer's Works," *English Historical Review* 98 (1983), 737–62; Sommerville, ed., *Sir Robert Filmer. Patriarcha and Other Writings* (Cambridge, 1991), pp. xxxiv–xxxvii.

[33] Filmer, "The Free-holders Grand Inquest," in *Patriarcha and Other Writings*, ed. Sommerville, pp. 76–80, 96–7, 115–18.

[34] *A Brief Survey of the Dangerous and pernicious Errors to Church and State, In Mr. Hobbes's Book, Entitled Leviathan* (Printed at the Theater, 1676), pp. 109–10, 112.

royalist response to the Nineteen Propositions which the two houses had sent to the king in early June of 1642. Here the Long Parliament issued a series of outrageous demands, including the right to name the king's counsellors, ministers, and judges, as well as the right to control the militia, reform religion, and oversee the education of his children.[35]

That Charles I rejected the demands of the two houses came as no surprise. But the precise language and arguments that he chose to justify his position must have shocked them. The king refused the Nineteen Propositions on the ground that to accept them would be to subvert the English government as established by law. Then, in a series of remarkable passages, Charles lectured the two houses on the proper theory and origin of the English constitution. England's government, he explained, was a "mixed monarchy," consisting of a happy mixture of the three main forms of government – absolute or pure monarchy, aristocracy, and democracy. This fortuitous equipoise could be seen in action when the three coordinate and coeval estates of the realm, King, Lords, and Commons, made law. Stressing their partnership in this endeavor, the king pointed to parliament, where "the laws are jointly made by a king, a house of peers, and by a house of commons chosen by the people, all having free votes and particular privileges." The virtue of such an admirable mixture, Charles I continued, lay in the fact that the king's prerogative and his subjects' liberties existed in a perfect balance – a balance which would be destroyed if Charles accepted the Nineteen Propositions. Further, he continued, the origin of this mixed monarchy could be found in the "wisdom and experience" of "your" – that is, his subjects' – "ancestors."[36]

When the king's *Answer* reached the Long Parliament on June 21, it was considered for a week in the House of Commons. Soon enough parliamentarians realized that certain portions readily lent themselves to exploitation. Much to their surprise Charles I had couched his declaration not in the order idiom of political thought, which so perfectly suited the royalist cause, but rather in terms that favored his rivals. The *Answer* contained several critical "errors."

---

[35] Weston and Greenberg, *Subjects and Sovereigns*, pp. 35–40. Michael Mendle, *Dangerous Positions. Mixed Government, the Estates of the Realm, and the Answer to the XIX propositions* (Tuscaloosa, Ala., 1985), Introduction, chapter I *passim*.

[36] *His Majesties Answer to the XIX. Propositions of Both Houses of Parliament* (London, 1642), pp. 17–18.

First, by choosing a model that made the king merely one of the three estates, Charles placed himself and the kingship at a severe disadvantage: he was now down in the arena with the two houses, and, should anyone be counting, outnumbered two to one. In restropect, the king and his advisers would have been better off selecting another description of the estates – one which gave far less away. Such a definition not only existed but enjoyed the blessings of a good many sixteenth- and early seventeenth-century lawyers and political writers. This was the well-known view that the three estates consisted of the lords spiritual – that is, the bishops – , the lords temporal, and the commons. In this version, the king stood at the apex of parliament. He was its head, the sovereign governor of parliament as well as the realm.[37]

Still, the slip might have gone unnoticed had it not been for the *Answer*'s talk about coordination. There was, after all, nothing new in its announcement that the king made law in parliament with the Lords and Commons. Indeed, throughout the middle ages lawyers and theorists in England and on the continent acknowledged that certain matters, in particular, law-making and taxation, must be dealt with by the king in consultation with a body that represented in some fashion or another the entire kingdom. But the *Answer* went far beyond this when its authors lowered the king to the level of the two houses and had Charles speak the language of an equality in government. King, Lords, and Commons, according to the *Answer*, enjoyed a coordination which revealed itself in law-making, the highest power within the state. If this were not enough, Charles then identified the people – "your ancestors" – and not God and king as the source of the mixed monarchy.[38] In other words, the *Answer*, when "properly" interpreted, provided an undergirding for a doctrine of popular sovereignty. And throughout the rest of the Stuart period it was frequently cited as proof that the "people," however defined, had some sort of right to participate in important affairs of government in one way or another.

Eventually royalists grasped the dangerous implications of the king's words. Writing around 1644, Heylyn warned that the king's definition of the three estates, along with the doctrine of coordina-

---

[37] Weston and Greenberg, *Subjects and Sovereigns*, pp. 41–6. *Cf.* Mendle, *Dangerous Positions*, chapters 1, 2, and 8 *passim*.
[38] Weston and Greenberg, *Subjects and Sovereigns*, pp. 35–40.

tion, opened the way for a superiority in the two houses, especially where law-making was concerned. In his words,

> If the king be granted once to be no more than one of the three estates, how can it choose but follow from so sad a principle, that he is of no more power and consideration in the time of parliament than the house of peers, which sometimes hath consisted of three lords, no more; or than the house of commons only, which hath many times consisted of no more than 80 or an hundred gentlemen . . . What else can follow hereupon but that the king must be coordinate with his two houses of parliament, and if coordinate, then to be over-ruled by their joint concurrence . . .

Placing the menacing implications of the coordination principle beyond doubt, Heylyn charged that its popularity provided the prime explanation for the beginning and continuance of the civil war.[39]

Despite royalist attempts to remedy the damage, the *Answer* soon became known throughout the country, Charles I himself ordering it to be read in the two houses of parliament and in churches and chapels in England and Wales. Published with his seal in at least seven editions, the *Answer* reached an ever-widening audience with this message: sovereignty now vested not in the monarch alone but in that holy trinity of law-makers, King, Lords, and Commons. And this on the word of a king.

Armed with Charles I's admission that the two houses possessed a coordinate share in government, parliamentarian polemicists soon linked it to the late medieval and Huguenot tag *singulis major, universis minor*. Taken together, these principles proved to their satisfaction that the king, though superior to individual subjects, occupied a position subordinate to the two houses who spoke for the kingdom.[40] Thus equipped, the Long Parliament now adroitly grafted the doctrine of coordination onto the ancient constitution. The mixture produced a powerful ideological weapon. For the Long Parliament, the matchless value of St. Edward's laws, the *Modus*, and the *Mirror* lay in the fact that, with the proper motivation, all could be read as confirming the antiquity of a parliament in which three coordinate estates shared equally in the government of the kingdom, especially in legislation. Such had been the case before 1066 as well as in the

---

[39] Heylyn, *The Stumbling-block of Disobedience and Rebellion, Cunningly laid by Calvin in the Subject's Way, Discovered, Censured, and Removed* (London, 1658), pp. 226–7, 230–1, 263–4.

[40] See Quentin Skinner, *The Foundations of Modern Political Thought* (Cambridge, 1978), vol. II, pp. 41, 45, 117–18, 120, 133, 181–2, 333–4, 342, 347; Mendle, *Henry Parker and the English Civil War*, 43, 86–7, 90; Weston and Greenberg, *Subjects and Sovereigns*, pp. 62–4, 75–8, 82, 114, 155–6, 210–14.

Stuart period, this by grant of successive Norman and English kings. Among the medieval sources, St. Edward's laws deserves pride of place, and for several reasons. First, the authenticity of the *Modus* and the *Mirror*, earlier questioned by Selden, now received even greater critical scrutiny. But no such skepticism attached to St. Edward's laws. Second, as we shall see, one particular part of St. Edward's laws, Chapter 17, proved indispensable to rebel theorizing: it took the blame for rebellion off the shoulders of parliamentarians and placed it instead on the king and his supporters. In addition, Chapter 17, by removing the taint of the Despencers' treason from the doctrine of the king's two bodies, enabled anti-royalists throughout the century to incorporate this absolutely essential construct into their theorizing. In turn, the blending of Chapter 17 with the doctrine of the king's two bodies allowed the Long Parliament to redefine the thorny issue of allegiance. This line of reasoning also shored up its case for the utter sovereignty of parliament and the right of the two houses to hold Charles I to account. These were the make or break issues for the Long Parliament, and without the fortification of the medieval canon, and St. Edward's laws in particular, parliamentarians could have made little headway. The role of the three sources became crystal clear as the Long Parliament more precisely articulated its theories of resistance.

ANCIENT CONSTITUTIONALIST SOURCES IN
PARLIAMENTARIAN THEORIZING

In the months immediately preceding and following the outbreak of civil war on August 22, 1642, parliamentarians churned out declarations and pamphlets that deftly grafted the doctrines of coordination and the king's two bodies onto an ancient constitutionalist view of political society. The earliest parliamentarian tracts responded to the particularly pressing circumstances in which the Long Parliament found itself. One of its main concerns was to find a convincing justification for carrying on the business of governing without the king, who in February of 1642 had left Westminster for York and later Oxford. The most exigent issues, control of the militia and the making of law in the king's absence, came to the fore in the spring and summer of that year. In April Sir John Hotham, accompanied by London trained bands, seized the magazine at Hull in parliament's name and refused to turn it over to Charles I. Acting on the claim that, in dire circumstances, the two houses could legislate without the king, the Long Parliament converted the militia bill into an ordinance for which its members claimed the force of statute. In response, Charles I replied that "we are still a part of parliament, and shall be till this well founded monarchy be turned into a democracy." Pointedly, he and his supporters reminded the two houses that no bill could become law without the royal assent.[41]

Undeniably, centuries of legal learning told in the king's favor. To justify its blatant breach of English law, the Long Parliament and its supporters turned to medieval history in an attempt to make the new appear old. From the very beginning, the rebel defense reflected a strong Saxonist flavor. And from the very beginning rebels took aim at the royalist claim that because William I ruled as a conqueror, so too did Charles I. Indeed, some of the earliest parliamentarian pamphlets followed in the historical tradition so well known to Tudor and early Stuart Englishmen, their authors assuming as a matter of course that the most vital political and legal institutions existed before 1066 and survived the arrival of the Normans.

The Long Parliament's affinity for the ancient constitution appeared clearly when it ordered the republication of several leading works from earlier in the century. One was Ralph Starkey's *The Priviledges and Practice of Parliaments in England*, first printed in 1628 and republished in 1640. Another, William Hakewill's 1610 speech against impositions, appeared in 1641 under the title *The Libertie of the Subject against the pretended Power of Imposition*. In the same year the respected antiquary and common lawyer brought out his own version of the *Modus*. Then came William Prynne's *An Humble Remonstrance against Ship-Money*, written in 1636 and reprinted in 1641 and 1643. But most important of all was the posthumous appearance of Coke's *Second, Third,* and *Fourth Part* of the *Institutes of the Laws of England*. Hitherto unpublished, the *Second* was printed by order of the Long Parliament in 1642, with the *Third* and *Fourth* appearing under the same auspicies in 1644.[42] Circulating now with the imprimatur

---

[41] Edward Husband, *An Exact Collection of all Remonstrances, Declarations . . . and other Remarkable Passages between the Kings Most Excellent Majesty, and His High Court of Parliament* (London, 1642), p. 262. See also, *A Letter sent From A Private Gentleman To A Friend in London, In justification of his owne adhering to His Majestie in these times of Distraction* (n.p., 1642), p. 4.

[42] See, for example, *Second Part of the Institutes of the Laws of England*, 4th. edn. (London, 1671), pp. 22–5; *Fourth Part of the Institutes of the Laws of England*, ed. Francis Hargreave (London, 1797), p. 36.

of the Long Parliament, these various works relied on the *Modus*, the *Mirror*, and St. Edward's laws to preach the high power of parliament and the common law as against over-mighty kings. All found these institutions in place as early as the Saxon period. And all found them surviving the Norman conquest and descending intact to the people of Stuart England.

In addition to these earlier works, new tracts also appeared, the king's opponents rushing into print with their most persuasive political arguments. These pamphlets spoke to a special and compelling need: if the Long Parliament could not in these early and most perilous days persuade Englishmen to support the good old cause, the rebels stood no chance whatsoever. It is, then, of some significance that many of the tracts appearing in the months immediately before and after the commencement of civil war relied on ancient constitutionalist arguments and sources. Thus, the author of *The Privilidges of Parliament* (1642) vouched the antiquity and longevity of parliament to demonstrate that the Long Parliament possessed the power to alter the governments of both state and church. "Since William the Conqueror," he wrote, the institution "hath been in use . . . and before his reign, from King Lucius to Edward the Confessor." Indeed, it was "this constancy of parliaments," which consisted of the three estates of King, Lords, and Commons, that "made this nation secure."[43]

Also to the point were the remarks of the anonymous author of *The Definition of a Parliament*, published in January of 1643. In his defense of the Long Parliament's right to make war on Charles Stuart, the author considered it relevant that parliaments had existed in the reigns of Ine, Athelstan, and Cnut. "In one word," he wrote, "time out of mind this high court and its judicature hath flourished before the conquest, although *silent leges inter arma*, and ever since the conquest until this present house."[44] Still another writer found continuity of law and legal institutions across the divide of 1066. To those who spoke of England as "a conquered nation" on whom "the Conqueror might have made what alterations in the law, or state, he pleased," the author answered that William did nothing of the sort. Instead, he retained the law and subjected himself to it.[45]

---

[43] *The Privilidges of Parliament: Or a Modest Answer to Three Questions* (London, 1642), pp. 1–3.

[44] *The Definition of a Parliament Or, A Glosse upon the Times* (London, 1643), A3.

[45] [John Marsh], *An Argument or, Debate in Law. of the Great Question concerning the Militia; As it is now settled by Ordinance of both Houses of Parliament* (London, 1642), pp. 25–6. For the identity

Yet another pamphleteer defended the parliamentarian cause by quoting Fortescue's late fifteenth-century description of the continuity of law and institutions from Roman to Stuart times. Although "we have had many changes; as first the Romans, then the Saxons, then the Danes, and lastly the Normans; yet in the time of all these nations, and during their reigns, the kingdom was for the most part governed in the same manner as it is now."[46]

Henry Parker, though by no means an ancient constitutionalist in the broader sense, also referred to parliament as existing in Saxon times. Described by Michael Mendle as "the most aggressive, thoughtful, and provocative parliamentarian writer in early years of the Long Parliament," Parker penned several highly influential tracts. In his *Observations upon some of his Majesties late Answers and Expresses* (1642), he wrote that "this admirably composed court which is now called a parliament" used to be known as "the mickel synod, or Witenagemot."[47] Parker's *Jus Populi*, published in 1644, relied more heavily on historical sources. In order to refute royalist use of conquest theory, he assailed his opponents' frequent boast that England had suffered three conquests – by the Saxons, the Danes, and the Normans. In none of the three, Parker wrote, "was the whole nation defeated and subdued, nor scarce any part of it altered by conquest." On the contrary, "all our conquerors themselves did rather lose themselves and their customs, and their laws to us, than assimilate us to themselves." Indeed, as regarded William I, the single county of Kent would have delivered a "fatal check" had he "not prudently betaken himself to a mild way of treaty, and composition."[48]

Philip Hunton wrote similarly of the origins of English government. A leading Puritan divine on close terms with leaders in the Long Parliament, he published his *Treatise of Monarchie* in 1643. The tract enjoyed much influence throughout the century. It was rep-

---

of the author see Alan Cromartie, "The Constitutional Revolution: the Transformation of Political Culture in Early Stuart England," *Past and Present* 163 (1999), 115.

[46] "Examples for Kings; or rules for Princes to govern by . . . (1642)," in *Harleian Miscellany*, vol. II, (London, 1809), pp. 224–7.

[47] Parker, *Observations upon some of his Majesties late Answers and Expresses* (London, 1642), p. 15. Mendle, *Henry Parker and the English Civil War*, p. xi, chapter 5. See also Robert Zaller, "Henry Parker and the Regiment of True Government," in *Proceedings of the American Philosophical Society* 135 (1991), 255–85. But *cf.* Cromartie, "The Constitutional Revolution," pp. 81, 114–15.

[48] Parker, *Jus Populi. Or, A Discourse Wherein clear satisfaction is given, as well concerning the Right of Subjects, as the Right of Princes* (London, 1644), pp. 14–15.

rinted in 1689, and Anthony Wood described it as "in great vogue
among many persons of commonwealth and leveling principles."[49]
Here Hunton credited the Saxons with introducing both parliament
and the common law. Indeed, from these Germanic peoples he
traced "the antiquity of our liberties, and frame of government. So
they were governed in Germany, and so here, to this day; for, by
transplanting themselves, they changed their soil, not their manner
and government." This manner of government included holding
meetings of estates, where "all weighty matters were dispatched."
True, William I introduced some changes and dispossessed many
English of their lands. Nevertheless, he took the crown as the heir of
Edward the Confessor, his goal "not to gain a new absolute title, but
to vindicate the old limited one, whereby the English-Saxon kings,
his predecessors, held this kingdom." Moreover, after Harold's death
at Hastings "the people chose rather to submit" than to risk further
bloodshed. In fact, it was "the people's voluntary acceptance of him
and his claim" that gave him the kingdom. In sum, because William
took his title as the "rightful successor to Edward . . . he was indeed
king, not as a conqueror, but as Edward's successor; and on the same
right, as he and his predecessors held the crown." Importantly, by
confirming the Saxon laws and Saxon ways of governing "he did
equivalently put himself and his successors into the state of legal
monarchs: and in that tenure have all kings of this land held the
crown till this day."[50]

The affinity for the medieval English past also appeared in early
parliamentarian tracts written to justify the Long Parliament's
seizure of the militia. Once again, when parliamentarians deployed
such records they did so in the expectation that the aura surrounding
the works they cited would obscure the outright illegality of their
actions. In particular, polemicists cited portions of St. Edward's laws
and the *Mirror of Justices* to prove that parliamentary control of the
militia, far from being an innovation, had existed in ancient times.
As Prynne wrote in August of 1642, the antiquity of this right
appeared from "King Edward's laws, that in his and former ages the

---

[49] Wood, *Athenae Oxonienses*, ed. Philip Bliss (London, 1820), vol. IV, p. 40. See also William
Nicholson, *The English Historical Library* (London, 1699), vol. III, p. 19.
[50] Hunton, *A Treatise of Monarchie*, pp. 34–7. See also Hunton, *A Vindication of the Treatise of
Monarchy* (London, 1644), pp. 33–7. Hunton did not, however, go so far as to embrace the
doctrine of coordination. Still, this made his work no less incendiary to royalists throughout
the century. See Weston and Greenberg, *Subjects and Sovereigns*, pp. 59–61.

lieutenants and supreme commanders of the militia in every county, were elected . . . by the common council, for the common utility of the realm; through every province, country, and county, in a full folkmoot or county court by the freeholders of the county." Just as the freeholders elected these officers, so, according to Saxon laws, did they choose their lieutenants, captains, and sheriffs too. St. Edward's laws, then, proved the right of the Long Parliament to control the militia, "without any impeachment of his majesties prerogative."[51] The anonymous author of *A Brief and Exact Treatise*, published in December 1642, cited St. Edward's laws to the same purpose, as did the Long Parliament's *Second Remonstrance or Declaration* of January 1643.[52]

Another polemicist took issue with those royalists who argued that Charles I controlled the militia because his ancestor William I reigned as a conqueror. Not so, the author insisted, since the first Norman ruler retained St. Edward's laws and subjected himself to them.[53] According to still another anonymous author, the inestimable John Pym mounted a similar defense of parliament's right to control the militia, citing both St. Edward's laws and the *Mirror of Justices* to prove his point. Further, the author implied, if subjects exercised this right in Saxon times, so must they, and their representatives, exercise it still.[54]

Medieval sources, and St. Edward's laws in particular, performed an equally essential service when they fortified an element of argumentation critical to the rebel cause. This was the theory of the

[51] [William Prynne], *A Soveraign Antidote to Prevent, Appease, and Determine our unnaturall and destructive Civill Warres and Dissentions* (London, 1642), pp. 9–10. These pages are misnumbered. Prynne also denounced Charles I's commissions of array as being contrary to his coronation oath. *Ibid.*, pp. 10, 29. For the authorship of this tract see William Lamont, *Marginal Prynne* (London, 1963), p. 113, n. 2; Mendle, *Henry Parker and the English Civil War*, p. 93 and n. 13. Prynne made the same argument regarding the militia in "A short, legal, medicinal, useful, safe and easy prescription to recover our Kingdom, Church, and Nation," in *Harleian Miscellany*, vol. VIII (London, 1811), p. 83. See also Michael Mendle, "The Great Council of Parliament and the First Ordinances: The Constitutional Theory of the Civil War," *Journal of British Studies* 31 (1992), 133–62.

[52] *A Brief and Exact Treatise Declaring How the Sheriffs, and all other the great Officers of this Kingdome have been Anciently elected and chosen* (London, 1642), pp. 4–6. *A Second Remonstrance or Declaration of the Lords and Commons Assembled in Parliament, Concerning the Commission of Array* (London, 1643), p. 44.

[53] [Marsh], *An Argument or, Debate in law: of the Great Question concerning the Militia*, p. 25.

[54] "Certain select Observations on the several Offices, and Officers, in the Militia of England; with the Power of the Parliament to raise the same, as they shall judge expedient; etc. Collected and found among the Papers of the late Mr. John Pym (1641)," in *Harleian Miscellany*, vol. VI (London, 1810), pp. 303–4.

king's two bodies, which the Long Parliament first articulated several months before the war broke out. Although absolutely essential to the success of the parliamentarian ideology, the notion of the king's two bodies might have remained in the shadows were it not for the sanctifying influence of Holy Edward. First fully articulated in the mid-sixteenth century, the idea itself dated back to the middle ages. Since the twelfth century, theorists in Western Europe had distinguished between the person and the office of a king, emphasizing the private nature of the one and the public nature of the other. Both Chapter 11 and Chapter 17 of St. Edward's laws – Pope Eleutherius's alleged correspondence with King Lucius and the "Office of a King" – had spoken to this distinction.

In addition, there were the influential writings of the Scottish theorist George Buchanan, tutor to the young James VI. As James Burns notes, Buchanan contrasted "the authority" with "the man who wielded the authority," invoking the canonists' distinction between "the pope" and "the man who is pope."[55] Stuart Englishmen also knew of the idea from the law reports of the respected Elizabethan jurist Edmund Plowden, as well as through the writings of Sir Edward Coke and Sir Francis Bacon. According to these early modern lawyers, the king possessed two bodies, one natural and private, the other political and public. As a natural person he, like any mortal, began life as an infant, progressed to the age of majority, and succumbed to disease and death. But in his politic body he enjoyed such transcendent powers as timelessness – he was always of age – , immortality – he never died, perfection – he could do no wrong, and ubiquity – in law he was considered virtually present in all of his courts even though personally absent. While his natural body consisted of flesh and blood, his politic body was invisible and incorporeal. The latter was, in fact, in the nature of a corporation; it was a juristic person created by the policy of man. As for the relationship between the king's two bodies, Plowden viewed the politic body as superior to the natural body. It was "more ample and large" because to it government adhered.[56]

---

[55] Burns, *The True Law of Kingship*, p. 205.
[56] Plowden, *Commentaries or Reports* (London, 1816), pp. 212a, 213, 200a, 238a. Coke, *Seventh Part of the Reports*, p. 32. Bacon, "The Case of the Post-Nati in Scotland," in *The Works of Francis Bacon*, ed. James K. Spedding, Robert L. Ellis, and Douglas D. Heath (London, 1879), vol. VII, pp. 667–8. See also Ernst Kantorowicz, *The King's Two Bodies: A Study in Medieval Political Thought* (Princeton, 1957), chapter 1, especially p. 9; F. W. Maitland, "The Corporation Sole," in *The Collected Papers of Frederic William Maitland*, ed. H. A. L. Fisher (Cambridge,

This idea became indispensable to the rebel cause, enabling parliamentarians and later whigs to claim that they supported the kingship and opposed only the person of the king. But before they could safely deploy the doctrine of the two bodies, they had to detoxify it, since contemporaries associated it with the Despencers' treason. In the early fourteenth century, the Despencer brothers led a baronial revolt against Edward II. In order to justify their rebellion, they turned to a distinction similar to that of the king's two bodies. Claiming that they owed allegiance less to the king's person than to the crown, they concluded that they could depose the one while remaining loyal to the other. With the failure of the revolt, this reasoning was denounced as treasonous.[57] In the sixteenth and seventeenth centuries, attempts to justify separating the king's natural and politic bodies were often condemned by reference to the Despencers' treason – that "damnable and damned opinion" that had earlier produced such "execrable and detestable consequences."[58]

One way to decontaminate the theory was to present the same idea in a different guise. This was where St. Edward's laws came in. Both Chapters 11 and 17 drew the distinction between a king and a tyrant. Both could be read as implying that subjects need obey only the former, while they might actually depose the latter. By citing these chapters, which, as earlier mentioned, contained a version of what Burns calls "the ground bass" of early modern political thought, parliamentarians could avoid the contamination of the Despencers' treason.[59] This move also permitted them to sidestep royalist attempts to link them to Jesuits and Calvinists who deployed the idea to justify the killing of kings who subscribed to the wrong religion.

Although it is impossible to demonstrate that Stuart rebels had this precise strategy in mind when they invoked Chapters 11 and 17 of St. Edward's laws in this context, indirect evidence suggests that they probably did. Thus, when they linked the doctrine of the king's two bodies to the idea that kings, not tyrants, merited allegiance, they could have cited a wide range of sources to prove their case.

1911), pp. 210–43; Maitland, "The Crown as Corporation," in *ibid.*, pp. 244–70; Frederick Pollock and Frederic William Maitland, *History of English Law*, 2nd. edn. (repr. Cambridge, 1968), vol. I, pp. 511–26.

[57] Kantorowicz, *The King's Two Bodies*, pp. 364–72.

[58] Coke, *Seventh Part* of the *Reports*, p. 11. Sir Francis Bacon, "The Case of the Post-Nati in Scotland," pp. 669–70.

[59] Burns, *The True Law of Free Monarchy*, p. 284.

After all, Aristotle, Conciliarists, Jesuits, and French and Scottish Calvinists all made use of the notion that a king who misruled unkinged himself. And, indeed, whenever royalists attacked this line of reasoning they themselves attributed the idea only to these foreign sources, never to St. Edward whom their opponents constantly cited. Griffith Williams and John Maxwell, for example, traced the idea to the "Sorbonists," from whom the Jesuits and eventually the English rebels borrowed. As regarded the story of Pepin, the pope, and Childeric, Maxwell charged that "this precedent was made a leading case in the after ages, both for popish and popular usurpation to intrude, nay, to invade upon the sacred right of sacred kings. Nay, our puritans have from hence learned to color and lustre their ugly treasons and seditions with the cloak of religious righteousness."[60] By associating the idea of the office with such sources, royalists probably sought to strip the argument of its ideological appeal, insinuating that there was something suspiciously and dangerously un-English about it.

The revolutionary potential of Chapters 11 and 17 of St. Edward's laws first appeared in the declarations issued by the Long Parliament in May of 1642 and in early civil war tracts. In the spring of that year, the two houses declared that when the king had earlier abandoned Westminster for York and Oxford, he did so only in his personal capacity. However, his politic body, superior in all respects because essential to his public office, remained in the safe keeping of his high court of parliament. This argument, it will be recalled, rang true because, according to the doctrine of the king's two bodies, he was always considered virtually present in his courts. As Samuel Rutherford, the leading Scottish Protestant polemicist of the period, explained, while the king "is absent from his parliaments as a man, he is legally and in his law-power present, and so the parliaments are as legal as if he were personally present with them."[61]

The parliamentarian interpretation of the distinction between the

---

[60] Maxwell, *Sacro-Sancta*, pp. 9–17, especially 17. Williams, *Jura Majestatis*, pp. 117–19, 207.

[61] Rutherford, "Lex Rex," pp. 146, 219. See also John Coffey, *Politics, Religion, and the British Revolutions: the Mind of Samuel Rutherford* (Cambridge, 1997), chapter 6; Husband, "A Declaration of the Lords and Commons in Parliament concerning his Majesties Proclamation, May 27, 1642," in *An Exact Collection*, p. 304; "The Third Remonstrance, May 26, 1642," in *ibid.*, p. 267; Charles Herle, *A Fuller Answer to a Treatise Written by Doctor Ferne, Entituled The Resolving of Conscience upon this Question* . . . (London, 1642), pp. 10–12; *The Subjects Liberty* (London, 1643), pp. 17–20, 25; *The Maximes of Mixt Monarchy* (London, 1643), pages unnumbered; *The Subject of Supremacy* (London, 1643), p. 65; *Maximes Unfolded*, pp. 11–12, 17; *An Answer to Mis-led Doctor Ferne* (London, 1644), pp. 17, 25, 27.

king's person and his office soon entered the mainstream of anti-monarchical discourse.[62] This line of reasoning characterized a number of parliamentarian tracts written in the months preceding and following the eruption of war. As an anonymous author wrote in August of 1642, although subjects had sworn an oath of allegiance to Charles I as king, by deserting the parliament at Westminster the king deserted his "kingly office" and so freed his subjects from allegiance. In order for the king to redeem himself, he must, in the author's words, "return to your parliament, and so unto your people; return to your parliament, and so unto your lawful power."[63] Another writer put it more succinctly. If Charles I refused to be ruled by law, he was no king but a tyrant, "and my obedience is due to him, as a king, not as a tyrant."[64]

Although few of the early parliamentarian tracts cited sources for this theorizing, some referred specifically to Chapters 11 and 17 of St. Edward's laws. In one tract, published in August of 1642, Prynne quoted extensively from Pope Eleutherius's letter to Lucius in order to prove that kings who departed from their office freed their subjects from allegiance. He also noted that the kings of England knew well the idea that a king who misgoverned thereby lost the very name of a king. After all, at least as early as Henry I they had sworn in their coronation oaths to govern according to its precepts – a clear reference to St. Edward's laws.[65] Another pamphlet, dated September 2, 1642, quoted Chapter 17 of St. Edward's laws at length, noting that a king who departed from his office "loseth the very name of a king." Citing Foxe's *Acts and Monuments* as his source, the anonymous author further explained that when kings promised at their coronations to submit themselves to their office, they entered into a covenant with their subjects, who owed them allegiance only so long as they kept their end of the bargain.[66]

---

[62] See, for example, *The unlimited Prerogative of Kings subverted* (n.p., 1642), A1ᵛff; *Some Special Arguments for the Scottish Subjects lawfull defence of their Religion and Liberty* (n.p., 1642), pp. 3–8; *The Dutie of a King in His royall Office . . . Written by the High and Mightie Prince James* (London, 1642), pp. 1, 4–5; *The Aphorisms of the Kingdome* (London, 1642), p. 4; "Of the Fundamental Laws of the Politick Constitution (1643)," in *State Tracts. Being a Further Collection of Several Choice Treatises Relating to the Government. From the Year 1660 to 1689* (London, 1689), pp. 24, 26.

[63] *Vox Populi: or the Peoples Humble Discovery of Their own Loyaltie, and His Majesties ungrounded Jealousies* (London, 1642), pp. 4–5.

[64] [Marsh], *An Argument or, Debate in Law*, p. 3.

[65] [Prynne], *A Soveraign Antidote*, pp. 4–5, 6–7, 29–31.

[66] *A Collection of the Rights and Priviledges of Parliament* (London, 1642), pp. 4–5, 11. See also "Of the Fundamental Laws of the Politick Constitution," pp. 24, 26.

To royalist attempts to tar the two houses with the Despencers' treason, parliamentarians responded that it was not they who separated the king's two bodies but Charles I himself. He had, after all, deserted his parliament and refused to join with his people – once again, an assertion that made sense because the king was always presumed to be present in his courts. Equally to the point, the Long Parliament's bill of 1641, to which Charles I had consented, declared that this parliament could not be dissolved without its own consent. The king, then, had no choice but to attend. If he abrogated his legal responsibility, that is, if he departed from his kingly office, he unkinged himself – a line of argumentation backed by respected medieval sources which neatly let parliamentarians off the hook.[67]

Equally valuable, the distinction between the king's office and person helped parliamentarians deal with the thorny problem of allegiance. Citing the doctrine, they argued that subjects owed allegiance to the royal politic body, which in law could do no wrong, and not to the king in his personal capacity, which now made war against kingdom and parliament.[68] This argument was given wide publicity by Charles Herle, a Presbyterian clergyman whose writings the Long Parliament held in high esteem. A rather obscure countryman from Lancashire, Herle first appeared on the political scene in London in the fall of 1642, when he was invited to preach a fast sermon before the House of Commons at St. Margaret's. The invitation came from John Moore, a wealthy Liverpool merchant who served on key house committees and eventually became a regicide. Herle's obscurity soon ended, as he showed himself capable of constructing arguments indispensable to the rebel cause. In a much-cited tract published just months after the war began, Herle noted that when English law and history referred to the king as "the only supreme head and governor; it is not to be understood that he is so in his single or natural capacity, for then he should govern by his own personal will as the supreme rule, but in his politic or mixed capacity, which takes in law and parliament."[69] Or, as another writer expressed it, the people owed allegiance not to the king as a

---

[67] See, for example, *The Subject of Supremacy*, p. 65; *The Maximes of Mixt Monarchy*, pages unnumbered; *A Discourse Upon Questions in Debate between the King and Parliament* (n.p., [1643]), pp. 7, 10, 11–12; *Maximes Unfolded*, pp. 11–12, 17, 47.

[68] Husband, *An Exact Collection*, pp. 267, 304.

[69] Herle, *An Answer to Dr. Ferne's Reply, Entitled Conscience Satisfied* (London, 1643), pp. 18, 20–1, 36, 39.

private person but to the king in his public body, now under the firm control of the coordinate and coeval estates of Lords and Commons.[70]

This same line of reasoning allowed parliamentarians, in particular the clergy among them, to refute scriptural injunctions which seemed, on their face, to command unqualified obedience to the king. Here the stakes were particularly high, because, according to Phillip Hunton, such injunctions, especially Romans 13:1, constituted a principal royalist argument against resistance. Hunton's opinion is confirmed by the fact that, as Ian Gentles notes, royalist standards themselves sometimes carried the words "Romans xiii," "Touch not mine anointed," and "Render unto Caesar."[71] Like his brethren, Hunton found an answer to these biblical passages in Bishop Bilson's implied distinction between the king's two bodies. "It is," Bilson wrote, "the prince's will not against his laws; but agreeing to his laws," that subjects must obey.[72] In other words, when God commanded subjects to obey the powers that be, he meant only the lawful powers. Other parliamentarians argued similarly. Indeed, as Herle put it, 1 Peter 2:13 and Romans 13:1 obligated Christians to obey not the king but rather those three coordinate estates in parliament who constituted the legal sovereign.[73]

Jeremiah Burroughes, chaplain to the countess of Warwick and member of the Westminster Assembly, agreed. Described by Nigel Smith as the first person to suggest in print that England could function without a monarchy, he cited Romans 13 in parliament's cause. According to Burroughes, Paul did not write that "Whosoever resists the highest men shall receive damnation, but whosoever shall resist the power." It fell to subjects to distinguish between lawful and unlawful power, and if parliamentarians determined that Charles I acted illegally, they could resist him "without the least offending

---

[70] *Maximes Unfolded*, pp. 5–7, 11–12, 17, 47–8. See also *Vox Populi*, pp. 4–5; "Of the Fundamental Laws of the Politick Constitution," pp. 24, 26; *A Discourse Upon Questions in Debate between the King and Parliament*, pp. 6–7, 11–12; John Bellamy, *A Iustification of the City Remonstrance and Its Vindication* (London, 1646), pp. 33–4, 37–8; *A Declaration Against Prince Rupert* (London, 1643), p. 7; *A New Plea for the Parliament* (London, 1643), p. 10; *The Subjects Liberty*, pp. 5–6, 14, 16, 18–20; *The unlimited Prerogative of Kings subverted*, B2.

[71] Gentles, "The Iconography of Revolution: England 1642–1649," in *Soldiers, Writers and Statesmen of the English Revolution*, ed. Ian Gentles, John Morrill, and Blair Worden (Cambridge, 1998), pp. 91–113, especially 98.

[72] Hunton, *A Vindication of the Treatise of Monarchy*, pp. 57–8.

[73] Herle, *A Fuller Answer to A Treatise Written by Doctor Ferne*, pp. 1–18 *passim*. Herle, *An Answer to Dr. Ferne's Reply*, pp. 39–41.

against the text."[74] Writing in agreement was Stephen Marshall. Another protégé of Warwick, he was a close associate of the Essex grandees who worked intimately with John Pym. "Pym's favorite preacher," as Hugh Trevor-Roper describes him, Marshall enjoyed a place of honor in the inner circle that managed the Commons during the early years of the war. Along with Pym, Hampden, and Sir Robert Harley, he helped write the Root and Branch bill which abolished the episcopacy. In addition, he served as chaplain to the earl of Essex's regiment and also attended the negotiations of the Solemn League and Covenant as a commissioner.[75] Marshall wrote to remind his audience that the term "supreme power," which God commanded subjects to obey, referred to "that power, which by the original and fundamental constitution of any people and nation, hath authority to make laws which shall bind the whole nation." In England this "highest power" resided not in the "king's absolute or illegal will . . . but his legal will in the highest court, or the king and parliament." It was "to king and parliament" that God enjoined obedience and allegiance. Whoever resisted them "resisteth the ordinance of God, and they that resist shall receive to themselves damnation."[76] This view was later repeated by the esteemed Puritan clergyman Richard Baxter.[77]

Predictably, such reasoning led parliamentarians to conclude that subjects could wage war against Charles I without committing

---

[74] Burroughes, *The Glorious Name of God, The Lord of Hosts. Opened in two Sermons, at Michaels Cornhill, London* (London, 1643), pp. 112–14, 123. Burroughes, *A briefe Answer to Doctor Fernes Book* (n.p., n.d.), pp. 2–3, 7, 8. Pages are misnumbered at this point. Writing at the end of the Interregnum, the Lancashire clergyman Edward Gee cited Burroughes to make the same point. Gee, *The Divine Right and Original of the Civill Magistrate from God* (London, 1658), pp. 136–43, especially 139–40. See also Smith, *Literature and Revolution in England, 1640–1660*, p. 143; Sommerville, "English and European Political Ideas in the Early Seventeenth Century," p. 188.

[75] Trevor-Roper, *Religion, the Reformation and Social Change* (London, 1967), p. 264. *Biographical Dictionary of British Radicals in the Seventeenth Century,* ed. Richard L. Greaves and Robert Zaller (Brighton, 1984), vol. II, p. 217.

[76] Marshall, *A Copy of a Letter Written by Mr. Stephen Marshall* (London, 1643), pp. 1–12, 14, 15. See also Rutherford, "Lex Rex," p. 144; *The unlimited Prerogative of Kings subverted*, A1ᵛ-A3; *The Sovereignty of Kings: Or An absolute Answer and Confutation of that Groundlesse Vindication of Psalme 105.15* (London, 1642); *A Vindication of Psalme 105.15* (London, 1642); Herle, *A Fuller Answer to a Treatise Written by Doctor Ferne*, p. 20; *An Answer to Mis-led Doctor Fearne*, pp. 1–5; and *The Subject of Supremacie*, pp. 4, 9, and 53, where the author wrote that Romans 13.1 meant that parliament, which was composed of three coordinate estates, "is transcendant to the king in the legislative power."

[77] Baxter, *A Holy Commonwealth, or Political Aphorisms opening the True Principles of Government* (London, 1659), p. 477 and *passim*.

treason. As the Long Parliament's declaration of May 26 put it, by levying war against Charles I's "personal commands, though accompanied by his presence," parliamentarians fought for him as a king. In fact, according to Edward III's statute of treason, to fight for the king's "laws and authority" but against his "personal commands, though accompanied with his presence," was to fight for the kingship.[78] Herle made the point with equal force. "A parliament of England," he wrote, "may with good conscience in defence of king, laws, and government established, when imminently endangered, especially when actually invaded, take up arms without, and against the king's personal command, if he refuses."[79] In the present circumstances, this meant that "in fighting for the preservation of the land and kingdom they [parliamentarians] fight for him" in his politic capacity and not against him.[80] From this it also followed that royalists and not parliamentarians committed treason. Indeed, the king's army, even though "raised by his personal command, are enemies to him in his politic capacity, as king, because they are in arms against the law and so against the kingdom, and so against him as king."[81]

The distinction between the person and office of the king accomplished one other vital task. It helped refute the royalist claim that the two houses possessed no legislative power without the king. Because the doctrine of the king's two bodies permitted parliament to supply any deficiency in government which occurred as a result of the king's youth or disability, rebels now argued that the two houses could act without the personal presence of the king. Their right to do so Herle expressed in the phrase, "*co-ordinata invicem supplent,* coordinates supply each other." This doctrine became operable when the kingdom faced grave danger. At such a time the two coordinate and

[78] Husband, *An Exact Collection of All Remonstrances*, p. 276. See also pp. 208, 279, and 304. In the Third Remonstrance of May 26, 1642 the two houses defended acting without Charles I in the following way: "we shall never allow a few private persons about his majesty, nor his majesty himself in his own person, and out of his courts to be judge of the law, and that contrary to the judgment of the highest court of judicature." *Ibid.*, p. 267.

[79] Herle, *A Fuller Answer to a Treatise Written by Doctor Ferne*, pp. 1–2, 3, 10. See also *Some Special Arguments For the Scottish Subjects lawfull defence of their Religion and Liberty*, pp. 3, 5.

[80] Herle, *A Fuller Answer to a Treatise Written by Doctor Ferne*, p. 12. See also *An Answer to Mis-led Doctor Fearne*, pp. 9, 14, 17; *XI. Queries Propounded and Answered, Shewing Whether it bee Treason to bee for or against the King* (London, 1642), pp. 3, 5.

[81] Herle, *A Fuller Answer to a Treatise Written by Doctor Ferne*, p. 10. See also *A Declaration Against Prince Rupert*, p. 7.

coeval estates might – indeed, must – issue ordinances that bound subjects.[82]

The Long Parliament's claim to make law in the personal absence of the king gained even greater credence when parliamentarians put their own peculiar spin on that part of the coronation oath in which kings promised to abide by the law, in particular, the laws associated with St. Edward. The exact phrase on which parliamentarians focused was that in which the king solemnly promised to *"corroborare justas leges & consuetudines quas vulgus elegerit."* Throughout the century anti-court writers translated *"vulgus"* as "people" and *"elegerit"* as "shall choose" or "should choose." Such an interpretation allowed them to conclude that the king must assent to whatever bills the two houses sent him. As Parker wrote, the language of the coronation oath bound kings "to consent to new laws, if they be necessary, as well as defend the old"[83] – a view earlier put forward in 1308.

To the king's supporters, all such theorizing was ludicrous and absurd. For one thing, as Heylyn sarcastically wrote with regard to the theory of the king's two bodies, the Long Parliament pretended that it "might destroy Charles Stuart without hurting the king."[84] Or, as Digges put it, the two houses fantasize that they could "shoot at him as at Edgehill for his preservation" and try "to kill him in his own defense."[85] Equally specious, according to Charles I, was the parliamentarian interpretation of the coronation oath. For, "unless they have a power of declaring Latin, as well as law," *elegerit* meant "hath chosen as well as will choose." In fact, Charles continued, by swearing to uphold the laws of "the glorious King Saint Edward your predecessor," kings merely swore to uphold custom. In no way did the language of the coronation oath diminish the royal right to

---

[82] Herle, *A Fuller Answer to a Treatise Written by Doctor Ferne*, pp. 1–13 *passim*. See also the May 19 declaration of the Lords and Commons, "The Declaration or Remonstrance of the Lords and Commons, in Parliament Assembled," in Husband, *An Exact Collection*, p. 208; Ferne, *A Reply unto Severall Treatises*, pp. 52–3; Brian Tierney, *Religion, Law, and the Growth of Constitutional Thought, 1150–1650* (Cambridge, 1982), p. 83.

[83] Parker, *Observations upon some of his Majesties late Answers and Expresses*, pp. 2–8 *passim*. See also the two houses' declaration of May 26, in Husband, *An Exact Collection of all Remonstrances*, pp. 268–70; and Natalie Fryde's and J. R. Maddicott's description of Edward II's barons as being similarly motivated when they rewrote the coronation oath in 1308, chapter 2 above.

[84] Heylyn, *Aerius redivivus, or, The History of the Presbyterians* (London, 1672), pp. 438–9. See also Spelman, *A View of a Printed Book*, p. 28; Jenkins, "Lex Terrae," pp. 100–3.

[85] Digges, *The Unlawfulnesse of Subjects taking up Armes*, pp. 84–5. See also Rutherford, "Lex Rex," p. 146.

turn mere bills into statutes or to prevent them from becoming such.[86]

Obviously, much more than grammar was at stake in the debate over the coronation oath. By translating *elegerit* in the past tense, royalists preserved the king's role in making law. By translating the verb in the future tense, parliamentarians, following in the steps of the barons in Edward II's reign, stripped him of his veto power. This move, in turn, bolstered the argument for a coordination in the legislative power which gave the two houses, as two coequal estates, the lion's share of sovereignty. As the anonymous author of *Maximes Unfolded* wrote in 1643, although the king had departed parliament in his personal body, his authority remained in his office now under the control of parliament. In this politic body, he must consent to whatever measures the two houses sent him. And this by his own coronation oath.[87]

The parliamentarians' combination of the doctrine of coordination and ancient constitutionalism quickly became the mainstay of rebel theorizing. Fortified by St. Edward's laws, the *Modus*, and the *Mirror*, the king's enemies now began to hammer out unremitting defenses of resistance and, soon, regicide. Sir Roger Twysden, the learned common lawyer and Saxon scholar, lent his voice to the cause. Closely connected with Selden and the Saxonist William Somner, he sided with the Long Parliament only to fall out of favor when he refused to pay his taxes and take the Covenant. This obstinancy led to his imprisonment at Lambeth Palace from 1643 to 1647. But Twysden did not abandon his ancient constitutionalist stance in revenge for his treatment. With numerous records and manuscripts now at his disposal, he prepared a new edition of Lambarde's *Archaionomia*, adding to it the laws of Henry I as well as the Conqueror's laws and the tale of Sharnborn's case.[88]

From prison Twysden also began writing *Certaine Considerations Upon the Government of England*, an uncompromisingly ancient constitutionalist account of English history. Although not completed until

[86] "His Majesty's Answer to a Printed Book ... In Answer to a Declaration under His Majesties Name concerning the Business at Hull," in Husband, *An Exact Collection*, pp. 289–91.

[87] *Maximes Unfolded*, pp. 9–10, 11–12, 17, 47. See also *The Subjects Liberty*, pp. 5, 18–22; *An Answer to Mis-led Doctor Fearne*, p. 31.

[88] For Twysden's life and career see Frank W. Jessup, *Sir Roger Twysden, 1597–1672* (New York, 1965), especially chapters 5 and 6. But *cf.* Mendle, "Review of David L. Smith: Constitutional Royalism," *Albion* 27 (1995), 490–1.

the 1650s and not published until the nineteenth century, the work dates from the years 1642 to 1644. In *Certaine Considerations* Twysden deployed St. Edward's laws and the *Modus* to prove the contractual origins of the English government and the concomitant right of parliament, and the Commons in particular, to resist a king who broke the terms of the agreement. Concerned to answer Ferne, who argued that the Norman conquest had defeated any right in the people to empower kings, Twysden insisted that medieval history proved the contrary. William I, after all, claimed his title from St. Edward. Then came his promise at Swanscombe Down, his ruling in Sharnborn's case, and finally the confirmation of St. Edward's laws in 1070. Such actions created a contract between king and community. Citing Chapter 17 of St. Edward's laws, Twysden wrote that "both king and subject did, by swearing to each other, mutually make a solemn compact together, and establish their agreements on his taking the crown."[89]

And so it went in subsequent reigns. Although kings did not always honor the terms of the contract, giving the Commons cause to complain mightily at times, the coronation oath in general, and Chapter 17 in particular, nevertheless "tied" them to the observance of the contract. In such confirmations "was a plain stipulation between the king and the subject, their old laws restored, their ancient liberties asserted, and he received king." An especially notable confirmation occurred in 1215. At that time King John "was pressed to confirm Magna Carta, containing for the most part no other than the ancient rights and customs of the realm, extracted out of the laws of the Confessor and Henry the first . . ." And so it was with Henry III's Magna Carta, leading Twysden to call St. Edward's laws "the foundation of our common law; and . . . I should say that never people in Europe have had the rights of monarchy better limited, with the preservation of the subjects' liberty, than the English . . ." In the final analysis, the survival of St. Edward's laws throughout the centuries meant that, just as William I did not reign as a conqueror, neither did Charles Stuart.[90]

As for the origins of parliament, Twysden credited the Saxons

---

[89] Twysden, *Certaine Considerations upon the Government of England*, ed. John Mitchell Kimbell, Camden Society, vol. XLV (London, 1849), pp. 35–7, 40–1, 70–1, 75–6. See also Alan Cromartie, *Sir Matthew Hale, 1609–1676* (Cambridge, 1995), p. 51.

[90] Twysden, *Certaine Considerations Upon the Government of England*, ed. Kimbell, pp. 35–7, 40, 43–4, 56–8, 59–60, 70–1, 75–6.

with introducing it into England. He believed, too, that the people made laws there which bound both king and kingdom. Although some misled royalists pointed to 1265 as the date when the Commons first became a part of parliament, St. Edward's laws demonstrated its presence in Saxon times. This must be the meaning of the words that described those laws as "*concessa a rege, baronibus, et populo.*"[91] Even the term *baro*, when properly interpreted, included ordinary citizens such as Londoners. So it was with the similar term *proceres*. Prescription, too, told for the Commons. Since statutes of Edward III and Richard II referred to the lower house as "ever" present and as enjoying a customary right to be summoned, and since all Englishmen knew that "no custom can begin since Richard I," then "it must of necessity follow" that the Commons was summoned before 1189.[92]

The *Modus*, said to have been shown to the Conqueror, also attested to the presence of the Commons in Saxon times. Although that treatise's frequent use of the word "parliament" made Twysden suspicious as to its antedating the conquest, he nevertheless read it as consisting of the "ancient customs of the kingdom extracted out of the laws of King Edward and Henry the I."[93] The *Modus* served the parliamentarian cause in another way. It demonstrated that Charles I had no power to dissolve the Long Parliament until all petitions were heard and public acts had been passed. A king who acted otherwise committed perjury.[94] Much to Twysden's point was the reason for the lower house's presence in parliament: because England was "governed by no other than *quas vulgus elegerit,*" that is, "a concurrence of the people with the king in making the laws," he had no choice but to summon the Commons.[95]

The medieval English past also told Twysden how the people could preserve their laws and liberties. Here he found *Curtana*, which the earl of Chester carried before the king at his coronation, relevant. Although he did not know whether the earls of Chester had ever exercised the power implied in the display of St. Edward's sword, he did know that the coronation oath, in which kings promised to govern according to Chapter 17 of St. Edward's laws, constituted a contract between king and people. This convinced him that "there is no question . . . but it is lawful for subjects to oppose

[91] *Ibid.*, pp. 121–2, 125.   [92] *Ibid.*, pp. 125–6.
[93] *Ibid.*, p. 127. See also pp. 84, 88–9, 141.
[94] *Ibid.*, p. 141.   [95] *Ibid.*, p. 84.

their prince not observing his paction." After all, "no man can renounce his natural defence."[96]

The most forceful and consequential deployment of the radical ancient constitution appeared in two tracts of conspicuous importance – William Prynne's *Soveraigne Power of Parliaments and Kingdomes* (1643) and Nathaniel Bacon's *An Historical Discourse of the Uniformity of the Government of England* (1647–51). Both were singled out by Richard Baxter as among those works most advantageous to the parliamentarian cause; and both rested solidly on a Saxon foundation.[97] Cited and republished throughout the century and feared by generations of royalists, the two tracts contain the fullest and most mature statements of radical ancient constitutionalism written during the civil wars. They also demonstrated just how lethal the combination of medieval English history and the doctrine of coordination could be.

Prynne's *Soveraigne Power of Parliaments and Kingdomes* bore the imprimatur of the Long Parliament, which commissioned him early in 1643 to write the work. This tract, soon to be notorious, therefore constituted an *official* justification for warring against Charles Stuart. The extent of Prynne's success appeared from the animosity with which royalists throughout the century greeted the work. Writing in 1685, the high tory John Northleigh spoke for generations of Stuart loyalists when he described Prynne as "the most malicious miscreant of the pen" and a "seditious dolt," whose *Soveraigne Power* merited the name "vomit."[98]

Prynne was by any measure an extraordinary figure. Trained in common law at Lincoln's Inn and a member of the Commons in the Long Parliament, he enjoyed a long and tumultuous political career scarcely matched in the century of revolution. An early opponent of Charles I, he pestered the king throughout the early years of his reign, taking on issues from masques at court to ship money. By the end of the civil war, however, Prynne had done an about face.

---

[96] *Ibid.*, pp. 92–3.
[97] Baxter, *Reliquiae Baxterianae: or, Mr. Richard Baxter's Narrative of the most Memorable Passages of his Life and Times*, ed. Matthew Sylvester (London, 1696), pp. 1, 41. Baxter, *A Holy Commonwealth*, p. 458. The other two tracts singled out by Baxter were Parker's pre-civil war tract *Observations upon Some of His Majesties Late Answers and Expresses* and Hunton's *A Treatise of Monarchie*.
[98] Northleigh, *Remarks Upon the most eminent of our Antimonarchical Authors and Their Writings* (Westminster, 1699), pp. 290, 292, 424, 571. This work was first published in 1685 under the title *The Triumph of Our Monarchy*.

Genuinely committed to a mixed monarchy, he came to fear the extremist views of the army. He was excluded from the House of Commons at Pride's Purge, and he vigorously opposed the execution of Charles I and the destruction of government by King, Lords, and Commons. At the Restoration, Charles II rewarded him with the office of Keeper of the Tower Records, from which position he proceeded to attack the radical ancient constitutionalism he had earlier helped to shape.[99]

Until 1649, however, Prynne occupied a place of great honor among parliamentarian polemicists. Even the most cursory examination of *Soveraigne Power of Parliaments and Kingdomes* indicates why this was so. Here Prynne, a fervent believer in the doctrine of coordination, created out of the usual medieval sources a convincing cover for making war against the king. And he did so in a way that made rebellion and treason appear as the just restoration of ancient practices. Prynne's basic theme, which ran consistently through the tract, was the utter sovereignty of kingdom and parliament over kings and their concomitant right to call tyrants to account. In his words, "the whole kingdom and parliament representing it, are the most sovereign power; and above the king himself." That is, supreme authority "legally and really . . . reside[s] in the whole kingdom, and parliament, which represents it, not in the king's person, who is inferior to the parliament."[100]

For proof of his position Prynne relied on a number of sources, including St. Edward's laws, the *Modus*, and the *Mirror*. These he found useful both in establishing the general principles of English government and in justifying specific policies of the Long Parliament. The *Modus* and the *Mirror*, for example, spoke unequivocally of the high power of parliament. According to the *Mirror*, in Saxon times parliament had been considered so vital to the governance of the kingdom that it met regularly and frequently. Indeed, King Alfred "in an assembly of parliament enacted for a perpetual custom; That a parliament should be called together twice every year," or more often if necessary. Two statutes of Edward III had

[99] *Biographical Dictionary of British Radicals in the Seventeenth Century*, ed. Greaves and Zaller, vol. II, pp. 112–13. Lamont, *Marginal Prynne*.

[100] Prynne, *The Soveraigne Power of Parliaments and Kingdomes: Divided into Four Parts together with an Appendix* (London, August 2, 1643), p. 91. This work was published in serial form throughout 1643. Each of its four parts had a different title, and some carry the month of the year. Pages are frequently misnumbered.

confirmed Alfred's earlier ordinance, and kings were "obliged by their coronation oaths to observe these laws."[101] The *Modus*, too, offered proof of parliament's commanding presence within the English state. Dating from the Confessor's reign and enjoying the blessings of William I, it depicted parliament as "above the law itself, having power upon just grounds to alter the very common law of England . . . Yea, it hath power . . . so far as finally to oblige both king and subject."[102]

Prynne also noted that these sources addressed the issue of taking up the sword against Charles I. According to his reading, both St. Edward's laws and the *Mirror* sanctioned resistance on the part of subjects. This conclusion followed from that fact that in England, kingdom and parliament constituted "the most sovereign and primitive power from whence all other powers were, and are derived." That is, people and parliament created and therefore antedated kings.[103] Prynne recognized, of course, that God played a vital role in constituting government. Indeed, he was the author and ultimate source of all power. But God had left it to each community to decide exactly what form of government it wished to live under, and in England the people elected kings, while parliament, as its representative, empowered them.[104] Thus, Prynne concluded, "Their royal authority . . . is of human institution properly, not divine; from their people, who both elect, constitute them kings, and give them all their regal authority by human laws enacted, not from God as the only efficient cause."[105]

English history, Prynne continued, afforded many examples of people and parliament electing their rulers. The *Mirror*, for its part, told how the forty Saxon princes, presumably acting on behalf of the community, chose one to rule over all. Moreover, the people confirmed Cnut's title in 1017, and "by a general consent of the nobles, clergy, and people" chose Edward the Confessor as king. And so it went with Henry I, Maude, and Stephen who also attained

---

[101] Prynne, *The Treachery and Disloyalty of Papists to Their Soveraignes*, 2nd. edn. enlarged (London, 1643), p. 12. The statutes were 4 Edw. 3. c. 4 and 36 Edw. 3. c. 10. See also Prynne, *The Third Part of a Seasonable, Legal, and Historical Vindication of the good old Fundamental Liberties, Franchises, Rights, Properties, Laws, Government of all English Freemen* (London, 1657), pp. 74–5, 80.

[102] Prynne, *The Treachery and Disloyalty of Papists to Their Soveraignes*, pp. 39, 43, 45.

[103] *Ibid.*, p. 39. *The Soveraigne Power of Parliaments or Kingdomes. Or Second Part of the Treachery and Disloialty of Papists to their Soveraignes* (London, March 28, 1643), p. 82.

[104] *The Treachery and Disloyalty of Papists to Their Soveraignes*, pp. 35–6, 39, 49.

[105] *The Third Part of the Soveraigne Power of Parliaments and Kingdomes*, pp. 118–19.

the crown by election after promising to keep St. Edward's laws. Finally, Prynne described how, after the deposition of Edward II, parliament, "in the great hall at Westminster, with the universal consent of the people there present," elected his eldest son king.[106]

It almost went without saying that, when the people chose their king, they imposed conditions upon him. These conditions they specified in the coronation oath, which embodied Chapter 17 of the Confessor's laws. Citing Foxe's *Acts and Monuments* throughout, Prynne wrote that the ruler who swore to uphold the "Office of a King" thereby committed himself to govern "according to the universal common law for all people." This appeared unmistakably when, at the bishop's request, the king confirmed by oath "the laws and customs granted to the people of England . . . especially the laws, and customs and ancient liberties granted by glorious King Edward to the clergy and people."[107] In so swearing, he recognized his subservience to people and parliament. As Prynne put it, "the whole kingdom and parliament are the supreme sovereign authority, and paramount the king, because they may lawfully, and do usually prescribe such conditions, terms, and rules of governing the people to him, and bind them thus by oath, faithfully to perform the same, as long as he shall continue king."[108]

Their relationship with him was, then, contractual, and their obligation to obey entirely dependent upon his ruling as a king rather than a tyrant. Prynne recognized, of course, that some royalists acknowledged the possibility of an elective monarchy but insisted on the irrevocable nature of the community's grant of power to the sovereign. In this royalist reading of the *lex regia*, the people possessed no right to call an errant ruler to account. Nonsense, Prynne responded. The fact that king after king swore anew to govern according to the "Office of a King" proved the absurdity of the royalist position. After all, St. Edward's laws stated unequivocally "that a king governing in a settled kingdom, ceaseth to be a king, and degenerates into a tyrant, so soon as he leaves to rule by his laws" and when he attempts to "destroy his people in a hostile manner." In such circumstances, he unkinged himself and the

---

[106] *The Treachery and Disloyalty of Papists to Their Soveraigne*, pp. 54, 79–100 *passim*.
[107] *Ibid.*, p. 56.
[108] *Ibid.*, pp. 32–40 *passim*, 51, 56–8, 75, 87–100 *passim*. In addition, Prynne also cited Bracton's and Fleta's versions of the "Office of a King." *Ibid.*, p. 34.

kingdom could call him to account.[109] More than this. If the king in his personal capacity made war against the kingdom, all subjects were obligated to come to parliament's defense. This conclusion followed from "the original compact and mutual stipulation of every member of any republic, state, or society of men."[110] In Prynne's view, then, the people took care to leave "a just authority, power, and remedy residing in them, whereby to preserve themselves, the nation kingdom, from utter desolation, ruin, and vassalage." Here, surely, was "impregnable evidence" that "parliament," which consisted of three coordinate and coeval estates, "may, as they are the highest sovereign power and judicature, resist the king and his forces, though he be their father, head, shepherd, lords, as they are private men."[111]

The *Mirror*, as fortified by Bracton and Fleta, also validated the right of kingdom and parliament to limit the power of kings. Noting that in some situations parliament needed to "bridle" an errant ruler, Prynne deployed the *Mirror* to show how this right had come about. When, after conquering the Britons, the Saxons installed forty princes, they saw to it that each Saxon prince had "companions" who insured that he governed justly. The system carried over to the Saxon king, who met at least twice a year with his parliament. In these assemblies companions, now called counts, heard and determined "all the writs and plaints of the wrongs of the king, the queen, and their children," especially those of ordinary subjects who could not otherwise receive justice. The purpose of the companions and parliament itself was "to restrain and bridle the king when he casts off the bridle of the law, and invades the subjects' liberties, especially with open force of arms in a hostile manner."[112]

Thus, Prynne told his readers, the practice of calling errant kings to account was a familiar practice in ancient England, and it remained so after the arrival of the Normans. In response to those who refused to see things parliament's way, Prynne delved deeper into his history books for specific examples. First came parliament's deposition of two British kings, Archigallo and Emerian, for violating

---

[109] *The Third Part of the Soveraigne Power of Parliaments and Kingdomes*, pp. 3–6, 9. *The Treachery and Disloyalty of Papists to Their Soveraignes*, pp. 51, 87.

[110] *The Third Part of the Soveraigne Power of Parliaments and Kingdomes*, pp. 10–13, 132.

[111] *Ibid.*, p. 132. *The Soveraigne Power of Parliaments and Kingdomes Divided into Four Parts* (London, August 2, 1643), pp. 91–2.

[112] *The Treachery and Disloyalty of Papists to Their Soveraignes*, pp. 36–7. *The Third Part of the Soveraignty of Parliaments and Kingdomes* (London, May 8, 1643), p. 3.

their coronation oaths. Next Prynne called attention to Edwin of Mercia who also lost his crown for misrule. And he reminded readers of the example of King John, from whom Magna Carta and the Charter of the Forest, "with other fundamental liberties, [were] . . . forcibly extorted . . . at first."[113]

Although devoted to the principle of coordination, Prynne knew the Commons possessed ultimate supremacy. In language he would live to regret and in due course recant, he turned to the *Modus*, which dictated that when the king summoned his parliament, all parties had to attend. No one could be absent without special license. Not even the king, who in case of illness must meet with a special body of visitors from the two houses to verify that he was indeed sick. If, however, the Lords, for whatever reason, chose to stay away, the business of parliament, according to the *Modus*, could be carried on by king and Commons alone. If, on the other hand, the Lords attended and the members of the lower house absented themselves, no parliament existed. The preeminence of the Commons stemmed from the fact that it alone represented the kingdom, whereas each baron represented only himself. This meant, in turn, that king and Commons possessed "a sufficient and full authority to make, ordain, and establish good and wholesome laws for the commonwealth of this realm."[114]

The king, then, reigned as the creature of kingdom and parliament, performing his office under their close scrutiny. He could do very little without them, and certainly nothing as important as making law. Once again Prynne emphasized the link between Chapter 17 and the coronation oath, especially the *quas vulgus elegerit* clause. In his view, when the king promised to abide by the "Office," he bound himself not only to the ancient laws of Holy Edward but also to whatever future laws parliament should send to him. Interpreting *elegerit* in the future tense, Prynne insisted that the king "hath little or no hand in making, but only in assenting to laws, when they are made by the houses." Still, in a sleight of hand he denied that he completely stripped the king of law-making power, since the royal assent remained necessary to the legislative process. But the king could not withhold it. Thus, in Prynne's view Chapter 17, as it was expressed in the coronation oath, effectively deprived

---

[113] *Ibid.*, p. 26. See also pp. 78–86 *passim.*
[114] *The Treachery and Disloyalty of Papists to Their Soveraignes*, pp. 42–3, 78–86 *passim.*

the king of his negative voice. Completely at the mercy of the two houses or the lone Commons, he must rubber-stamp whatever measures they sent him.[115]

Like other parliamentarian writers, Prynne found medieval sources, especially the Chapter 17, helpful in sorting out the problem of allegiance. Understanding that subjects might be confused as to which side to back as the civil war ground on, he attempted to ease troubled consciences by reminding doubters of the distinction between the office and person of a king. It was the king in his politic capacity who promised in the coronation oath to govern according to his office, and it was also in this body that he was considered virtually present in all of his courts. Thus, Charles I was legally present in the Long Parliament though personally absent. Indeed, the king in his politic capacity "cannot be severed from the parliament," for in law "the king himself and whole realm . . . are ever legally present in and with his parliament when they sit . . . wherever the king's person is; and his royal legal will (of which alone the law takes notice) is ever presumed to concur with his greatest council the parliament."[116]

According to Prynne's reading of history, this pattern of power, in which kingdom and parliament and in the last analysis the lone Commons took precedence over the king, was no recent innovation. On the contrary, the major features of the government in his own day could be found at least as early as the Saxon period. As for the role of parliament, chroniclers such as Paris, Eadmerus, Huntingdon, Holinshed, and Speed told of assemblies playing an active role in all phases of government, including law-making. Further, the composition of these primitive bodies was the same as in Prynne's day, such assemblies being "no other than parliaments, wherein the king and all temporal estates assembled." Indeed, parliaments consisting of three coordinate estates could be found in the reigns of Vortigern and Siegbert as well as in Cnut's and the Confessor's times.[117]

The nature of the English government, Prynne continued, remained unchanged after the planting of the Norman dynasty, for, William's destructive policies notwithstanding, Saxon laws and

---

[115] *Ibid.*, pp. 47–52 *passim*. *The Soveraigne Power of Parliaments and Kingdomes. Or Second Part of the Treachery and Disloialty of Papists to their Soveraignes*, pp. 75–82 *passim*.

[116] *The Treachery and Disloyalty of Papists to Their Soveraignes*, pp. 105, 109–11.

[117] *The Soveraigne Power of Parliaments and Kingdomes* (August), pp. 7–10 *passim*, 12–13, 94–5.

institutions endured. Witness, for example, William's oath to keep Saxon laws, which, of itself, amply demonstrated that he was no conqueror. Witness, too, the repeated confirmations of St. Edward's laws by Henry I, King Stephen, and Henry II in their coronation charters. Prynne also told how King John swore twice to uphold St. Edward's laws, once when he was crowned "with a great oath solemnly taken upon the altar and coffin of Saint Edward," and again at Runnymede. Indeed, this practice had continued unabated since the coronation of Edward II's reign.[118]

Prynne understood, of course, that kings had not always honored such promises. William the Conqueror, for one, confirmed St. Edward's laws in the fourth year of his reign, only to renege on his promise almost immediately. But such acts of perjury always caused the Saxons to rise up in arms against him, forcing still further confirmations. At St. Albans in 1072, for example, William gave way before the Saxon rebels because he feared losing the crown "with shame, which he had gotten with effusion of so much blood." Hence his oath to Abbot Frederick "swearing to observe and inviolably to keep the ancient laws of this land, and most especially those compiled by Edward the Confessor."[119] Prescription, then, told for the English, whose refusal to surrender quietly kept Saxon laws and institutions alive. And alive they remained in Prynne's day, protecting subjects from royal tyranny.

Although Prynne showed the world how easily medieval history could be used to justify rebellion against Charles I, he remained, as previously mentioned, committed to some version of mixed government and had nothing to do with the new Commonwealth government. The task of extending the reach of St. Edward's laws, the *Modus*, and the *Mirror* to encompass regicide, the destruction of government by King, Lords, and Commons, and the establishment of a republic fell to other polemicists. One of these was Nathaniel Bacon, whose *An Historical Discourse of the Uniformity of Government* deployed medieval sources and the doctrine of coordination to prove not only the kingdom's right to hold kings accountable but also its duty to replace them if they governed as tyrants. Published in 1647, with a "Continuation" appearing in 1651, the tract quickly became a favorite among radicals and was steadily republished well into the

[118] *Ibid.*, pp. 9–13 *passim*. *The Treachery and Disloyalty of Papists to Their Soveraignes*, pp. 49–56 *passim*, 79ff.
[119] *Ibid.*, pp. 51–2.

eighteenth century. It was secretly reprinted in 1672, in 1682 at the time of the exclusion crisis, in 1689 at the Glorious Revolution, again in 1739, and by 1750 in a fifth edition. The tract's persuasive power was attested after the Restoration, when Charles II's government made efforts to suppress it. Thus, the king ordered the prosecution of the radical printer John Starkey, a member of the Green Ribbon Club, who dared to publish the "dangerous work." Fearing for his life, Starkey fled to Amsterdam.[120]

A Suffolk lawyer, Bacon was a member of the Rump Parliament, and he later served the Commonwealth and Protectorate as a judge in Admiralty and a master of Requests.[121] Obviously well read in English history, his *Historical Discourse* brimmed with references to St. Edward's laws and the *Mirror of Justices*. Bacon's eminence, combined with the great popularity of his tract, must have done much to familiarize Englishmen with the radical potential of the English past. He wrote to help those who required guidance in the turbulent days that accompanied the end of the civil war. In order to act appropriately, they need only read their own history, in particular the parts that dealt with Saxon England. Because the Saxon monarchy had been elective and the relationship between king and people contractual, the same was true of their own age. The *Mirror of Justices* and St. Edward's laws provided compelling evidence of this continuity. The same sources demonstrated the legitimacy of the parliamentary cause, proving unmistakably the right of the people and its representative to depose tyrannical rulers and settle the government to their liking.

Referring expressly to Chapter 17, which he knew from Foxe and Lambarde, Bacon noted that in Saxon times the people exercised precisely these powers. The *Mirror*, too, supported this contention, as when, for example, it described how the people elected Cnut king and made him swear to govern "according to the laws of God and the whole nation . . ." The subject's allegiance was, then, condi-

---

[120] *Calendar of State Papers Domestic, 1677–78*, pp. 446, 449, and vol. 23, pp. 236, 608. The British Library *Catalogue* lists these three editions, but *cf. D.N.B.* See also Melinda S. Zook, *Radical Whigs and Conspiratorial Politics in Late Stuart England* (University Park, Pa., 1999), p. 27; Richard L. Greaves, *Enemies Under His Feet. Radicals and Nonconformists in Britain, 1664–1677* (Stanford, 1990), p. 234; Richard Tuck, *Philosophy and Government, 1572–1651* (Cambridge, 1993), pp. 221–40; Samuel Kliger, *The Goths in England* (Cambridge, Mass., 1952); R. J. Smith, *The Gothic Bequest* (Cambridge, 1987).

[121] For Bacon's career see A. Blair Worden, *The Rump Parliament 1648–1653* (Cambridge, 1974), pp. 73, 109, 127, 130.

tional. Indeed, if the king failed to defend his people, and especially his churchmen, he lost his crown. No mere "dead word," Bacon continued, the people's right to make and unmake kings was often put into practice in Saxon times, as the nation "made the monarchical crown in this land to walk circuit into all parts of the country to find heads fit to wear itself until the Normans came." The Saxons, then, "hammered their kings in their elections, and made [them] . . . properly their own." This piece of the English past led Bacon to conclude that "a Saxon king was no other than a *primum mobile* set in a regular motion, by laws established by the whole body of the kingdom."[122]

Bacon labored to impart one vital message to his readers: because the Saxon kingship was elective and firmly under the thumb of the people, so too was the Stuart kingship. But Bacon's medieval sources told him of another contemporary institution that dated to the Saxon past, namely, that "grand assembly" which "was holden sacred." Like its modern counterpart, the ancient parliament consisted of "*king, baronibus, and populo*," as Lambarde had noted in *Archaionomia*. And, like its modern counterpart, parliament's business consisted of governing the kingdom, a task which included sitting in judgment of the king. So much was clear from the *Mirror*, which reminded king and kingdom that rulers could not be a judge in their own cause.[123] As for the power of the king in parliament, Bacon vouched the coronation oath, with its *quas vulgus elegerit* clause, to prove that he had no veto power. He must pass those measures sent to him by the two houses.[124]

Bacon ended the 1647 portion of his tract with a chapter entitled "An Epilogue to the Saxon Government." Noting, first of all, that the kingdom underwent an assault by the Danes, he insisted that this particular invasion "trenched not upon the fundamental law of the people's liberty." The Danish military success notwithstanding, "the liberty of the Saxon freeman, which the Danes could never conquer," survived, and the crown soon returned to the Saxon line. "To sum up all," Bacon concluded, "the Saxon commonweal was a

---

[122] Bacon, *An Historical Discourse of the Uniformity of the Government of England* (London, 1647–51), pp. 49–51, 53, 112ff.

[123] *Ibid.*, pp. 59–60.

[124] *Ibid.*, "The Continuation of an Historical Discourse of the Government of England, Untill the end of the Reigne of Queene Elizabeth. With a Preface, being a Vindication of the ancient way of Parliaments in England" (1651), pp. 303–4.

building of greatest strength downward even to the foundation, arched together both for peace and war . . . It was a beautiful composure, mutually dependent in every part from the crown to the clown, the magistrates being all choice men, and the king the choicest of the chosen . . ." "Thus" the Saxon government became "above all other likest unto that of Christ's kingdom, whose yoke is easy and burthen light."[125]

Nor was this situation altered by the coming of the Normans, royalist claims to the contrary. William I never shook "off the clog of Saxon law . . ." or "raise[d] the title of conquest." Indeed, he followed the Saxon coronation ceremony, making "a solemn covenant to observe those laws which were *bone & approbate & antiquae leges Regni*," that is, St. Edward's laws. Not content with this measure, William even commended these laws to his own justices, ordering that they be translated into French so that the Normans might read them. Hence the law by which William ruled England was "not the law of the conqueror's own will, nor the law that suits with his desire; but the ancient law of the kingdom."[126] As for William's two sons and successors, both William Rufus and Henry I came to the throne by election and only after promising, as did their father, to govern according to ancient Saxon laws. "Thus," Bacon continued, "these three Norman kings made their way to the throne . . . by capitulation, election, and stipulation."[127]

Just as William I kept St. Edward's laws, so did he govern as the Saxons had done, that is, with parliament, whose "footprints" Bacon found in the Conqueror's time. Indeed, the "grand council" which William, in 1070, summoned from all the counties, was itself a parliament – and a parliament with "the legislative power and right of cognizance, and judicature in those laws that concerned the kingdom in general . . ." In this "representative body of the kingdom" he reserved to himself only the free services of free men, in return for which he and his parliament granted them their lands in inheritance. This was also the occasion for collecting the various Saxon customs known as the *Leges Edwardi Confessoris*. The products of the assembly of 1070 deserved, in Bacon's view, to "be called the first Magna Carta in the Norman times." Henry I also treated "his people in a parliamentary way," making his confirmation of St.

---

[125] *Ibid.*, pp. 111–12.   [126] *Ibid.*, pp. 115–16, 155ff, 160ff.   [127] *Ibid.*, pp. 118–19.

Edward's laws in a parliament. Thus, William I governed by compact and so did his successors.[128]

Writing a summation to his tract in 1651, Bacon emphasized once more the continuity of Saxon laws and institutions across the divide of 1066 and their descent to the English people of his own day and age. Saluting both past and present, he wrote at the very end of his tract: "as I found this nation a commonwealth, so I leave it, and so may it be forever; so will it be, if we may attain the happiness of our forefathers' ancient Saxons, *Quilibet contentus sorte propria*" – "let everyone be content with his own lot." Since the present "commonwealth" referred to no mere utopia but to the government established after the regicide, Bacon's words must have provided no small measure of comfort.[129]

The works of Prynne and Bacon occupied a place of great prominence in civil war ideology, demonstrating just how easily the canonical medieval sources could be exploited for extremist purposes. The Levellers, who had even more radical goals, also turned to early English sources in search of legitimacy. Indeed, their anti-Normanism made Holy Edward and his laws especially appealing. To suggest that the Levellers found historical sources relevant to their cause goes somewhat against the grain of modern scholarship, which often emphasizes their political rationalism.[130] But an influential article by R. B. Seaberg suggests that they, like other opponents of the Stuart monarchy, found argument from history useful. Indeed, in Seaberg's opinion their articulation of the theory of the Norman yoke proved perfectly compatible with the traditional view that William I had conquered only the Saxon army and King Harold. Like the Tudor chroniclers such as Holinshed, Speed, Daniel, and Martyn whom they cited, the Levellers found the Conqueror confirming the laws of St. Edward. And, also like earlier writers,

[128] *Ibid.*, pp. 120–1.
[129] Bulstrode Whitelocke, called by David Underdown the most representative of the Rumpers, used St. Edward's laws to precisely the same effect in order to buttress the right of the lone House of Commons to govern in the absence of the king and upper house. *Notes Uppon the Kings Writt For choosing Members of Parliament XIII Car. II* (London, 1766), vol. II, pp. 98, 115–16, 134, 139–40, 256–7, 417–18. Underdown, *Pride's Purge: Politics in the Puritan Revolution* (Oxford, 1971), p. 296.
[130] See, for example, Christopher Hill, "The Norman Yoke," in *Puritans and Revolution* (London, 1968), pp. 76, 81; Skinner, "History and Ideology in the English Revolution," pp. 160–1; Austin Woolrych, "Political Theory and Political Practice," in *The Age of Milton: Backgrounds to Seventeenth-Century Literature*, ed. C. A. Patrides and R. B. Waddington (Manchester, 1980), p. 38.

they downplayed the changes that the Normans introduced by reference to two historical facts. First, in their view most of the legal changes that came in the aftermath of 1066 were of an administrative, not a substantive nature. Second, when William and his successors went too far in the process of altering Saxon laws, English protests succeeded in forcing the conquerors to back down.[131]

Thus, John Lilburne, Richard Overton, William Walwyn, and John Wildman believed that St. Edward's laws, that is, the common law, had survived the conquest and continued to flourish in their own day. To Lilburne, the "iron Norman yoke" consisted of the introduction of Norman procedural rules and practices, which "to this day remain in the administration of the common law at Westminster." But although the "process" had been corrupted, the "fountain" remained. That is, the events of 1066 did not touch the substance of St. Edward's laws. For Lilburne, even a document as highly prized as Magna Carta paled in comparison to the Confessor's legal legacy.[132] Richard Overton and William Walwyn concurred. Overton, for example, noted that, although William I entered by force, he confirmed the laws of St. Edward upon petition of the Lords and Commons, as did later kings in their coronation oaths. Further, he agreed with Lilburne that the changes introduced into common law were of a procedural nature. Walwyn wrote to the same effect and, moreover, linked the Saxon laws with Magna Carta and the Petition of Right.[133] Indeed, the steady beat of confirmations, bolstered by the coronation oath, amounted to a mutual contract between king and people, which Lilburne tellingly identified with the Agreement of the People. Nor did it matter that Norman kings sometimes went back on their word, for the important point was that the Saxons repeatedly laid "claim unto the fundamental laws and liberties of England," and had done so "throughout all

[131] Seaberg, "The Norman conquest and the Common Law: the Levellers and the Argument from Continuity," *Historical Journal* 24 (1981), 791–806.
[132] Lilburne, *The Just Man's Justification* (London, 2nd edn, 1647), p. 14. Cited in Seaberg, "The Norman Conquest and the Common Law," pp. 795–6. See also Diane Parkin-Speer, "John Lilburne: a Revolutionary Interprets Statutes and Common Law Due Process," *Law and History Review* I (1983), 276–96; Andrew Sharp, "John Lilburne and the Long Parliament's *Book of Declarations*: a Radical's Exploitation of the Words of Authorities," *History of Political Thought* 9 (1988), 19–44. But *cf.* Burgess, *The Politics of the Ancient Constitution*, pp. 90–3.
[133] Overton, *Vox Plebis* (London, 1646), p. 6. Walwyn, *Juries Justified* (London, 1651), p. 5. On occasion, however, Walwyn and Overton wrote critically of Magna Carta. Seaberg, "The Norman Conquest and the Common Law," pp. 798–800.

succession of governments and changes." Prescription, then, told for the rebels.[134]

Then there was the Leveller John Hare, author of *St. Edward's Ghost*. Written in 1642 but not published until 1647, the work advocated a complete and thorough-going reform of the law for the purpose of restoring legal equality and securing a redistribution of property. Because present inequities stemmed from the imposition of a Norman yoke, the remedy lay in rolling back the clock to the days of St. Edward and his most equitable laws. The Confessor was, after all, the last rightful king of England. Therefore, the catalogue of kings should be altered so that he, and not William the Conqueror, stood as the first. Indeed, William had only defeated the usurper Harold, whom the English soldiers considered unworthy of their support. Even if the English people eventually admitted William to the throne, they did so only after he first promised to obey St. Edward's laws. These events had significance for Hare's own day. He urged Charles I to acknowledge that he derived "his right from St. Edward's legacy." And Hare further demanded "that all laws and usages introduced from Normandy, be (*eo nomine*) abolished and supply made from St. Edward's laws or the civil, and that our laws be divested of their French rags."[135] In another tract published in 1648 Hare repeated these arguments. William I was merely a "pretended conqueror" who in point of fact "was admitted as legatee of St. Edward, and upon his oath to preserve our laws and liberties."[136]

To the extent that Seaberg's interpretation is correct, ancient constitutionalism enjoyed a life alongside the natural law and reason theorizing of the Levellers. They did indeed believe in the existence of a "Norman yoke." But it was a yoke tempered by the Conqueror's confirmations of St. Edward's laws and the subsequent confirma-

---

[134] Lilburne, *The Legal and Fundamental Liberties* (London, 1649), p. 44. *The Fundamental Laws and Liberties of England* (London, 1653), p. 2. Quoted in Seaberg, "The Norman Conquest and the Common Law," pp. 801, 803–4.

[135] Hare, *St. Edward's Ghost* (London, 1647), pp. 15, 18–19. For the identification of Hare as a Leveller see *Biographical Dictionary of British Radicals in the Seventeenth Century*, ed. Greaves and Zaller, vol. I, p. 53; Christopher Hill, "Gerrard Winstanley and Freedom," in Hill, *A Nation of Change and Novelty: Radical Politics, Religion and Literature in Seventeenth-Century England* (London, 1993), p. 136; Burgess, *The Politics of the Ancient Constitution*, pp. 92–3. Colin Kidd identifies Hare as a "radical Saxonist." *British Identities Before Nationalism. Ethnicity and Nationhood in the Atlantic World, 1600–1800* (Cambridge, 1999), pp. 77–8.

[136] Hare, "England's proper and only Way to an Establishment in Honour, Freedom, Peace and Happiness (1648)," in *Harleian Miscellany*, vol. VI (London, 1810), pp. 36–42 *passim*.

tions carried in the coronation oath. In this understanding, Leveller interpretations of 1066 and its aftermath appear somewhat more compatible with the traditional view of medieval history than is often allowed. As Seaberg puts the matter, the Levellers could "believe in a kind of continuity to English history because they did not view the Norman conquest as the fatal breach in English tradition." Perhaps, however, Quentin Skinner deserves the last word. Although, in his opinion, both radical and royalist writers continued to rely heavily on historical frameworks, they no longer viewed history as imbued with "prescriptive force." They saved it instead for purposes of illustration.[137]

THE RADICAL ANCIENT CONSTITUTION DURING THE INTERREGNUM

A new era opened with the victory of the New Model Army in 1648. The Rump, that part of the Long Parliament left sitting after Pride's purge, carried out a political revolution in early 1649. Declaring England a republic in which the House of Commons exercised supreme authority, it erected the High Court of Justice that tried and executed the king. Although medieval historical sources did not figure prominently in the case against Charles I, John Bradshaw, president of the High Court, alluded to one of them. Referring to the *Mirror* in an effort to justify the Rump's authority, Bradshaw cited the ancient practice of bi-annual parliaments. He also noted that parliament and people had in the past called errant kings to account, "as may appear if we look into the Saxons' time," and since the conquest as well. Witness, for example, the fate of Edward II and Richard II.[138]

The killing of the best of kings sent shock waves throughout Europe, and in England Charles soon achieved the status of martyr. But the Rump did more than kill the king. Not content with regicide, it proceeded to abolish the monarchy itself, along with the House of Lords.[139] The nation now confronted a problem of allegiance

---

[137] Seaberg, "The Norman conquest and the Common Law," p. 801.

[138] *A Complete Collection of State Trials*, ed. T. B. Howell (London, 1816), vol. v, pp. 1010, 1012. *The Trial of King Charles the First* (Edinburgh, 1928), pp. 120–1.

[139] See G. E. Aylmer, *Rebellion or Revolution? England from 1640–1660* (Oxford, 1987), pp. 97–101; Underdown, *Pride's Purge*; Blair Worden, *The Rump Parliament*. Howard Nenner describes how Charles I's enemies flirted with the notion of elective monarchy in this period. *The*

unprecedented in its history. And the stability of the revolutionary government depended in large measure on its ability to persuade English people of its legitimacy. The new republic faced formidable obstacles, since moderate parliamentarians as well as royalists shrank with contempt and horror from those responsible for the death of the king and the destruction of government by King, Lords, and Commons. The problem became particularly acute when the government mandated the swearing of an oath to be "true and faithful to the Commonwealth of England, as it is now established, without a king or a House of Lords." Englishmen justified submission to the new government in various ways. Some argued, for example, that the parliamentarian victory was an act of providence, a palpable manifestation of God's will. Others suggested that allegiance followed protection: subjects should obey a government that protected them.

Such appeals, drawing on combinations of natural law theories, continental sources, and Biblical materials have been studied, with impressive results, by Skinner and John Wallace, among others.[140] But scholars have neglected one important element in the Commonwealth's arsenal of arguments. This was the appeal to English law and history, in particular, St. Edward's laws, the *Modus*, and the *Mirror*. Nowhere was their extremist potential more plainly displayed than in the work of publicists who wrote at the government's behest. Fully mindful of the high stakes, the republican government mounted a polemical offensive aimed at convincing the nation and the world of its legitimacy. Spearheading the drive were John Sadler and John Milton, two of the most eminent and active of commonwealthmen. Their tracts in defense of the good old cause and the new order demonstrated, in language familiar to their readers, that the English past could be deployed for the most radical of all ends – regicide and the utter and complete transformation of the ancient government.

A wealthy landowner and lawyer with close ties to Oliver Cromwell, Sadler enjoyed a career which was, in Austin Woolrych's words, "remarkable by any standard." As a member of the council

Right to be King. The Succession to the Crown of England 1603–1714 (Chapel Hill, 1995), pp. 68–71.

140 Wallace, *Destiny His Choice: the Loyalism of Andrew Marvell*. Skinner, "Conquest and Consent: Thomas Hobbes and the Engagement Controversy," in *The Interregnum: the Quest for Settlement 1646–1660*, ed. G. E. Aylmer (London, 1972), pp. 790–8.

of state, his legal talents were highly valued by the new government. He served as a member of the Hale commission on law reform, and he also sat, along with Bacon, as a judge in Admiralty and a master of requests in Chancery. Moreover, in the Barebone's Parliament he served on numerous committees and was greatly in demand for drafting bills.[141]

Sadler also made a significant contribution to the defense of the commonwealth. His *Rights of the Kingdom and People*, written in the months following the king's execution, won the praises of Milton, the commonwealthman Marchamont Nedham, George Lawson, and John Locke – a radical quartet if ever there was one.[142] Much cited in the late seventeenth century, the *Rights of the Kingdom and People* was reprinted in 1682 as germane to the exclusion crisis. It is, then, of the greatest interest that Sadler chose English history, in general, and St. Edward's laws, the *Modus*, and the *Mirror*, in particular, as perfectly suited to persuade Englishmen to support the new revolutionary government. Sadler's stated goal was two-fold: first, to learn how "the laws and customs of our ancestors" defined the rights of king and parliament; and, second, to discover the appropriate responses if a king failed to perform his duty. Sadler's unequivocal answer was that, because the people elected their kings in parliament, parliament – now a remnant of the House of Commons – must judge them if they violated their trust. His proof rested squarely on Saxon and early Norman history. Indeed, there is scarcely a word of Charles Stuart in this mind-numbing historical account of some 250 pages. Still, the obvious implication of Sadler's words was that the king's death, however lamentable, constituted no impediment to transferring allegiance to the commonwealth.

Running through the tract, from beginning to end, was the sustaining and unifying thread of St. Edward's laws, the *Modus*, and the *Mirror*. These Sadler deployed to demonstrate the king's subservience to his people, their contractual relationship, and the antiquity

---

[141] Woolrych, *Commonwealth to Protectorate* (Oxford, 1982). See also *Calendar of State Papers Domestic, 1651–1652*, p. 36; *ibid., 1652–1653*, p. 433; *ibid., 1653–1654*, pp. 237, 280, 281, 282; *ibid., 1655*, p. 91.

[142] Locke recommended Sadler's work (along with those of Bracton, Fleta, and Coke) to those who desired to understand "the ancient constitution of the government of England." Locke, *Educational Writings*, ed. James L. Axtell (Cambridge, 1968), p. 401. Nedham, who was also capable of pleading the royalist cause, advised readers who "would know more of the customs and constitutions of this nation" to see Sadler's "excellent piece." *The Excellencie of a Free State* (London, 1767), pp. viii–ix. See also Milton, *Eikonoklastes* (London, 1649), pp. 41, 234; George Lawson, *Politica Sacra et Civilis* (London, 1660), p. 151.

and supremacy of the House of Commons. This uncompromising historical focus renders the work quaintly antiquarian to modern eyes. Woolrych, for example, has described it as "one of the more curious defences of the new commonwealth," characterized as it was by Sadler's "fantastic excursions into 'precedents' furnished by mythical ancient British kings."[143] But this would not have been the contemporary response. Sadler's appeal to history, pitched in these terms, would have had considerable purchase. Contemporaries likely saw in him an eminent lawyer and trusted member of the Commonwealth government, urging them in a troubled and uncertain time, to transfer allegiance from God's anointed to the republic on historical grounds. And doing so in language of the utmost familiarity.

According to Sadler, English history taught that the people and their representatives had every right to judge Charles I and, if necessary, alter the government. They had this right because in Saxon times the kingship was elective and the relationship between king and people contractual. And what was true then was true now. Abundant proof existed in the *Mirror* and St. Edward's laws, both of which spoke about elective monarchy and made it perfectly clear that all kings, including the Confessor, had been chosen by the people in full parliaments. Here Sadler directed readers' attention to St. Edward's laws as referred to in the coronation oath: the king was elected by a council of the kingdom, that is "*per consilium Procerum Regni.*" So, too, were William I, sometimes mistakenly called the conqueror, and all of his successors. In fact, never in England's history had the crown devolved by "blind succession."[144] Because people and parliaments elected their rulers, they could impose on them whatever conditions they pleased. In England, these conditions appeared in the coronation oath and Chapter 17 of St. Edward's laws, which together constituted an original contract. In this oath, the man who would be king promised to abide by the ancient laws of the realm, as well as those which the people "shall choose." This done, the archbishop went to the four sides of the scaffold and asked those assembled whether they accepted the candidate as king. If, after he agreed to their terms, they consented, then the people

---

[143] Woolrych, *Commonwealth to Protectorate*, p. 206.
[144] Sadler, *Rights of the Kingdom and People*, pp. 1–2 and preceding unnumbered introductory pages, p. 74. See also pp. 14–20, 31–42 *passim*, 52, 53, 55, 56, 60, 63, 68, 83, and *passim*. Pagination is irregular. Citations here refer to correct page numbers.

offered up to him their homage and fealty. In other words, the people's promise to obey depended upon the king's promise to govern by St. Edward's laws. Here, in this most critical of public ceremonies, the contractual relationship between ruler and ruled was dramatically displayed for all to see.[145]

However, Sadler continued, the people swore their allegiance not to the king alone but also "to the laws, to the kingdom, and the kingdom's good, or profit." This followed from the fact that St. Edward's laws were made "*ad Honorem Corona, & ad Utilitatem Regni*," as were those of later kings. It was, then, to the community of the realm that allegiance was due, and the people were obliged to see that these laws were kept. Moreover, according to the *Modus*, such had been the practice "in all ages."[146]

Just as the people had anciently elected their kings, so they had been represented in parliaments. In Sadler's words, "the track of parliaments, is visible enough, in all the Saxons reigning here." Indeed, as the *Mirror* made clear, parliaments played such a vital role in government that King Alfred ordained that they be held at least twice a year.[147] Sadler also knew that, then, as now, the primary business of parliaments was law-making. One had only to recall the words of the ancient coronation oath, which obligated the king to accept those laws *quas vulgus elegerit*, to know this was true.[148] Edward the Confessor, for example, made his laws, including the coronation oath, "by the common council of the whole kingdom. Or by parliament." So, too, had kings Ine, Alfred, Edgar, and Ethelred.[149]

Moreover, as St. Edward's laws, the *Modus*, and the *Mirror* made clear, these early parliaments consisted of both Lords and Commons. Once more the Latin tag from the coronation oath proved apt, helping Sadler nail down another point central to his defense of the commonwealth government – the superiority of the Commons over both king and Lords. To understand the proper relationship between King, Lords, and Commons, Englishmen had only to remember that St. Edward's laws obligated the king "to confirm the just laws which the Commons (not the Lords, but the Commons) shall elect or choose." He could not have produced

---

[145] *Ibid.*, pp. 19ff, 31–3, 53–6, 75, 86, 90, and *passim*.
[146] *Ibid.*, pp. 20–31 *passim*, 83.   [147] *Ibid.*, pp. 150–160 *passim*.
[148] *Ibid.*, pp. 88, 143, 150–60 *passim*, 171. See also pp. 52, 59–66, 146–8 *passim*, 166, 167.
[149] *Ibid.*, pp. 150, 151, 156, 158, 159–160.

better evidence with which to show the unequivocal prominence of the Commons over the other two estates.[150]

The *Mirror* and *Modus* provided further confirmation of this power relationship. According to Sadler's reading of the former, the Commons predated the Lords, who were, as it turned out, raised out of the Commons and endowed with judicial power. But not with legislative power. While Sadler admitted that the Lords played some role in legislation, he insisted that the king called them primarily to give counsel, not to make law. Only the Commons possessed this highest of powers, as the coronation oath made clear. The "old *Modus*" explained the reason for this disparity: "the Commons," Sadler paraphrased, "have better, and stronger votes" because they were more essential to government than the Lords. Indeed, according to both the English and Irish *Modi*, there was a time when parliaments had no Lords at all; but never was the Commons absent. For this reason, as the *Modus* made clear, the king could hold a parliament that included only the Commons.[151]

Sadler understood that some of his contemporaries failed to grasp the superiority of the Commons because of a linguistic misunderstanding: they translated medieval references to peers and proceres to mean the Lords. This led them to conclude, incorrectly, that in Stuart England the lower house took a back seat to king and Lords, and had always done so. Here Sadler had in mind the recent convert Prynne as well as royalist writers such as Filmer. However, Sadler possessed a powerful antidote to such a dangerous view of English history. As luck had it, the *Mirror* and the *Modus* interpreted these terms to include the Commons as well as the other two estates. Further, he pointed out that the *Modus* described how, in case of disagreement, the two houses might reduce themselves to a committee of twenty-five, and from thence to fewer and fewer. Importantly, the composition of the committee of twenty-five was such that the Commons possessed a majority – telling evidence of where superiority resided.[152]

Predictably, Sadler addressed the question of who within the kingdom possessed the right to judge the king. And predictably he found that if the king broke his coronation oath, thereby betraying his trust, parliament must judge him. After all, Chapter 17 of St. Edward's laws pointed out with utmost clarity and precision the fate

---

[150] *Ibid.*, pp. 87–91 *passim*.   [151] *Ibid.*, pp. 86–92 *passim*.   [152] *Ibid.*, pp. 77–8, 260.

of a ruler who failed to live up to the "Office of a King": they prescribed that such a king "*should not retain so much as the name of a king.*"[153] Moreover, according to the *Mirror*, the Commons, as well as the Lords, possessed judicial authority. Their right to sit in judgment of the king became operative not only when he failed to comport himself in a manner commensurate with the "Office," but also when he found himself in a dispute with a subject. Because a man could not be a judge in his own cause, he had "companions" in the two houses who would do it for him. If the Lords failed in their duty, it fell to the Commons to see that justice was done. The same rule applied to the king's wife and children.[154]

The trio of medieval sources also demonstrated the power of parliament, and especially the House of Commons, over the king in other ways. Focusing now on the thorny matter of allegiance, Sadler raised the question of the Rump Parliament's right to govern without the king. The *Modus*, for example, "tells us, that if the king dissolved the parliament, before all petitions had been considered, etc. It was plain down right perjury." This meant that the present House of Commons, first summoned in 1640, continued to exist in law, since Charles I could not legally send it home before its business was concluded. In a related vein, these same sources proved that parliament possessed both the power of the militia and the exclusive right to levy taxes.[155] Given the "facts" as Sadler laid them out, subjects should have no qualms about transferring allegiance from that man of blood to the new regime.

One major task remained before Sadler's plea for the commonwealth was complete. In order to prove his major point – that Stuart Englishmen and their parliament now reigned supreme because such had been the case in Saxon days – , he needed to demonstrate the continuity of basic legal and political institutions through the centuries. And this meant, of course, coming to terms with the royalist interpretation of 1066. For a lawyer imbued with ancient constitutionalist learning, this proved an easy assignment. Calling upon the usual medieval sources, Sadler proceeded to present William, miscalled by some the conqueror, and his successors as following directly in the footsteps of the late, great Saxons. This appeared incontrovertably from William I's confirmations of Holy

---

[153] *Ibid.*, pp. 2, 31–2.   [154] *Ibid.*, pp. 24, 30, 78, 121, 185, and *passim*.
[155] *Ibid.*, pp. 129–31, 137, 140, 147–8, 176, 182, 186, 223, 261.

Edward's laws, both in his coronation oath and also after receiving an account of these laws from a jury called together to collect them for his benefit. William even brought out his own edition of these laws, which readers could see for themselves in the works of Lambarde, Twysden, and Whelocke.[156]

The unrelenting historical approach in *Rights of the Kingdom and People* demonstrates the ease with which medieval English legal and historical sources could be put to radical, even republican, ends. Yet Sadler's extremism pales by comparison with that of a distinguished contemporary. This was John Milton, secretary of state for foreign tongues. Entering the lists about the same time as Sadler and clearly indebted to him, Milton developed his own brand of radicalism when he put forward an incisive defense of regicide and the new order. He did so in three tracts of conspicuous importance commissioned by the Commonwealth government. These were *The Tenure of Kings and Magistrates* (1649), probably conceived during Charles I's trial and completed after his execution; *Eikonoklastes* (1649), containing Milton's response to the *Eikon Basilike* that had elevated Charles I to martyrdom; and, most famous of all, the notorious *Defence of the English People* (1651), Milton's answer to Salmasius, the French classical scholar who had written a passionate defense of the late king. Milton's tracts went through numerous editions, his *Defence of the English People* alone achieving more than a dozen in the first two years after its publication.[157]

While Milton's classical learning shaped his justification of recent revolutionary events, he, like Sadler, appreciated the polemical value of English history. In making this claim, I take issue with scholars who suggest that he neglected English history for continental sources, natural law, reason, the scriptures, and, of course, classical sources.[158] To be sure, Milton relied heavily on these sources, but the English past mattered as much to him as it did to Sadler. Moreover, whereas a certain muddiness rising out of an oblique approach occasionally blurred Sadler's radical message, Milton met

---

[156] *Ibid.*, pp. 21, 60, 69–82 *passim*, 131ff, 139, 150ff, 173–5 and *passim*.

[157] F. F. Madan, "Milton and Salmasius, and Dugard," *The Library* 4 (1923–24), 4th series, 119–45. Madan, "A Revised Bibliography of Salmasius's *Defensio Regia* and Milton's *Pro Populo Anglicano Defensio*," *The Library* 5th series, 9 (1954), 112–20.

[158] See, for example, Hill, *Milton and the English Revolution* (Harmondsworth, 1979), pp. 95, 100, 170; Arthur Barker, *Milton and the Puritan Dilemma* (Toronto, 1942), p. 148; William Grace, "Milton, Salmasius, and the Natural Law," *Journal of the History of Ideas* 14 (1963), 324; Don M. Wolfe, *Milton and the Puritan Revolution* (New York, 1941), pp. 260–1, 326–7.

the problem of regicide head on. His unflinchingly public justification of Charles's execution, along with the clarity of his presentation, rendered his works especially dangerous to the kingship. As Christopher Hill writes, "Short of signing the death warrant, Milton could hardly have done more."[159]

In defense of recent events, Milton seized the high ground with the claim that the English people, whom God had invested with original power, were legally superior to the king. Of the several medieval sources which he cited as proof, he made particular use of St. Edward's laws and their subsequent confirmations in royal charters and in the coronation oath. But he went far beyond this when he demonstrated with chilling clarity the radical possibilities of Chapter 17, the "Office of a King." Here he put in the most explicit language ideas only hinted at in Sadler's tract. Elevating people and parliament, or its remnant, above the king, Milton referred to "the greatest thing of all, amongst the laws of King Edward, commonly called the Confessor," namely, the "very excellent . . . kingly office; which office, if a king do not discharge as he ought; Then says the law, he shall not retain so much as the name of a king." Taking care that his words be understood, Milton noted that the people had previously deposed kings if they ruled tyrannically. "Our laws," he wrote, "plainly, and clearly declare, that a king may violate, diminish, nay, and wholly lose his royalty. For that expression in the law of *St. Edward*, of *losing the name of a king* [Milton's emphasis], signifies neither more nor less, than being deprived of the kingly office and dignity." He then cited as an example Childeric, king of France, which "is taken notice of in the law itself." Milton drove the point home relentlessly, emphasizing once more that "truly royal law of Edward, that basic precept of our law," which stated that "a wicked king is liable to punishment." He found this to be the clear meaning of King Edward's sword, "*Curtana*," which "the earl of Chester used to carry in the solemn procession at a coronation." Matthew Paris considered it "a token" that the king was subject to punishment "if he will not do his duty." And, as though intent on not leaving one scintilla of doubt in the reader's mind as to his meaning, Milton added that punishment by sword was rarely short of capital.[160]

---

[159] Hill, *Milton and the English Revolution*, p. 207. See also Annabel Patterson, *Early Modern Liberalism* (Cambridge, 1997), chapter 2.
[160] Milton, *A Defence of the English People* (n.p. 1692), pp. 193–5. *The Tenure of Kings and Magistrates*

He then turned to the many confirmations of the Confessor's laws, which he regarded as fundamentally important to English liberties. One such confirmation occupied a special place in English history because it dispelled any doubts about the title by which William the Conqueror ruled. In 1070 William, "in a very full council," ratified the Saxon laws "with a most solemn oath: And by so doing, he not only extinguished his right of conquest, if ever he had any over us, but subjected himself to be judged according to the tenor of this very law." Only then did the Saxons agree to accept him as king, and when he broke his word, they took up arms, forcing him to renew his oath to observe St. Edward's laws. And so it went on reign after reign, proving that neither Charles I nor any of his ancestors ever governed by conquest.[161] In sum, unless kings promised to abide by the Confessor's laws at their coronation, the people would withhold their consent. And unless kings kept their promise, the people would withdraw their allegiance. Indeed, the incessant drumbeat of confirmations guaranteed the people's right to depose and punish kings who defied St. Edward's laws, a right intact in Milton's own day.[162]

In addition to conferring a general right of deposition, Milton continued, St. Edward's laws endowed people and parliaments with powers often mistakenly considered part of the royal prerogative. He had in mind control of the militia and the right to make war and peace. Anciently, as the Confessor's laws made clear, the people commanded the militia. If the king possessed this power, then parliaments would have obviously been unsuccessful in their fight to preserve "the liberty and laws of St. Edward." Milton admitted that the monarch could command the militia, but only against those whom parliament designated enemies. But "if he acted otherwise," as Charles Stuart did, then he "himself was to be accounted an enemy; since according to the very law of St. Edward, or according

(London, 1649), p. 23. While Milton relied more heavily on the Confessor's "Office" in *A Defence of the English People*, Merritt Hughes suggests that the idea that a ruler who became a tyrant merited deposition also constituted the central proposition of *The Tenure of Kings and Magistrates*. *Complete Prose Works*, vol. III, ed. Hughes (New Haven, 1966), p. 104.

[161] Milton, *A Defence of the English People*, pp. 159, 178–9, 193–4, 237–9. *The Tenure of Kings and Magistrates*, pp. 10–11, 13, 23–4.

[162] Milton, *A Defence of the English People*, pp. 178–9, 206, 208, 210, 233–4, 238–9. Milton also vouched Bracton and Fleta, both of whom remembered the "Office of a King." As Bracton wrote, "the king should exercise the power of law as God's agent and servant; the power to do wrong is of the devil, not of God. When the king stoops to crime, he is the devil's servant." *Ibid.*, pp. 194–5. See also *The Tenure of Kings and Magistrates*, pp. 10–11, 13, 23–4.

to a more sacred law than that, the law of nature itself, he lost the name of a king, and was no longer such."[163]

Milton found the *Modus* and the *Mirror* conducive to his entire line of argumentation. They proved particularly helpful when it came to demonstrating the superior power of parliament in general and the House of Commons in particular. Milton recognized that, in the royalist view of English history, parliaments did not exist before William the Conqueror. But, he lectured, "the thing was always in being" in Saxon times, where it was known as *Concilia sapientum Wittena-gemot*.[164] Alluding to the *Mirror*, Milton pointed to the ancient practice which obliged parliaments to meet twice a year. The importance of this body to the governing of the kingdom also appeared from the *Modus*, which compelled the king to keep parliament in session until all its business was complete. Otherwise, Milton continued, he committed perjury, "and shall be reputed to have broken his coronation oath," which "has always been looked upon by our lawyers, as a most sacred law." Unless the king kept parliament in session as long as its members wanted, "how can he be said to grant those good laws, which the people choose, as he is sworn to do, if he hinders the people from choosing them, either by summoning the parliaments seldomer, or by dissolving them sooner than the public affairs require, or admit."[165]

As for the composition of early parliaments and the relationship among their various components, Milton turned again to the *Modus*. In answer to those who insisted that only the barons and earls were present, Milton countered that all sorts of people were called "barons" in medieval times, including guardians of the Cinque Ports, magistrates of cities, even tradesmen. In fact, every member of the Commons could "reasonably" be called a baron. The word *sapientes* also encompassed the commons. Further, the *Modus* told him that "the king, and the commons may hold a parliament, and enact laws, though the lords and bishops are absent." But without the

---

[163] Milton, *A Defence of the English People*, pp. 206, 208, 210.
[164] *Ibid.*, pp. 184–5.
[165] *Ibid.*, pp. 181, 192–3, 199. *Eikonoklastes*, pp. 41, 44, 45. One of Charles I's offenses, according to Milton, was to alter the coronation oath, in particular the *quas vulgus elegerit* phrase. This Milton condemned in the strongest of language: "Unworthy and abominable action! The act was wicked in itself . . . for, by the eternal God, what greater breach of faith, and violation of laws can possibly be imagined? What ought to have been more sacred to him, next to the Holy Sacraments themselves, than that oath." *A Defence of the English People*, pp. 237–9. *Eikonoklastes*, pp. 58, 61, 219.

presence of the lower house, no parliament existed. The reason, Milton explained, could be found in the fact that "kings held parliaments and councils with their people, before any lords or bishops were made; besides, the Lords serve for themselves only, the Commons each for the country, city, or borough that sent them." Therefore, "the Commons in parliament represent the whole body of the nation; in which respect they are more worthy, and every way preferable to the house of peers."[166]

The *Modus* and the *Mirror* also reinforced the message of the "Office of a King": a ruler who degenerated into a tyrant deposed himself and must be judged by the people. The *Mirror*, for example, told how the Saxons, when they defeated the Britons, "chose a king, required an oath of him, that he would submit to judgment of the law." The *Mirror* further prescribed how the peers, a term that included the Commons, should judge and punish him if he harmed his subjects. But among the peers, the Commons possessed "sovereign power . . . and a power of judging the king himself, because before there was ever a king, they in the name of the whole body of the nation held councils and parliaments, had the power of judicature, made laws, and made the kings themselves . . ."[167]

For Milton, then, a king who contravened the Saxon laws referred to in St. Edward's laws, the *Modus*, and the *Mirror* committed treason against the kingdom and dethroned himself. Travelling this road, Charles Stuart had become an enemy of state and a prisoner of war, his final doom sealed "by that sacred law of Saint Edward, which denies that a bad king is a king at all, or ought to be called so."[168] Finally, at the close of a crucial chapter in *A Defence of the English People*, Milton confirmed precisely and unequivocally his devotion to English law and history when he wrote in a summary statement:

By all this evidence and citation of laws I believe I have at last successfully completed my task, because I have shown that, since the commons have full right to judge a king, and did in fact execute a king who had deserved so ill of church and state and shown no signs of improvement, they acted rightly and regularly and were faithful to their state and to themselves, to their position and to their country's laws. Here I cannot fail to voice my pride in our fathers who, in establishing this state, displayed a wisdom and a sense of freedom equal to that of the ancient Romans or the most

---

[166] Milton, *A Defence of the English People*, pp. 184–5, 197.
[167] *Ibid.*, pp. 192, 195–7 *passim*, 199, 233. *Eikonoklastes*, p. 234.
[168] Milton, *A Defence of the English People*, pp. 224–5.

illustrious Greeks; and these our fathers in their turn, if they know anything of our actions, cannot but rejoice in their sons who, when they had well nigh been made slaves, did with such courage and good sense save that state which had been wisely planned and so founded on liberty, from the unbridled tyranny of the king.[169]

By putting his case in the familiar ancient constitutionalist idiom, Milton rendered it much more meaningful to his English audience than he could ever have done by way of illustrations drawn from classical Greece and Rome. He acted with the conviction that the proper study and interpretation of the English past made respectable even regicide as a court of last resort. Even if we grant that Milton's appeal to the past was merely a rhetorical move, he nevertheless succeeded, as did no other contemporary, in demonstrating how ruthlessly and effectively Englishmen could tailor their own history and law to ultra-radical ends.

That Milton had hit his target appeared at the Restoration. Acknowledging the danger inherent in his words, Charles II's government ordered that *A Defence of the English People* and *Eikonoklastes* be burned by the common hangman at the assizes and at the Old Bailey. An accompanying royal proclamation prohibited the two tracts being printed, sold, or dispersed, lest "such wicked and traitrous principles" corrupt the king's subjects.[170] Indeed, Milton's name had become so notorious that he was almost exempted from the Act of Indemnity. And so greatly did the government fear his polemical power that in 1683 James Parkinson was dismissed from his fellowship at Lincoln College, Oxford, for, among other alleged actions, recommending Milton's political writings to his students.[171] The Oxford University Judgment and Decree points to that part of Milton's political writings deemed most menacing to the Stuart kingship. Among the ideas condemned as "pernicious," "dam-

---

[169] *A Defence of the People of England*, in *Complete Prose Works of John Milton*, vol. IV, ed. Don Wolfe (New Haven, 1966), pp. 494–5. For Milton's use of Saxon sources in his *History of Britain* see Nicholas von Maltzahn, *Milton's History of Britain. Republican Historiography in the English Revolution* (Oxford, 1991), chapter 10.

[170] Charles Gilbert, *Burned Books* (Port Washington, NY, 1964), pp. 429–31. *Calendar of State Papers Domestic, Charles II, 1660–1661*, p. 189.

[171] Hill, *Milton and the English Revolution*, pp. 206–8. That the uproar occasioned by Parkinson's political views was more than a local matter is clear from the interest taken by Charles II's government. *Calendar of State Papers Domestic, 1683*, pp. 319, 320, 325, 326, 350, 351, 370, 382, 415. *The Life and Times of Anthony Wood*, ed. Andrew Clark (Oxford, 1894), vol. III, pp. 62–4. At the Glorious Revolution Parkinson wrote his own account of the affair. [James Parkinson], *An Account of Mr. Parkinson's Expulsion from the University of Oxford in the late Times* (London, 1689).

nable," and "destructive to the sacred persons of princes, their state and government, and of all human society," was the message inherent in the "Office of a King." Milton's name, along with several others, was expressly associated with this notion.[172]

The public and official condemnation of Milton's tracts and the idea inherent in the "Office of a King" occasions no surprise. He had, after all, covered the "Office" with the blood of the best of kings, and that part of the Confessor's laws – indeed, the whole – must henceforth bear an indelible stain, its extremist implications plain to all observers. Similarly, Milton's deployment of the *Modus* and the *Mirror* stigmatized them just as badly. Yet despite the use made of these medieval sources in the 1640s and 1650s, their popularity continued, and in some ways even increased, after Charles II's Restoration in 1660. Indeed, the enemies of the Stuarts, remarkably undeterred by the lurid light now surrounding St. Edward's laws, the *Modus*, and the *Mirror*, pressed them into the service of anti-monarchical causes until the end of the century. So great, in fact, was their persuasive power that royalist writers soon attempted to commandeer them for the king's cause. However, as we shall see, the effort never came to much, for the trio of medieval sources was already the intellectual property of radical ancient constitutionalists.

[172] Gillett, *Burned Books*, pp. 429–31. David Wootton, ed., *Divine Right and Democracy* (Harmondsworth, 1986), p. 121. Other authors associated with the doctrine were Rutherford, Baxter, Goodwin, Buchanan, and the author of *Vindiciae contra Tyrannos*.

CHAPTER 6

"That noble transcript of the original contract, the Confessor's laws": the radical ancient constitution in the late Stuart period

> Every time a society finds itself in crisis, it instinctively turns its
> eyes towards its origins and looks there for a sign.
>
> Octavio Paz

INTRODUCTION

When Charles II entered London in May of 1660, he might reasonably have anticipated governing a people who lauded the kingship
and exalted the royal authority. Indeed, royalist fervor ran so high
that the political nation imposed hardly any official conditions upon
his return. Moreover, the Convention, which met from March to
December of 1660, rolled back the clock by restoring the monarchy,
the church, and the House of Lords. Still, Charles II could by no
means claim an unalloyed victory. In the first place, most early
reforms of the Long Parliament stood, denying him extra-parliamentary levies and recourse to the old prerogative courts. In addition,
the Triennial Act of 1641 remained in force for the time being. But
most telling of all, from the very beginning of the Restoration signs
pointed unmistakably to the tenacity of radical ancient constitutionalism. The extent to which its language and ideas had taken root
appears from a resolution passed by the Convention Parliament on
May 1, 1660, the eve of the king's return. Here the two houses resolved
that "according to the ancient and fundamental laws of the kingdom,
the government is, and ought to be, by King, Lords, and Commons."
Further, on May 30 the earl of Manchester, speaker of the House of
Lords, told the peers that with Charles II's restoration, the business of
the kingdom would be "carried on according to the ancient government of this realm, by King, Lords and Commons."[1]

---

[1] William Cobbett, *Parliamentary History of England* (London, 1806), vol. IV, p. 25. *Calendar of State
Papers Domestic, 1660*, p. 428. See also Andrew Swatland, *The House of Lords in the Reign of*

Surely memories were not so short as to have forgotten the implications of such language: it would have reminded many Englishmen of the main tenets of parliamentarian theorizing, in particular, the principle of coordination. Indeed, evidence shows that contemporaries themselves interpreted these words in precisely this way. Thus, the resolution of May 1 was evoked in the 1673 House of Commons to defeat Charles II's Declaration of Indulgence. Because, in the words of one member, the May declaration proved that "the legislative power resides in King, Lords, and Commons," Charles II could not dispense with statutes enjoining religious conformity.[2] And in 1689 a member of the Convention interpreted the measure as a sound basis for deposing James II and replacing him with William and Mary.[3] Clearly, then, the resolution of May 1 provided the monarchy's enemies with a potent authority for a basic assumption of rebel ideology – the idea that, since antiquity, King, Lords, and Commons shared equally in the government of the kingdom.

That the wording of the Convention's address and Manchester's speech was no accident appears from the "act for the preservation of the king," passed in 1661 by the royalist Cavalier Parliament which replaced the Convention. The only offical measure to define the legal nature of the restoration, this statute condemned as illegal the proceedings of the rebels who had opposed and executed Charles I. In addition, it singled out for censure certain ideas prevalent in the revolutionary period, among them the view "that both houses of parliament or either house of parliament have or hath a legislative

Charles II (Cambridge, 1996). The continuing influence of radicals is discussed by Corinne C. Weston and Janelle Greenberg, *Subjects and Sovereigns: the Grand Controversy over Legal Sovereignty in Stuart England* (Cambridge, 1981), chapter 6; Richard L. Greaves, *Deliver Us from Evil: the Radical Underground in Britain, 1660–1663* (Oxford, 1986); Greaves, *Enemies Under His Feet: Radicals and Nonconformists in Britain, 1664–1677* (Stanford, 1990); Greaves, *Secrets of the Kingdom: British Radicals from the Popish Plot to the Revolution of 1688–89* (Stanford, 1992); Richard Ashcraft, *Revolutionary Politics and Locke's Two Treatises of Government* (Princeton, 1986); Gary S. De Krey, "London Radicals and Revolutionary Politics, 1675–1683," in *Politics of Religion in Restoration England*, eds. Tim Harris, Paul Seaward, and Mark Goldie (Oxford, 1990), pp. 132–62; De Krey, "Rethinking the Restoration: Dissenting Cases for Conscience, 1667–1672," *Historical Journal* 38 (1995), 53–83; Tim Harris, " 'Lives, Liberties and Estates': Rhetorics of Liberty in the Reign of Charles II," in *Politics of Religion*, ed. Harris, Seaward, and Goldie, pp. 217–41.

2 Anchitell Grey, *Debates in the House of Commons, from the year 1667 to the year 1694* (London, 1763), vol. II, pp. 67–8. D. T. Witcombe, *Charles II and the Cavalier House of Commons, 1663–1674* (New York, 1966), Appendix 1, p. 208.

3 "Some short considerations relating to the settling of the government; humbly offered to the Lords and Commons of England," in *Somers Tracts. A Second Collection* (London, 1809), ed. Walter Scott vol. IV, p. 256.

power without the king."[4] Here, in the guise of a restoration of royal powers, was the Cavalier Parliament's tacit recognition of the doctrine of coordination: the act it passed for the preservation of the king assumed as a matter of course that law-making resided in King, Lords, and Commons. Once again there is evidence that contemporaries themselves interpreted the words in precisely this way. Writing in 1683, a critic commented that before the act of 1661 was passed, some believed "that both or either houses of parliament, had a legislative power without the king: since which time the like principle hath been revived, that both or either houses of parliament hath a coordinate power and share in the government with the king and that this is the ancient constitution of the government of this kingdom."[5] In other words, the point so vigorously urged in parliamentarian writings and so much resisted by royalists was now conceded without a struggle. More specifically, the parliamentarian version of the ancient constitution, of which the principle of coordination was now a significant part, received official sanction in a statute enacted by a parliament often described as more royalist than the king.[6]

True, the framers of the resolution of May 1 intended to welcome back the monarchy and the House of Lords, while the act for the king's preservation guaranteed the king at least an equal share in law-making and a power of veto. Further, because neither the Convention nor the Cavalier Parliament made any reference to the supremacy of the two houses, we can assume that the coordination principle was shedding some of its radical overtones – a process that would make it more acceptable to the new political generation. It is always possible, of course, that the Convention and Cavalier Parliament acted without full awareness and understanding of the implications of their words. But if this were the case, then we can assume that by the early 1660s, the language of radical ancient constitutionalism had become so routine that the resolutions seemed

---

[4] Weston and Greenberg, *Subjects and Sovereigns*, pp. 149–50. See also Howard Nenner, *The Right to Be King. The Succession to the Crown of England 1603–1714* (Chapel Hill, 1995), pp. 93–6; Nenner, *By Colour of Law. Legal Culture and Constitutional Politics in England, 1660–1689* (Chicago, 1977), pp. 124–31; Paul Seaward, *The Cavalier Parliament and the Construction of the Old Regime, 1661–1689* (Cambridge, 1989).

[5] *The Arraignment of Co-ordinate Power* (London, 1683), p. 13. See also Roger Acherley, *The Britannic Constitution: or, The Fundamental Form of Government in Britain*, 2nd. edn. (London, 1759), p. 145; Weston and Greenberg, *Subjects and Sovereigns*, pp. 149–51.

[6] *Ibid.*, pp. 150–1.

unexceptional, perhaps even conventional. Indeed, it appears that many members of the political nation had grown comfortable with the idea of an ancient constitution characterized by a legal sovereignty in King, Lords, and Commons.[7]

However routine such language might have become, those at the center of the Restoration government possessed a full awareness of the deadly ends to which it could be put. In particular, they understood that regicides and republicans espoused a version of English history that had little or no place for the king. Even if they had been capable of forgetting the trauma of the civil wars and Interregnum, vivid reminders remained close at hand. Thus, the fiery Edmund Ludlow, who sat on the High Court of Justice and signed Charles I's death warrant, based his defense of the regicide on just such an appeal to the past. Writing shortly after the Restoration from his sanctuary on the continent, the unrepentant republican defended king-killing by reminding his countrymen back home that rulers could be called to account by the highest authority in the nation. So much Ludlow knew from reading Matthew Paris, who described "the sword of St. Edward that the *Comes Palatii* did carry before" the king at his coronation – a "token that if the king himself did transgress, he had of right a power to restrain him; which law William the Conqueror confirmed." Ludlow then quoted Bracton's "Office" as well as the similar section of Fleta.[8]

However, with the exception of Ludlow, who wrote from his safe perch in Holland, we hear almost nothing about civil war and Interregnum interpretations of St. Edward's laws. Although both *Curtana* and Chapter 17 would find renewed polemical life at the Glorious Revolution, for the time being they probably smacked too much of regicide and republicanism to be safely deployed. That royalists feared the threat posed by such a rebel reading of English history appeared during the trials of the regicides. When at one point in the proceedings the regicide Thomas Scot attempted to vouch Saxon history to justify king-killing, chief justice Orlando Bridgeman cut him off. In his view, Scot ought to confine himself to the period since the conquest, rather than speaking "of those times wherein things were obscure."[9]

---

[7] *Ibid.*, pp. 151 and 326 n. 6.

[8] Ludlow, *A Voyce from the Watch Tower*, ed. Blair Worden (London, Camden Society, 1978), pp. 201–5.

[9] *A Complete Collection of State Trials*, ed. T. B. Howell (London, 1816), vol. v, pp. 1059, 1065–7 *passim*.

Of much greater significance is the fact that royalist polemicists such as Edward Bagshaw the Elder, Roger Coke, William Dugdale, Fabian Philipps, and Robert Sheringham recognized and conceded the polemical power of the Saxon past.[10] Writing early in the Restoration, they attempted to neuter the radical ancient consti- tution. More particularly, they transformed it into an historical construction that made Charles II, not the three coordinate estates of King, Lords, and Commons, the sovereign governor of the realm. Whether they enjoyed the king's blessings and governmental spon- sorship, we do not know. However, several of these authors had close ties both to Charles I and Charles II. Thus, the renowned scholar William Dugdale held a heraldic office under Charles I and, after the civil war began, attended the king at Oxford. Enjoying the admiration and friendship of the earl of Clarendon, a close adviser to both kings, he regained his heraldic function at the Restoration. Bagshaw also served Charles I at Oxford. Philipps held office in the Court of Wards and evoked gratitude at Charles II's court with his ultra-royalist writings. Further, in a 1687 tract that dealt extensively with Charles II's reign, Philipps indicated that he had enjoyed the king's assistance in his polemical efforts. Sheringham, too, had royal connections. A royalist divine from Norfolk who went into exile in Holland after the civil war, he was rewarded for his loyalty in 1660. At that time Charles II restored him to the fellowship at Caius College, Cambridge which he had lost in 1644. Also pertinent is the interest that the king himself showed in ancient historical records. Philipps, for one, noted that in 1676 Charles II ordered him, along with Dugdale and Dugdale's son-in-law Elias Ashmole, "to examine the state and conditions of the records in the Tower of London." Their goal might well have been the construction of an English history favorable to the royalist cause.[11]

Regardless of whether Charles II was personally involved in such matters early on, he could only have been pleased with the line of argumentation now put forward on his behalf. In a series of lengthy and well-argued tracts, royalists turned the ancient constitution and

---

[10] Pocock discusses the royalists' use of the ancient constitution after 1660 in *The Ancient Constitution and the Feudal Law. A Study of English Historical Thought in the Seventeenth Century. A Reissue with a Retrospect* (Cambridge, 1987), chapter 7.

[11] Philipps, *The Established Government of England, Vindicated from All Popular and Republican Principles and Mistakes: With a Respect to the Laws of God, Man, Nature and Nations* (London, 1687), "The Preface to the Reader."

St. Edward's laws on their heads, deploying them as proof of the order theory of kingship. Moreover, they did so by reinterpreting Chapter 17, the "Office of a King." Their focus on this particular section probably owed much to the parliamentarian usage during the civil wars and Interregnum, especially Milton's notorious defenses of regicide that Charles II's government condemned. Attempting to beat the rebels at their own game, royalist polemicists now set out to reclaim the Confessor's laws for Charles II. They accomplished this feat in two ways. First, they castrated Chapter 17, excising the most offensive part which told the story of Pepin, Childeric, and the fate of kings who misgoverned. Next, they disembedded the dangerous idea expressed in the deleted portion and linked it not to Holy Edward but to writers whom they could more easily condemn, in particular, Roman Catholics and French and Scottish Calvinists. In so doing, early Restoration royalists put their own spin on early English history, reading the sources in ways that maintained the utter sovereignty of kings as against the perniciously radical version of the ancient constitution. At the same time they preserved an institutional continuity of sorts from Saxon times to Stuart England.

Sheringham adopted precisely this strategy in his construction of an ancient constitution in which a sovereign king reigned supreme. This work, *The Royal Supremacy Asserted*, first appeared in 1660 and was reprinted in 1682. Sheringham earned the admiration of the late Stuart historian Bishop William Nicholson, who cited his work as a learned critique of the restless and anti-monarchical scribblers who had "distracted the age with their impertinent and mad discourses about coordination of the three estates."[12] In this tract, Sheringham wrote that the nature of all governments, which was settled once and for all at their foundation, was immutable. Those interested in determining the original frame of the English government had only to consult St. Edward's laws, which, in his view, constituted "the fundamental laws" of the kingdom. Castigating those who believed that "the fundamental laws are not written (so they might cover their fraud and deceit)," Sheringham pointed "to all histories, and records of those times" which told of the Confessor's laws and William the Conqueror's confirmation. Both king and subject were bound by these laws, the king promising to uphold them in his

---

[12] Nicholson, *The English Historical Library* (London, 1699), vol. III, p. 204.

coronation oath and the subject in the oath of allegiance. The king's obligation found explicit expression in Chapter 17, which Sheringham quoted at length, but not in its entirety, in Latin and English. Stopping before he reached the offending part that mentioned the certainty with which an errant king lost the very name of king, he noted that this chapter committed the monarch to maintaining and defending "all the lands, honors, dignities, rights and liberties of the crown" without diminution. Moreover, "this hath been the known law of the land ever since the time of William the Conqueror," who confirmed these laws in 1070.[13]

And why should William not have done so, given that he found "nothing in them prejudicial to his crown and royal authority." Chapter 17, after all, referred to the king as God's vicegerent on earth. Indeed, Sheringham continued, nothing in the Saxon laws "can give the least color or pretence for such a coordination, as is conceited." To the contrary, the Confessor's laws established the king's supremacy and reinforced the idea that "the crown hath *legibus solutam potestatem*, which is a prerogative compatible to none but the supreme power." Pointedly, Sheringham reminded his readers that what was true of the Saxon and Norman kingship was true of the Stuart, "for the common law was the same it is now, before the conquest, and is the base and pillar of royal power." Again Sheringham referred specifically to the "Office of a King," which he once more quoted at length, though without the offending words.[14]

Sheringham understood, of course, that the king's enemies vouched both St. Edward's laws and William's confirmation as proof that monarchs came to the throne by election and that they shared power equally with the Lords and Commons. Not so, he countered. Although William entered into a "composition" with the Saxons, granting that they could be governed by St. Edward's laws, he nevertheless took the crown as conqueror. This historical fact in and of itself told against coordination. In Sheringham's words, William, who "last fashioned and reformed the English monarchy, obtained the crown by conquest; he had it not by election as a gift and gratuity of the people, but made his passage by the sword: and conquerors

---

[13] Sheringham, *The Kings Supremacy Asserted* (Little Britain, 1682), pp. 41–2, 44, 55–6. Much of this tract, which was written in the 1650s, was directed at the civil war writings of Charles Herle and Philip Hunton.

[14] *Ibid.*, pp. 54–6.

are not wont to allow of such coordinations, or admit so many sharers in the rights of sovereignty as it is fantasized."[15]

Sheringham also recognized that some among the king's enemies claimed "that conquest is no good title," while still others insisted "that the conquest was not full and entire, but a partial conquest" mitigated by a "final composition and agreement" circumscribing the royal power. Wrong again, he answered. Although William I did come to an agreement, he did so "after a victory; and it is not probable that the conqueror having been at such expense of blood in gaining the crown and rights of sovereignty, should after his victory give them away again, and agree to such a mixture as is pleaded for."[16]

The antiquity of parliament also figured in Sheringham's defense of the Stuart monarchy. Granting that parliaments existed long before the Norman conquest, when kings such as Edward the Confessor used them to make law, Sheringham insisted that only the king and the nobles were present. For proof he turned to Lambarde's *Archaionomia*, which, he pointed out, made no explicit mention of the Commons.[17] Polydore Vergil, too, denied the presence of the Commons in Saxon times, leading Sheringham to conclude, along with the Italian historian, that kings only "occasionally" summoned the representatives of the people until the reign of Henry I.[18]

Constructing a virtually identical version of the ancient constitution was the elder Edward Bagshaw. In *The Rights of the Crown of England*, written when he was a prisoner of the Long Parliament and published in 1660, Bagshaw, too, found medieval sources conducive to royalist argumentation. In particular, St. Edward's laws, especially, the first part of Chapter 17, appeared to him compatible with royal sovereignty and inimical to the doctrine of coordination and its close companion, the principle of *singulis major, universis minor*.[19] Historical sources also told against the rebels' use of the theory of the king's two bodies, since they supported the contention that the office of a king attached to the king's natural body. To this, and not the politic body, subjects owed allegiance. Indeed, Bagshaw

---

[15] *Ibid.*, p. 53.

[16] *Ibid.*

[17] *Ibid.*, pp. 61–5. Sheringham recognized that Lambarde, in his *Archeion*, included the Commons among the *sapientes* who were present in Saxon parliaments. But in his view the great antiquary erred. *Ibid.*, p. 65.

[18] *Ibid.*, p. 66.

[19] Bagshaw, *The Rights of the Crown of England* (London, 1660), pp. 7, 9–12, 18, 66–70, 90.

condemned in the strongest language the "damnable doctrine" which held that a king who, in his subjects' judgment, failed "to govern according to his kingly office" thereby freed his subjects to "rise up in arms against him."[20]

Writing in the same vein was Roger Coke, whose *Justice Vindicated* also appeared in 1660. Citing the *Mirror* and *Modus*, Coke acknowledged the existence of parliaments in Saxon times but insisted that these two sources proved the supremacy of kings, who summoned, presided over, and ended their sittings.[21] Equally valuable was Chapter 17 of St. Edward's laws, because it clearly demonstrated both the supremacy of kings and their complete immunity from earthly judgment. Kings, after all, reigned by virtue of God's ordinance. Like Sheringham and Bagshaw, Coke gave the "Office of a King" in Latin and English, though without the incendiary part. However, the idea embedded within the omitted portion of Chapter 17 he vigorously condemned. Associating the notion with Calvin, he wrote that the very idea that a king could unking himself by breaking the law was "mad and wild." It amounted to claiming that a man who did something wrong ceased to be a man, that a father who did something wrong ceased to be a father, and so on. Put simply, kings were under no obligation to obey their own laws. Subjects might hope and expect that their monarch ruled well, but they could not compel him. Those who argued otherwise expressed "a seditious opinion."[22]

For Fabian Philipps, St. Edward's laws proved the king's right to command his people and the people's duty to obey their king. Philipps wrote to demonstrate that the basis of allegiance lay in the feudal ties between medieval kings and their vassals, a relationship which had existed at least as early as Saxon times. So much was proved by Chapter 35 of the Confessor's laws. Carrying a description of how St. Edward's people swore annually in their assemblies to be faithful to the king and defend the kingdom, this chapter became the basis of a similar oath that William the Conqueror exacted after confirming the Confessor's laws. Philipps did not find William's

---

[20] *Ibid.*, p. 35.

[21] Coke, *Justice Vindicated From the False Fucus put upon it, By Thomas White Gent. Mr. Thomas Hobbs, and Hugh Grotius. As also Elements of Power and Subjection; Wherein is demonstrated the Cause of all Humane, Christian, and Legal Society* (London, 1660), pp. 105–6, 108. The material cited here is from the section entitled *Elements of Power and Subjection*.

[22] *Ibid.*, pp. 51–3, 66–7.

action in the least surprising, since the Normans already knew about Saxon laws, having earlier adopted English customs when the Confessor had first brought them to Normandy.[23] These laws, which included English liberties, were greatly venerated after the Norman invasion. Indeed, Philipps told how, as their country lay in ruins, the English hid the Confessor's laws "under his shrine at Westminster and thought themselves happy, when as with tears and importunities they obtained of William the Conqueror to be restored to them, and left them as rich heir-looms, and a precious legacy to their posterity."[24] With these words Philipps signaled that the cult of St. Edward's laws had now entirely supplanted the cult of kingship, since medieval writers had placed the Confessor's bones in the shrine.

Continuing in this vein, Philipps noted that the Saxons, not content to provide for their own liberty, looked to the future and secured "the care and observation" of St. Edward's laws by inserting them into the coronation oath of the succeeding kings of England. Philipps thought it no surprise that the English held the Confessor's laws in such high esteem: after all, "they were *Leges propriae*, laws of their own country, and . . . the ancient customs in which their forefathers were born or bred up in . . ." Later generations also venerated St. Edward's laws, "adventuring their lives and all that they had at the making of Magna Carta, and in the Barons' Wars."[25]

Dugdale, perhaps the greatest medievalist of the seventeenth century, also entered the fray soon after the return of Charles II. In his *Origines Juridicales*, first published in 1666 and reprinted in 1680 during the exclusion crisis, Dugdale deployed the Confessor's laws to reinforce the royal supremacy. Although he credited the Saxons, and St. Edward in particular, with establishing the common law, and although he knew that William and his successors confirmed St. Edward's laws on numerous occasions, he insisted that these laws originated with kings. Of course, Saxon kings legislated with their assemblies of wise men, assemblies which included "representatives of the people, or commons." Dugdale had learned as much from Lambarde, who had described the Confessor's laws as being made

[23] Philipps, *Tenenda non Tollenda* (London, 1660), pp. 8, 9–10.
[24] Philipps, *The Established Government of England*, p. 759.
[25] Philipps, *Tenenda non Tollenda*, pp. 18, 73–4. See also Philipps, *The Established Government of England*, p. 759.

"*a Rege, Baronibus & populo.*" Numerous other Saxon records carried the same language. However, Dugdale argued, with William's conquest of England the practice changed considerably, for Norman kings, with an eye toward feudal customs, summoned parliaments in which the tenants-in-chief represented the Commons.[26]

Other royalists expressed similar views throughout Charles II's reign. John Nalson, whose work the government sometimes sponsored, condemned both coordination and the notion that the people and the Commons could call unlawful kings to account. The unworthiness of the latter argument should be evident, he suggested, in the fact that it flowed from the pens of Knox, Calvin, Buchanan, Goodman, and Bellarmine.[27] Moreover, in a history dedicated to Charles II, Sir Winston Churchill explained that William I confirmed St. Edward's laws upon "finding his prerogative sufficiently guarded by the ancient laws of the land." Chapter 17, in particular, proved the king's supremacy in ecclesiastical matters. Indeed, so impressed was William that "he suffered himself to be so far conquered by them, that instead of giving to, he took the law from them, and contentedly bound himself up." For that matter, the Saxons should have considered themselves fortunate to have the Norman duke as king, especially given that Edward the Confessor was "one of our weakest kings." But then they should be grateful for the introduction of all things French, for this new influence vastly improved on English civilization.[28] Similar interpretations of St. Edward's laws and the idea associated with Chapter 17 could also be found in the works of William Assheton, John Brydall, Edward Hyde, earl of Clarendon, and Edward Stillingfleet.[29]

Still, royalists' efforts to commandeer the ancient constitution lacked polemical staying power. Their future lay instead with the

---

[26] Dugdale, *Origines Juridicales; or, Historical Memorials of the English Laws* (London, 1680), pp. 3–18 *passim.*

[27] Nalson, *The Common Interest of King and People* (London, 1677), pp. 115–40 *passim*, 189–93 *passim*, 201–28 *passim.* See also Nalson, *An Impartial Collection of the Great Affairs of State* (London, 1682), vol. i.

[28] Churchill, *Divi Britannici: Being a Remark Upon the Lives of Kings of this Isle* (London, 1675), pp. 33, 34–6, 19–99 *passim.*

[29] Assheton, *The Royal Apology: Or, An Answer to the Rebels Plea* (London, 1684), pp. 2–6, 23, 38–40 *passim.* Brydall, *Jura Coronae. His Majesties Royal Rights and Prerogatives Asserted* (London, 1680), pp. 51, 56, 68–70, 76, 103, 145, 146. Edward Hyde, earl of Clarendon, *A Brief Survey of the Dangerous and pernicious Errors to Church and State, In Mr. Hobbes's Book, Entitled Leviathan* (Printed at the Theater, 1676), pp. 109–10. Stillingfleet, *The Grand Question concerning the Bishops Right to Vote in Parliament in Cases Capital* (London, 1680), pp. 74–6, 181.

very different historical construction of Dr. Robert Brady, who put forward a remarkably accurate and thoroughly un-ancient constitutionalist view of the English past.[30] A physician with close ties to Charles II and his avowedly Catholic brother James duke of York, Brady was motivated to take pen in hand by the struggle over the succession to the throne. During the exclusion crisis, as it is usually known, the nation again confronted the prospect of civil disorder; and rebels again found in radical ancient constitutionalism and its medieval sources formidable weapons with which to assault the Stuart kingship.[31] Although they went to great lengths to dissociate themselves from the sins of '41 and '49, their arguments in favor of exclusion came directly from ancient constitutionalist theorizing. Indeed, that particular historical construction figured just as prominently now as during the civil wars. It was to this line of argumentation that Brady had to respond.

At issue during the late 1670s and early 1680s was the right of parliament to meddle in the succession, a matter that necessarily involved a more general discussion of the power of the two houses *vis à vis* the king. The exclusion controversy itself concerned whig attempts to exclude James duke of York from the throne.[32] The story began with Charles II's desire to enact a measure of religious toleration. In order to secure this goal, the king set about issuing declarations of indulgence in which he dispensed with the numerous statutes enjoining adherence to the established church. The two houses, however, refused to countenance such moves, turning him back in 1662, 1672, and 1673. Their opposition came not only from a virulent anti-Catholic phobia but also from a dislike of the dispensing power that the king would use to bring about toleration.

---

[30] See Pocock, *The Ancient Constitution*, chapter 8 *passim*; Weston and Greenberg, *Subjects and Sovereigns*, chapter 7 *passim*.

[31] In this section on the exclusion crisis I follow Melinda S. Zook, *Radical Whigs and Conspiratorial Politics in Late Stuart England* (University Park, Pa., 1999), Introduction and chapters 2, 3 and 4.

[32] Some modern scholars question whether exclusion constituted the major theme during these years and also whether there was indeed a "crisis." See, for example, Jonathan Scott, *Algernon Sidney and the Restoration Crisis, 1677–1683* (Cambridge, 1991), part I; Ronald Hutton, *Charles II: king of England, Scotland and Ireland* (Oxford, 1989), p. 357 and *passim*. For the contrary view see Zook, *Radical Whigs and Conspiratorial Politics in Late Stuart England*; Mark Knights, *Politics and Opinion in Crisis, 1678–81* (Cambridge, 1994); Tim Harris, *London Crowds in the Reign of Charles II: Propaganda and Politics from the Restoration until the Exclusion Crisis* (Cambridge, 1994); Harris, "Party Turns? Or, Whigs and Tories Get Off Scott Free," *Albion* 25 (1993), 581–90; Harris, "Sobering Thoughts, But the Party is Not Yet Over: A Reply," *ibid.*, 645–7; and Harris, "What's New About the Restoration?," *ibid.* 29 (1997), 187–222.

Parliament's main objection to this prerogative, the legality of which had gone virtually unchallenged for centuries, involved a question now considered of major constitutional import: did English law permit the king, who, according to many, possessed only one share of the legislative authority, to dispense with a statute that had been made by all three? "No," answered a majority in both houses of this thoroughly royalist body. In the view of the Cavalier Parliament, Charles II could not legally dispense with statutes because he alone did not make them. Law, according to the two houses, must be dispensed with by the same authority that created it, that is, King, Lords, and Commons.[33]

Not content to defy Charles II's efforts to bring religious toleration, parliament passed two measures designed to impose even greater restrictions on Catholics – the 1673 Test Act, which prohibited Charles II from appointing them to political office, and the corresponding act of 1678, which extended the restrictions to members of parliament. Yet even these measures failed to placate leading members of the political nation, whose fears stemmed not from their colleagues in parliament or even from papists at court. Rather, their concerns centered on a far more imminent and menacing threat: since Charles II had fathered no legitimate children, the throne would descend by hereditary right to his Catholic brother. Although the two houses agreed to a proviso in the Test Act of 1678 that allowed James to sit in the House of Lords, a strong majority drew the line when it came to the throne. How secure, many asked rhetorically, would the liberty and religion of England be with a son of Rome wearing the crown? Accordingly, on May 15, 1679 Richard Hampden, grandson of the great civil war leader, introduced the first of three exclusion bills. Although the whigs eventually failed in their attempts to deny James the throne, their persistence and popularity within much of the country gravely threatened the government. Indeed, on occasion Charles II felt such pressure from the two houses that he sent parliament home rather than risk further damage to the crown. To make matters worse, his political enemies lobbied for an end to the Cavalier Parliament and new elections, which would, they hoped, return a lower house even more favorable to the whig cause. So high did tensions run that many recalled the dark days of 1642.

[33] Weston and Greenberg, *Subjects and Sovereigns*, chapter 6.

The attempt to bar the duke of York from the throne, combined with the lapse of censorship in 1679, loosed a veritable flood of tracts, their number and variety unmatched since the 1640s. The early history of parliament and its fate in 1066 appeared front and center, as whigs consistently justified altering the succession on the familiar ground that parliament and the common law reigned supreme because they were immemorial. Indeed, both had coexisted with kings at least since the Saxon period, which lay safely outside 1189, the date of legal memory. Little doubt surrounded the antiquity of the upper house, most polemicists agreeing that early kings summoned barons to their councils. The problem now, even more so than during the civil wars and Interregnum, centered on the longevity of the House of Commons. Put simply, if the lower house could be shown up as a latecomer to the political scene, summoned into existence only in the late thirteenth century, then the doctrine of prescription told against the whigs. That is, the Commons could not claim to be immemorial. From this two conclusions ineluctably followed. First, no equality marked the relationship between King, Lords, and Commons, that is, the lower house relinquished all claim to a coordinate share in sovereignty. And second, without coordination the Commons possessed no right to participate in the alteration of the succession. The task at hand would have been difficult for the exclusionists under any circumstances, but it became all the more daunting with the reprinting of Filmer's *The Free-holder's Grand Inquest* in 1679 and the publication of his *Patriarcha* in 1680. Both attacked the parliamentarian, and now whig, assertion that while government in general was from God, the particular form proceeded from the people. In the *Free-holder's*, it will be recalled, Filmer argued that kings reigned by divine ordinance. In *Patriarcha* he found the absolute power of monarchs analogous to the father's authority within the family, a power relationship that God himself countenanced. The *Free-holder's* proved particularly damaging to the exclusionist cause because it cogently attacked the antiquity of the lower house. Indeed, according to Filmer, the Commons became a part of parliament only in 1265, the date of the earliest extant writ of summons.[34]

To make matters worse, the formidable Brady soon entered the

---

[34] Filmer, "The Freeholder's Grand Inquest," in *Patriarcha and Other Writings*, ed. Johann P. Sommerville (Cambridge, 1991), pp. 89, 99–100, 114–17, 120–1, and *passim*. Filmer, "Patriarcha," in *ibid.*, pp. 6, 33, 35, 41–4, 52–6, 66–8.

lists. Enjoying the patronage of Charles II himself, this highest of high tory historians endorsed and embellished existing arguments against the antiquity of parliament and in the process launched one of the most daunting attacks yet on the ancient constitution. Beholden to Prynne's later writings, in which the apostate of the Long Parliament had himself undermined the antiquity of the Commons, Brady located sovereignty solely in the king. Coordination was a lie concocted by those who denied God, nature, and their own history. Articulating a particularly accurate account of how things used to be, Brady argued that kings predated and created parliaments, which possessed only those rights that kings deigned to grant them. For proof one had to look no further than 1066, when William the Conqueror, after obliterating the Saxon nation and its laws, imposed Norman customs upon the vanquished. As for the pedigree of the lower house, it appeared late on the political scene, summoned only in 1265 during a time of rebellion.

For proof of his theorizing, Brady met ancient constitutionalists on their own ground, which he proceeded to cut out from under them by articulating an antithetical version of the past. Turning to early English history, he described how William I stripped the Saxons of their estates and bestowed them on his French followers. Such behavior, Brady smirked, characterized an absolute monarch, not a mere invader who graciously agreed to govern by a contract with his new neighbors. The king's enemies, he knew, tried to prove otherwise with their story of Edwin of Sharnborn. But this was nothing more than a "trite fable" introduced by desperate men who could dig up no better evidence. In sum, Brady confidently concluded, William and his successors reigned as absolute conquerors whose will was law and whose heirs enjoyed an indefeasible right to the crown.[35]

The cogency of the assault launched on the ancient constitution by Filmer, Prynne, and, eventually Brady placed whigs in a distressingly vulnerable position. Exclusionists now had to marshal both their forces and their sources in order to justify altering the succes-

---

[35] Brady, *A Full and Clear Answer to a Book lately written by Mr. Petyt*, published in 1681 and reprinted in a collection of Brady's tracts known as *An Introduction to the Old English History* (London, 1684). For Brady's career and views see Pocock, *The Ancient Constitution*, chapter 8 and 343ff; Weston and Greenberg, *Subjects and Sovereigns*, chapter 7 *passim*. See also the writings of John Guilford, who agreed in many particulars with Brady and Filmer. "A Small book, of John Guilford," B.L. Add. MSS 32. 518. fos. 26–173 *passim*.

sion. Predictably, they grounded their arguments in the historical tradition so familiar to them and their ancestors. Of the hundreds of exclusionist tracts published in the late 1670s and early 1680s, none boasted greater authority than William Petyt's treatise on the antiquity of the Commons. A learned whig lawyer, Petyt enjoyed the friendship and patronage of the earl of Essex, who was closely associated with the earl of Shaftesbury and John Locke. Since both Essex and Shaftesbury spearheaded the drive to exclude the duke of York from the throne, and since Brady wrote to counter Petyt, his words mattered. The title of his main exclusionist tract – *The Antient Right of the Commons of England Asserted, or, A Discourse proving by Records and the best Historians, that the Commons of England were ever an Essential Part of Parliament* – told the whole story. Here, in words bordering on insolence, Petyt made the case for a parliament which, because it was legally sovereign, possessed the right to alter the succession. He wrote primarily against Prynne and Filmer, both of whom had attacked the antiquity of the Commons on the ground that the first extant writ of summons dated only from 1265, that is, from 49 Henry III. In answer to this potentially fatal historical argument, Petyt evoked the standard anti-court rejoinder articulated earlier in the century and contained in medieval chronicles. Many rolls and records had been lost by negligent keepers, destroyed by fearful kings, or embezzled by attorneys and government officials. Indeed, if the records of 49 Henry III had not survived, the king's men would now be arguing that the Commons first attended parliament in the reign of Edward I. But this loss of official records should not cause despair, Petyt continued, because a solution lay close at hand: "those parliamentarian records being nowhere to be found, their defects must be supplied only out of such fragments and memorials of them as are extant in our other records and ancient historians." He had in mind Matthew Paris, Matthew of Westminster, Henry of Huntingdon, and Roger of Hoveden. In the works of such chroniclers, Englishmen could find proof that parliament, including the Commons, had exercised great power at least since Saxon times and continued to do so after the arrival of William I, sometimes mistakenly called the conqueror.[36]

Petyt might correctly have added that in Paris, Huntingdon, and

[36] Petyt, *A Discourse Wherein is proved, That the Commons of England were an essential part of the Parliament before the 49th year of Henry 3*, pp. 55, 64–6. This appears as the second part to *The Antient Right of the Commons of England Asserted; Or, A discourse Proving by Records and the best*

Hoveden people could read about St. Edward's laws and William I's confirmations for themselves. Of all the medieval works at his disposal, Petyt found those associated with the Confessor most illuminating: they conclusively proved the antiquity of the Commons and hence its right to participate as an equal with King and Lords in the legislative process. Citing Lambarde's *Archaionomia*, Petyt pointed out that the Confessor reformed and confirmed "the ancient Saxon laws and added new ones *a Rege, Baronibus & Populo*, that is, by king, barons, and people." Moreover, the correspondence between Pope Eleutherius and King Lucius, also contained in St. Edward's laws, suggested the existence of such a body even earlier. Therefore, Petyt concluded, "it is apparent and past all contradiction that the Commons in those ages were an essential part of the legislative power, in making and ordaining laws, by which themselves and their posterity were to be governed, and that the law was then the golden metawant and rule which measured out and allowed the prerogative of the prince and liberty of the subject."[37]

St. Edward's laws also suited Petyt's polemical purposes in another way. Their regular and constant confirmations throughout English history proved that the constitutional arrangements of Saxon government – including an elective kingship and a contractual relationship between ruler and ruled – lived on after the arrival of the Normans. William I's first confirmation came at his coronation, when he declared publicly "that he would confirm the laws of Saint Edward." Upon this promise "he was *electus a clero & populo*, and with all the ceremonies and solemnities then in use, was crowned at Westminster, the whole nation submitting to him."[38] This gave England its first Magna Carta, though William's purpose was "to fix himself more sure in that his new-got chair of sovereignty." When he reneged on his promises to the Saxons, they rose up against him and forced another confirmation of the Confessor's laws, this time at St. Albans. This was the second Magna Carta. And so it went with William's successors, Petyt recounting the long line of medieval confirmations, including King John's at Runnymede.[39]

Historians, that the Commons of England were ever an Essential part of Parliament (London, 1680). The pages of the two parts are numbered separately.

[37] Petyt, *The Antient Right of the Commons of England Asserted*, pp. 11–12. The reference to King Lucius is in *ibid.*, pp. 3–5.

[38] *Ibid.*, pp. 29–30, 67, 71–2.

[39] *Ibid.*, pp. 14, 32–7 *passim*.

Finally, there was the coronation oath, to which all kings swore and in so swearing committed themselves to enacting those laws that the two houses should choose.[40]

Still, Petyt recognized that William enjoyed great power and that he "introduced several arbitrary laws," such as new tenures. Nevertheless, he governed with a general council or parliament, leading Petyt to conclude "that freemen or commons of England, were there, and had a share in the making of laws; for what could the promised restitution of the laws of the Confessor signify, if their WitanaGemot, or Parliament . . . was destroyed and broken?"[41] Neither did William's introduction of new tenures amount to "an absolute conquest." Nor, for that matter, "did the kingdom receive so universal a change" as some "modern authors" suggested. The limited nature of William's victory appeared from the fact that he even permitted some Saxons, particularly those who had early accepted his rule, to keep their lands. As proof Petyt cited Sharnborn's case and the case at Penenden Heath.[42]

By confirming St. Edward's laws, William acknowledged both the high power of parliament and the monarchy's subservience to the law made there. The right of parliament to alter the succession was also reinforced by the *Mirror* and the *Modus*. Although Petyt followed Selden in dating the latter from the reign of Edward III, he nevertheless thought it worth citing, since it mandated the attendance of both Lords and Commons in parliament.[43] The *Mirror*, which Petyt accepted as "an ancient and learned treatise of the law," noted that "parliaments were instituted *pur oyer & terminer les plaintes de tort de la Roy, de la Roigne & de lour Infans* . . . against whom the subject otherwise could not have common justice."[44] Finally, Petyt wanted his readers to understand that parliament's right to alter the succession was not merely theoretical. It had been exercised on many occasions in English history. Indeed, early parliaments had frequently made kings of those who possessed no legitimate claim to the throne. Witness, for example, William II, Henry I, and King John, who "were elected and created kings of England, having no hereditary right."[45]

---

[40] *Ibid.*, pp. 37, 61. *A Discourse*, p. 60.
[41] Petyt, *The Antient Right of the Commons of England Asserted*, pp. 39–40.
[42] *Ibid.*, pp. 23–45 *passim.*   [43] Petyt, *A Discourse*, p. 22.
[44] Petyt, *The Antient Right of the Commons of England Asserted*, pp. 40–1.
[45] *Ibid.*, pp. 66–7.

The conclusion that Petyt drew from his reading of English history was "that in the British, Saxon, and Norman governments, the commons (as we now phrase them) had votes, and a share in the making and enacting of laws for the government of the kingdom, and that they were an essential part of the *Commune Concilium Regni*, WittenaGemot, or parliament, before and after the supposed conquest of King William the First."[46] For Petyt, then, the laws of the Confessor and their subsequent confirmations constituted a vital link in the chain of historical evidence that proved the principles of coordination and coevality and, therefore, the right of parliament to exclude James duke of York from the throne.

A blatantly Edwardian tone characterized Edward Cooke's *Argumentum Anti-Normanicum*, the title sheet of which gives this book its cover. Although modern scholars sometimes write dismissively about the work, Melinda Zook properly describes it as "one of the most important statements on ancient constitutionalism in the late Stuart era." Not only did Brady deem it worthy of rebuttal in his *Full and Clear Answer*, it was reprinted in time for the Convention's deliberations in 1689 under the title *A Seasonable Treatise Wherein is proved, that King William (commonly call'd the Conqueror) Did not get the Imperial Crown of England by the Sword, but by the Election and Consent of the People: To whom he swore to observe the Original Contract between King and People*. In addition, James Tyrrell, the prominent whig writer and close associate of John Locke and the earl of Shaftesbury, quoted the work frequently in his own justifications for the Glorious Revolution.[47]

As the title of the 1689 edition clearly indicates, Cooke wrote for the purpose of refuting those who, like Filmer and Brady, argued that Charles II reigned absolutely because his predecessor William the Conqueror had done so. Nothing could be further from Cooke's reading of the past. Indeed, William I's confirmation of St. Edward's laws, which Ingulf described as being "proclaimed authentic and perpetual all over England," meant that kings reigned by right, not

---

[46] *Ibid.*, p. 73. See also Petyt, *Miscellanea Parliamentaria: Containing Presidents 1. Of Freedom from Arrests. 2. Of Censures* (London, 1680), pp. 66–74 *passim*. The royalist John Northleigh demonstrated that he had taken the measure of exclusionists such as Petyt when he wrote that, although they said "parliament" had the power to alter the succession, they really meant the House of Commons. *The Parallel; Or, The New Specious Association An Old Religious Covenant* (London, 1682), p. 24.

[47] Zook, *Radical Whigs and Conspiratorial Politics in Late Stuart England*, p. 82. For Tyrrell's references see *The General History of England . . . to the Reign of William III* (London, 1696), vol. 1 *passim*.

conquest. After all, a study of the coronation oath indicated that
William had taken the same oath as Saxon kings. Although tempted
to introduce Norman laws, which was "thought a more killing blow
than that of his victory," William submitted to the English, who
begged on "the soul of King Edward . . . that he would not impose a
yoke upon them."[48] At length, the new king, "in a common council
of his kingdom," yielded, "and by his Magna Charta (the groundwork of all that followed) . . . confirmed to them their ancient laws,"
commanding "that all men keep, and observe duly the laws of King
Edward." Indeed, William's reverence for these laws led him to
make "them to be the common standing laws of the land, equally
observed by Norman and English."[49]

This meant, of course, that William was no conqueror. On the
contrary, "the mighty conqueror is himself conquered, and solemnly
renouncing all arbitrary will and power, submits his will to be
regulated and governed by justice, and the ancient rights of the
English men."[50] Not that William kept all the Saxon laws. Some he
did indeed change, but always *"per Commune Concilium totius Regni."*
Once again, so far was William from conquering England "that
instead of giving to, he took the law from them, and contentedly
bound himself up by those which they called St. Edward's laws."[51]

Finally, Cooke turned to the ever important question of the
antiquity of the Commons. Parliament, he wrote, "was in substance
the same that it was before the coming in of the Conqueror."
Constituting the representative body of the kingdom, it contained a
House of Commons many of whose members were English and not
Norman. Moreover, then as now parliament possessed the right to
alter law.[52] Other exclusionists sounded the same note. Petyt's
friends William Atwood, James Tyrrell, and John Somers defended
parliament's right to alter the succession by reference to the Saxon
origins of government, the antiquity of the Commons, and the
absence of a Norman conquest. Somers, whom Howard Nenner
describes as "one of the best constitutional scholars of his generation," was an eminent whig lawyer who later chaired the committee

---

[48] Cooke, *Argumentum Antinormanicum* (London, 1682), pp. xi–xii, xviii, xxii, xvii, xxxi–xxxii.
[49] *Ibid.*, pp. xxviii, liv.
[50] *Ibid.*, pp. xxix–xxxii *passim.*
[51] *Ibid.*, pp. lviii–lix.
[52] *Ibid.*, pp. xlv, xcvi, c, cx. See also Cooke, *Magna Carta, Made in the Ninth Year of King Henry the Third* (London, 1680), pp. 15, 29, 30.

that drafted the Declaration of Rights and also served William and Mary as solicitor general, attorney general, lord keeper, and chancellor.[53] In *A Brief History of the Succession Collected out of the Records, and the most Authentick Historians* (1680), he noted that Saxon kings, including Edward the Confessor, were sometimes chosen in full parliaments. This alone should be enough to convince Englishmen that "it is no strange thing to hear of a parliament's meddling with the succession." Moreover, the practice continued after the arrival of the Normans, who took pains to restore the ancient Saxon laws and promised in their coronation oath to uphold them. By so doing, Somers insisted, they acknowledged that they took the throne on condition and not by divine or patriarchal right or conquest.[54]

In a tract sometimes attributed to Somers, Charles II's attempts to save his brother by dissolving parliament also drew attention. The author(s) of *A Just and Modest Vindication of the Proceedings of the two last Parliaments of King Charles the Second*, published first in 1681 and again in 1689, vouched the *Modus* and the *Mirror* to prove the king's duty to summon parliaments annually and to keep them sitting until all petitions had been answered. The *Mirror*, for example, "tells us, That parliaments were ordained to hear and determine all complaints of wrongful acts, done by the king, queen, or their children, and such others against whom common right cannot be had elsewhere." This meant that parliament had the right and the duty to admonish a king who erred. Indeed, every king swore at his coronation to govern according to this limitation. To act otherwise, by dissolving parliament abruptly, at a time "when nothing but the legislative power and the united wisdom of the kingdom" could save the nation was "very unsuitable to the great trust reposed in the prince . . ."[55]

---

[53] Nenner, *The Succession to the Crown of England, 1603–1714*, p. 107.

[54] Somers, "A Brief History of the Succession, Collected out of the Records, and the most Authentick Historians," in *State Tracts: Being a Collection of Several Treastises Relating to the Government* (London 1689), vol. II, pp. 383–7, 397–8.

[55] "A Just and Modest Vindication of the Proceedings of the two last Parliaments of King Charles the Second," in *State Tracts*, vol. II, pp. 165, 180–1, 184. In addition to Somers, the names of Robert Ferguson, Sir William Jones, and Algernon Sidney are also associated with the work. See Lois G. Schwoerer, *The Declaration of Rights, 1689* (Baltimore, 1981), pp. 48–9; Nenner, *The Right to be King*, p. 289, n. 122; Scott, *Algernon Sidney and the Restoration Crisis, 1677–1683*, p. 186; Michael Landon, *The Triumph of the Lawyers* (Tuscaloosa, AL, 1970), p. 261, n. 22. The *Mirror* and the *Modus* were deployed to the same ends in anonymous works such as "Vox Populi: Or, The People's Claim to their Parliaments' Sitting, to Redress Grievances. . . ," in *State Tracts*, vol. II, pp. 221–4; "A Letter From a Parliament-Man to his Friend, Concerning the Proceedings of the House of Commons This last session, begun the 13th of October, 1675," in *ibid.*, p. 55.

Atwood too turned to St. Edward's laws as well as the tales of Sharnborn and the men of Swanscombe Down to prove parliament's right to alter the succession. Trained at Gray's Inn, he was a protégé of Petyt and perhaps connected with the Essex circle. His career as an ancient constitutionalist polemicist was long and distinguished, stretching from the exclusion crisis through the Glorious Revolution. With his mentor's encouragement, Atwood immersed himself in early English history, his purpose to learn the lessons contained in the chronicles, charters, and parliamentary rolls. Here he came to know St. Edward's laws, declared, he believed, in a full parliament and confirmed by William I and his successors in similar bodies. The Confessor's laws taught him that kings reigned by virtue of election and a contractual agreement with their people. This meant in turn that the parliaments of their own day and age possessed the power to alter the succession.[56] Tyrrell used the same sources to bolster the same arguments.[57] Although Atwood and Tyrrell steered clear of the explosive issue of whether parliament could compel a king, Tyrrell cited Bracton's and James I's "Office," which he linked to the coronation oath. And Atwood had the nerve to mention *Curtana*, which contemporaries almost certainly associated with regicide.[58]

All of these whig writers believed in an ancient constitution at the center of which stood a government composed of the three coordinate and coeval estates. However, some of the most noted and honored exclusionists and martyrs went further. Algernon Sidney, for one, advocated a scheme of government that flirted with republicanism. For this reason, Sidney, a radical by any standard, is usually seen as outside the mainstream of whig political thought. Yet he, like Milton, knew what to do with historical sources, and, in fact, his use of such sources contributed to his death. In 1683 Sidney was tried and executed for complicity in the Rye House Plot, part of the evidence against him being a work found among his private papers. Indeed, the court made his *Discourses Concerning Government* serve as

---

[56] Atwood, *Jani Anglorum Facies Nova: Or, Several Monuments of Antiquity touching the Great Councils of the Kingdom* (London, 1680), pp. 8, 31, 34–52 *passim*, 58. For the stories of the men of Swanscombe Down and Sharnborn see *ibid.*, pp. 49–58, 100–5. Atwood, *Jus Anglorum ab Antiquo. Or, A Confutation of an Important Libel Against the Government by King, Lords, and Commons* (London, 1681), Preface, pp. 9, 18, 20–1, 32–58 *passim*, 100, 104–5, 113–18, 124–7, 128–39 *passim*, 181, 191–6 *passim*, 215. Zook provides the fullest account of Atwood's career. *Radical Whigs and Conspiratorial Politics in Late Stuart England*, pp. 66ff, 161ff.

[57] Tyrrell, *Patriarcha non Monarcha* (London, 1681), pp. 67–8, 140–1, 149–51, 156–7, 221, 223, 227–8, 229.

[58] *Ibid.*, pp. 151, 159. Atwood, *Jani Anglorum Facies Nova*, p. 8.

the second witness – the first being Lord Howard – mandated by the law of treason. Although Sidney never admitted to writing this "false, seditious, and traitorous libel," it was widely believed to be his and was published in London in 1698, 1704, 1705, 1730, 1763, and 1772.[59]

Running to almost 500 pages, the tract brims with references to Saxon laws, which Sidney deployed to exalt the power of people and parliament over kings. Taking aim at Filmer, he argued that in England kings were chosen by the people, as medieval chronicles made clear. William I was a case at point, as he obtained the crown not by conquest but by compact with the realm. In Sidney's words,

William the Norman was not by force brought into England, but came voluntarily, and desired to be king: The nobility, clergy and commons proposed the conditions upon which they would receive him. These conditions were to govern according to their ancient laws, especially those that had been granted, or rather collected in the time of the famous King Edward.

William, for his part, "accepted the crown upon the conditions offered and swore upon the Evangelists to observe them." When, however, he departed from his oath, he found "the people would not endure it," and at St. Albans, where he probably examined the contents of St. Edward's laws, he swore once more to honor them. William's successors likewise swore in their coronation oaths to observe these laws, which meant that the Confessor's laws "continue to be of force amongst us." The laws were also kept alive through Magna Carta, which was "only an abridgment of our ancient laws and customs," as well as its subsequent confirmations.[60]

In Sidney's view, the laws of the Confessor, which stood at the center of the coronation oath, constituted a vital part of the contract between ruler and ruled. From the king's promise to observe and keep them inviolate flowed the community's promise to obey. The primacy of parliament in this scheme appeared from the fact that it, and only it, made laws, including those of St. Edward. Further, early parliaments had always contained a Commons, leading to the

---

[59] Zook, *Radical Whigs and Conspiratorial Politics in Late Stuart England*, pp. 123–6. Alan Craig Houston, *Algernon Sidney and the Republican Heritage in England and America* (Princeton, 1991), pp. 285–6. Scott, *Algernon Sidney and the Restoration Crisis, 1677–1683*. Annabel Patterson, *Early Modern Liberalism* (Cambridge, 1997), chapter 4.

[60] Sidney, *Discourses Concerning Government* (London, 1698), pp. 324–5, 327–8, 311, 455.

conclusion that the people, through their representatives in parliament, made the laws that bound the king.[61]

The republican Henry Neville's views echoed Sidney's. Neville knew from his studies that English history had bequeathed to Stuart Englishmen a form of government in which King, Lords, and Commons shared authority. And this by consent of the people themselves. However, the power of the king proved negligible, since the *quas vulgus elegerit* clause of the coronation oath effectively stripped him of his veto power. Nor did the king possess the power to summon and disband parliaments at will. Medieval statutes committed him to calling parliaments annually, and the *Modus tenendi Parliamentum* bound him to extend their life until all petitions had been heard. Such had been the case since antiquity. Not even the coming of the Normans affected the English government, since they entered by treaty. Indeed, "there was no conquest made upon any but Harold; in whose stead William the first came, and would claim no more after his victory, than what Harold enjoyed."[62]

Finally, William Disney, who would soon die for complicity in Monmouth's Rebellion, put medieval sources to similar uses in his tract *Nil dictum quod non dictum prius*. Intent on proving the superiority of the three coordinate and coeval estates to the king alone, Disney evoked the laws of Holy Edward. The history of these laws proved that the Saxon constitution, of which they constituted the key part, survived 1066 intact. Though some misguided writers claimed that William I "came in by arms," Disney believed that he entered "by election, capitulation or stipulation." This appeared from the fact that in 1070 he confirmed the laws of good King Edward in his parliament. In fact, so far was William from acting like a conqueror "or acting by the sole dictates of his own pleasure, that he

---

[61] *Ibid.*, pp. 14, 82ff, 88, 196, 247–87 *passim*.

[62] Neville, "Plato Redivivus, or, A Dialogue Concerning Government (c. 1681)," in *Two English Republican Tracts*, ed. Caroline Robbins (Cambridge, 1969), pp. 120–4, 128–30. The medieval canon also figured in the controversy over the right of the bishops to sit in capital cases in the case of the earl of Danby as well as in the defense of London's charter in Charles II's *quo warranto* proceedings. See William Atwood, *Considerations Touching that Question, Whether the Prelates Have Right to sit among the Lords, and Vote with them in Parliament in Capital Cases* (London, 1682), pp. 120–2, 129, 161–2, 180–2, 196, 202–3, 226, 229; Atwood, *Reflections upon Antidotum Britannicum, and Mr. Hunt's late Book and Post-script* (London, 1682), pp. 236, 252–5, 258–60, 271–2, 292–3; (These two works appear in *Lord Hollis His Remains* [London, 1682]); Thomas Hunt, *A Defence of the Charter, and Municipal Rights of the City of London* (London, n.d.), pp. 38–40; *The Triumph of Justice over Unjust Judges* (London, 1681), pp. 2–7 *passim*; *The English-man's Right* (London, 1680), pp. 4–7 *passim*, 39.

commended the laws of the Confessor to his justices, in the same language they were wont formerly to be written, least through ignorance the people rashly might offend." In addition, the new king even "had a desire to learn the Saxon tongue, that he might the better know their law, and judge according to it." William's heirs and successors likewise confirmed the Confessor's laws, both in their coronation oaths and in special charters, such as Henry I's Coronation Charter and King's John's Magna Carta.[63] History also showed the fate of the king who went back on his word: parliament rose up against him, "its power . . . unlimited and universal." Indeed, parliament possessed "power above the law itself, having power to alter the common law of England . . . not only without, but against the king's personal consent . . ."[64]

By vouching St. Edward's laws, the *Modus*, and the *Mirror* to prove the right of parliament to control kings and alter the succession, exclusionists played the trump card in their ideological deck.[65] They served, however, in a lost cause. The failure of exclusion and the discovery of the Rye House plot to kill Charles II and his brother led to a royalist reaction. With the whigs in retreat, the government moved to quash the major ideas and sources associated with the movement. On July 21, the same day that William Lord Russell lost his head for conspiring against the king, the Judgment and Decree of the University of Oxford condemned a number of principles as "pernicious," "damnable," and "destructive to the sacred persons of princes, their state and government and all human society." Among them was the idea inherent in Chapter 17 of St. Edward's laws, namely, "That if lawful governors become tyrants, or govern otherwise than by the laws of God and man they ought to do, they forfeit the right they had unto their government." However, the names associated with the doctrine included no mention of the Confessor, Bracton, Fleta, or Fortescue. Instead credit, or rather blame, went to the ignominious crowd of Milton, Rutherford, Goodwin, Buchanan, and the author of the *Vindiciae contra Tyrannos*.[66]

[63] Disney, *Nil dictum quod non dictum prius, the Case of the Government of England Established by Law* (London, 1681), pp. 31–3, 50–2, 79, 86–96, 139–50 *passim*.

[64] *Ibid.*, pp. 135–7.

[65] Royalists during these years did not entirely abandon Saxon sources. See, for example, Fabian Philipps, *A Plea for the Pardoning Part of the Soveraignty of the Kings of England* (London, 1682), pp. 1–2, 23, 31–5, 41, 42.

[66] *Divine Right and Democracy*, ed. David Wootton (Harmondsworth, 1986), p. 121.

Upon the death of Charles II, rebels schemed to place his illegitimate son the duke of Monmouth on the throne. Not only were they unsuccessful, but the crackdown came hard and swift, as hundreds of rebels suffered imprisonment and death by order of the new king, James II. Despite the dangers inherent in this atmosphere, dissidents continued to raise many of the same political issues that had proved troublesome in the previous reign. By 1688 and 1689 the main bone of contention was the right of parliament to alter the kingship as well as the succession. Once again, opponents of the Stuart monarchy pressed into action the medieval sources so familiar to both whigs and tories. By now St. Edward's laws, the *Modus*, and the *Mirror* surely triggered associations of an immemorial House of Commons, a shared and coordinate authority among King, Lords, and Commons, and a contractual relationship between ruler and ruled. *Curtana* and Chapter 17 in its entirety must have conjured up visions of the use of coercive force against the king, as well as images of regicide and republicanism. Despite, or perhaps because of, their pedigree, the heyday of these sources lay in the Glorious Revolution.

THE RADICAL ANCIENT CONSTITUTION IN THE GLORIOUS REVOLUTION AND REVOLUTION SETTLEMENT

Amid a show of popular support, James II ascended the throne on February 6, 1685. Within four years, however, he had transformed this support into a general hostility that permeated almost every sector of English society. Through a series of impolitic and ill-considered policies, James managed to engender such dislike that whigs and tories united to force his departure and to settle the crown on his eldest daughter, Mary, and her husband, William Prince of Orange, savior of Dutch Protestantism. To Bishop Gilbert Burnet, James II's sudden fall was one of the oddest events in history: "A great king, with strong armies and mighty fleets, a great treasure and powerful allies, fell all at once, and his whole strength, like a spider's web, was . . . irrecoverably broken at a touch."[67] The cause of James II's plummet could be traced to his Catholicizing policies, which he forwarded by means of the controversial dispensing power. Whether the political nation objected more to the former or to the latter, we cannot say. But clearly the combination of the two, which for

---

[67] Quoted in Weston and Greenberg, *Subjects and Sovereigns*, p. 222.

contemporaries raised the specter of arbitrary government, proved more than sufficient to destroy the king's support and unite whigs and many tories in a common cause. As Tim Harris writes, James II "was perceived to be acting in violation of the rule of law and against England's national interests."[68]

Almost as soon as he ascended the throne, the new king sought to introduce a general toleration by dispensing with those statutes that enjoined religious conformity. In so doing, he signaled his inclination to have his way with the law without regard to the two houses, which in turn imperilled the view of legislative sovereignty that now commanded wide support. According to his enemies who followed the logic of radical ancient constitutionalism, statutes must be dispensed with by the same ancient authority that created them – King, Lords, and Commons. Thus, to favor the king's dispensing power was to advance the view that the king alone possessed sole legislative power. Indeed, many of the king's friends consistently argued in this fashion. To make matters even worse, James II used the controversial prerogative to set aside those statutes prohibiting Catholics from serving in the military and in parliament. Protestant fears ran especially high at this time, exacerbated by Louis XIV's persecution of the Huguenots and the final revocation of the Edict of Nantes. The dangers inherent in this situation motivated even conservative Englishmen to look to the two houses as an effective counterweight to an overly ambitious and proudly papist ruler. So much became clear at the end of James II's reign, when even the Anglican clergy – hitherto the mainstay of the Stuart monarchy – deserted him.

But in 1685, this development lay in the future. In the early days of James II's short reign, royalist propaganda occupied the high ground. Tory polemicists such as Brady, John Wilson, and Dr. Nathaniel Johnston, working in an atmosphere of newly imposed censorship, wrote powerful tracts that enjoyed royal approval and sponsorship. Brady, now as close a friend to James II as he had been to his brother, was particularly fast off the starting block. Publishing the first volume of his *Complete History* in 1685, he dedicated his work to the new king, who rewarded him with an appointment as keeper

---

[68] Harris, "What's New About the Restoration?," p. 217. See also Steven C. A. Pincus, "The Universal Debate over Universal Monarchy," in *A Union for Empire: Political Thought and the British Union of 1707*, ed. John Robertson (Cambridge, 1995), pp. 37–62; Weston and Greenberg, *Subjects and Sovereigns*, chapter 8.

of the Tower records. James II had every reason to appreciate Brady's efforts on his behalf. After all, the polemicist mounted a defense of the Stuart kingship based on the absolute sovereignty of William the Conqueror, whose heir James was. On this ground Brady attacked the radical ancient constitution and championed the right of the king, as sole legislator, to dispense with and suspend statutes at his will and pleasure.[69]

Brady's like-minded friend, Dr. Nathaniel Johnston, also found favor with the king, whose secretary of state, Lord Sunderland, commissioned Johnston's *Excellency of Monarchical Government*. Published in 1686, this tract also turned to the Norman conquest for proof of the legality of the royal dispensing power. Because William conquered both England and its laws, he reigned as an absolute conqueror from whose will flowed the merely derivative powers of parliament and the law. Railing against "the serpent of co-ordinate power," Johnston concluded that James II, as sovereign legislator, could dispense with statutes at his will and pleasure.[70]

This was not, however, the view of the political nation, and when in April of 1687 James II suspended large numbers of statutes in his second Declaration of Indulgence, whigs and tories closed ranks. In November of 1688 James, fearing for his life, fled England for the last time, and William Prince of Orange set sail from Holland. In January of 1689 the Convention met to consider the nation's fate, and on the 28th the lower house accepted with hardly any negative votes a statement declaring

that James the Second, having endeavoured to subvert the constitution of the kingdom by breaking the original contract between king and people, and, by the advice of Jesuits and other wicked persons having violated the fundamental laws and having withdrawn himself out of this kingdom, has abdicated the government and that the throne is thereby become vacant.[71]

As Lois G. Schwoerer notes, this resolution "closely reflected the principles of radical whig members" of the House of Commons, its language suggesting "that James's *acts* had broken the original contract between king and people and violated the nation's funda-

---

[69] Pocock, *The Ancient Constitution and the Feudal Law*, pp. 212ff. Weston and Greenberg, *Subjects and Sovereigns*, chapter 8.

[70] Johnston, *The Excellency of Monarchical Government* (London, 1686), Introduction, pp. 127–8, 139, 145, 151–3, 155, 157, 301–7.

[71] *Commons Journal*, vol. x, p. 14. See also Schwoerer, *The Declaration of Rights*, pp. 24–5; Landon, *The Triumph of the Lawyers*, pp. 228–38.

mental laws." In so doing he abdicated his government and the throne was now vacant. The resolution's use of certain terms provoked extended debate in the Convention, especially among the Lords. Tories, for their part, disliked references to the "original contract" and the "fundamental laws," while whigs deplored a tory interpretation in which James merely withdrew from the kingdom, leaving the throne for the next legitimate successor. As a result of the debate, leaders in the two houses came to a compromise. "Original contract" and "fundamental laws" were dropped, but "abdicated" and "vacant" remained. Nevertheless, the compromise did not entirely mute the resolution's message. In Schwoerer's view, the changes strongly implied "that James's misdeeds had broken the original contract between king and people and violated the fundamental laws, as left-wing whigs had argued in debate and pamphlet."[72]

Moving immediately to fill the void left by James's abdication, the two houses declared William and Mary king and queen, but not without condition. As Schwoerer demonstrates, the two were proclaimed only after accepting the Declaration of Rights, a document which, in its statutory form as the Bill of Rights, changed the kingship in significant ways. First and foremost, the opening clauses of both documents abolished the dispensing power and its twin the suspending power, acknowledged for centuries as essential and inseparable attributes of sovereignty. Undoubtedly, their elimination constituted a revolution in the government as established by law. The same can be said of the abolition of the king's right to control the militia. Not only did this constitute yet another drastic constitutional revision, it linked the revolutionaries of 1689 with those of 1642.[73]

Having replaced the king, supporters of the Revolution settlement now faced an equally vital and even more intimidating task – persuading the nation that transferring allegiance from James to William and Mary was just and lawful as well as expedient. The task

---

[72] Schwoerer, *The Declaration of Rights*, p. 25. See also Landon, *The Triumph of the Lawyers*, chapt. 7.

[73] Schwoerer, *The Declaration of Rights*, pp. 71–4, 75–6, 227–8, 245–6, and *passim*. See also Schwoerer, *"No Standing Armies!" The Antiarmy Ideology in Seventeenth-Century England* (Baltimore, 1974). The term "dispensing power" referred to dispensations to individuals, while the term "suspending power" referred to the wholesale suspension of statutes. Legally, however, there was no difference between the two; the suspending power was simply the dispensing power exercised on a large scale.

became critical when in April 1689 the Convention Parliament mandated that, before August 1, all civil and ecclesiastical office holders had to take a new oath of allegiance or face suspension. Almost everyone complied. But, as Mark Goldie writes, while "the expediential grounds for doing so were clear, the philosophical grounds" required substantial thought and explanation. The scene of battle now shifted to the polemical arena, where the printing press emerged as the weapon of choice.[74]

The outpouring of Revolution tracts numbered in the thousands, contemporaries themselves stunned by the enormous proliferation of political literature.[75] Goldie suggests that by the end of 1689 some 2,000 separate titles had appeared, about two-thirds dealing with the Glorious Revolution. This made 1689 one of perhaps only five years to have attained such an output before the mid-eighteenth century, the other years being 1642, 1648, 1660, and 1710. A normal crop, on the other hand, consisted of around 700 pamphlets annually. Although we do not know the exact numbers of a given printing, a sensible estimate runs around one thousand, leading Goldie to suggest that by the mid-1690s, approximately 300,000 copies of Revolution tracts circulated in England. As for the size of the market, he estimates that between 40,000 and 100,000 readers "engaged in an extraordinarily intensive program of reading." These statistics lead Goldie to conclude that "the Revolution provided its generation with a political education," a sentiment echoed by a contemporary who noted that politics was "'a science never so common as it has been within these three years'" – 1689 to 1692. Indeed, Goldie estimates that there was probably one allegiance tract for every two literate adult males, more than one for every elector, and approximately eight for every adult who received a higher education.[76] Although we know little about the purchasers, many tracts sold for only a penny and would have therefore been affordable to a number of people. In addition to those who bought the works and loaned them to friends, many

---

[74] Goldie, "The Revolution of 1689 and the Structure of Political Argument," *Bulletin of Research into the Humanities* 83 (1980), 476–7. He suggests that about 400 out of 10,000 clergy and an unknown number of laymen refused to take the oath. *Ibid.*, 479.

[75] This discussion follows Goldie, "The Revolution of 1689"; and Schwoerer, "Press and Parliament in the Revolution of 1689," *Historical Journal* 20 (1977), 545–67; Schwoerer, "Propaganda in the Revolution of 1688–89," *American Historical Review* 82 (1977), 545–67.

[76] Goldie, "The Revolution of 1689," pp. 478, n. 14, n. 15, 479, 480–3.

must have heard them read aloud in the coffee houses where politics were hotly debated.[77]

The writers of allegiance tracts aimed first at convincing the political nation of the propriety of taking the new oath, and second at explaining the principles by which Englishmen ought to do so. Toward this end, the Revolution's supporters rushed into print with works that drew upon a wide range of sources and argumentation. As in the civil wars, polemicists found natural law and natural reason, the Bible, and, of course, their own national history suitable to the cause. The major arguments of this literature also echoed civil war ideology. Thus, whigs, as well as the occasional tory, claimed that while government in general was from God, the particular form proceeded from the people, who therefore constituted the human source of political authority. The people, in order to secure their lives, liberties, and properties, instituted the form of government that suited them. Some polemicists described a precedent philosophical or social contract by which the people agreed to leave their state of nature, while others referred to a rectoral or governmental contract by which a specific government was established. Many supporters of the Revolution settlement agreed that in England, the community instituted a mixed government in which the king shared authority equally and coordinately with parliament, which represented the people. Because the community existed before kings and empowered them, the relationship between ruler and ruled was contractual. In England this contract found expression in the ancient coronation oath, in which kings promised to abide by both ancient customs, especially St. Edward's laws, and those statutes which the Lords and Commons chose. The king who broke his oath thereby broke the contract which empowered him in the first place, and in so doing he freed his subjects from allegiance. Finally, many Revolution tracts, including some of the most prominent, argued that these features of English government enjoyed the approbation of time: they had themselves existed in Saxon times, from whence they descended to Stuart Englishmen. As in the civil wars, the king's enemies found St. Edward's laws, the *Modus*, and the *Mirror* ideally suited to their polemical ends.

By suggesting that whigs took advantage of the radical potential of

---

[77] Schwoerer, *The Declaration of Rights*, pp. 126–7, 344, n. 29 and n. 31. Schwoerer, "Press and Parliament in the Revolution of 1689," p. 556. Goldie, "The Revolution of 1689," pp. 481–3.

the English historical past to justify the Glorious Revolution, I am advancing an interpretation of late Stuart ideology and politics different from that often expressed in modern scholarship. Many historians view mainstream whig ideology as fundamentally conservative, and on several grounds. First, they point out that radical theories of contract, resistance, and deposition appear to have little purchase in the Convention and little impact on the Revolution settlement itself. To be sure, the two houses of the Convention voted that James II, by violating the original contract between ruler and ruled, had abdicated the government. But, these historians add, this action came to nothing after all, despite the fact that such a vote signaled an affectionate awareness of the idea of an original contract and an acceptance of its basic premises. In the end, however, the vote appeared to be no more than a formal obeisance to the idea, rather than a genuine expression of dedication to the right of the community to resist and depose a tyrannical king. After all, neither the Declaration of Rights nor the Bill of Rights mentioned such a contract.

Second, a number of scholars assess the Glorious Revolution as conservative because so few of its supporters followed Locke's example. Only fringe groups, the "True Whigs" or "Old Whigs," whose roots stretched backward to exclusion and forward to the republicanism of the eighteenth century, defended the Revolution with Lockean theories that located the origins of government in "popular" or philosophical contracts. According to these radical views, James II had forfeited his kingly rights and abdicated the government by his illegal actions. Power therefore devolved upon the people, who could settle the government as they pleased. Such reasoning, many scholars argue, went too far for most whigs, who justified the events of 1689 by reference to a governmental contract and who postulated a devolution of power not to the people but only to parliament. Moreover, whereas natural law well suited the more extremist forms of argumentation, English law and history better suited the latter. This follows from the fact that history tied men to a static constitution, whereas natural law left them free to make truly radical alterations. That mainstream whigs turned their backs on Lockean reasoning made sense, because, many scholars further reason, the Revolution settlement itself introduced few significant changes. The political nation settled for remedying James's worst excesses. Thus, a more conservative ideology befitted a primarily conservative event such as the Glorious Revolution. Put differently, while there was a change of kings, there was no change in the kingship.[78]

But, as this study has shown, radicalism comes in many guises, and if late seventeenth-century whigs had little to say about power devolving to the people on the Lockean model, they did indeed spend much time discussing resistance, deposition, and parliament's right to choose a new king – radical notions all. Moreover, when the Convention debates are reviewed in the light of medieval sources, and when the meaning these held for contemporaries is kept steadily in view, the tone of the Convention seems undeniably extremist. True, the Confessor's laws, the *Modus*, and the *Mirror* are rarely mentioned by name in surviving records of the debates. But these are fragmentary and incomplete, and it is inconceivable that St. Edward's ghost in particular did not haunt the proceedings when contract, abdication, and the coronation oath came under discussion. Petyt, for one, noted that St. Edward, as well as other kings, had been chosen in parliament. Further, because historians make so much of the fact that contract theory dropped out of sight, it is worth noting that the coronation oath, much commented upon in the Convention debates, had long been associated with the laws of the Confessor. And in the eyes of many these laws stood as concrete proof of the contractual relationship between king and people. As the moderate theologian Samuel Masters wrote in defense of the Revolution, there was no need to search the records of English history for a definitive description of the contract between ruler and ruled. For

when at a coronation we see a king presented to the people, and their consent solemnly asked and given, what can we reasonably infer from thence, but that anciently kings were advanced to their thrones by the

[78] See, for example, Goldie, "The Roots of True Whiggism," *History of Political Thought* (1980), 209–10; Goldie, "The Revolution of 1689 and the Structure of Political Argument," pp. 486–7; H. T. Dickinson, *Liberty and Property* (New York, 1977), chapter 2; J. P. Kenyon, "The Revolution of 1688: Resistance and Contract," in *Historical Perspectives. Studies in English Thought and Society in Honour of J. H. Plumb*, ed. Neil McKendrick (London, 1974), pp. 43–70; Ashcraft, *Revolutionary Politics and Locke's Two Treatises of Government*, pp. 208–9, 210–11, 560–2, 572; Nenner, "Constitutional Uncertainties and the Declaration of Rights," in *After the Reformation: Essays in Honor of J. H. Hexter*, ed. Barbara Malament (Philadelphia, 1980), pp. 291–308; John Morrill, "The Sensible Revolution of 1688," in *The Nature of the English Revolution*, ed. Morrill (London, 1993); Tony Claydon, *William III and the Godly Revolution* (Cambridge, 1995). See also Tim Harris, "The People, the Law, and the Constitution in Scotland and England," *Journal of British Studies* 38 (1999), 28–58.

consent and agreement of the people. When we hear the king solemnly promise and swear to maintain to the people their rights and liberties, to conserve the laws and cause them to be observed; must we not conclude from thence, that there are rights and liberties reserved to the people, that the will of the king is limited by the law of the realm, and that he is bound to protect us all in our rights, as we are bound to obey in all his laws?[79]

The inextricable connection between the coronation oath, contract, and the Confessor's laws was also made by the author of *The Late King James's Letter to his Privy-Counsellors.* Here the author argued that the king's promise in his coronation oath to obey the Confessor's laws, if broken, warranted deposition.[80] Other polemicists writing in defense of the Glorious Revolution connected the coronation oath, St. Edward's laws, the contract between ruler and ruled, and the right of resistance, suggesting that whenever the coronation oath was mentioned in the debates of 1689, it probably carried explicitly radical connotations.[81] This speculation is made the more plausible by the ways in which the Confessor's laws had been deployed throughout the seventeenth century: in any number of scholarly as well as polemical writings, the cult of Holy Edward's laws had been linked to a contractual view of government. It would have taken no great stretch of imagination to make such a connection in 1689. Indeed, members of the Convention would have made it automatically.[82]

Especially relevant is the fact that parliamentary speakers sometimes discussed the vital issues of original contract and abdication in

[79] Masters, "The Case of Allegiance in our present Circumstances consider'd," in *A Collection of State Tracts, Published on Occasion of the late Revolution in 1688, and during the Reign of William III* (London, 1705), vol. I, pp. 321–2, 325, and *passim.*

[80] "The Late King James's Letter to his Privy-Counsellors. With just Reflections upon it, and upon the pretended Prince of Wales," in *ibid.*, vol. II, p. 235.

[81] See, for example, "The Oaths of Allegiance and Supremacy no Badges of Slavery," in *State Tracts*, vol. II, pp. 492–9; [Daniel Defoe?], "The Letter which was sent to the Author of the Doctrine of Passive Obedience and Jure Divino disprov'd etc.," in *A Collection of State Tracts*, vol. I, pp. 378 and *passim*; [Daniel Whitby], "Agreement betwixt the Present and the former Government," in *ibid.*, vol. I, pp. 413–14, 418–19; [Thomas Long], "A Resolution of Certain Queries concerning Submission to the present Government," in *ibid.*, vol. I, pp. 443–4 and *passim*; [White Kennett], "A Dialogue between Two Friends, a Jacobite and a Williamite," in *ibid.*, vol. II, pp. 288–9; "An Historical Account of some Things relating to the Nature of the English Government," in *ibid.*, vol. I, pp. 576, 578, 580, 581–2, 591–2; "Plain English: or an Inquiry concerning the Real and Pretended friends to the English Monarchy. With an appendix, concerning the Coronation-oath administered to King James the Second," in *ibid.*, vol. II, pp. 79–94.

[82] See Lois G. Schwoerer, "The Coronation of William and Mary, April 11, 1689," in *The Revolution of 1688–1689. Changing Perspectives*, ed. Lois G. Schwoerer (Cambridge, 1992), pp. 120–3.

language distinctly reminiscent of Chapter 17, the "Office of a King." Importantly, they included leading whig lawyers and politicians intimately connected with the drafting of the Declaration of Rights, its passage through the two houses, and its transformation into the Bill of Rights. A prime example is Sir George Treby, who boasted impeccable radical credentials. Counsel and friend of John Starkey, who was prosecuted in 1677 for attempting to publish Bacon's *Historical Discourse of the Uniformity of Government*, Treby played a role in the exclusion controversy and had close ties to Shaftesbury as well as to Petyt. He had also defended the London charter in Charles II's *quo warranto* proceedings against the city. At the Revolution, he chaired the committee that drafted the first two versions of the Declaration of Rights, which he helped steer through the House of Commons. Speaking in the crucial debates of January 28, when the lower house voted almost unamimously that James II, by violating the original contract, had "abdicated" the government, Treby pointed to the dispensing power as key to James's misgovernment. Because the king's use of that prerogative amounted "to a manifest declaration of his will, no longer to retain the exercise of his kingly office, thus limited, thus restrained, then in common sense, as well as legal acceptations, he has sufficiently declared his renouncing of the very office." Moreover, Treby continued, it mattered not whether James II had left the kingdom voluntarily or involuntarily. What mattered was that he had gone away when he found that he could not do what he desired because of "the duty of his office and relation, and the obligation of the original contract, as likewise his own coronation oath." Putting it differently, Treby found that the king "has renounced his legal government, and fallen from it." Then came the verdict. He that would not exercise that power according to law "is no longer king." It was as if James had said: "'My administration must be a contradiction to my office.'" "Is it not," Treby asked rhetorically, 'a renouncing'?"[83]

This view was echoed by Sir John Somers, whose exclusionist tracts were discussed earlier. Chairman of the second committee concerned with the Declaration of Rights and the man responsible

---

[83] Cobbett, *Parliamentary History of England*, vol. v, pp. 81–2. *Miscellaneous State Papers*, ed. Philip Yorke, earl of Hardwicke (London, 1778), vol. II, pp. 409–10. Lois G. Schwoerer, ed., "A Journal of the Convention at Westminster begun the 22 of January 1688/89," in *Bulletin of the Institute of Historical Research* 49 (1976), 259. Treby's role is discussed in Schwoerer, *The Declaration of Rights, passim*.

for linking the Bill of Rights to the proffer of the crown to William and Mary, he charged that James II had subverted the government and broken the original contract between king and people. Somers concluded that in so doing the king had "renounced to be a king according to the law, such a king as he swore to be at his coronation." It mattered not whether the renunciation had taken place by an express declaration or by acting contrary to the royal office. Either way, James II's subjects no longer owed him allegiance.[84] Others reiterated the point. Justice Gilbert Dolben noted that "a prince ceasing to administer justice . . . ceases to be a king."[85] Sir Robert Howard, active in the opposition to Charles II and James II, told the Convention that for a king to break the law was "to quit the part of a king, to act that of a tyrant." He cited as his authorities Bracton and Fortescue, presumably their own versions of the "Office of a King."[86] Sir Richard Temple, also closely associated with the drafting of the Declaration of Rights, and Justice Henry Pollexfen and Serjeant John Maynard, both experienced and respected lawyers, expressed similar sentiments. Indeed, on April 28 Maynard responded to the charge that subjects could not depose the king with these words: "The question is not whether we can depose the king, but whether the king has deposed himself. It is no new project; our government is mixed – not monarchical and tyrannous, but had its beginning from the people. There may be such a transgression in the prince, that the people will be no more governed by him." Moreover, Maynard continued, when James II broke the contract between king and parliament, he made himself "*civiliter mortuus*." Finally, the esteemed common lawyer John Holt, one time recorder of London and soon to be chief justice of King's Bench, expressed the sense of the argument in these terms: "the doing an act inconsistent with the being and end of a thing, or that shall not answer the end of that thing, but quite the contrary, that shall be construed as an *Abdication* and formal *Renunciation* of that thing."[87]

Admittedly, St. Edward's name is rarely mentioned in the debates,

---

84 Cobbett, *Parliamentary History*, vol. v, p. 70. For Somers's career see Schwoerer, *Declaration of Rights, passim*; Landon, *The Triumph of the Lawyers*, p. 231 and *passim*.

85 *Miscellaneous State Papers*, ed. Hardwicke, vol. ii, p. 401.

86 *Ibid.*, p. 402.

87 *Ibid.*, pp. 401–2, 407–8. Cobbett, *Parliamentary History*, vol. v, pp. 36, 40, 45, 87–8. *A Collection of Parliamentary Debates in England from the Year MDCLXVIII to the Present Time*, ed. J. Torbuck (London, 1741), vol. ii, pp. 184–256 *passim*. Landon, *The Triumph of the Lawyers*, p. 231.

and, as earlier noted, the idea that a king who governed tyrannically thereby renounced the throne could be supported by sources other than English law and history. Further, the idea could be read in a conservative fashion: if James II had deposed himself, then there had been no resistance. Still, the notion had patent and prominent ties to St. Edward, and by this time contemporaries well understood its most radical implications. After all, Charles II's government had publicly banned and burned Milton's *Defence of the English People*, in which the "Office of a King" justified resistance and regicide. And then there was the decree of Oxford University, which explicitly condemned the main tenet in Chapter 17, associating it with Milton, Buchanan, Rutherford, and the author of *Vindiciae contra Tyrannos*. Further, *A Defence of the English People* appeared in an English translation in 1692 and was apparently circulating long before. Finally, Milton's *Tenure of Kings and Magistrates*, in which the theme of the "Office" constituted a principal argument, was reprinted early in January of 1689, when the Convention was meeting, as well as in 1691. In the wake of the Glorious Revolution, few could claim to vouch Chapter 17 or its premise innocently and casually. For all kinds of people, that particular part of the Confessor's laws must have implied, at the very least, a right of resistance and deposition. We can surely assume, then, that when the major tenet associated with the "Office of a King" found voice in the Convention, it signaled a radicalism in that body. Given its intimate and immediate association with regicide, it could hardly mean anything else.

Yet one particular action of the Convention seemingly places the Confessor's influence in doubt. When in March of 1689 it rewrote the coronation oath, mention of his laws, long at the center of the king's promise to his people, was deliberately omitted. According to the preamble of the new oath, because it had previously "been framed in doubtful words and expressions, with relation to ancient laws and constitutions at this time unknown," henceforth kings must swear to govern by "the statutes in parliament agreed on, and the laws and customs of the same."[88] Schwoerer suggests the new oath excised St. Edward's laws because contemporaries objected to the phrase describing English laws as "granted" to the people "by the ancient kings." After all, such words could be interpreted as

---

[88] St. 1 Wm. and Mary, c. 6. *The Eighteenth Century Constitution, 1688–1815*, ed. E. N. Williams (Cambridge, 1960), pp. 36–9. This discussion follows Schwoerer, "The Coronation of William and Mary, April 11, 1689," pp. 120–30.

acknowledging that the king constituted the human source of law and therefore placed both statutes and common law within his possession. The new oath therefore reinforced the Bill of Rights' condemnation of the dispensing and suspending powers. It also confirmed the political nation's insistence upon a sovereignty vested in that holy trinity of law makers, King, Lords, and Commons.[89]

Whatever the case, the excision of St. Edward's laws from the new coronation oath by no means spelled the end of their ideological influence, nor that of the *Modus* and *Mirror*. On the contrary, these medieval sources reached their zenith in the political literature written to justify the Revolution, demonstrating beyond a shadow of a doubt their thoroughly radical pedigree. Now whigs of various stripes found them absolutely essential to proving the validity of their key arguments – the right of parliament and/or the people to depose and replace unlawful rulers, the validity of the new oaths of supremacy and allegiance, and the legality of the Convention that met without royal summons. In an effort to put the best possible face on the whig cause, writer after writer made plentiful use of all three, and especially St. Edward's "Office of a King," the most radical source of all. Moreover, St. Edward's laws, the *Modus*, and the *Mirror* suited the purposes not only of writers on the fringe but also those who are generally considered to be within the mainstream. Undoubtedly, the polemicists who penned these works evoked the canon in the well-founded expectation that their readers would know exactly what was being discussed and would find the arguments solid and convincing.

Prominent among the spokesmen for the offical whig position, as opposed to the extremist fringe, were Atwood and Tyrrell, as well as the eminent whig jurist Sir Robert Atkyns.[90] Both Atwood and

---

[89] Greenberg, "The Confessor's Laws and the Radical Face of the Ancient Constitution," *English Historical Review* 104 (1989), 634–35. David Ogg, *England in the Reigns of James II and William III* (London, 1969), pp. 35–9; *The Eighteenth Century Constitution*, ed. Williams, pp. 3–4. Pocock and Schwoerer suggest that the omission of the Confessor's laws from the new coronation oath perhaps signaled the declining polemical power of history. Pocock, *Ancient Constitution and the Feudal Law*, pp. 239–41. Schwoerer, "The Coronation of William and Mary, April 11, 1689," pp. 123–4.

[90] Ashcraft designated Atwood, Tyrrell, and Bishop Burnet as the spokesmen for the mainstream, or orthodox, whig position, as distinguished from the radical fringe that Locke represented. They were also, in Ashcraft's view, William III's official spokesmen. *Revolutionary Politics*, pp. 586–9 and n. 257. *Cf.* Goldie, "The Revolution of 1689 and the Structure of Political Argument," p. 508; Pocock, *Virtue, Commerce, and History*, p. 226; and Pocock, *Ancient Constitution*, p. 360. Both Goldie and Pocock find Atwood and Tyrrell more radical than Ashcraft suggests.

Tyrrell had demonstrated their understanding of the polemical potential of St. Edward's laws, the *Modus*, and the *Mirror* during the exclusion controversy, and both now vouched the same sources and rehearsed many of the same arguments to justify the Revolution settlement. In particular, the medieval sources proved the existence of an elective kingship, a contractual relationship between king and subject, and the community's right, through its sovereign parliament, to resist a ruler who broke the contract and replace him with another king more to their liking. Moreover, Atwood and Tyrrell judged that these features of English government dated from Saxon times and remained alive in their own day and age.

For Atwood, St. Edward's laws and the *Mirror* proved incontrovertibly that the nation might lawfully transfer allegiance from James II to the new king and queen. This conclusion followed from the stipulations of the original contract between ruler and ruled, which could be found in Chapter 17 of the Saxon laws. As Atwood expressed it, "that noble transcript of the original contract, the Confessor's laws . . . shows that if a king does not answer the true end for which he was chosen, he loses the name, or ceases to be a king."[91] Citing it at length, Atwood linked Chapter 17 to the coronation oath, at the center of which stood "the laws, customs, and freedoms granted (the clergy and people) by the most glorious and holy King Edward." The *Mirror*, too, spoke pointedly to this issue. Referring to its description of the election of the first Saxon king, Atwood noted that the work charged the king's companions with making sure that he did "right and justice." And "what right and justice was in the last result, the Confessor's laws explain when they show, that he may lose the name of king." In order that the king did indeed govern justly, St. Edward's sword *Curtana* was carried before him at his coronation, "a known emblem and remembrancer" of his office.[92]

Atwood firmly believed that the original contract expressed in Chapter 17 of St. Edward's laws had never been undone by conquest. Noting that there were two kinds of submission which a people might make to a ruler – simple and conditional – he concluded that the latter characterized the relationship between William I and the English nation. This was surely the meaning of William's coronation

[91] Atwood, *Fundamental Constitution of the English Government* (London, 1690), p. 73.

[92] *Ibid.*, pp. iv, 28–30, 31–6, 39, 72–3.

oath, which was essentially the same as that taken by his Saxon predecessors. In fact, "Every election of a king truly so called, is an evidence of a compact; . . . ancient authors tell us, that W. I. was elected king, nay they are express that he was received upon a mutual contract, and that . . . he made a league with the people, which comes to the same thing . . . That the people made a league with him." Lest the nature of William's contract be left in doubt, Atwood concluded: "And if the compact were not sufficiently expressed at the first, at least it was made so by his several confirmations of the Confessor's laws, which he received with that very clause, which shows in what case he would cease to be the king of England."[93] For Atwood, then, St. Edward's laws and their confirmations, which he identified with the common law itself, combined with the coronation oath to produce a mutual compact that lasted through the centuries. In his words, "The Confessor's laws received by William I and continued downwards as the noblest transcript of the common law, shows that the kings of England were to be elected, and the end for which they are chosen by the people."[94]

Just as the usual medieval sources proved the existence of an original contract, so did they provide evidence that parliament, including the Commons, existed in pre-conquest England. Such, Atwood continued, was surely the message of the *Modus*, which also suggested a mechanism by which disputes among the different parts of parliament could be resolved. Referring to the council of twenty-five, Atwood described how this body, if it could not agree, might be steadily reduced to a single person, who had the power to make a determination. Although the king and his council could, if they chose, amend the decision, they must do so "in full parliament, and with the consent of the parliament, and not out of parliament."[95] As for the relative power of the three parts of parliament, the medieval sources had invested the lower house "with supreme judicature," including the right to judge the king.[96]

Finally, Atwood, like many supporters of William and Mary, found St. Edward's laws, the *Modus*, and the *Mirror* useful in sorting out a critical issue now confronting the political nation – the right of the

---

[93] *Ibid.*, p. 73.
[94] *Ibid.*, Appendix, p. 34.
[95] *Ibid.*, pp. 69–70. He gave this part of the *Modus* in full in the Appendix, pp. 28–9.
[96] *Ibid.*, pp. 34–5.

Convention to assemble without a royal summons. In answer to those who opposed its proceedings on this ground, Atwood pointed to St. Edward's laws, "received by W. I. and continued downwards by the coronation oaths required to this very day." The oath mandated that "the general Folcmot ought to be annually, without any formal summons." Such had been the case since the Saxon government "was transplanted hither out of Germany." Atwood also referred to the statute of the Long Parliament, which in 1641 did away with the necessity of writs of summons, as well as to the Convention of 1660, which was summoned by the keepers of the liberties of England, not by the king's writs.[97]

Tyrrell argued similarly in his massive *Bibliotheca Politica*, published in the years from 1692 through 1694. The work, which Julian Franklin describes as "perhaps the most comprehensive of the whig apologics," is in the form of thirteen dialogues between Mr. Meanwell, a civil lawyer who supported James II, and Mr. Freeman, a gentleman who backed the Revolution settlement and who represented Tyrrell's own views.[98] Citing St. Edward's laws and the *Mirror*, Freeman noted that the power of kings was limited by an original compact entered into at the first institution of government. The purpose of the contract, he continued, was "the maintenance and observation of . . . fundamental rights . . ." Moreover, the original contract reserved to the people and their representative assemblies "a power of deposing their kings for tyranny and misgovernment." So much appeared from Chapter 17 of St. Edward's laws, which he quoted, adding that Bracton too had written that "He is not a king (that is, ceases to be a king) when his will, and not the law governs."[99] The *Mirror* told the same story when it pointed to the king's companions who, because a man could not be both judge and jury, must hear and determine in parliaments complaints against the king and his family.[100]

---

[97] *Ibid.*, pp. 103–4, Appendix, p. 33. Atwood repeated these arguments in *The Superiority and Direct Dominion of the Imperial Crown of England over the Crown and Kingdom of Scotland* (London, 1704), pp. 231–569 *passim*. See also "A Lord's Speech Without Doors, To the Lords upon the present Condition of the Government," in *A Tenth Collection of Papers Relating to the Present Juncture of Affairs in England* (London, 1689), p. 26.

[98] Franklin, *John Locke and the Theory of Sovereignty: Mixed Monarchy and the Right of Resistance in the Political Thought of the English Revolution* (Cambridge, 1978), p. 109.

[99] Tyrrell, *Bibliotheca Politica: or, An Enquiry into the Antient Constitution of the English Government . . . Wherein all the Chief Arguments both for and against the Late Revolution, are Impartially Represented and Consider'd* (1692–94), p. 705. See also p. 697.

[100] *Ibid.*, pp. 354, 356, 364.

Tyrrell linked the Confessor's laws directly to an elective kingship and a right of deposition when he had Freeman conclude that

the king was at first elected, and created for this end, that he may do justice to all men; . . . So that it is plain, that if he either command or permit these willful injuries generally, or all over his kingdom, he fails to defend it, according to K. Edward's laws, and if he thus fail to defend it, he thereupon loses or forfeits his very title or office of a king, since he cannot keep or hold his crown, or royal dignity, for without justice it cannot subsist, and this by the original contract; since upon whatever terms the first king of this race, took the crown, upon the same terms all his posterity who succeed either by election or right of blood, by virtue of that first compact are to hold it under the like penalty of a forfeiture, in case of a willful neglect, or violation of his duty.[101]

Mr. Meanwell, clearly equal to the task, responded with all the standard tory arguments. In particular, he insisted that even if William the Conqueror and his successors had confirmed St. Edward's laws, the telling historical event was the conquest of England. Whatever rights the people had enjoyed ended at the point of the sword. Indeed, Meanwell continued, the confirmations themselves attested to this judgment, for what were they if not royal concessions to the people, who prayed for relief from burdensome policies? Far from proving that the kingship was elective, the confirmations of the Confessor's laws throughout the centuries demonstrated that the king ruled by the sword, which meant in turn that his will was law.[102]

Not content to make this telling point, Meanwell, in an unusual move, proceeded to attack Chapter 17 of St. Edward's laws. Labeling it a forgery, he charged that the monks must have tampered with it, since the chapter mistakenly described Pope John instead of Pope Zachary as deciding against King Childeric. In response, Freeman admitted that that particular part of Chapter 17 which described the deposition of the French king might have been added later by monks. But, he insisted, the law of the "Office of a King" was genuine.[103]

Freeman repeatedly challenged Meanwell's charge that the Normans conquered English law and therefore governed not by law but by the sword. In fact, William I, "whom you call the conqueror

---

[101] *Ibid.*, p. 712. See also p. 706.
[102] *Ibid.*, pp. 320–1, 355–6, 358–9.
[103] *Ibid.*, pp. 707, 709–10.

. . . had no more power of making laws without the consent of his great council, than any of his successors . . . As for the liberties of Englishmen, as embodied in the Great Charters, these were won by force of arms, they being merely confirmations of their ancient rights and liberties."[104] The role of St. Edward's laws stood at the heart of Tyrrell's argument. "Though it is true," he wrote,

that William the Conqueror re-granted and confirmed them: Yet was it no more than what he was obliged in conscience and honor to perform and observe, since he was admitted to the crown by the general consent of the clergy, nobility, and people, and at his coronation (as well as afterward) swore to observe the laws of King Edward; And by the way, tho' these laws are called the laws of King Edward, yet William of Malmesbury long since observed, That they were called his laws, *Non quas tulit, sed quas observaverit*, that is, he had only collected them into one body, and ratified them with the assent of his Great Council.

Moreover, William and his successors were forced on more than one occasion to observe these laws, "for fear of a general insurrection of the people." When subsequent monarchs violated those liberties, they, too, were compelled to restore them "by the Magna Chartas of Hen. I, K. Stephen, K. Hen. II, K. John, and K. Hen. the III. And those oppressions contrary thereunto, are branded by all historians as notorious perjuries, and wrongs to the subjects."[105]

Central to Tyrrell's case was the argument that St. Edward's laws had been made, codified, and confirmed in parliaments, or councils, that included the Commons. To Meanwell's charge that the king's absolute power remained intact because neither Englishmen nor commoners attended those assemblies, Freeman responded that ancient historians wrote of kings legislating with the "common council of the whole kingdom," which surely included the Commons. Indeed, the Confessor was himself elected by a full parliament while still in his mother's womb. This in and of itself gave the lie to those who, like Meanwell and his hero Brady, dated the arrival of the commons in 1265. Certainly "the king could not alter K. Edward's laws without their consent."[106] The *Modus*, too, proved as much, though Freeman granted, following Selden, that it dated

---

[104] *Ibid.*, p. 321. See also pp. 757–60.

[105] *Ibid.*, pp. 321–2, 362–3.

[106] *Ibid.*, pp. 391–2. See also pp. 368–9. For further proof of the antiquity of the Commons, Freeman pointed to the history of all neighboring countries with Gothic constitutions. These nations had always been governed by assemblies of estates that included representatives from the community. *Ibid.*, pp. 544, 757–60.

not from Saxon times but from the reign of Edward III.[107] In sum, the Confessor's laws and their subsequent confirmations exemplified "the fundamental constitution of the government," which "neither K. William the I. nor his successors, ever changed."[108]

Sir Robert Atkyns likewise relied on the trinity of medieval sources in two tracts published at the Revolution. A noted jurist, he had been removed from the court of Common Pleas during the exclusion crisis, and he would soon become lord chief baron of the Exchequer and speaker of the House of Lords. He was also one of the lawyers consulted by the Lords when the issue of contract was being debated at the Revolution. It is, then, of some interest that he turned to the *Mirror*, the *Modus*, and St. Edward's laws to prove that when James II dispensed with statutes, he broke the pact between king and people. Putting forward an ancient constitutionalist view of English law, he wrote that "We ourselves . . . chose our common law, and consented to the most ancient acts of parliament, for we lived in our ancestors one thousand years ago, and those ancestors are still living in us."[109] Most of the common law, he continued, flowed from Saxon times, when full parliaments governed alongside kings. Indeed, St. Edward's laws themselves were chosen by the common council for the common utility of the realm.[110] The dispensing power, however, constituted no part of the common law, for it dated only from the reign of Henry III and was therefore within legal memory, which Atkyns defined as the coronation date of Richard I. Further, its very existence carried a grave threat to the government as established in the original pact between king and people, since it allowed kings to call parliaments infrequently. Here Atkyns cited the *Mirror* as his authority for the ancient practice of frequent parliaments.[111]

Other supporters of the Revolution settlement also vouched St. Edward's laws in making their case. One was Thomas Comber, dean of Durham and chaplain in ordinary to William and Mary. His *Letter*

---

[107] *Ibid.*, Appendix, pp. 71–2. See also pp. 335, 353, 378.

[108] *Ibid.*, p. 541 and *passim*.

[109] Atkyns, "An Enquiry into the Power of Dispensing with Penal Statutes (London, 1689)," in Howell, *A Complete Collection of State Trials*, vol. XI, pp. 1204–5, 1218–19, 1221, 1234–5. This work appeared in two editions in 1689.

[110] *Ibid.*, pp. 1225, 1226. See also Atkyns, *The Power, Jurisdiction, and Privileges of Parliament and the Antiquity of the House of Commons Asserted* (London, 1689), pp. 25, 59.

[111] *Ibid.*, pp. 17, 51, 59. See also Atkyns, "An Enquiry into the Power of Dispensing with Penal Statutes," pp. 1225, 1226.

to a Bishop concerning the Present Settlement was so popular that it appeared in four editions in 1689. In Comber's opinion, by dispensing with the law James II had broken the hinges of government, in which sovereignty was divided between the three coordinate estates of King, Lords, and Commons. In so doing, he ceased to be king. Citing both the Confessor's and Bracton's "Office," the author admonished nonjurors to heed the laws of St. Edward, "since by them a king by misgovernment, *verum nomen perdit*, forfeits the title of king as well as the power."[112] Samuel Masters echoed these views. Identifying the coronation oath with a tacit compact, symbolic of the original agreement, Masters noted that the "Office of a King" in the Confessor's laws obliged subjects to depose a king who ruled despotically.[113] Edmund Hickeringill, bishop of Colchester, described whig supporters of the Revolution as championing the right of parliament, in particular, the three coordinate estates of King, Lords, and Commons, by vouching the *Mirror* and the *Modus*. The *Modus*, for example, assured that the king could not dissolve parliament while petitions pended, while the *Mirror* mandated that the king call bi-annual parliaments. Taken together, these two sources proved to the whigs that parliament possessed the right to settle the government as it pleased.[114] A spate of anonymous tracts adhered to the same line.[115]

Writers on the fringes of whig political thought also found historical sources relevant to their argumentation. One was the reverend Samuel Johnson, who boasted impressive radical credentials. Chaplain to William Lord Russell who, like Sidney died for participation in the Rye House plot, Johnson provoked much hostility at the courts of both Charles II and James II. Indeed, he was twice convicted of seditious libel and suffered a public whipping

---

[112] Comber, "A Letter to a Bishop concerning the Present Settlement, and the New Oaths (1689)," in *Somers Tracts*, ed. Walter Scott (London, 1813), vol. IX, pp. 374–8, 385–7. Goldie identifies Comber as the likely author of this tract. "The Revolution of 1689 and the Structure of Political Argument," p. 508.

[113] Masters, "The Case of Allegiance in our present Circumstances consider'd," p. 325 and *passim*.

[114] "The History of the Whigs," in *The Works of the Reverend Mr. Edmund Hickeringill, Late Rector of All Saints Colchester* (London, 1709), pp. 146–57 *passim*.

[115] See, for example, "The Supremacy Debated: Or, The Authority of Parliaments (formerly owned by Romish Clergy) the Supremest Power," in *A Collection of State Tracts*, vol. I, pp. 231–3; "An Inquiry; or a Discourse between a Yeoman of Kent, and a Knight of the Shire, upon the Prorogation of the Parliament to the second of May, 1693," in *ibid.*, vol. II, pp. 330–1, 333–7.

for his troubles.[116] Johnson justified resistance to James II by referring pointedly to St. Edward's "Office," which he linked to the similar passage in Fortescue. Here Englishmen could learn about the relationship between king and subject, which, Johnson explained, was grounded in the king's proper fulfilling of his public office. Both Chapter 17 of St. Edward's laws and Chapter 13 of Fortescue's treatise made it clear that, because kings received their power from their people, they must govern according to the law their subjects made. Johnson closed this section of his work with words evocative of a contractarian view of government: "Corollary, A Bargain's a Bargain."[117]

He also vouched medieval sources in one of the best-selling tracts to appear in the aftermath of the Glorious Revolution. In *An Argument Proving, That the Abrogation of King James by the People of England . . . was according to the Constitution*, published in five editions by 1693, Johnson wrote that the people dethroned James II for misgovernment, an action prescribed by the constitution. Proof that they indeed possessed such a right could be found in the St. Edward's "Office of a King" as well as in Bracton and Fortescue.[118] The *Mirror* also suited Johnson's purposes, for when it described the election of the first king, it reflected "the original contract . . . which contract is still continued in the coronation oath, and the oath of allegiance." Tellingly, subjects swore their oath only after the king took the coronation oath. The *Mirror* also demonstrated that parliament, as the representative of the people who constituted the fountain of civil power, must meet annually.[119]

The radical Huguenot theologian Peter Allix found the *Mirror* and Chapter 17 of the Confessor's laws equally to his liking. Writing to justify the Revolution in general and the taking of the oath of allegiance to the new king and queen in particular, Allix linked the "Office" to the fundamental laws of the kingdom. Proof that the government of England originated in a contract between king and people could be found in the coronation oath, where all kings, including William I, swore to observe the laws of the Confessor. The

---

[116] Zook, *Radical Whigs and Conspiratorial Politics in Late Stuart England*, pp. 56–62, 143–4. Ashcraft, *Revolutionary Politics*, pp. 594–5.

[117] Johnson, *A Compleat Collection of Papers, in Twelve Parts . . . A Fifth Collection* (London, 1688), pp. 16–17.

[118] *Ibid.*, pp. 16–17, 54–7.

[119] *Ibid.*, pp. 51–4, 58–60.

meaning of the oath could be ascertained by that part of St. Edward's laws stating "that if the king do not govern according to the end for which he was constituted, he shall not so much as retain the name of a king, but forfeits his title. So that we see how the fundamental laws of the nation do decide the point." Allix reinforced his position with the similar passage from Fortescue which "agrees very well with the description of the duty of a king, which we find in the 17th chapter of St Edward."[120] In another tract he linked St. Edward's laws, the coronation oath, and subsequent confirmations, all of which proved the community's right to depose an errant king. Much to the point was the story of *Curtana*, which "signified that the king . . . was liable to the same penalties" as private persons "whenever he transgressed the laws of the state, whereof he was the keeper and defender." Such was also the implication of Magna Carta, itself a confirmation of St. Edward's laws. Allix even included a lengthy appendix in which he gave Magna Carta in two English versions, one from the Latin and the other from French. Originally, he suggested, an English edition had existed, which the king ordered sent to every county.[121]

Robert Ferguson supported the Revolution settlement on precisely the same grounds. Ferguson enjoyed a rather spectacular career. In addition to serving Shaftesbury as chaplain and propagandist, he joined the Rye House conspiracy, marched with Monmouth at Sedgemoor, and accompanied William of Orange's army to Torbay. Described by Zook as "a prolific and ingenuous propagandist," he produced numerous tracts during the exclusion crisis and at the Glorious Revolution.[122] Many of his works relied heavily on Saxon history in general and the *Mirror* and St. Edward's laws in particular to prove the essential elements of his theorizing: the people's right since time immemorial to elect kings and depose those who violated the terms of their contract as specified in the coronation oath. This was the line he took in *A Brief Justification*, which, according to

---

[120] Allix, "An Examination of the Scruples of Those who refuse to take the Oath of Allegiance," in *A Collection of State Tracts*, vol. I, pp. 302–3, 312–13. According to Ashcraft, when Allix argued that James II had forfeited the crown even before he left England, he used a Lockean argument. *Revolutionary Politics*, p. 594.

[121] Allix, "Reflections upon the Opinions of some Modern Divines, concerning the Nature of Government in general, and that of England in particular," in *A Collection of State Tracts*, vol. I, pp. 505–6, 519ff.

[122] Zook, *Radical Whigs and Conspiratorial Politics in Late Stuart England*, p. 94. See also pp. 93–109.

Franklin, enjoyed a "quasi-official . . . status" and was published with William III's approval.[123] Writing in the same vein was Daniel Defoe, whose radical credentials were also impeccable. In his *Reflections upon the Late Great Revolution* he quoted the *Mirror* to demonstrate that the Saxons elected the first king "and made him swear, that he would be obedient to suffer right, as well as his people should be." Upon these terms the first rulers took office, and so, too, did their successors when they swore to govern by St. Edward's laws. The king who went back on his word, as James II had done by dispensing with parliamentary statutes, "actually unkings himself by it."[124]

Still other radical tracts deployed medieval history to prove the right of the people to call errant rulers to account and to resume complete political authority once they had done so. The author of *Four Questions Debated* found the *Mirror of Justices* particularly helpful in this regard, since it demonstrated that "the ancient constitution of the government of England" exalted the power of the people and their representatives in parliament. Such was the *Mirror*'s purpose in mandating bi-annual meetings in King Alfred's day. Had the late king of England adhered to this rule, he could not have subverted the government through the use of the dispensing power.[125]

Two other tracts designated as radical by Ashcraft and M. M. Goldsmith used the trinity of medieval sources to the same effect. In *Political Aphorisms*, which Ashcraft calls a Lockean piece, the author recited English history from the Saxons onward to prove the community's right to alter the succession. William the Conqueror himself "made a league or compact" in which he promised at his coronation to govern by St. Edward's laws, and William Rufus, Henry I, King Stephen, Richard I, and King John did likewise. Only then did the archbishops offer them the crown. The drumbeat of royal promises meant that obedience was conditional upon the king ruling well, which the author defined by reference to Chapter 17 of

---

[123] Ferguson, *A Brief Justification of the Prince of Orange's Descent into England, And of the Kingdoms Late Recourse to War* (London, 1689). See also *A Brief Vindication of the Parliamentary Proceedings against the Late King James* (n.p., 1689); *A Representation of the Threatening Dangers, Impending over Protestants in Great Britain, Before the Coming of His Highness the Prince of Orange* (n.p., 1689). Franklin, *John Locke and the Theory of Sovereignty*, p. 99.

[124] Defoe, "Reflections upon the Late Great Revolution Written by a Lay-Hand in the Country for the Satisfaction of some Neighbors," in *A Collection of State Tracts*, vol. 1, pp. 254–9, 264. Defoe also cited Bracton's "Office."

[125] "Four Questions Debated," in *ibid.*, vol. 1, pp. 163–5.

St. Edward's laws: "'Tis not the title of a king, but the power (which is the laws) that is invested in him, which makes the differences betwixt him and other men."[126] Another tract, perhaps written by the same author, cited the same sources, including Chapter 17 of St. Edward's laws, to the same effect.[127]

Then there was George Lawson's *Politica Sacra et Civilis*. Described by Richard Baxter as the divine from whom "I have learned more than from . . . any other," Lawson wrote the tract in the late 1650s, though it did not appear until 1660. At the Glorious Revolution it was considered sufficiently relevant to merit republication on two occasions, first in *A Collection of State Tracts 1660–1689*, and second in *A Collection of Tracts . . . During the Reign of William III*. I have chosen to discuss the work here because of Lawson's strong influence on John Locke, who, as Franklin has noted, took many of his political ideas from the *Politica Sacra et Civilis*.[128] In particular, Locke borrowed Lawson's claim that "the community and people of England gave both the king and parliament their being." In Lawson's view, the community made of England a mixed monarchy in which neither King, Lords, nor Commons could act alone. This meant that when Charles I left Westminster in 1642, both his authority and parliament ceased to exist, and power reverted to the people. Equally valuable was Lawson's description of legislative sovereignty: although King, Lords, and Commons made law jointly, in practice the lower house, because it represented the people, trumped the other two estates. Witness the *quas vulgus elegerit* clause of the coronation oath, which bound the king in his politic capacity to pass whatever legislation the Commons sent him. Witness, too, Charles I's *Answer to the XIX Propositions*. Indeed, according to Lawson, England was a monarchy "only in respect of the executive part" and then only "in the intervals

---

[126] "Political Aphorisms: Or, the True Maxims of Government display'd. By way of Challenge to Dr. William Sherlocke, and Ten other New Dissenters," in *ibid.*, vol. I, pp. 389–402. Ashcraft and Goldsmith, "Locke, Revolution Principles, and the Formation of Whig Ideology," *Historical Journal* 26 (1983), 773–800.

[127] "The Letter which was sent to the Author of the doctrine of Passive Obedience and Jure Divino disprov'd, etc. Answered and Refuted," in *A Collection of State Tracts*, vol. I, pp. 378–80. Ashcraft and Goldsmith, "Locke, Revolutionary Principles, and the Formation of Whig Ideology," 773–800.

[128] Franklin, *John Locke and the Theory of Sovereignty. Biographical Dictionary of British Radicals in the Seventeenth Century*, ed. Richard Greaves and Robert Zaller (Brighton 1984), vol. II, pp. 177–8. A. H. McLean, "George Lawson and John Locke," *Cambridge Historical Journal* 9 (1947), 69–77.

of parliament." Even the royal prerogative proceeded from "the Commons of England."[129]

However, unlike Locke, Lawson used the English past and its revered sources to prove his radical claims. He turned, for example, to the *Mirror*, which described how the Saxons elected their rulers. And he also found there proof of the superiority of people over kings, for the *Mirror* explained that when the people placed a ruler on the throne, they "made a bridle to keep him in, and put it upon him." In addition, Lawson appreciated the value of "King Edward the Confessor's *Modus*," to which "the Conqueror bound himself." Though he knew that some doubted its authenticity, both Coke and Spelman had recommended it. Within its pages Englishmen could learn why the Commons took precedence over the other two estates in the making of law. Finally, both the *Mirror* and the *Modus* convinced Lawson that the way the English government worked now was the way it worked in Saxon times. In his words, "I will suppose the government of England to have been by king and parliament before the conquest, and to have continued so till our days: and whosoever will not grant this, must either be very ignorant, or very partial."[130] The ease with which Lawson blended radical argumentation with an appeal to the English past demonstrates once and for all how well the two lines of argumentation meshed.

At the very end of the century came Sir William Temple's *An Introduction to the History of England*, a version of the past which rehearsed all the ancient constitutionalist story lines contained in medieval and early modern literature. First published in 1695 in London, the work reappeared in 1699, and in 1708 it was printed in France and Holland. Temple was a man of practical politics, wise in the ways of the continent as well as the British Isles. He had served Charles II as envoy at the Congress of Aix-la-Chappelle, ambassador at the Hague, and master of the rolls in Ireland. Sitting in both the Irish and English parliaments, he was actively courted by William at the Glorious Revolution, and, after turning down an offer to serve as secretary of state, continued in his position as master of the rolls. His history of medieval England can be read as a panegyric to William I and, by association to that more recent arrival from the continent, William III. Both entered England by the assent of nobles and

---

[129] Lawson, *Politica Sacra et Civilis* (London, 1660), pp. 92, 95, 97. *Ibid.* (London, 1689), pp. 66ff, 88–105 *passim*, 150–66 *passim*, 175. Pages are sometimes misnumbered.
[130] *Ibid.*, pp. 80–105 *passim*, 147–76 *passim*, 371–87 *passim*, 401.

people. Both governed not as conquerors but according to the laws of Edward the Confessor. And both gave their second homeland cause to rejoice at their coming.

England, Temple began, had been conquered on several occasions, by the Romans, the Saxons, and the Danes. The stain of the last conquest faded with the return from Normandy of Edward the Confessor, whom the nobles and people chose as king. Edward, who placed many Normans in high positions in government, had tapped William duke of Normandy as his successor, notwithstanding the rightful claim of his brother Edgar the Atheling. This historical association alone would have been welcome to the prince of Orange.[131] But there was more. Temple went on to describe the Conqueror, and by analogy William III, as among the best things that had ever happened to England and the English. His story began with Harold taking the throne notwithstanding his own and the Confessor's promise to William. But when the duke sailed to make good his claim, he came in peace. Camping out in Sussex in full expectation that the English would elect him king, William I ordered his troops to treat the people well. Even when Harold sent spies into the Norman camp, William treated them "courteously" and showed them around his base. Upon their return to Harold, the spies told the king "that the Normans looked rather like an army of priests than of soldiers, by their great silence and order . . . as well as their faces being shaved." Indeed, so peaceful was William that, in Temple's telling, he offered to settle matters by individual combat with Harold rather than risk the shedding of blood. Upon Harold's refusal, the English prepared for battle by singing and feasting, while the Normans passed the night "in much devotion."[132]

Continuing his story, Temple admitted that after Hastings William behaved with great cruelty on his way to London, at least until he arrived in Kent. There the Kentish men forced him to grant them their ancient laws and customs, a promise that he repeated when he came to London. After consulting with the people, William was acknowledged by the citizens and clergy as their "just and lawful king." Thus received "with open gates and open arms," he "claimed the crown . . . by testament of Edward the Confessor, without any

[131] Temple, *An Introduction to the History of England* (London, 1695), pp. 2, 74–9 *passim*, 81, 83–4, 100. See also Colin Kidd, *British Identities Before Nationalism. Ethnicity and Nationhood in the Atlantic World, 1600–1800* (Cambridge, 1999), pp. 78, 90, 196, 244–5.

[132] Temple, *An Introduction to the History of England*, pp. 112–15.

mention of conquest." He proceeded to take the old Saxon coronation oath and to confirm St. Edward's laws, that is, "the common
law of the kingdom." Now king by concurrence of the Londoners,
William issued two resolutions throughout the kingdom. The first
demanded that "all inhabitants . . . with universal consent, submit
. . . to his government," the second that the English barons who had
taken up arms against him lose their lands to his Norman
followers.[133] As for the majority of the English, who had peacefully
submitted and "liked their new king," they should continue to enjoy
their property rights as before. Indeed, "justice was administered
[as] equally to the English men" who suffered injuries at the hands
of the Normans as to the Normans who had suffered at the hands of
the Saxons. As proof of this contention Temple cited a particularly
"memorable instance . . . upon the record," namely, the case of the
earl of Sharnborn and the earl of Warren. The case ended with the
Saxon put back into possession and "the Norman cast and condemned to the costs of the suit."[134]

Temple knew that some writers "make the Conqueror to have
broken or changed the laws of England, and introduced those of
Normandy," for example, knights service, baronage, scutage, and
trial by jury. Historical records, however, indicated that the "feudal
laws were all brought into Europe by the ancient Goths," from whom
the Saxons and Normans inherited them. The same held for
assemblies of estates.[135] True, Temple continued, William did introduce some Norman customs. Thus, he caused the Saxon laws,
including those published by the Confessor in Latin, to be translated
into French. He also ordered pleas of the crown held in that language
and in addition introduced new terms, new forms of pleading,
process, and new names for offices and courts. More important still,
the Normans, "who were a witty but contentious people," replaced
the simplicity of Saxon folks with complicated litigation. In the end,
however, these changes never amounted to much, since "all was
frustrated by the overall balance of numbers in the nation, in the
proportion of strangers." Moreover, the English refused to give up
their language because they recognized that "their laws and liberties"
might soon follow. And so it came to pass that the Normans began
speaking English, instead of the other way around.[136]

[133] *Ibid.*, pp. 124–7, 133–9, 154, 160–1, 163–4.   [134] *Ibid.*, pp. 164–5.
[135] *Ibid.*, pp. 154–63 *passim*, 171.   [136] *Ibid.*, pp. 240–1.

Indeed, in all important matters Saxon ways and institutions continued to flourish. Not that William always had smooth sailing. On the contrary, from time to time rebellious lords rose up and forced the new king "to change the whole frame of the English government, to abolish their ancient laws and customs and introduce those of Normandy, by which he thought he should be more absolute, and too powerful to be again disturbed." But "the whole people, sad and aggrieved . . . with universal agreement" petitioned William to renew his coronation oath, "and by the soul of St. Edward, from whom he had the crown and kingdom, under whose laws they were born and bred," to continue to govern as the Confessor's heir. After meeting with Lanfranc William relented, and "by a public and open charter" renewed the ancient laws "and thereby purchased the hearts, as well as the satisfaction of his English subjects . . ."[137] Indeed, in the fourth year of his reign William I "summoned out of every county, the nobles, wise men, and such as were learned in their own law; that he might from them learn what were their ancient laws and customs." Thus did he confirm and conserve "the laws of St. Edward . . . throughout the whole kingdom."[138]

What, then, did England lose at the conquest? First, the brave men who fell at Hastings and during subsequent revolts. Second, the line of ancient Saxon kings. And third, much of "the old plainess and simplicity of the Saxon times and customs of life, who were generally a people of good meaning, plain dealing, contented with their own, little coveting or imitating their neighbors, and living frugally upon the product of their own fruitful soil." But, continued Temple, "what we preserved is remarkable in three particulars not usual upon great conquests." The first "our name"; the second the Saxon language, though now augmented with Latin and French. Most of all, "we preserved our form of government, our laws and institutions, which have been so much celebrated by ancient writers, and . . . so obstinately defended by our ancestors." Here Temple found Fortescue apt, for he had described how these laws and institutions "have been preserved through five several governments in this island: of Normans, Danes, Saxons, Romans, and Britains." This meant that England had endured longer than any other nation known in history. Then, with a clear nod to William III, he told how in 1066 the Saxons gained "both dominion and power abroad, and also in dignity and

[137] *Ibid.*, pp. 187–209 *passim*, 230–3, 235–6, 239–40.   [138] *Ibid.*, pp. 297–8.

state at home, by the accession of so much territory upon the Continent." And, if this were not enough, "by the conquest we gained more learning, more civility, more refinement of language, customs, and manners" as well as more territory and glory abroad – "all these happy circumstances of this famous conquest."[139]

That Temple should tell such stories and draw such conclusions comes as no surprise. He simply followed in the footsteps of medieval chroniclers and early modern historians and antiquaries who had made the ancient constitutionalist story line common coin. Small wonder, then, that Englishmen of various political leanings found in it a persuasive ideology with which to justify the Glorious Revolution. By the end of the seventeenth century this familiar narrative and the trio of medieval sources on which it rested had demonstrated once and for all the plasticity of appeals to the past. Arguing from St. Edward's laws, the *Modus*, and the *Mirror*, rebels and dissidents vindicated the propositions they held nearest and dearest: an elective kingship, a contractual relationship between ruler and ruled, and the right of the community or its representatives to resist and depose a tyrannical ruler. Admittedly there were more radical views around, especially those Lockean arguments that postulated a devolution of power to the people. Nevertheless, St. Edward's laws, the *Modus*, and the *Mirror* sanctioned deposing one king and replacing him with another. That these tasks were to be undertaken by parliament instead of the people scarcely qualifies radical ancient constitutionalist thought as moderate, much less conservative. Mainstream whig ideology was as radical as it needed to be, and to label it otherwise, even in comparison to more extremist views, is to miss the meanings that it held for many English people. Theirs was indeed an appeal to history, but not one that tied them to a static and immutable constitution. On the contrary, the venerated medieval sources to which they looked allowed them to appeal to the past even as they molded the future. In closing, we can hardly do better than to quote an influential seventeenth-century writer who lay well outside the bounds of ancient constitutionalist thought. This was Thomas Hobbes, who in *The Elements of Law* proclaimed that "of our conceptions of the past, we make a future."[140]

---

[139] *Ibid.*, pp. 308–17 *passim*.
[140] Hobbes, *The Elements of the Law Natural and Politic*, ed. M. M. Goldsmith, 2nd edn. (London, 1969), p. 15.

Bibliography

MANUSCRIPT SOURCES

Bodleian Library, Oxford University
  Ashmolean MSS 1141. v. 7362
  Tanner MSS 88
British Library, London
  Additional MSS 41, 48
  Cotton MSS Cleo. A. xvi
  Cotton MSS Cleo. E. vi
  Cotton MSS Faustina. E. v
  Cotton MSS Titus. Λ. xxvii
  Cotton MSS Vit. E. v
  Harleian MSS 5520, 6018
  Landsdowne MSS 213, 646
  Stowe MSS 302, 366, 423
Cambridge University Library
  Dd. xi. 73

PRINTED PRIMARY SOURCES

Acherley, Roger. *The Britannic Constitution: or, The Fundamental Form of Government in Britain*. 2nd. edn. London, 1759.

An Account of Mr. Parkinson's Expulsion from the University of Oxford in the late Times. London, 1689.

Ailred of Rievaulx. *Vita Sancti Edward: Regis et Confessoris*. In Sir Roger Twysden, *Historiae Anglicanae Scriptores* x. London, 1652. Repr. in *Patrologia Latina*, ed. S. P. Migne, vol. cxcv. Paris, 1844.

Allix, Peter. "An Examination of the Scruples of Those who Refuse to Take the Oath of Allegiance." In *A Collection of State Tracts, Published on Occasion of the late Revolution in 1688, and during the Reign of William III*. 3 vols. London 1705–7, vol. i.

"Reflections upon the Opinions of some Modern Divines, concerning the Nature of Government in general, and that of England, in particular." In *A Collection of State Tracts, Published on Occasion of the late*

Revolution in 1688, and during the Reign of William III. 3 vols. London, 1705–7, vol. I.

The Anglo-Saxon Chronicle. Trans. G. N. Garmonsway. London, 1954.

Annales Prioratus de Dunstaplia. Ed. Henry R. Luard, vol. III. London, 1866.

An Answer to Mis-led Doctor Fearne. London, 1644.

The Aphorisms of the Kingdome. London, 1642.

An Argument or, Debate in Law: of the Great Question concerning the Militia; As it is now settled by Ordinance of both Houses of Parliament. London, 1642.

The Arraignment of Co-ordinate Power. London, 1683.

Assheton, William. *The Royal Apology: or, An Answer to the Rebel's Plea.* London, 1684.

Atkyns, Sir Robert. "An Enquiry into the Power of Dispensing with Penal Statutes." In T. B. Howell, *A Complete Collection of State Trials and Proceedings for High Treason and Other Crimes and Misdemeanors from the Earliest Period to the Year 1783.* 34 vols. London, 1809–28, vol. XI.

The Power, Jurisdiction, and Privileges of Parliament and the Antiquity of the House of Commons Asserted. London, 1689.

Atwood, William. *Considerations Touching that Question, Whether the Prelates have Right to sit among the Lords, and Vote with Them in Parliament in Capital Cases.* London, 1682.

Fundamental Constitution of the English Government. London, 1690.

Jani Anglorum Facies Nova: Or, Several Monuments of Antiquity touching the Great Councils of the Kingdom. London, 1680.

Jus Anglorum ab Antiquo: or, a Confutation of an Important Libel against the Government by King, Lords, and Commons. London, 1681.

Reflections upon Antidotum Britannicum, and Mr. Hunt's late Book and Post-script. London, 1682.

The Superiority and Direct Dominion of the Imperial Crown of England over the Crown and Kingdom of Scotland. London, 1704.

Aylmer, John. *An Harborowe for faithfull and Trewe Subjects, agynst the late Blowne Blaste, concerning the Government of Women.* Strassburg, 1559.

Ayscu, Edward. *A Historie Contayning the Warres, Treaties, Marriages, and other occurents betweene England and Scotland, from King William the Conqueror, untill the happy Union of them both in our gratious King James.* London, 1606.

Axtell, James, ed. *The Educational Writings of John Locke.* Cambridge, 1968.

Bacon, Sir Francis. "The Case of the Post-Nati in Scotland." In *The Works of Francis Bacon,* ed. James K. Spedding, Robert L. Ellis, and Douglas D. Heath. 7 vols., vol. VII. London, 1879.

Bacon, Nathaniel. *An Historical Discourse of the Uniformity of the Government of England.* 2 vols. in one. London, 1647–51.

Bagshaw, Edward (the Elder). *The Rights of the Crown of England as it is established by Law.* London, 1660.

Baker, J. H., ed. *Reports of Sir John Spelman.* Selden Society XCIV, London, 1978, vol II.

Baker, J. H. and S. F. C. Milsom, eds. *Sources of English Legal History: Private Law to 1750*. London, 1986.

Ball, William. "The Power of Kings Discussed" [1649]. In *Somers Tracts*, ed. Walter Scott. 13 vols., vol. v. London, 1811.

Barlow, Frank, ed. *Life of King Edward who rests at Westminster, attributed to a monk of Saint-Bertin*. 2nd. edn. Oxford, 1992.

Bate, George. *The Regal Apology. Or, The Declaration of the Commons, Feb. 11, 1647. Canvassed*. n.p., 1647.

Baxter, Richard. *A Holy Commonwealth, or, Political Aphorisms opening the True Principles of Government*. London, 1659.

   Reliquiae Baxterianae: or, Mr. Richard Baxter's Narrative of the most Memorable Passages of his Life and Times. Ed. Matthew Sylvester. London, 1696.

Bellamy, John. *A Iustification of the City Remonstrance and its Vindication*. London, 1646.

Bolton, Edmund. *Hypercritica or a Rule of Judgment for Writing or Reading our History's*. Oxford, 1722.

The Booke Called, The Mirrour of Justices: Made by Andrew Horne. With the Book, called, The Diversity of Courts, And Their Jurisdictions. Both translated out of the old French into the English Tongue. London, 1646.

Bowles, Edmund. "Plain English to our Wilful Bearers with Normanism (1647)." In *Harleian Miscellany*. 9 vols., vol. ix. London, 1810.

Bracton, Henry. *On the Laws and Customs of England*. Ed. Samuel E. Thorne. 4 vols. Cambridge, Mass., 1968.

Brady, Dr. Robert. *A Complete History of England ... (Wherein it is Shewed the Original of Our English Laws)*. London, 1685, vol. i.

   A Full and Clear Answer to a Book written by Mr. Petyt. London, 1681.

   An Introduction to the Old English History, Comprehended in Three several Tracts ... Together with An Appendix ... And a Glossary, expounding many Words used frequently in our Antient Records, Laws and Historians. London, 1684.

Bramhall, John. "The Serpent-Salve: Or, a Remedy for the Biting of an Aspe (1643)." In *The Works of the Most Reverent Father in God, John Bramhall*. Dublin, 1676.

A Breviat Chronycle, contayning all the Kynges, from Brute to thys Day. London, 1560.

Bridge, William. *The Wounded Conscience Cured*. London, 1643.

A Brief and Exact Treatise Declaring How the Sheriffs, and all other the great Officers of this Kingdome have been Anciently elected and chosen. London, 1642.

A Brief Vindication of the Parliamentary Proceedings against the Late King James. n.p., 1689.

Britannia, Passionately and Historically, Remembering her Majesty and Happiness in former Ages. London, 1644.

Brooke, Sir Robert. *La Graunde Abridgement*. London, 1573.

Brydall, John. *Jura Coronae. His Majesties Royal Rights and Prerogatives Asserted*. London, 1680.

Burroughes, Jeremiah. *A briefe Answer to doctor Fernes Book*. London, n.d.

The Glorious Name of God, The Lord of Hosts. Opened in two Sermons, at Michaels Cornhill, London. London, 1643.

Calendar of State Papers, Domestic Series. 81 vols. London, 1603–1714.

Camden, William. *Britain, Or a Chorographicall Description of the Most Flourishing Kingddomes, England, Scotland, and Ireland.* Trans. Philemon Holland. London, 1610, 1637.

Britannia. London, 1607.

Remains concerning Britain. Ed. R. D. Dunn. Toronto, 1984.

The Case of Allegiance in our Present Circumstances consider'd. London, 1689.

"Certain select Observations on the several Offices, and Officers, in the Militia of England; with the Power of the Parliament to raise the same, as they shall judge expedient; etc. Collected and found among the Papers of the late Mr. John Pym (1641)." In *Harleian Miscellany.* 9 vols., vol. VI. London, 1810.

Charles I. *His Majesties Answer to the XIX. Propositions of Both Houses of Parliament.* London, 1642.

"His Majesty's Reasons against the Pretended Jurisdiction of His Sacred Majesty of the High Court of Justice." In *Eikon Basilike. The Portraiture of His Sacred Majesty in His Solitudes and Sufferings,* ed. Philip A. Knachel. Ithaca, The Folger Shakespeare Library, 1966.

The Chronicle of Adam of Usk. A. D. 1377–1421. Ed. Chris Given-Wilson. Oxford, 1997.

The Chronicle of Jhon [sic] Hardyng. London, 1543.

Chronicles of the Revolution 1397–1399. The Reign of Richard II. Ed. Chris Given-Wilson. Manchester, 1993.

Churchill, Winston. *Divi Britannici: Being a Remark Upon the Lives of Kings of this Isle.* London, 1675.

Cleveland, John. *Majestas Intemerata. Or, The Immortality of the King.* n.p., 1649.

Cobbett, William. *Parliamentary History of England: From the Norman Conquest in 1066 to . . . 1803.* 44 vols. London, 1806–38.

Coke, Sir Edward. *The First Part of the Institutes of the Laws of England, or, A Commentary on Littleton.* Ed. Charles Butler. 19th. edn. London, 1832.

Fourth Part of the Institutes of the Laws of England. Ed. Francis Hargreave. London, 1797.

La Huict^{me} Part des Reports de Sr Edward Coke. London, 1611.

La Neuf^{me} Part des Reports de Sr. Edw. Coke. London, 1613.

The Reports of Sir Edward Coke. London, 1826.

Les Reports de Edward Coke. London, 1600–1615, 1656, 1659. 13 vols.

The Second Part of the Institutes of the Laws of England. 4th. edn. London, 1671.

The Third Part of the Institutes of the Laws of England. Ed. Francis Hargreave. London, 1797.

Le Tierce Part Des Reportes del Edward Coke. London, 1602.

Coke, Roger. *Justice Vindicated from the False Fucus put upon it, By Thomas White Gent. Mr. Thomas Hobbs, and Hugh Grotius. As also Elements of Power and*

Subjection; Wherein is demonstrated the Cause of all Humane, Christian, and Legal Society. London, 1660.

A Collection of Papers Relating to the Present Juncture of Affairs in England. n.p., 1688–9.

A Collection of the Rights and Priviledges of Parliament. London, 1642.

A Collection of State Tracts, Publish'd on Occasion of the late Revolution in 1688, and during the Reign of William III. 3 vols. London, 1705–7.

Comber, Thomas. "A Letter to a Bishop concerning the Present Settlement, and the New Oaths (1689)." In *Somers Tracts. A Collection of Scarce and Valuable Tracts, on the most Interesting and Entertaining Subjects,* ed. Walter Scott. 13 vols., vol. IX. London, 1813.

Commons Debates, 1621. Ed. Wallace Notestein, Hartley Simpson, and Frances Relf. New Haven, 1935.

Commons Debates, 1628. Ed. Robert C. Johnson and Maija Jansson Cole, assisted by Mary Frear Keeler and William B. Bidwell. 7 vols. New Haven, 1977–83.

A Complete Collection of State Trials and Proceedings for High Treason and Other Crimes and Misdemeanors from the Earliest Period to the Year 1783. Ed. T. B. Howell. 34 vols. London, 1809–28.

Cooke, Edward. *Argumentum Antinormanicum: Or An Argument Proving From Ancient Histories and Records, That William, duke of Normandy, Made no Absolute Conquest of England by the Sword; in the sense of our Modern Writers.* London, 1682.

    Magna Carta, made in the ninth year of King Henry the Third . . . faithfully translated for the benefit of those that do not understand the Latin. London, 1680.

    A Seasonable Treatise: wherein it is proved that King William, commonly called the Conqueror did not get the Imperial Crown of England by Sword. London, 1689.

[Cornwallis, Sir William]. *The Miraculous and Happie Union of England and Scotland.* London, 1604.

Cowell, John. *The Interpreter; or "Booke Containing the Signification of Words."* Cambridge, 1607.

    Institutes of the Lawes of England . . . Translated into English According to Act of Parliament for the Benefit of All. London, 1651.

    Institutiones Juris Anglicani. Cambridge, 1605.

Craig, Sir Thomas. *The Right of Succession to the Kingdom of England.* London, 1703.

    Scotland's Sovereignty Asserted. Trans. George Ridpath. London, 1695.

    De Unione Regnorum Britanniae Tractatus. Ed. C. Sanford Terry. Edinburgh, 1909.

Crompton, Richard. *The Mansion of Magnanimitie.* [London], 1599.

The Crowland Abbey Chronicle by Ingulph. Ed. Walter Gray de Birch. Wisbech, 1883.

Dallison, Charles. *The Royalists Defence: Vindicating the King's Proceedings in the late Warre Made against Him.* n.p., 1648.

Daniel, Samuel. *The Collection of the History of England.* London, 1618, 1626, 1634, 1650.

The First Part of the Historie of England. London, 1612, 1613.

Davies, Sir John. *Discovery of the True Causes why Ireland was never Entirely Subdued.* London, 1612, reprinted Shannon, 1969.

A Perfect Abridgment of the Eleaven Bookes of Reports of the Reverend, and Learned Kt. Sr. Edw. Cook. London, 1651.

Le Primer Report des Cases & Matters en Ley resolves & adiuges en les Courts del Roy en Ireland. Dublin, 1615.

The question concerning Impositions. London, 1656.

A Declaration Against Prince Rupert. London, 1643.

The Definition of a Parliament Or, A Glosse upon the Times. London, 1643.

[Defoe, Daniel?] "The Letter which was sent to the Author of the Doctrine of Passive Obedience and Jure Divino disprov'd etc." In *A Collection of State Tracts, Published on Occasion of the late Revolution in 1688, and during the Reign of William III.* 3 vols. London, 1705–7, vol. I.

"Reflections upon the Late Great Revolution Written by a Lay-Hand in the Country for the Satisfaction of some Neighbors." In *A Collection of State Tracts, Published on Occasion of the late Revolution in 1688, and during the Reign of King William III.* 3 vols. London, 1705–7, vol. I.

de Diceto, Ralph. *The Historical Works of Master Ralph de Diceto, Dean of London.* Ed. William Stubbs. 2 vols. London, 1876.

Digges, Sir Dudley. *An Answer to a Printed Book, Intituled, Observations upon some of His Majesties Late Answers and Expresses.* Oxford, 1642.

A Review of the Observations upon some of his Majesties late Answers and Expresses. Oxford, 1643.

The Unlawfulnesse of Subjects taking up Armes Against Their Soveraigne. n.p., 1644.

A Discourse Upon Questions in Debate between the King and Parliament. n.p., [1643].

Disney, William. *Nil dictum quod non dictum prius, or, the Case of the Government of England Established by Law.* London, 1681.

The Doctrine of the Church of England, Established by Parliament against Disobedience and wilful Rebellion. London, 1642.

Dodderidge, John. "A Breif Consideracion of the Unyon." In *The Jacobean Union. Six Tracts of 1604,* ed. Bruce Galloway and Brian Levack. Edinburgh, 1985.

The English Lawyer. London, 1631, repr. 1980.

Domesday-Book, sen Liber Censualis Willelmi Primi Regis Angliae. London, 1783.

Doughty, John. *The Kings Cause Rationally, briefly, and plainly debated, as it stands Defacto.* n.p., 1644.

Drayton, Michael. *Poly-Olybion,* vol. IV. Oxford, 1933.

Dugdale, William. *Monasticon Anglicanum.* London, 1654.

Origines Juridicales; or, Historical Memorials of the English Laws. London, 1666, 1680.

The Dutie of a King in His royall Office . . . Written by the High and Mightie Prince James. London, 1642.

The Ecclesiastical History of Orderic Vitalis. Ed. Marjorie Chibnall. 6 vols. Oxford, 1969–80, vol. II.

Egerton, Sir Thomas, Lord Ellesmere. *A Discourse upon the Exposicion and Understandinge of Statutes.* Ed. Samuel E. Thorne. San Marino, Ca., 1942.

English Historical Documents, 1042–1189. Ed. Douglas, David C. and George W. Greenaway. 2nd. edn. 3 vols., vol. I. London, 1981.

"Examples for Kings; or rules for Princes to govern by . . . (1642)." In *Harleian Miscellany.* 9 vols., vol. II. London, 1809.

Fabyan, Robert. *The New Chronicles of England and France.* London, 1516, repr. 1811.

Ferguson, Robert. *A Brief Justification of the Prince of Orange's Descent into England, And of the Kingdoms Late Recourse to War.* London, 1689.

Ferne, Henry. *A Reply unto Severall Treatises Pleading for the Armes now taken up by Subjects in the pretended defence of Religion and Liberty.* Oxford, 1643.

  The Resolving of Conscience. Cambridge, 1642.

Filmer, Sir Robert. "The Free-Holders Grand Inquest." In *Patriarcha and Other Writings*, ed. Johann P. Sommerville. Cambridge, 1991.

  Patriarcha and Other Writings. Ed. Johann P. Sommerville. Cambridge, 1991.

Fitz Nigel, Richard. *Dialogus de Scaccario. The Course of the Exchequer.* Ed. Charles Johnson, F. E. L. Carter, and D. E. Greenway. Oxford, 1983.

Forset, Edward. *A Comparative Discourse of the Bodies Natural and Politique.* London, 1606.

Fortescue, Sir John. *On the Laws and Governance of England.* Ed. Shelley Lockwood. Cambridge, 1997.

Foster, Elizabeth Read, ed. *Proceedings in Parliament 1610.* 2 vols. New Haven, 1966.

"Four Questions Debated." In *A Collection of State Tracts, Published on Occasion of the late Revolution in 1688, and during the Reign of William III.* 3 vols. London, 1705–7, vol. I.

Foxe, Edward. *The true Dyfferences betwen y regall power and the Ecclesiastical power translated out of Latyn by Henry lord Stafforde.* London, 1548.

Foxe, John. *The First Volume of the Ecclesiasticall history contaynyng the Actes and Monumentes of thynges passed in every kynges tyme in this Realme.* London, 1570.

Froissart, Sir John. *The Chronicle of Froissart.* Trans. Sir John Bouchier Lord Berners. New York, 1967.

Fuller, Nicholas. *The Argument of Master Nicholas Fuller, in the Case of Thomas Lad and Richard Maunsell, his Clients.* London, 1607.

Fulman, William. *Rerum Anglicarum Scriptorum Veterum.* Oxford, 1684.

"Of the Fundamental Laws of the Politick Constitution (1643)." In *State Tracts. Being a Further Collection of Several Choice Treatises Relating to the Government. From the year 1660 to 1689.* London, 1689.

The Fundamental Laws and Liberties of England. London, 1653.

Gardiner, S. R. ed. *Parliamentary Debates in 1610*. Camden Society, vol. LXXXI. London, 1862.

Gee, *The Divine Right and Original of the Civill Magistrate from God*. London, 1658.

Gervase of Canterbury. *The Historical Works of Gervase of Canterbury. The Minor Works Comprising the Gesta Regum with its Continuation, the Actus Pontificum, and the Mappa Mundi*. Ed. William Stubbs. 2 vols., vol. II. London, 1880.

Gibson, Edmund. "Life of Sir Henry Spelman." In *Reliquiae Spelmanniae. The Posthumous Works of Sir Henry Spelman Kt. Relating to the Laws and Antiquities of England*. Oxford, 1698.

The Golden Legend or Lives of the Saints as Englished by William Caxton. London, 1900.

Goodman, Christopher. *How Superior Powers Oght to be Obeyd*. Geneva, 1558. New York, Facsimile Text Society, 1931.

Gordon, John. *The Union of Great Brittaine*. London, 1604.

Grafton, Richard. *A Chronicle at large and Meere History of the Affayres of Englande and Kinges of the Same, deduced from the Creation of the Worlde, unto the First Habitation of Thys Yslande*. [London], 1568.

The Grand Question concerning Taking up Armes against the King answered. n.p., 1643.

Grey, Anchitell, ed. *Debates in the House of Commons, from the year 1667 to the year 1694*. 10 vols. London, 1763, vol. II.

Hakewill, William. "The Antiquity of the Laws of this Island." In *A Collection of Curious Discourses*, ed. Thomas Hearne. 2 vols., vol. I. London, 1775.

The Libertie of the Subject: Against the Pretended Power of Impositions. Maintained by an Argument in Parliament An. 7. Jacobi Regis. London, 1641.

Modus tenendi Parliamentum: the Old Manner of holding Parliaments in England. Extracted out of our Ancient Records. London, 1641.

Hale, Sir Matthew. *The History of the Common Law in England*. Ed. Charles M. Gray. Chicago, 1971.

Hare, Edward. "England's proper and only Way to an Establishment in Honour, Peace and Happiness (1648)." In *Harleian Miscellany*. 9 vols., vol. VI. London, 1810.

St. Edward's Ghost. London, 1647.

Hayward, John. *An Answere to the First Part of a Certaine Conference, Concerning Succession, Published not long since under the name R. Dolman*. London, 1603.

The Lives of the III. Normans, Kings of England. London, 1613.

A Treatise of Union of the Two Realmes of England and Scotland. London, 1604.

Herbert, William. *Prophecie of Cadwallder*. London, 1604.

Herle, Charles. *An Answer to Dr. Ferne's Reply, Entitled Conscience Satisfied*. London, 1643.

A Fuller Answer to a Treatise Written by Doctor Ferne, Entituled The Resolving of Conscience upon this Question . . . London, 1642.

Heylyn, Peter. *Aerius redivivus, or, The History of the Presbyterians*. London, 1672.

A Little Description of the Great World. Augmented and Revised. London, 1625.

"The Rebel's Catechism (1643)." In *Harleian Miscellany.* 9 vols., vol. VII. London, 1811.

The Stumbling-block of Disobedience and Rebellion, Cunningly laid by Calvin in the Subject's Way, Discovered, Censured, and Removed. London, 1658.

Hickeringill, Edmund. "The History of the Whigs." In *The Works of the Reverend Mr. Edmund Hickeringill, Late Rector of All Saints Colchester.* London, 1709.

Higden, Ranulph. *Polychronicon Ranulphi Higden Monachi Cestrensis; Together with the English Translations of John Trevisa and of an unknown writer of the Fifteenth Century.* Ed. Joseph R. Lumby, vol. VI. London, 1879.

"An Historical Account of some Things relating to the Nature of the English Government." In *A Collection of State Tracts, Published on Occasion of the late Revolution in 1688, and during the Reign of William III.* 3 vols. London, 1705–7, vol. I.

Historical Manuscripts Commission, Salisbury Manuscripts, vol. XV. London, 1930.

Thirteenth Report, Appendix, Part I. The Manuscripts of . . . the Duke of Portland, preserved at Welbeck Abbey. London, 1891.

Hobbes, Thomas. *The Elements of the Law Natural and Politic.* Ed. M. M. Goldsmith. 2nd. edn. London, 1969.

Holinshed, Raphael. *Holinshed's Chronicles.* Ed. Henry Ellis. 6 vols. London, 1807–8.

Holinshed's Chronicles. London, 1577.

Hoveden, Roger. *Chronica.* Ed. William Stubbs. 4 vols. London, 1868–71.

Hunt, Thomas. *A Defence of the Charter, and Municipal Rights of the City of London.* London, n.d.

Huntingdon, Henry of. *Historia Anglorum. The History of the English People.* Ed. Diana Greenway. Oxford, 1996.

Hunton, Philip. "A Treatise of Monarchy (1643)" 1689 edn. in *Harleian Miscellany.* 9 vols., vol. VI. London, 1810.

A Vindication of the Treatise of Monarchy. London, 1644.

Husband, Edward. *An Exact Collection of all Remonstrances, Declarations . . . and other Remarkable Passages between the Kings Most Excellent Majesty, and His High Court of Parliament.* London, 1642.

Hyde, Edward earl of Clarendon. *A Brief Survey of the Dangerous and pernicious Errors to Church and State, In Mr. Hobbes's book, Entitled Leviathan.* Printed at the Theatre, 1676.

Ingulf of Croyland. The Chronicle of Croyland Abbey. Ed. Walter de Gray Birch. Wisbech, 1883.

"The History of Ingulf." In *The Church Historians of England,* ed. and trans. Joseph Stevenson. London, 1854.

Ingulf and the Historia Croylandensis. Ed. W. G. Searle. Cambridge, 1894.

Ingulf's Chronicle of the Abbey of Crowland with the Continuation by Peter of Blois. Trans. H. T. Riley. London, 1854.

"An Inquiry; or a Discourse between a Yeoman of Kent, and a Knight of the Shire, upon the Prorogation of the Parliament to the second of May, 1693." In *A Collection of State Tracts, Published on Occasion of the late Revolution in 1688, and during the Reign of William III*. 3 vols. London, 1705–7, vol. I.

An Introduction to a Breviary of the History of England. London, 1693.

The Ioiefull and Blessed Reuniting of the two mighty kingdomes. Oxford, 1604.

James I. "A speech, As It Was Delivered in the Upper House of Parliament to the Lords Spirituall and Temporall, and to the Knights, Citizens and Burgesses there assembled." In *King James VI and I. Political Writings*. Ed. Johann P. Sommerville. Cambridge, 1994.

"The Treu Law of Free Monarchies." In *King James VI and I. Political Writings*. Ed. Johann P. Sommerville. Cambridge, 1994.

Jenkins, David. "Lex Terrae; or, Laws of the Land." In *Somers Tracts*, ed. Walter Scott. 2nd. edn. 13 vols., vol. V. London, 1810.

Jewell, John. "The Defence of the Apologie of the Church of England, conteining an Answer to a certaine Booke lately set forth by M. Harding, and entituled, A Confutation of etc." In *The Works of John Jewell, Bishop of Salisbury*, ed. John Ayre, part VI. Cambridge, Parker Society, 1850.

Johnson, Samuel. *A Compleat Collection of Papers, in Twelve Parts . . . A Fifth Collection*. London, 1688.

Johnston, Nathaniel. *The Excellency of Monarchical Government*. London, 1686.

[Kennett, White]. "A Dialogue between Two Friends, a Jacobite and a Williamite." In *A Collection of State Tracts, Published on Occasion of the late Revolution in 1688, and during the Reign of William III*. 3 vols. London, 1705–7, vol. II.

Kenyon, J. P. ed. *The Stuart Constitution*. 2nd. edn. Cambridge, 1986.

Knighton, Henry. *Chronicon*. Ed. J. R. Lumby, vol. I. London, 1889.

Knyghton's Chronicle, 1337–1396. Ed. G. H. Martin. Oxford, 1995.

Knox, John. "The First Blast of the Trumpet Against the Monstrous Regiment of Women." In *Works of John Knox; Collected and Edited by David Laing*. 6 vols., vol. IV. New York, 1966.

Lambarde, William. *Archaionomia, sive de priscis anglorum legibus libri*. London, 1568.

Archeion or, A Discourse upon the High Court of Justice in England. Ed. Charles H. McIlwain, and Paul L. Ward. Cambridge, Mass., 1957.

Eirenarcha or the Office of Justices of the Peace [1581]. London, 1972.

A Perambulation of Kent: Containing the Description, Hystorie, and Customes of that Shire. London, 1576.

Lanquet, Thomas. *Cooper's Chronicle*. London, 1560.

"The Late King James's Letter to his Privy-Counsellors. With just Reflections upon it, and upon the pretended Prince of Wales." In *A Collection of State Tracts, Published on Occasion of the late Revolution in 1688, and during the Reign of William III*. 3 vols. London, 1705–7, vol. II.

The Laws of Edward the Confessor. Ed. Bruce R. O'Brien. Philadelphia, 1999.

Lawson, George. *Politica Sacra et Civilis*. London, 1660, 1689.

Leges Henrici Primi. Ed. L. J. Downer. Oxford, 1972.

Legg, J. Wickham, ed. *Three Coronation Orders*. Henry Bradshaw Society, vol. XIX, London, 1891.

"A Letter from a Parliament-Man to his Friend, Concerning the Proceedings of the House of Commons This last session, begun the 13th of October, 1675." In *State Tracts: Being a Collection of Several Treatises Relating to the Government. Privately Printed in the Reign of K. Charles II*, vol. II. London, 1689; republished two vols. in one, 1693.

A letter sent by F. A. touchying the proceedings in a private quarell and unkindnesse, betweene Arthur Hall, and Melchisedech Mallerie Gentlemen, to his very friende L. B. being in Italie. With an admonition to the Father of F. A. to him being a Burgesse of the Parliament, for his better behavior therein. n.p. 1579.

A Letter sent From A Private Gentleman To A Friend in London, In justification of his owne adhering to His Majestie in these times of Distraction. n.p., 1642.

"The Letter which was sent to the Author of the doctrine of Passive Obedience and Jure Divino disprov'd, etc. Answered and Refuted." In *A Collection of State Tracts, Published on Occasion of the late Revolution in 1688, and during the Reign of William III*. 3 vols., London, 1705–7, vol. I.

Lewis, John. *The History of Great-Britaine from the First Inhabitants Thereof*. London, 1729.

Liber Albus: the White Book of the City of London. Compiled A.D. 1419 by John Carpenter, Common Clerk, and Richard Whitington, Mayor. Ed. Henry Thomas Riley. London, 1861.

Liebermann, F. *Die Gesetze der Angelsachsen*. 2 vols., vol. I. Halle, 1903.

Lilburne, John. *The Just Man's Justification*. 2nd. edn. London, 1647.
　　The Legal and Fundamental Liberties. London, 1649.

Littleton, Thomas. *Tenures*. Ed. E. Wambaugh. Washington, D. C., 1903.

Le Livere de Reis de Brittanie e le Livere de Reis de Engleterre. Ed. John Glover. London, 1865.

[Long, Thomas]. "A Resolution of Certain Queries concerning Submission to the present Government." In *A Collection of State Tracts, Published on Occasion of the late Revolution in 1688, and during the Reign of William III*. 3 vols. London, 1705–7, vol. I.

"A Lord's Speech Without Doors, To the Lords upon the present Condition of the Government." In *A Tenth Collection of Papers Relating to the Present Juncture of Affairs in England*. London, 1689.

Ludlow, Edmund. *A Voyce from the Watch Tower*. Ed. Blair Worden. London, Camden Society, 1978.

Lydgate, John. *The Minor Poems of John Lydgate*. Ed. Henry N. McCracken. Early English Text Society, no. 192. London, 1934.

Malmesbury, William of. *Gesta Regum Anglorum, atque Historia Novella*. Ed. Thomas Duffus Hardy. 2 vols. London, 1840.
　　Historia Novella. Ed. K. R. Potter. London, 1995.

[Marsh, John.] *An Argument or, Debate in Law: of the Great Question concerning the*

Militia; As it is now settled by Ordinance of both the Houses of Parliament. London, 1642.

Marshall, Stephen. *A Copy of a Letter Written by Mr. Stephen Marshall.* London, 1643.

Martyn, William. *The Historie, and Lives, of the Kings of England; From William the Conqueror, unto the end of the Raigne of King Henrie the Eight.* London, 1615.

Masters, Samuel. "The Case of Allegiance in our present Circumstances consider'd." In *A Collection of State Tracts, Published on Occasion of the late Revolution in 1688, and during the Reign of William III.* 3 vols. London, 1705–7, vol. I.

"The Oaths of Allegiance and supremacy no Badges of Slavery." In *State Tracts: Being a Collection of Several Treatises relating to the Government.* London, 1689, vol. II. Republished two volumes in one, 1693.

The Maximes of Mixt Monarchy. London, 1643.

Maximes Unfolded. London, 1643.

Maxwell, John. *Sacro-sancta Regum Majestas: or, The Sacred and Royall Prerogative of Christian Kings.* Oxford, 1644.

Milton, John. *Complete Prose Works of John Milton.* 10 vols., vol. III, ed. Merritt Hughes; vol. IV, ed. Don. M. Wolfe. New Haven, 1966.

A Defence of the English People. n.p., 1692.

Eikonoklastes. London, 1649.

The Tenure of Kings and Magistrates. London, 1649.

Minsheu, John. *Ductoris in Linguas, The Guide into Tongues.* London, 1617, 1625.

The Mirror of Justices. Ed. William Joseph Whittaker. Selden Society, vol. VII. London, 1895.

Miscellaneous State Papers. Ed. Philip Yorke, earl of Hardwicke, vol. II. London, 1778.

Mundy, Anthony. *The Triumphes of a re-united Britania.* London, 1605.

Nalson, John. *The Common Interest of King and People.* London, 1677.

An Impartial Collection of the Great Affairs of State. London, 1682.

Nedham, Marchamont. *The Excellencie of a Free State.* London, 1767.

Neville, Henry. "Plato Redivivus, or, A Dialogue Concerning Government (c. 1681)." In *Two English Republican Tracts*, ed. Caroline Robbins. Cambridge, 1969.

A New Plea for the Parliament. London, 1643.

Nichols, John. *The Progresses, and Public Processions, of Queen Elizabeth ... to Which are subjoined some of the Early Progresses of King James.* London, 1705.

Nicholson, William. *The English Historical Library.* London, 1699.

Northleigh, John. *The Parallel; Or, The New Specious Association An Old Religious Covenant.* London, 1682.

Remarks Upon the most eminent of our Antimonarchical Authors and Their Writings. Westminster, 1699.

Noy, William. *The Principal Grounds and Maximes, with an Analysis; and A Dialogue and Treatise of the Laws of England.* Abingdon, 1821, repr. 1985.

Osbert of Clare. "La vie de s. Edouard le Confesseur par Osbert de Clare." Ed. Marc Bloch. *Analecta Bollandiana* 41 (1973).

[Overton, Richard]. *Vox Plebis.* London, 1646.

Paris, Matthew. *Chronica Majora.* Ed. H. R. Luard. 7 vols. London, 1872–1883.

La Estoire de Seint Aedward le rei. Ed. K. Y. Wallace. Anglo-Norman Text Society 41. London, 1983.

Historia Anglorum. Ed. Sir Frederic Madden. 3 vols. London, 1866–9.

Matthew Paris's English History. Ed. J. A. Giles. 2 vols. London, 1849.

Vitae Viginti Truum Abbatum S. Albani. In *Historia Major,* ed. William Wats. London, 1684.

Parker, Henry. *Jus Populi. Or, A Discourse Wherein clear Satisfaction is given, as well concerning the Right of Subjects, as the Right of Princes.* London, 1644.

Observations upon some of his Majesties late Answers and Expresses. London, 1642.

[Parkinson, James]. *An Account of Mr. Parkinson's Expulsion from the University of Oxford in the late Times.* London, 1689.

Parliamentary Texts of the Later Middle Ages. Ed. Nicholas Pronay and John Taylor. Oxford, 1980.

Parsons, Robert. *An Answere to the fifth part of reports of Sir Edward Coke.* n.p., 1606.

A Conference About the Next Succession to the Crowne of England. London, 1594.

Petyt, William. *The Antient Right of the Commons of England Asserted; or, A Discourse Proving by Records and the best Historians, that the Commons of England were ever an Essential part of Parliament.* London, 1680.

Miscellanea Parliamentaria: Containing Presidents 1. Of Freedom from Arrests 2. Of Censures. London, 1680.

Philipps, Fabian. *The Established Government of England, Vindicated from All Popular and Republican Principles and Mistakes: With a Respect to the Laws of God, Man, Nature and Nations.* London, 1687.

A Plea for the Pardoning Part of the Soveraignty of the Kings of England. London, 1682.

Tenenda non Tollenda. London, 1660.

A Pious and Learned speech Delivered in the High Court of Parliament, 1 Henry 4. by Thomas Mercks then Bishop of Carlisle. London, 1642.

"Plain English: or an Inquiry concerning the Real and Pretended friends to the English Monarchy. With an appendix, concerning the Coronation-oath administered to King James the Second." In *A Collection of State Tracts, Published on Occasion of the late Revolution in 1688, and during the Reign of William III.* 3 vols. London, 1705–7, vol. II.

Plowden, Edmund. *Commentaries or Reports.* London, 1816.

"Political Aphorisms: Or, the True Maxims of Government display'd. By way of Challenge to Dr. William Sherlocke, and Ten other New Dissenters." In *A Collection of State Tracts, Published on Occasion of the late Revolution in 1688.* 3 vols. London, 1705–7, vol. I.

The Political Works of James I. Ed. C. H. McIlwain. Cambridge, Ma., 1918.

Polydore's English History, vol. I. *Containing the First Eight Books, Comprising the Period Prior to the Norman Conquest.* Ed. Sir Henry Ellis. London, Camden Society, 1846.

Polydore Vergil. *Urbinatis Anglicae historiae libri uigintisex.* Book IX. Basle, 1546.

Ponet, John. *A Short Treatise of Politic Power* [1556]. Menston, Yorkshire, 1970.

The Priviledges and Practice of Parliaments in England. Collected out of the Common Lawes of the Land. Seene and allowed by the Learned in the Lawes. Commended to the High Court of Parliament now Assembled. London, 1628.

The Privilidges of Parliament: Or a Modest Answer to Three Questions. London, 1642.

Proceedings of the Short Parliament of 1640. Ed. Esther S. Cope and Willson H. Coates. Camden Society, 4th series, vol. XIX. London, 1977.

Prynne, William. *Brief Animadversions on, Amendments of, and Additional Explanatory Records to, the fourth Part of the Institutes of the Lawes of England.* London, 1669.

——— *The Fourth Part of the Soveraigne Power of Parliaments and Kingdomes.* 2nd. edn. London, 1643.

——— *An Humble Remonstrance Against Ship-money Lately imposed: Laying Open the Illegality, Injustice, Abuse, and Inconvenience thereof.* London, 1643.

——— "A short, legal, medicinal, useful, safe and easy prescription to recover our Kingdom, Church, and Nation." In *Harleian Miscellany.* 9 vols., vol. VIII. London, 1811.

——— *A Soveraign Antidote to Prevent, Appease, and Determine our unnaturall and destructive Civill Warres and Dissentions.* London, 1642.

——— *The Soveraigne Power of Parliaments and Kingdomes: Divided into Four Parts together with an Appendix.* London, 1643.

——— *The Soveraigne Power of Parliaments and Kingdomes, or, Second Part of the Treachery and Disloyalty of Papists to their Soveraignes.* 2nd. edn. enlarged London, 1643.

——— *The Third Part of a Seasonable, Legal, and Historical Vindication of the good old Fundamental Liberties, Franchises, Rights, Properties, Laws, Government of all English Freemen.* London, 1657.

——— *The Third Part of the Soveraigne Power of Parliaments and Kingdomes.* 2nd. edn. London, 1643.

——— *The Treachery and Disloyalty of Papists to their Soveraignes, in Doctrine and Practice. Together with The First Part of the Soveraigne Power of Parliaments and Kingdomes.* 2nd. edn. London, 1643.

The Public Confider. Oxford, 1643.

XI. Queries Propounded and Answered, Shewing Whether it bee Treason to bee for or against the King. London, 1642.

Rastall. John. *The Chronycles of Englande and of dyvers other realmes.* London, 1530.

A Representation of the Threatening Dangers, Impending over Protestants in Great Britain, Before the Coming of His Highness the Prince of Orange. n.p., 1689.

Roger of Wendover. *Flowers of History.* Trans. J. A. Giles. London, 1849.

Rolle, Sir Henry. *Un Abridgment des plusiers Cases et Resolutions del Commun Ley.* Ed. Matthew Hale. London, 1668.

Le Roman de Rou de Wace. Ed. A. J. Holden. Paris, vol. II, 1971.

Rutherford, Samuel. "Lex, Rex." In *The Presbyterian's Armoury.* Edinburgh, 1843.

Sadler, John. *Rights of the Kingdom and People.* London, 1649.

Saltern, George. *Of the Ancient Laws of Greate Britaine.* London, 1605.

Savile, Sir Henry. "Historical Collections." In *The Jacobean Union,* ed. Bruce Galloway and Brian Levack. Edinburgh, 1985.

Rerum Anglicarum Scriptores post Bedam praecipui. London, 1596.

Schwoerer, Lois G., ed. "A Journal of the Convention at Westminster begun the 22 of January 1688/89." *Bulletin of the Institute of Historical Research* 49 (1976).

A Second Remonstrance or Declaration of the Lords and Commons Assembled in Parliament Concerning the Commission of Array. London, 1643.

Selden, John. *Eadmeri . . . historiae novorum sive sui saeculi libri vi . . .* London, 1623.

The Historie of Tithes. London, 1618.

Jani Anglorum Facies Altera, rendered into English, with large Notes thereupon, by Redman Westcott, Gent. London, 1683.

"Notes on Fortescue." In Sir John Fortescue, *De Laudibus Legum Angliae,* trans. Robert Mulcaster. London, 1616, repr. 1672.

Titles of Honor. London, 1614, 1631.

A Sermon Preached in the Citie of London By a Lover of Truth. London, 1643.

Several Speeches Delivered At a Conference concerning the Power of Parliaments, to proceed against their Kings for Misgovernment. London, 1648.

Sheringham, Robert. *The Kings Supremacy Asserted.* London, 1660, 1682.

Sidney, Algernon. *Discourses Concerning Government.* London, 1698.

Snow, Vernon, ed. *Parliament in Elizabethan England: John Hooker's Order and Usage.* New Haven, 1977.

"Some short considerations relating to the settling of the government; humbly offered to the Lords and Commons of England." In *Somers Tracts,* ed. Walter Scott. 13 vols., vol. IV. London, 1809.

Some Special Arguments for the Scottish Subjects lawfull defence of their Religion and Liberty. n.p., 1642.

Somers, John. "A Brief History of the Succession, Collected out of the Records, and the most Authentick Historians." In *State Tracts: Being a Collection of Several Treatises Relating to the Government. Privately Printed in the Reign of K. Charles II,* vol. II. London, 1689, republished two vols. in one, 1693.

"A Just and Modest Vindication of the Proceedings of the two last Parliaments of King Charles the Second." In *State Tracts: Being a Collection of Several Treatises Relating to the Government. Privately Printed in the Reign of K. Charles II,* vol. II. London, 1689, republished two vols. in one, 1693.

La Somme appelle Mirroir Des Iustices vel Speculum Iusticiariorum, Factum per Andream Horne. London, 1642.

The Sovereignty of Kings: Or An absolute Answer and Confutation of the Groundless Vindication of Psalme 105.15. London, 1642.

Speed, John. *History of Great Britaine.* London, 1611.

Theater and History. London, 1611.

Spelman, Sir Henry. *Archaeologus. In Modum Glossarii ad rem antiquam posteriorem.* London, 1626.

The English Works of Sir Henry Spelman, Kt. Published in his Life-Time; Together with his Posthumous Works, Relating to the Laws and Antiquities of England; First Publish'd by the Present Lord Bishop of Lincoln, in the Year 1695. London, 1723.

"Of the Ancient Government of England." In *The English Works of Sir Henry Spelman, Kt. Published in his Life-Time; Together with his Posthumous Works, Relating to the Laws and Antiquities of England; First Publish'd by the Present Lord Bishop of Lincoln, in the Year 1695.* London, 1723.

"Of the Antiquity and Etymology of Terms and Times for Administration of Justice in England." In *A Collection of Curious Discourses Written By eminent Antiquaries upon several Heads in Our English Antiquities.* Ed. Thomas Hearne. 2 vols., vol. II. London, 1775.

De Non Temerandis Ecclesiis. London, 1613, 1646.

"The Origin, Growth, Propagation and Condition of Feuds and Tenures by Knights-Service, in England." In *Reliquiae Spelmanniae. The Posthumous Works of Sir Henry Spelman Kt. Relating to the Laws and Antiquities of England,* ed. Edmund Gibson. Oxford, 1698.

"Of the Union." In *The Jacobean Union. Six Tracts of 1604,* ed. Bruce Galloway and Brian Levack. Edinburgh, 1985.

Spelman, John. *The Case of Our Affaires, in Law, and Religion, and other Circumstances briefly examined, and Presented to the Conscience.* Oxford, 1643.

Certain Considerations upon the Duties both of Prince and People. London, 1643.

A View of a Printed Book Intituled Observations upon His Majesties Late Answers and Expresses. Oxford, 1643.

[Spelman, John.] *A Review of the Observations upon some of his Majesties late Answers and Expresses.* Oxford, 1643.

St. German, Christopher. *Doctor and Student.* Ed. T. F. T. Plucknett and J. L. Barton. Selden Society, vol. XCI. London, 1974.

Steele, Robert, ed. *A Bibliography of Royal Proclamations of the Tudor and Stuart Sovereigns.* 2 vols. Oxford, 1910.

Stillingfleet, Edward. *The Grand Question concerning the Bishops Right to Vote in Parliament in Cases Capital.* London, 1680.

Origines Brittannica. London, 1710.

Stow, John. *The Annales of England.* London, 1605.

The Chronicles of England, from Brute unto this present Yeare 1580. London, 1580.

The Subject of Supremacy. London, 1643.

The Subjects Liberty. London, 1643.

"The Supremacy Debated: Or, The Authority of Parliaments (formerly owned by Romish Clergy); the Supremest Power." In *A Collection of State Tracts, Published on Occasion of the late Revolution in 1688, and during the Reign of William III.* 3 vols. London, 1705–7, vol. I.

Temple, William. *An Introduction to the History of England.* London, 1695.

Textus Roffensis. Ed. Peter Sawyer. Copenhagen, 1957.

Thornborough, John. *A Discourse Plainely Proving the evident utilitie and urgent necessitie of the desired happie Union of the two famous Kingdomes of England and Scotland: by way of answer to certaine objections against the same.* London, 1604.

Thorne, William. *William Thorne's Chronicles of Saint Augustine's Abbey Canterbury.* Ed. A. H. Davies. Oxford, 1934.

"A Treatise of the Happie and Blessed Union." In *The Jacobean Union. Six Tracts of 1604*, ed. Bruce Galloway and Brian Levack. Edinburgh, 1985.

The Trial of King Charles the First. Edinburgh, 1928.

The True Law of Free Monarchy, Or the reciprocall and mutuall duty betwixt a free King and His naturall Subjects. London, 1642.

Two Lives of Charlemagne. Einhard and Notker the Stammerer. Ed. Lewis Thorpe. London, 1969.

Twysden, Sir Roger. *Archaionomia, sive De Priscis Anglorum.* Cambridge, 1644.

    Certaine Considerations upon the Government of England. Ed. John Mitchell Kimbell. Camden Society, vol. XLV. London, 1849.

    Historiae Anglicanae Scriptores X. London, 1652.

Tyrrell, James. *Bibliotheca Politica: or, An Enquiry into the Antient Constitution of the English Government . . . Wherein all the Chief Arguments both for and against the Late Revolution, are Impartially Represented and Consider'd.* London, 1692–4.

    General History of England . . . to the Reign of William III, vol. I. London, 1698.

    Patriarcha non Monarcha. London, 1680.

The Unlawfulnesse of Subjects taking up Armes. n.p. 1644.

The unlimited Prerogative of Kings subverted. n.p., 1642.

Verstegan, Richard the Elder. *A Restitution of Decayed Intelligence: In Antiquities. Concerning the most noble and renoued English nation.* Antwerp, 1605.

A Vindication of Psalme 105.15. London, 1642.

"Vox Populi: Or, The People's Claim to their Parliaments' Sitting, to Redress Grievances . . ." In *State Tracts: Being a Collection of Several Treatises Relating to the Government. Privately Printed in the Reign of K. Charles II.* vol. II. London, 1689; republished two vols. in one, 1693.

Vox Populi: Or the Peoples Humble discovery of Their own Loyaltie, and His Majesties ungrounded Jealousies. London, 1642.

Walker, George. *Anglo-Tyrannus, Or the Idea of a Norman Monarch, Represented in the parallel Reignes of Henrie the Third and Charles Kings of England.* London, 1650.

Walsingham, Thomas. *Chronica Monasterii St. Albani.* Ed. Henry T. Riley. London, 1876.
    Gesta Abbatum Monasterii Sancti Albani. Ed. Henry T. Riley, vol. i. London, 1867.
Walwyn, William. *Juries Justified.* London, 1651.
The Westminster Chronicles. Ed. L. C. Hector and Barbara Harvey. Oxford, 1982.
Whelocke, Abraham. *Archaionomia, Sive De Priscis Anglorum Legibus libri.* Cambridge, 1644.
The Whipper Whipt. London, 1644.
[Whitby, Daniel]. "Agreement betwixt the Present and the former Government." In *A Collection of State Tracts, Published on Occasion of the late Revolution in 1688, and during the Reign of William III.* 3 vols. London, 1705–7, vol. i.
Whitelocke, Bulstrode. *Notes Uppon the King's Writt For Choosing Members of Parlement XIII Car. II. Being Disquisitions on the Government of England by King, Lords, and Commons.* 2 vols. vol. ii. London, 1766.
Williams, E. N., ed. *The Eighteenth Century Constitution, 1688–1815.* Cambridge, 1960.
Williams, Griffith. *Jura Majestatis, the Rights of Kings Both in Church and State.* Oxford, 1644.
Wood, Anthony. *Athenae Oxonienses: An Exact History of all the Writers and Bishops who have had their Education in the University of Oxford.* Ed. Philip Bliss. 4 vols. London, 1820.
    The Life and Times of Anthony Wood. Ed. Andrew Clark, vol. iii. Oxford, 1894.
Woodhouse, A. S. P., ed. *Puritanism and Liberty.* 2nd. edn. London, 1974.
Wootton, David, ed. *Divine Right and Democracy.* Harmondsworth, 1986.
Worcester, John of. *The Chronicle of John of Worcester.* Ed. R. R. Darlington and P. McGurk and trans. Jeniffer Bray and P. McGurk. Oxford 1995.
Year Books of Edward II. The Eyre of Kent 6 and 7. A.D. 1313–1314. Ed. William Bolland. Selden Society, vol. xxix. London, 1913.

SECONDARY SOURCES

Adamson, J. S. A. "The Baronial Context of the English Civil War." *Transactions of the Royal Historical Society* 5th series, 40 (1990).
Anglo, Sydney. *Spectacle, Pageantry, and Early Tudor Policy.* 2nd. edn. Oxford, 1997.
Armitage, David, Armand Himy, and Quentin Skinner, eds. *Milton and Republicanism.* Cambridge, 1996.
Armstrong, J. A. "The Inauguration Ceremonies of the Yorkist Kings and Their Title to the Throne." *Transactions of the Royal Historical Society,* 4th series, 30 (1948).

Ashcraft, Richard. *Revolutionary Politics and Locke's Two Treatises of Government.* Princeton, 1986.

Ashcraft, Richard and M. M. Goldsmith. "Locke, Revolution Principles and the Formation of Whig Ideology." *Historical Journal* 26 (1983), 773–800.

Aston, Margaret. "Lollardy and Literacy." *History* 62 (1977), 347–71.

Axtell, James, ed. *The Educational Writings of John Locke.* Cambridge, 1968.

Aylmer, G. E. *Rebellion or Revolution? England from 1640–1660.* Oxford, 1987.

ed. *The Interregnum. The Quest for Settlement 1646–1660.* London, 1983.

Baker, J. H. *An Introduction to English Legal History.* 2nd. edn. London, 1979.

Baker, J. H. and S. F. C. Milsom. *Sources of English Legal History: Private Law to 1750.* London, 1986.

Barker, Arthur. *Milton and the Puritan Dilemma.* Toronto, 1942.

Barlow, Frank. *Edward the Confessor.* Berkeley, 1970.

"The King's Evil." *English Historical Review* 95 (1980), 3–27.

"The Vita Aedwardi (Book II); the Seven Sleepers: Some Further Evidence and Reflections." *Speculum*, 40 (1965).

Bates, David R. "The Land Pleas of William I's Reign: Penenden Heath Revisited." *Bulletin of the Institute of Historical Research* 51 (1978), 1–19.

Beddard, Robert. "The Unexpected Whig Revolution of 1688." In *The Revolution of 1688.* Ed. Robert Beddard. Oxford, 1981.

Beeson, Trevor. *Westminster Abbey.* 8th. edn. London, 1989.

Behrens, B. "The Whig Theory of the Constitution in the Reign of Charles II." *Cambridge Historical Journal* 8 (1941–3), 42–71.

Binski, Paul. "Abbot Berkyng's Tapestries and Matthew Paris's Life of St. Edward the Confessor." *Archaeologia* 109 (1991), 85–100.

The Painted Chamber at Westminster. Society of Antiquaries. Occasional Paper, n.s. IX. London, 1986.

"Reflections on *La Estoire de Seint Aedward le Rei.* Hagiography and Kingship in Thirteenth-Century England." *Journal of Medieval History* 16 (1990), 335–50.

Westminster Abbey and the Plantagenets. New Haven and London, 1995.

Biographical Dictionary of British Radicals in the Seventeenth Century. Ed. Richard Greaves and Robert Zaller. 3 vols. Brighton, 1984.

Blaas, P. M. *Continuity and Anarchronism: Parliamentary and Constitutional Development in Whig Historiography and in the Anti-Whig Reaction Between 1890 and 1930.* The Hague, 1978.

Bloch, Marc. *The Royal Touch. Sacred Monarchy and Scrofula in England and France.* London, 1973.

Brand, Paul. "The Age of Bracton." In *The History of English Law: Centenary Essays on "Pollock and Maitland".* Ed. John Hudson. *Proceedings of the British Academy* 89 (1996).

The Making of the Common Law. London, 1992.

"'Time Out of Mind': the Knowledge and Use of the Eleventh- and Twelfth-Century Past in Thirteenth-Century Litigation." *Anglo-Norman Studies* 16 (1994), 37–54.

Brieger, Paul. *English Art 1216–1307.* Oxford, 1968.

Brooks, Christopher W. *Pettyfoggers and Vipers of the Commonwealth: The "Lower Branch" of the Legal Profession in Early Modern England.* Cambridge, 1986.

"The Place of Magna Carta and the Ancient Constitution in Sixteenth-Century English Legal Thought." In *The Roots of Liberty. Magna Carta, Ancient Constitution, and the Anglo-American Tradition of Rule of Law,* ed. Ellis Sandoz. Columbia, Mo., and London, 1993, 57–88.

Brooks, Christopher W. and Kevin Sharpe. "History, English Law and the Renaissance." *Past and Present* 72 (1976), 133–42.

Brown, Elizabeth A. R. *The "Lit de Justice": Semantics, Ceremonial, and the Parlement of Paris, 1300–1600.* Sigmaringen, 1994.

Burgess, Glenn. *Absolute Monarchy and the Stuart Constitution.* New Haven, 1996.

The Politics of the Ancient Constitution. An Introduction to English Political Thought 1603–1642. University Park, Pa., 1992.

Burns, J. H. "George Buchanan and the Anti-Monarchomachs." In *Political Discourse in Early Modern Britain.* Ed. Nicholas Phillipson and Quentin Skinner. Cambridge, 1993, 3–23.

"Scholasticism: Survival and Revival." In *The Cambridge History of Political Thought,* vol. II. *1450–1700,* ed. J. H. Burns and Mark Goldie. Cambridge, 1991.

The True Law of Kingship. Concepts of Monarchy in Early-Modern Scotland. Oxford, 1996.

Burns, J. H. ed. *The Cambridge History of Political Thought,* vol. I. *Medieval Political Thought, c. 350–c. 1450.* Cambridge, 1988.

and Mark Goldie. *The Cambridge History of Political Thought,* vol. II *1450–1700.* Cambridge, 1991.

Camille, Michael. *The Gothic Idol: Ideology and Image-Making in Medieval Art.* Cambridge, 1989.

Carpenter, David. "Kings, Magnates, and Society: The Personal Rule of Henry III, 1234–1258." *Speculum* 60 (1985), 59–62.

Carswell, John. *The Porcupine: The Life of Algernon Sidney.* London, 1989.

Cato, J. "Andrew Horn: Law and History in Fourteenth-Century England." In *The Writing of History in the Middle Ages: Essays Presented to Richard William Southern,* ed. R. C. Davis and J. M. Wallace-Hadrill. Oxford, 1981.

Cheshire, G. C. *The Modern Law of Real Property.* 6th. edn. London, 1949.

Chibnall, Marjorie, ed. *The Ecclesiastical History of Orderic Vitalis.* 6 vols. Oxford, 1969–80.

Chrimes, S. B. "The Constitutional Ideas of Dr. John Cowell." *English Historical Review* 59 (1949), 461–87.

Christianson, Paul. "Ancient Constitutions in the Age of Sir Edward Coke and John Selden." In *The Roots of Liberty. Magna Carta, Ancient Constitution, and the Anglo-American Tradition of Rule of Law,* ed. Ellis Sandoz. Columbia, Mo. and London, 1993.

Discourse on History, Law, and Governance in the Public Career of John Selden, 1610–1635, Toronto, 1996.

"John Selden, the Five Knights' Case, and Discretionary Imprisonment in Early Stuart England." *Criminal Justice History* 6 (1985), 65–87.

Reformers and Babylon: English Apocalyptic Visions from the Reformation to the Eve of the Civil War. Toronto, 1978.

"Young John Selden and the Ancient Constitution, ca. 1610–1618." *Proceedings of the American Philosophical Society* 128 (1984).

Clanchy, M. T. *England and Its Rulers 1066–1272.* 2nd. edn. Oxford, 1998.

From Memory to Written Record. England 1066–1307. 2nd. edn. Oxford, 1993.

Clark, J. C. D. *English Society 1688–1832.* Cambridge, 1985.

Clarke, Maude V. *Medieval Representation and Consent.* London, 1936, repr. 1964.

Claydon, Tony. *William III and the Godly Revolution.* Cambridge, 1995.

Clegg, Cynthia Susan. *Press Censorship in Elizabethan England.* Cambridge, 1997.

Coffey, John. *Politics, Religion, and the British Revolutions: The Mind of Samuel Rutherford.* Cambridge, 1997.

Cogswell, Thomas. *The Blessed Revolution.* Cambridge, 1989.

"A Low Road to Extinction? Supply and Redress of Grievances in the Parliaments of the 1620s." *Historical Journal* 33 (1990), 283–303.

"War and the Liberties of the Subject." In *Parliament and Liberty. From the Reign of Elizabeth to the English Civil War*, ed. J. H. Hexter. Stanford, 1992.

Collinson, Patrick. "Truth, Lies, and Fiction in Sixteenth-century Protestant Historiography." In *The Historical Imagination in Early Modern Britain. History, Rhetoric, and Fiction, 1500–1800*, ed. Donald R. Kelley and David Harris Sacks. Cambridge, 1997, pp. 37–68.

"Truth and Legend: The Veracity of John Foxe's *Book of Martyrs*." In *Clio's Mirror: Historiography in Britain and the Netherlands*, ed. A. C. Duke and C. A. Tamse. Zutphen, 1985.

Condren, Conal. *The Language of Politics in Seventeenth-Century England.* New York, 1995.

The Coronation Chair. London, 1953.

Cressy, David. *Literacy and the Social Order. Reading and Writing in Tudor and Stuart England.* Cambridge, 1980.

Cromartie, Alan. "The Constitutional Revolution: the Transformation of Political Culture in Early Stuart England." *Past and Present* 163 (1999), 76–120.

Sir Matthew Hale, 1609–1676. Law, Religion, and Natural Philosophy. Cambridge, 1995.

Cronne, H. A. "The Study and Use of Charters by English Scholars in the Seventeenth Century: Sir Henry Spelman and Sir William Dugdale." In *English Historical Scholarship in the Sixteenth and Seventeenth Centuries*, ed. Levi Fox. Oxford, 1956.

Cust, Richard. *The Forced Loan and English Politics, 1626–1629.* Oxford, 1987.

Cust, Richard and Ann Hughes. "Introduction: After Revisionism." In *Conflict in Early Stuart England: Studies in Religion and Politics 1603–1642*, ed. Richard Cust and Ann Hughes. London, 1989.

Daly, James. "Some Problems in the Authorship of Sir Robert Filmer's Works." *English Historical Review* 98 (1983), 737–62.

Davies, R. R. *Domination and Conquest. The Experience of Ireland, Scotland, and Wales, 1100–1300.* Cambridge, 1990.

Davis, J. C. "Radicalism in Traditional Society: the Evaluation of Radical Thought in the English Commonwealth, 1649–1660." *History of Political Thought* 3 (1982), 193–213.

De Krey, Gary. "London Radicals and Revolutionary Politics, 1675–1683." In *Politics of Religion in Restoration England*, ed. Tim Harris, Paul Seward, and Mark Goldie. Oxford, 1990.

"The London Whigs and the Exclusion Crisis Reconsidered." In *The First Modern Society: Essays in English History in Honour of Lawrence Stone*, ed. A. L. Beier, D. Cannadine, and J. M. Rosenheim. Cambridge, 1989.

"Rethinking the Restoration: Dissenting Cases for Conscience, 1667–1672." *Historical Journal* 38 (1995), 53–85.

"Revolution *Redivivus*: 1688–89 and the Radical Tradition in Seventeenth-Century London Politics." In *The Revolution of 1688–1689: Changing Perspectives*, ed. Lois G. Schwoerer. Cambridge, 1992.

Dickinson, H. T. "The Eighteenth-Century Debate on the 'Glorious Revolution.'" *History* 6 (1976), 28–45.

"The Eighteenth-Century Debate on the Sovereignty of Parliament." *Transactions of the Royal Historical Society*, 5th. series, 26 (1976).

Liberty and Property. New York, 1977.

Digby, K. E. *An Introduction to the History of Real Property.* 5th. edn. Oxford, 1897.

Douglas, David C. *English Scholars.* London, 1939.

Time and the Hour. Collected Studies in Legal and Constitutional History. London, 1977.

William the Conqueror. Berkeley, 1964.

Eadie, Carolyn A. "Succession and Monarchy: The Controversy of 1679–1681." *American Historical Review* 70 (1964–5), 350–70.

Elton, G. R. "Arthur Hall, Lord Burghley and the Antiquity of Parliament." In *Studies in Tudor and Stuart Government and Politics.* 3 vols., vol. III. Cambridge, 1983.

"High Road to Civil War?" In *Studies in Tudor and Stuart Politics and Government.* 3 vols., vol. II. Cambridge, 1974.

"The Stuart Century." In *Studies in Tudor and Stuart Politics and Government.* 3 vols. vol. II. Cambridge, 1974.

Evans, E. "Of the Antiquity of Parliaments in England: Some Elizabethan and Early Stuart Opinions." *History* 23 (1938), 206–21.

Evans, Joan. *English Art 1307–1461*. Oxford, 1949.

A History of the Society of Antiquaries. Oxford, 1956.

Farmer, David, ed. *The Oxford Dictionary of Saints*. Oxford, 1978.

Finley, M. I. "The Ancestral Constitution." In *Uses and Abuses of History*. Harmondsworth, 1971.

Finucane, Ronald. *Miracles and Pilgrims*. Totowa, NJ, 1997.

Firth, Katherine. *The Apocalyptic Tradition in Reformation Britain, 1530–1645*. Oxford, 1979.

Fleming, Robin. *Domesday Book and the Law: Society and Legal Custom in Medieval England*. Cambridge, 1998.

Foster, Elizabeth Read. *The House of Lords 1603–1649*. Chapel Hill, 1983.

"The Painful Labour of Mr. Elsyng." *Transactions of the American Philosophical Society*, n.s. 62, pt. 8, 1972.

"Petitions and the Petition of Right." *Journal of British Studies* 14 (1974), 21–45.

Franklin, Julian. *John Locke and the Theory of Sovereignty: Mixed Monarchy and the Right of Resistance in the Political Thought of the English Revolution*. Cambridge, 1978.

Fryde, Natalie. *The Tyranny and Fall of Edward II 1321–1326*. Cambridge, 1979.

Furley, O. W. "The Whig Exclusionists: Pamphlet Literature in the Exclusion Campaign, 1679–81," *Cambridge Historical Journal* 13 (1957), 19–36.

Galbraith, V. H. *Roger of Wendover and Matthew Paris*. Glasgow, 1944.

Galloway, Bruce. *The Union of England and Scotland 1603–1608*. Edinburgh, 1986.

Gardiner, S. R. *History of England from the Accession of James I to the Outbreak of the Civil War, 1603–1642*. 10 vols. New York, 1909.

Garnett, George. "Coronation and Propaganda: Some Implications of the Norman Claim to the Throne of England in 1066." *Transactions of the Royal Historical Society*, 5th series, 36 (1986), 91–113.

Gentles, Ian. "The Iconography of Revolution: England 1642–1649." In *Soldiers, Writers and Statesmen of the English Revolution*, ed. Ian Gentles, John Morrill, and Blair Worden. Cambridge, 1998.

Gilbert, Charles. *Burned Books*. Port Washington, NY, 1964.

Goldie, Mark. "The Revolution of 1689 and the Structure of Political Argument." *Bulletin of Research into the Humanities* 83 (1980), 473–564.

"The Roots of True Whiggism." *History of Political Thought* 1 (1980), 195–236.

Gordon, Dillian. *Making and Meaning. The Wilton Diptych*. London, 1993.

Gough, J. W. "James Tyrrell, Whig Historian, and Friend of John Locke." *Historical Journal* 19 (1976), 581–610.

Grace, William. "Milton, Salmasius and the Natural Law." *Journal of the History of Ideas* 14 (1963).

Gransden, Antonia. "The Continuation of the *Flores Historiarum* from

1265–1327." In *Legends, Traditions, and History in Medieval England*, ed. Antonia Gransden. London and Rio Grande, 1992, 245–66.

English Historical Writing. 2 vols. Ithaca, 1974.

Gray, Charles M. "Parliament, Liberty, and the Law." In *Parliament and Liberty from the Reign of Elizabeth to the English Civil War*, ed. J. H. Hexter. Stanford, 1992.

"Reason, Authority, and Imagination: The Jurisprudence of Sir Edward Coke." In *Culture and Politics from Puritanism to the Enlightenment*, ed. Perez Zagorin. Berkeley, 1980.

Greaves, Richard. *Deliver Us from Evil: The Radical Underground in Britain, 1660–1663.* Oxford, 1986.

Enemies Under His Feet: Radicals and Nonconformists in Britain, 1664–1677. Stanford, 1990.

Secrets of the Kingdom: British Radicals from the Popish Plot to the Revolution of 1688–89. Stanford, 1992.

Green, Judith. *The Government of England under Henry I.* Cambridge, 1986.

Greenberg, Janelle. "The Confessor's Laws and the Radical Face of the Ancient Constitution." *English Historical Review* 104 (1989), 611–37.

"Our Grand Maxim of State, 'The King Can Do No Wrong.'" *History of Political Thought* 12 (1991), 210–28.

Greenberg, Janelle and Laura Marin. "Politics and Memory: Sharnborn's Case and the Role of the Norman conquest in Stuart Political Thought." In *Politics and Imagination in Later Stuart Britain. Essays Presented by Lois Green Schwoerer*, ed. Howard Nenner. Rochester, NY, 1997.

Guy, John. "The Origins of the Petition of Right Reconsidered." *Historical Journal* 25 (1982), 289– 312,

"Thomas Cromwell and the Intellectual Origins of the Henrician Revolution." In *Reassessing the Henrician Age. Humanism, Politics and Reform, 1500–1550*, ed. Alistair Fox and John Guy. Oxford, 1986.

Tudor England. Oxford, 1990.

Guy, John and John Morrill. *The Tudors and the Stuarts.* Oxford, 1992.

Hall, D. J. *English Medieval Pilgrimage.* London, 1965.

Haller, William. *Foxe's Book of Martyrs and the Elect Nation.* London, 1963.

Halliday, Robert. "The Norman Doorways at Wordwell and West Stow Churches." *Proceedings of the Suffolk Institute of Archaeology and History* 37 (1992), 367–9.

Harding, Alan. *England in the Thirteenth Century.* Cambridge, 1993.

Harris, Tim. "Introduction: Revising the Restoration." In *The Politics of Religion in Restoration England*, ed. Tim Harris, Paul Seaward, and Mark Goldie. Oxford, 1990.

"'Lives, Liberties and Estates': Rhetorics of Liberty in the Reign of Charles II." In *Politics of Religion in Restoration England*, ed. Tim Harris, Paul Seaward, and Mark Goldie. Oxford, 1990.

London Crowds in the Reign of Charles II: Propaganda and Politics from the Restoration until the Exclusion Crisis. Cambridge, 1994.

"Party Turns? Or, Whigs and Tories Get Off Scott Free." *Albion* 25 (1993), 581–90.

"The People, the Law, and the Constitution in Scotland and England: a Comparative Approach to the Glorious Revolution." *Journal of British Studies* 38 (1999), 28–58.

"Sobering Thoughts, But the Party is Not Yet Over: A Reply." *Albion* 25 (1993), 645–7.

"What's New About the Restoration?" *Albion* 29 (1997), 187–222.

Harris, Tim, Paul Seaward and Mark Goldie, eds. *Politics and Religion in Restoration England.* Oxford, 1990.

Harriss, G. L. "The Formation of Parliament." In *The English Parliament in the Middle Ages*, ed. R. G. Davies and J. H. Denton. Philadelphia, 1981.

Hay, Denys. *Polydore Vergil. Renaissance Historian and Man of Letters.* Oxford, 1952.

Hayton, David J., ed. *Megarry's Manual of the Law of Real Property.* 6th. edn. London, 1982.

Head, Thomas. *Hagiography and the Cult of Saints.* Cambridge, 1990.

Helgerson, Richard. *Forms of Nationhood. The Elizabethan Writing of England.* Chicago, 1992.

Herman, Peter C. "Rastell's *Pastyme of People*: Monarchy and the Law in Early Modern Historiography." *Journal of Medieval and Early Modern Studies*, forthcoming.

Hexter, J. H. "The Early Stuarts and Parliament: Old Hat and *Nouvelle Vague*." *Parliamentary History* I (1981), 181–215.

Hill, Christopher. *The English Bible and the Seventeenth-Century Revolution.* London, 1993.

"The First Century of the Church in England." In *Collected Essays*, vol. II *Religion and Politics in Seventeenth-Century England.* Hassocks and Amhurst, 1986.

"Gerard Winstanley and Freedom." In *A Nation of Change and Novelty: Radical Politics, Religion and Literature in Seventeenth-Century England.* London, 1993.

Milton and the English Revolution. Harmondsworth, 1979.

"The Norman Yoke." In *Puritanism and Liberty.* London, 1958.

"Parliament and the People in Seventeenth-Century England." *Past and Present* 92 (1981), 100–24.

Hirst, Derek. *Authority and Conflict. England, 1603–1658.* Cambridge, Mass., 1986.

"Freedom, Revolution, and Beyond." In *Parliament and Liberty from the Reign of Elizabeth to the English Civil War*, ed. J. H. Hexter. Stanford, 1992.

"Revisionism Revised: The Place of Principle." *Past and Present* 92 (1981), 79–102.

Holdsworth, William S. *A History of English Law.* 17 vols. London, 1966.

An Historical Introduction to Land Law. London, 1927.

Holt, J. C. "The Ancient Constitution in Medieval England." In *The Roots of Liberty. Magna Carta, Ancient Constitution, and the Anglo-American Tradition of Rule of Law*, ed. Ellis Sandoz. Columbia, Mo. and London, 1993.

Colonial England, 1066–1215. London and Rio Grande, 1997.

"The Origins of the Constitutional Tradition in England." In *Magna Carta and Medieval Government. Studies Presented to the International Commission for the Study of Parliamentary Estates*. London, 1985.

Magna Carta. 2nd. cdn. Cambridge, 1992.

"1086." In *Domesday Studies. Papers read at the Novocentenary Conference of the Royal Historical Society and the Institute of British Geographers, Winchester, 1986*. Woodbridge, 1987.

Houston, Alan Craig. *Algernon Sidney and the Republican Heritage in England and America*. Princeton, 1991.

Howarth, David. "Sir Robert Cotton and the Commemoration of Famous Men," *British Library Journal* 18 (1992).

Hudson, John. "Administration, Family and Perceptions of the Past in Late Twelfth-Century England: Richard Fitz Nigel and the *Dialogue of the Exchequer*." In *The Perceptions of the Past in Twelfth-Century Europe*, ed. Paul Magdalino. London, 1992.

Hughes, Andrew, "The Origins and Descent of the Fourth Recension of the English Coronation." In *Coronations. Medieval and Early Modern Monarchic Ritual*, ed. Janos Bak. Berkeley, 1990, pp. 197–216.

Hughes, Ann. *The Causes of the English Civil War*. London, 1991.

Hunt, William. *The Puritan Moment: the Coming of Revolution in an English County*. Cambridge, Ma., 1983.

Hutton, Ronald. *Charles II: King of England, Scotland and Ireland*. Oxford, 1989.

Jacob, E. F. *The Fifteenth Century 1399–1485*. Oxford, 1961.

Jessup, Frank W. *Sir Roger Twysden 1597–1672*. New York, 1965.

Kantorowicz, Ernst. *The King's Two Bodies: a Study in Mediaeval Political Theology*. Princeton, 1957.

Kearney. Hugh. *The British Isles. A History of Four Nations*. Cambridge, 1989.

Kelley, Donald A. "Elizabethan Political Thought." In *The Varieties of British Political Thought, 1500–1800*, ed. J. G. A. Pocock. Cambridge, 1993.

"Ideas of Resistance before Elizabeth." In *The Historical Renaissance: New Essays on Tudor and Stuart Literature and Culture*, ed. Heather Dubrow and Richard Strier. Chicago, 1988.

and David Harris Sacks, eds. *The Historical Imagination in Early Modern Britain. History, Rhetoric, and Fiction, 1500–1800*. Cambridge, 1997.

Kemp, Betty. *King and Commons, 1660–1832*. London, 1957.

Kemp, Eric W. *Canonization and Authority in the Western Church*. London, 1948.

Kenyon, J. P. "The Revolution of 1688: Resistance and Contract." In *Historical Perspectives. Studies in English Thought and Society in Honour of J. H. Plumb*, ed. Neil McKendrick. London, 1974.

Revolution Principles. Cambridge, 1977.

Ker, N. R., ed. *Medieval Libraries of Great Britain. A List of Surviving Books.* 2nd. edn. London, 1964.

Kidd, Colin. *British Identities Before Nationalism. Ethnicity and Nationhood in the Atlantic World, 1600–1800.* Cambridge, 1999.

King, John N. *English Reformation Literature.* Princeton, 1983.

Kingdon, Robert. "Calvinism and Resistance Theory, 1550–1580." In *The Cambridge History of Political Thought*, vol. II *1450–1700*, ed. J. H. Burns and Mark Goldie. Cambridge, 1991.

Kishlansky, Mark. "The Emergence of Adversary Politics in the Long Parliament." *Journal of Modern History* 49 (1977), 617–40.

"Tyranny Denied: Charles I, Attorney General Heath, and the Five Knights' Case." *Historical Journal* 42 (1999), 53–83.

Klein, William. "The Ancient Constitution Revisited." In *Political Discourse in Early Modern Britain*, ed. Nicholas Phillipson and Quentin Skinner. Cambridge, 1993.

Kliger, Samuel L. *The Goths in England.* Cambridge, Mass., 1952.

Knights, Mark. *Politics and Opinion in Crisis, 1678–81.* Cambridge, 1994.

Lamont, William. *Godly Rule: Politics and Religion, 1603–1660.* London, 1969.

Marginal Prynne. London, 1963.

Landon, Michael. *The Triumph of the Lawyers: Their Role in English Politics, 1678–89.* Tuscaloosa, Al., 1970.

La Patourel, John. "The Reports of the Trial on Penenden Heath." In *Studies in Medieval History Presented to F. M. Powicke.* Oxford, 1948, 15–26.

Laslett, Peter. "Introduction" to *Patriarcha and Other Political Works by Robert Filmer.* Oxford, 1949.

ed. *Locke's Two Treatises of Government.* Cambridge, 1960.

Lemmings, David. *Gentlemen and Barristers: The Inns of Court and the English Bar, 1680–1730.* Oxford, 1990.

Lethaby, W. L. "English Primitives. The Painted Chamber and the Early Masters of the Westminster School." *Burlington Magazine* 7 (1905).

"Medieval Paintings at Westminster." *Proceedings of the British Academy* 13 (1927).

Westminster Abbey and the King's Craftsmen. London, 1906.

Levack, Brian P. *The Formation of the British State.* Oxford, 1987.

"Law, Sovereignty and the Union." In *Scots and Britons. British Political Thought and the Union of 1603*, ed. Roger A. Mason. Cambridge, 1994.

Levy, F. J. "Hayward, Daniel, and the Beginnings of Politic History in England." *Huntington Library Quarterly* 50 (1987), 1–34.

Tudor Historical Thought. San Marino, Ca., 1967.

Lewis, Suzanne. *The Art of Matthew Paris in the Chronica Majora.* Berkeley, 1987.

Madan, F. F. "Milton and Salmasius, and Dugard." *The Library*, 4th series, 4 (1923–4), 119–45.

"A Revised Bibliography of Salmasius's *Defensio Regia* and Milton's *Pro Populo Anglicano Defensio*." *The Library*, 5th series, 9 (1954), 112–20.

Maddicott, J. R. *Thomas of Lancaster 1307–1322. A Study of the Reign of Edward II*. Oxford, 1970.

Maitland, F. W. "The Corporation Sole." In *The Collected Papers of Frederic William Maitland*, ed. H. A. L. Fisher. Cambridge, 1911, pp. 244–70.

Malcolm, Joyce Lee. "Doing No Wrong: Law, Liberty, and the Constraint of Kings." *Journal of British Studies* 38 (1999), 161–86.

Mason, Roger A. "Imagining Scotland: Scottish Political Thought and the Problem of Britain 1560–1650." In *Scots and Britons. British Political Thought and the Union of 1603*, ed. Roger A. Mason. Cambridge, 1994.

"Scotching the Brut: Politics, History and National Myth in Sixteenth-Century Britain." In *Scotland and England 1286–1815*, ed. Roger A. Mason. Edinburgh, 1987.

"The Scottish Reformation and the Origins of Anglo-British Imperialism." In *Scots and Britains. British Political Thought and the Union of 1603*, ed. Roger A. Mason. Cambridge, 1994.

McCusker, H. "Books and Manuscripts Formerly in the Possession of John Bale." *The Library* 16 (1935), 144–65.

McKisack, May. *The Fourteenth Century, 1307–1399*. Oxford, 1959.

Medieval History in the Tudor Age. Oxford, 1971.

McLean, A. H. "George Lawson and John Locke." *Cambridge Historical Journal* 9 (1947), 69–77.

Megarry, R. E. and H. W. R. Wade. *The Law of Real Property*. 2nd. edn. London, 1959.

Mendle, Michael. *Dangerous Positions. Mixed Government, the Estates of the Realm, and the Answer to the XIX Propositions*. Tuscaloosa, Al., 1985.

"The Great Council of Parliament and the First Ordinances: the Constitutional Theory of the Civil War." *Journal of British Studies* 31 (1992), 133–62.

Henry Parker and the English Civil War: the Political Thought of the Public's "Privado." Cambridge, 1995.

"Parliamentary Sovereignty: a Very English Absolutism." In *Political Discourse in Early Modern Britain*, ed. Nicholas Phillipson and Quentin Skinner. Cambridge, 1993.

Review of David L. Smith, *Constitutional Royalism. Albion* 27 (1995), 490–1.

Mendyk, Stan A. E. *"Speculum Britanniae." Regional Study, Antiquarianism, and Science in Britain to 1700*. Toronto, 1989.

Morrill, John. *The Revolt of the Provinces*. London, rev. ed., 1980.

"The Sensible Revolution of 1688." In *The Nature of the English Revolution*, ed. J. S. Morrill. London, 1983.

Murphy, Virginia. "The Literature and Propaganda of Henry VIII's First Divorce." In *The Reign of Henry VIII: Politics, Policy, and Piety*, ed. Diarmaid MacCulloch. New York, 1995.

Neale, J. E. *Elizabeth I and Her Parliaments, 1559–1581*. New York, 1953.

Nelson, Janet L. "The Rites of the Conqueror." In *Politics and Ritual in Early Medieval Europe*. London, 1986.

"Royal Saints and Early Medieval Kingship." In *Sanctity and Secularity. Studies in Church History*, ed. D. Baker, 10 (1973).

Nenner, Howard. *By Colour of Law: Legal Culture and Constitutional Politics in England, 1660–1689*. Chicago, 1977.

"Constitutional Uncertainties and the Declaration of Rights." In *After the Reformation: Essays in Honor of J. H. Hexter*, ed. Barbara Malament. Philadelphia, 1980.

ed. *Politics and the Political Imagination in Later Stuart Britain. Essays Presented to Lois Green Schwoerer*. Rochester, NY, 1997.

"Pretence and Pragmatism: the Response to Uncertainty in the Succession Crisis of 1689." In *The Revolution of 1688–1689. Changing Perspectives*, ed. Lois G. Schwoerer. Cambridge, 1992.

The Right to Be King. The Succession to the Crown of England 1603–1714. Chapel Hill, 1995.

Noppen, J. G. *Royal Westminster and the Coronation*. New York, 1937.

Oakley, Francis. "Christian Obedience and Authority, 1520–1550." In *The Cambridge History of Political Thought*, vol. II *1450–1700*, ed. J. H. Burns and Mark Goldie. Cambridge, 1991.

Omnipotence, Covenant, and Order: An Excursion in the History of Ideas from Abelard to Leibnitz. Ithaca, NY, 1984.

O'Brien, Bruce R. "The Becket Conflict and the Invention of the Myth of Lex Non Scripta." In Jonathan A. Bush and Alain Wijffels, eds. *Learning the Law. Teaching and Transmission of Law in England 1150–1900*. London and Rio Grande, 1999.

"Forgery and the Literacy of the Early Common Law." *Albion* 97 (1995), 1–18.

God's Peace and King's Peace. Philadelphia, 1999.

"The Origin of a Legal Literature of Complaint in England." Forthcoming.

"Studies in the '*Leges Edwardi Confessoris*' and Their Milieu." Unpublished PhD Dissertation, Yale University 1990.

O'Day, Rosemary. *The Debate on the English Reformation*. London, 1986.

Education and Society in Britain, 1500–1800. London, 1982.

Ogg, David. *England in the Reigns of James II and William III*. London, 1969.

The Oxford Dictionary of Saints. Ed. David Hugh Farmer. Oxford, 1978.

Parkin-Speer, Diane. "John Lilburne: a Revolutionary Interprets Statutes and Common Law Due Process." *Law and History Review* 1 (1983), 276–96.

Parry, Graham. *The Trophies of Time. English Antiquarians of the Seventeenth Century*. Oxford, 1995.

Partner, Nancy. *Serious Entertainments. The Writing of History in Twelfth-Century England*. Chicago, 1977.

Patterson, Annabel. *Censorship and Interpretation. The Conditions of Writing and Reading in Early Modern England*. Madison, Wis., 1990.

Early Modern Liberalism. Cambridge, 1997.

"Foul, his Wife, the Mayor, and Foul's Mare: the Power of Anecdote in Tudor Historiography." In *The Historical Imagination in Early Modern Britain. History, Rhetoric, and Fiction, 1500–1800*, ed. Donald R. Kelley and David Harris Sacks. Cambridge, 1997.

Reading Holinshed's Chronicles. Chicago, 1994.

Pawlisch, Hans. *Sir John Davies and the Conquest of Ireland*. Cambridge, 1985.

Peck, Linda Levy. "Kingship, Counsel and Law in Early Stuart Britain." In *The Varieties of British Political Thought, 1500 1800*. Cambridge, 1993.

Northampton: Patronage and Policy at the Court of James I. London, 1982.

ed. *The Mental World of the Jacobean Court*. Cambridge, 1991.

Petti, A. G. "Richard Verstegan and the Catholic Martyrologies of the Later Elizabethan Period." *Recusant History* 5 (1959–60), 64–90.

Pevsner, Nikolaus. *The Buildings of England. I. The Cities of London and Westminster*, revised Bridget Cherry. 3rd. edn. Harmondsworth, 1973.

Pincus, Steven C. A. "The Universal Debate over Universal Monarchy." In *A Union for Empire: Political Thought and the British Union of 1707*, ed. John Robertson. Cambridge, 1995.

Pocock, J. G. A. *The Ancient Constitution and the Feudal Law: a Study of English Historical Thought in the Seventeenth Century. A Reissue with a Retrospect*. Cambridge, 1987.

"Robert Brady, 1627–1700. A Cambridge Historian of the Restoration." *Cambridge Historical Journal* 10 (1951), 186–204.

"Two Kingdoms and Three Histories? Political Thought in British Contexts." In *Scots and Britons*, ed. Roger A. Mason. Cambridge, 1994.

Virtue, Commerce, and History. Cambridge, 1985.

Pollock, Frederick and Frederic William Maitland. *A History of English Law*, vol. II. 2nd. edn. Cambridge, 1898, repr. 1968.

Pond, C. C. *The Palace of Westminster*. Westminster, 1994.

Popofsky, Linda. "The Crisis over Tonnage and Poundage in Parliament in 1629." *Past and Present* 126 (1990), 44–75.

"Habeas Corpus and 'Liberty of the Subject:' Legal Arguments for the Petition of Right of 1628." *The Historian* 41 (1979), 257–75.

Powicke, Maurice. *England in the Thirteenth Century*. 2nd edn. Oxford, 1962.

Prest, Wilfred. *The Inns of Court under Elizabeth and the Early Stuarts, 1590–1640*. London, 1972.

"Lawyers." In *The Professions in Early Modern England*. London, 1987.

The Rise of the Barristers. Oxford, 1986.

Rabb, Theodore K. *Jacobean Gentleman: Sir Edwin Sandys, 1561–1629*. Princeton, 1998.

"Revisionism Revised: Two Perspectives on Early Stuart Parliamentary History." *Past and Present* 92 (1981), 55–91.

Relf, Frances H. *The Petition of Right*. Minneapolis, 1917.

Remensnyder, Amy G. *Remembering Kings Past. Monastic Foundation Legends in Medieval Southern France*. Ithaca, 1995.

"Legendary Treasure at Conques: Reliquaries and Imaginative Memory." *Speculum* 71 (1996), 884–906.

Reuschlein, Harold G. "Who Wrote the *Mirror of Justices?*" *Law Quarterly Review* 58 (1942).

Reynolds, Susan. *Kingdoms and Communities*. Oxford, 1984.

Richards, Mary P. "Texts and Their Traditions in the Medieval Library of Rochester Cathedral Priory." *Transactions of the American Philosophical Society* n.s. 78, pt. 3 (1988).

Richardson, H. G. "Early Coronation Records." *Bulletin of the Institute of Historical Research* 13 (1935–6).

"The English Coronation Oath." *Transactions of the Royal Historical Society* 4th series, 23 (1941), 129–58.

Richardson, H. G. and G. O. Sayles. *The Governance of Mediaeval England from the Conquest to Magna Carta*. Edinburgh, 1963.

Richardson, R. C. *The Debate on the English Revolution Revisited*. 2nd. edn. London, 1988.

Ridyard, Susan. "Condigna Veneratio: Post-Conquest Attitudes to the Saints of the Anglo-Saxons." *Anglo-Saxon Studies* 9 (1987), 179–206.

The Royal Saints of Anglo-Saxon England. Cambridge, 1998.

Robbins, Caroline. *The Eighteenth-Century Commonwealthman*. Cambridge, Mass., 1959.

Roberts, Clayton. *The Growth of Responsible Government*. Cambridge, 1966.

Rochelle, Mercedes. *Post-Biblical Saints Art Index*. Jefferson, NC, 1994.

Rollason, David. "Relic-cults as an Instrument of Royal Policy c. 900–c. 1050." *Anglo-Saxon England* 15 (1986), 91–103.

Rose, Tessa. *The Coronation Ceremony of the Kings and Queens of England and the Crown Jewels*. London, HMSO, 1992.

Rosenthal, Joel T. "Edward the Confessor and Robert the Pious: Eleventh-Century Kingship and Biography." *Medieval Studies* 30 (1971), 7–20.

Roskell, J. S. "A Consideration of Certain Aspects and Problems of the English *Modus Tenendi Parliamentum*." *Bulletin of the John Rylands Library* 1 (1968).

Rosser, Gervase. *Medieval Westminster, 1200–1540*. Oxford, 1989.

Russell, Conrad. "The Addled Parliament of 1614: The Limits of Revision." The Stenton Lecture of 1991. Reading, 1992.

"English Parliaments 1593–1606: One Epoch or Two?" In *The Parliaments of Elizabethan England*, ed. D. M. Dean and N. L. Jones. Oxford, 1990.

"Parliament in Perspective, 1604–1629." *History* 51 (1976), 1–27.

Parliaments and English Politics 1621–1629. Oxford, 1979.

Unrevolutionary England, 1603–1642. London, 1990.

Salmon, J. H. "Catholic Resistance Theory, Ultramontanism, and the Royalist Response, 1580–1620." In *The Cambridge History of Political Thought*, vol. II *1450–1700*, ed. J. H. Burns and Mark Goldie. Cambridge, 1991.

Salmond, J. W. *Salmond on Jurisprudence*, ed. P. J. Fitzgerald. 12th. edn. London, 1966.

Sanderson, John. *"But the People's Creatures": the Philosophical Basis of the English Civil War.* Manchester, 1989.

"Conrad Russell's Ideas." *History of Political Thought* 14 (1993), 85–102.

Saul, Nigel. *Richard II.* New Haven, 1997.

Sayles, G. O. "Modus Tenendi Parliamentum: Irish or English." In *England and Ireland in the Later Middle Ages*, ed. J. F. Lydon. Dublin, 1981.

Schochet, Gordon. *Patriarchalism in Political Thought.* Oxford, 1975.

Schoeck, R. "Early Anglo-Saxon Studies and Legal Scholarship in the Renaissance." *Studies in the Renaissance* 5 (1958), 2–10.

Schofield, R. S. "The Measurement of Literacy in Pre-Industrial England." In *Literacy in Traditional Societies*, ed. J. R. Goody. Cambridge, 1968.

Schramm, Percy E. *History of the English Coronation.* Trans. Leopold G. Wickham Legg. Oxford, 1937.

Schwoerer, Lois G. "The Coronation of William and Mary, April 11, 1689." In *The Revolution of 1688–1689. Changing Perspectives*, ed. Lois G. Schwoerer. Cambridge, 1992.

The Declaration of Rights, 1689. Baltimore, 1981.

"No Standing Armies!" The Antiarmy Ideology in Seventeenth-Century England. Baltimore, 1974.

"Press and Parliament in the Revolution of 1689." *Historical Journal* 20 (1977), 545–67.

"Propaganda in the Revolution of 1688–89." *American Historical Review* 82 (1977), 545–67.

ed. *The Revolution of 1688–89: Changing Perspectives.* Cambridge, 1992.

Scott, Jonathan. *Algernon Sidney and the Restoration Crisis, 1677–1683.* Cambridge, 1991.

Seaberg, R. B. "The Norman Conquest and the Common Law: the Levellers and the Argument from Continuity." *Historical Journal* 24 (1981), 791–806.

Seaward, Paul. *The Cavalier Parliament and the Construction of the Old Regime, 1661–1689.* Cambridge, 1989.

Sharp, Andrew. "John Lilburne and the Long Parliament's *Book of Declarations*: a Radical's Exploitation of the Words of Authorities." *History of Political Thought* 9 (1988), 19–44.

Sharpe, Kevin. "A Commonwealth of Meanings: Languages, Analogues, Ideas and Politics." In *Politics and Ideas in Early Stuart England.* London, 1989.

"Crown, Parliament and Locality: Government and Communication in Early Stuart England." *English Historical Review* 39 (1986), 321–50.

"Crown, Parliament and Locality." In *Politics and Press in Early Stuart England.* London, 1989.

"Culture, Politics, and the English Civil War." In *Politics and Ideas in Early Stuart England.* London, 1989.

"Introduction: Parliamentary History In or Out of Perspective?" In *Faction and Parliament: Essays on Early Stuart History*, ed. Kevin Sharpe. Oxford, 1978.

Sir Robert Cotton 1586–1631. History and Politics in Early Modern England. Oxford, 1979.

Simpson, A. W. B. *A History of the Land Law.* 2nd. edn. Oxford, 1986.

Skinner, Quentin. "Conquest and Consent: Thomas Hobbes and the Engagement Controversy." In *The Interregnum: the Quest for Settlement 1646–1660*, ed. G. E. Aylmer. London, 1972.

The Foundations of Modern Political Thought, 2 vols., vol. II. Cambridge, 1978.

"History and Ideology in the English Revolution." *Historical Journal* 8 (1965), 151– 78.

Smith, David L. *Constitutional Royalism and the Search for Settlement, c. 1640–1649.* Cambridge, 1994.

Smith, Nigel. *Literature and Revolution in England, 1640–1660.* New Haven, 1994.

Smith, R. J. *The Gothic Bequest.* Cambridge, 1987.

Snow, Vernon F. *Parliament in Elizabethan England: John Hooker's Order and Usage.* New Haven, 1977.

Sommerville, Johann P. "Absolutism and Royalism." In *The Cambridge History of Political Thought*, vol. II *1450–1700*, ed. J. H. Burns and Mark Goldie. Cambridge, 1991.

"The Ancient Constitution Reassessed: the Common Law, the Court and the Language of Politics in Early Modern Europe." In *The Stuart Court and Europe. Essays in Politics and Political Change*, ed. Malcolm Smuts. Cambridge, 1996.

"English and European Political Ideas in the Early Seventeenth Century: Revisionism and the Case of Absolutism." *Journal of British Studies* 35 (1996), 168 94.

"History and Theory: the Norman Conquest in Early Stuart Political Thought." *Political Studies* 24 (1986), 249–61.

"James I and the Divine Right of Kings: English Politics and Continental Theory." In *The Mental World of the Jacobean Court*, ed. Linda Levy Peck. Cambridge, 1991.

"John Selden, the Law of Nature, and the Origins of Government." *Historical Journal* 27 (1984).

ed. *King James VI and I: Political Writings.* Cambridge, 1994.

"Parliament, Privilege, and the Liberties of the Subject." In *Parliament and Liberty from the Reign of Elizabeth to the English Civil War*, ed. J. H. Hexter. Stanford, 1992.

Politics and Ideology in England, 1603–1640. London, 1986.

Southern, R. W. "Aspects of the European Tradition of Historical Writing: 4. The Sense of the Past." *Transactions of the Royal Historical Society* 5th series 23 (1973), 243–63.

Speck, William. *Reluctant Revolutionaries: Englishmen and the Revolution of 1688.* Oxford, 1988.

Spencer, B. *Souvenirs and Secular Badges*, pt. 2. Salisbury, 1990.

Spufford, Margaret. *Contrasting Communities. English Villagers in the Sixteenth and Seventeenth Centuries.* Cambridge, 1974.

Stanley, Arthur P. *Historical Memorials of Westminster Abbey.* 5th. edn. New York,1882.

Stephen's Commentaries on the Laws of England. Ed. A. D. Hargreaves. 21st. edn. London, 1950.

Stone, Lawrence. *The Causes of the English Revolution, 1529–1642.* London, 1972.

"The Educational Revolution in England, 1560–1650." *Past and Present* 28 (1964), 49–80.

"The Results of the English Revolution of the Seventeenth Century." In *Three Revolutions*, ed. J. G. A. Pocock. Princeton, 1980.

Stones, Alison. Review of Paul Binski, *The Painted Chamber at Westminster.* In *Burlington Magazine* 130 (1988), 259.

Strong, Roy. *Art and Power. Renaissance Festivals 1450–1650.* Berkeley, 1984.

Sturdy, David J. "'Continuity' Versus 'Change:' Historians and English Coronations of Medieval and Early Modern Periods." In *Coronations. Medieval and Early Modern Monarchic Ritual*, ed. Janos Bak. Berkeley, 1990.

Styles, Philip. "Politics and Historical Research in the Early Seventeenth Century." In *English Historical Scholarship in the Sixteenth and Seventeenth Centuries*, ed. Levi Fox. London, 1956, 49–72.

Sumption, Jonathan. *Pilgrimage. An Image of Medieval Religion.* Totowa, NJ, 1975.

Sutton, Anne F. and P. W. Hammond. *The Coronation of Richard III. The Extant Documents.* New York, 1983.

Swatland, Andrew. *The House of Lords in the Reign of Charles II.* Cambridge, 1996.

Tanner, Lawrence. "Some Representations of St. Edward the Confessor in Westminster Abbey and Elsewhere." *Journal of the British Archaeological Association* 3rd series, 15 (1952).

Taylor, John. *English Historical Literature in the Fourteenth Century.* Oxford, 1987. "The Manuscripts of the *Modus Tenendi Parliamentum.*" *English Historical Review* 83 (1968), 673–88.

Thomas, Keith. "The Perception of the Past in Early Modern England." University of London, The Creighton Trust Lecture, 1983.

Thompson, Martyn. "The History of Fundamental Law." *American Historical Review* 91 (1986), 1103–28.

"A Note on 'Reason' and 'History' in Late Seventeenth-Century Political Thought." *Political Theory* 4 (1976), 491–503.

"Significant Silences in Locke's *Two Treatises of Government.*" *Historical Journal* 31 (1988), 275–94.

Tierney, Brian. *The Middle Ages. Volume I: Sources of Medieval History.* 5th. edn. New York, 1992.

Religion, Law, and the Growth of Constitutional Thought (1150–1650). Cambridge, 1982.

Tomlinson, Howard, ed. *Before the English Civil War*. London, 1983.

Toy, John. *A Guide and Index to the Windows of York Minster*. York, 1985.

Trevor-Roper, Hugh. *Religion, the Reformation and Social Change*. London, 1967.

Tristam, E. W. *English Medieval Wall Paintings. The Thirteenth Century*. London, 1950.

Tuck, Richard. *Philosophy and Government, 1572–1651*. Cambridge, 1993.

Tucker, E. F. J. "*The Mirror of Justice*: Its Authorship and Preoccupations." *The Irish Jurist* n.s. 9, pt. 1 (1974), 99–109.

Underdown, David. *Pride's Purge: Politics in the Puritan Revolution*. Oxford, 1971.

Van Caenegem, R. C. *The Birth of the English Common Law*. 2nd. edn. Cambridge, 1988, repr. 1997.

Van Houts, Elizabeth C. "Camden, Cotton and the Chronicles of the Norman conquest of England." *British Library Journal* 18 (1992), 148–62.

"The Trauma of 1066." *History Today* 46 (1996), 9–15.

Van Norden, Linda. "Celtic Antiquarianism." In *Essays Dedicated to Lily B. Campbell*. Berkeley and Los Angeles, 1950.

"Sir Henry Spelman on the Chronology of the Elizabethan College of Antiquaries." *Huntington Library Quarterly* 13 (1949–50), 131–60.

Von Maltzahn, Nicholas. *Milton's History of Britain. Republican Historiography in the English Revolution*. Oxford, 1991.

Walker, David. *The Oxford Companion to Law*. Oxford, 1980.

Wallace, John. *Destiny His Choice: the Loyalism of Andrew Marvell*. Cambridge, 1968.

Wander, Steven. "Westminster Abbey: a Case Study in the Meaning of Medieval Architecture." Unpublished PhD Dissertation, Stanford University, 1974.

Warren, W. L. *Henry II*. Berkeley, 1973.

Watt, J. A. "Spiritual and Temporal Powers." In *The Cambridge History of Medieval Political Thought*, vol. 1 *c. 350–c. 1450*, ed. J. H. Burns. Cambridge, 1988.

Weston, Corinne C. "England: Ancient Constitution and Common Law." In *Cambridge History of Political Thought*, vol. II *1450–1700*, ed. J. H. Burns and Mark Goldie. Cambridge, 1991.

"The Authorship of the *Free-holders Grand Inquest*." *English Historical Review* 95 (1980), 74–98.

"The Case for Sir Robert Holbourne Reasserted." *History of Political Thought* 8 (1987), 435–60.

"'Holy Edward's Laws': the Cult of the Confessor and the Ancient Constitution." In *Restoration, Ideology, and Revolution*, ed. Gordon J. Schochet. *Proceedings of the Folger Institute Center for the History of British Political Thought* 4. Washington, DC, 1990.

Weston, Corinne C. and Janelle Greenberg. *Subjects and Sovereigns: the Grand Controversy over Legal Sovereignty in Stuart England*. Cambridge, 1981.

White, Stephen D. *Sir Edward Coke and "The Grievances of the Commonwealth," 1621–1628*. Chapel Hill, 1979.

Wickham Legg, L. G. *Coronation Records*. Westminster, 1901.

Williams, Ann. *The English and the Norman Conquest*. Woodbridge, 1996.

Wilson, Christopher. *The Gothic Cathedral. The Architecture of the Great Church 1130–1530*. London, 1990.

Wilson, David, ed. *The Bayeau Tapestry*. New York, 1985.

Wilson, Robert. *The Houses of Parliament*. Norwich, 1994.

Witcombe, D. T. *Charles II and the Cavalier House of Commons, 1663–1674*. New York, 1966.

Wolfe, Don M. *Milton in the Puritan Revolution*. New York, 1941.

Woolf, D. R. "Edmund Bolton, Francis Bacon and the Making of Hypercritica, 1618–1621," *Bodleian Library Record* 11 (1983), 162–8.

  The Idea of History in Early Stuart England. Erudition, Ideology, and "The Light of Truth" from the Accession of James I to the Civil War. Toronto, 1990.

  "Little Crosby and the Horizons of Early Modern Political Culture." In *The Historical Imagination in Early Modern Britain. History, Rhetoric, and Fiction, 1500–1800*, ed. Donald R. Kelley and David Harris Sacks. Cambridge, 1997.

  "Memory and Historical Culture in Early Modern England." *Journal of the Canadian Historical Association* 2 (1991), 293–308.

  "The Power of the Past." In *Political Thought and the Tudor Commonwealth. Deep Structure, Discourse and Disguise*, ed. Paul A. Fiedler and T. F. Mayer. London, 1992.

Woolrych, Austin. *Commonwealth to Protectorate*. Oxford, 1982.

  "Political Theory and Political Practice." In *The Age of Milton: Backgrounds to Seventeenth-Century Literature*, ed. C. A. Patrides and R. B. Waddington. Manchester, 1980.

Wootton, David, ed. *Divine Right and Democracy*. Harmondsworth, 1986.

Worden, A. Blair. "The Commonwealth Kidney of Algernon Sidney." *Journal of British Studies* 24 (1985), 1–40.

  The Rump Parliament 1648–1653. Cambridge, 1974.

Wormald, Jenny. "The Creation of Britain: Multiple Kingdoms or Core and Colonies." *Transactions of the Royal Historical Society*, 6th series, 2 (1992).

  "The Union of 1603." In *Scots and Britons. British Political Thought and the Union of 1603* ed. Roger A. Mason, 17–40.

Wormald, Patrick. "*Laga Edwardi*: the Textus Roffensis and Its Context." *Anglo-Norman Studies* 17 (1994), 243–66.

  The Making of English Law: King Alfred to the Twelfth Century, vol. 1 *Legislation and its Limits*. Oxford, 1999.

  "*Quadripartitus*." In *Law and Government in Medieval England and Normandy. Essays in Honour of Sir James Holt*, ed. George Garnett and John Hudson. Cambridge, 1994, pp. 111–47.

Wright, C. E. "The Dispersal of the Monastic Libraries and the Beginnings of Anglo-Saxon Studies." *Transactions of the Cambridge Bibliographical Society* (1951), 208–37.

Wright, H. G. *The Life and Works of Arthur Hall of Grantham, Member of Parliament, Courtier, and First Translator of Homer into English.* London, 1919.

Young, Michael B. "The Origins of the Petition of Right Reconsidered Further." *Historical Journal* 27 (1984), 449–52.

Zaller, Robert. "The Figure of the Tyrant in English Revolutionary Thought." *Journal of the History of Ideas* (1993), 585–610.

"Henry Parker and the Regiment of True Government." *Proceedings of the American Philosophical Society* 135 (1991), 255–85.

The Parliament of 1621. A Study in Constitutional Conflict. Berkeley, 1971.

Zook, Melinda. "Early Whig Ideology: Ancient Constitutionalism and the Reverend Samuel Johnson." *Journal of British Studies* 32 (1993), 139–65.

Radical Whigs and Conspiratorial Politics in Late Stuart England. University Park, Pa., 1999.

Zwicker, Steven. *Lines of Authority: Politics and English Literary Culture, 1649–1689.* Ithaca, N., 1993.

Index

335